First World War
and Army of Occupation
War Diary
France, Belgium and Germany

37 DIVISION
63 Infantry Brigade
Headquarters
1 July 1916 - 31 January 1919

WO95/2528/1

The Naval & Military Press Ltd
www.nmarchive.com
Published in association with The National Archives

Published by

The Naval & Military Press Ltd

Unit 10 Ridgewood Industrial Park,
Uckfield, East Sussex,
TN22 5QE England
Tel: +44 (0) 1825 749494

www.naval-military-press.com

www.nmarchive.com

This diary has been reprinted in facsimile from the original. Any imperfections are inevitably reproduced and the quality may fall short of modern type and cartographic standards.

© **Crown Copyright**
Images reproduced by permission of The National Archives, London, England, 2015.

Contents

Document type	Place/Title	Date From	Date To
Heading	WO95/2528/1 63 Inf Bde Headquarters July 1916-Mar 1919		
Heading	37th Division 63rd Infy Bde Bde Headquarters. Jly 1916-Mar 1919 From 21 Div		
Heading	63rd Infantry Brigade. War Diary July 1916		
War Diary	Assembly Area	01/07/1916	01/07/1916
War Diary	Vaux	04/07/1916	06/07/1916
War Diary	Talmas	07/07/1916	07/07/1916
War Diary	Mondicourt	08/07/1916	10/07/1916
War Diary	Bienvillers	11/07/1916	13/07/1916
War Diary	Humbercamp	14/07/1916	14/07/1916
War Diary	Houvin	15/07/1916	15/07/1916
War Diary	Chelers	16/07/1916	17/07/1916
War Diary	Chateau De La Haie	18/07/1916	24/07/1916
War Diary	Villa D'Acq	25/07/1916	31/07/1916
Heading	63rd Infantry Brigade. War Diary August 1916		
War Diary	Villa d'Acq	01/08/1916	12/08/1916
War Diary	Chateau De La Haie	13/08/1916	13/08/1916
War Diary	Chateau Du Bois Des Monts	14/08/1916	23/08/1916
War Diary	Chateau De La Haie	24/08/1916	31/08/1916
Miscellaneous	63rd Infantry Brigade.	08/07/1916	08/07/1916
Miscellaneous	Subject:- Officer Casualties	08/07/1916	08/07/1916
Miscellaneous	63rd Infantry Brigade Headquarters.	31/07/1916	31/07/1916
Miscellaneous	63rd Infantry Brigade. Reinforcements Arrived During July 1916		
Miscellaneous	Casualties During July 1916		
Miscellaneous	Summary of Casualties in Brigade During July 1916		
Miscellaneous	Strength of Units on 31st July 1916		
Miscellaneous	21st Division.	06/07/1916	06/07/1916
Miscellaneous	Nominal Roll of Officers of 8th Lincoln Regiment.		
Miscellaneous	Nominal Roll of Officers of 8th Somerset L. Infantry.		
Miscellaneous	Nominal Roll of Officers of 4th Middlesex Regiment.		
Miscellaneous	Nominal Roll of Officers of 10th York & Lancs Regiment.		
Miscellaneous	Nominal Roll of Officers of 63rd Machine Gun Company.		
Miscellaneous	Nominal Roll of Officers of 63rd Trench Mortar Battery.		
Miscellaneous	Nominal Roll of Officers. 4th Battalion Middlesex Regiment.		
Miscellaneous	Nominal Roll of Officers of 8th (Service) Battalion Lincolnshire Regiment.		
Miscellaneous	Nominal Roll of Officers. 8th (S) Battalion Somerset Light Infantry.		
Miscellaneous	Nominal Roll of Officers 4th Battalion Middlesex Regiment.		
Miscellaneous	Nominal Roll of Officers. 10th (S) Battalion York & Lancaster Regiment.		
Miscellaneous	Nominal Roll of Officers. 63rd Machine Gun Company.		

Miscellaneous	Nominal Roll of Officers. 63rd Infantry Brigade Headquarters.		
Miscellaneous	Casualties During November, 1916		
Miscellaneous	63rd Infantry Brigade. Reinforcements Received During November, 1916		
Miscellaneous	63rd Infantry Brigade Strength of Units November 30th, 16.		
Miscellaneous Heading	War Diary 63rd Infantry Brigade December 1916		
War Diary	Beauquesne	01/12/1916	13/12/1916
War Diary	Remaisnil	14/12/1916	14/12/1916
War Diary	Boubers Valhuon	15/12/1916	16/12/1916
War Diary	Fontaines Lez Hermans	17/12/1916	17/12/1916
War Diary	Busnes	18/12/1916	20/12/1916
War Diary	Vieille Chapelle	22/12/1916	31/12/1916
Miscellaneous	War Diary 63rd Infantry Brigade.		
Miscellaneous	Nominal Roll of Officers. 63rd Infantry Brigade Headquarters.		
Miscellaneous	Nominal Roll of Officers. 8th Battalion Lincolnshire Regiment.		
Miscellaneous	Nominal Roll of Officers. 8th Battalion Somerset Light Infantry		
Miscellaneous	Nominal Roll of Officers. 10th Battalion York & Lancaster Regiment.		
Miscellaneous	Nominal Roll of Officers. 63rd Machine Gun Company		
Miscellaneous	Casualties During December 1916		
Miscellaneous	Reinforcements Received During December, 1916		
Miscellaneous	Strength, December 1916		
Heading	War Diary. 63rd Infantry Brigade. January 1917 Vol 17		
War Diary	Vieille Chapelle	01/01/1917	01/01/1917
War Diary	Neuve Chapelle	02/01/1917	27/01/1917
War Diary	Ferme Du Bois Sect	28/01/1917	31/01/1917
Miscellaneous	63rd Infantry Brigade. Nominal Roll of Officers 8th (S) Bn. Somerset L.I.		
Miscellaneous	63rd Infantry Brigade. Nominal Roll of Officers 4th Bn. Middlesex Regiment.		
Miscellaneous	63rd Infantry Brigade. Nominal Roll of Officers 18th (s) Bn. York & Lancaster Regiment.		
Miscellaneous	Nominal Roll of Officers. 63rd Machine Gun Company.		
Heading	War Diary 63rd Infantry Brigade. February 1917		
War Diary	Ferme Du Bois Bethune	01/02/1917	12/02/1917
War Diary	Mazingarbe	13/02/1917	28/02/1917
Miscellaneous	Report on Dummy Raid Carried Out on the Night of 27/28th. February 1917. Observed from 'Man Trap' O.P., G.28.c.1.7	28/02/1917	28/02/1917
Miscellaneous	Nominal Roll of Officers. 63rd Infantry Brigade Headquarters.		
Miscellaneous	Nominal Roll of Officers. 8th Battalion (S) Lincolnshire Regiment.		
Miscellaneous	Nominal Roll of Officers. 8th (S) Battalion, Somerset Light Infantry		
Miscellaneous	Nominal Roll of Officers. 4th Battalion Middlesex Regiment.		
Miscellaneous	Nominal Roll of Officers. 10th (S) Battalion, York & Lancaster Regiment.		
Miscellaneous	Nominal Roll of Officers. 63rd Machine Gun Company		

Type	Description	From	To
Miscellaneous	Casualties During February 1917		
Heading	63rd Infantry Brigade War Diary March 1917 Vol 19		
War Diary	Mazingarbe	01/03/1917	02/03/1917
War Diary	Bethune Robecq Rely	03/03/1917	08/03/1917
War Diary	La Thieueloye	09/03/1917	09/03/1917
War Diary	Houvin-Houvigneul	10/03/1917	31/03/1917
War Diary	Houvin Houvigneul	01/04/1917	04/04/1917
War Diary	Manin	05/04/1918	06/04/1918
War Diary	Lattre St. Quentin	07/04/1918	07/04/1918
War Diary	Duisans.	08/04/1917	11/04/1917
War Diary	Arras	12/04/1917	12/04/1917
War Diary	Duisans	13/04/1917	13/04/1917
War Diary	Agnez Lez	13/04/1917	13/04/1917
War Diary	Duisans	14/04/1917	14/04/1917
War Diary	Manin	15/04/1917	18/04/1917
War Diary	Montenescourt	19/04/1917	20/04/1917
War Diary	Trenches	21/04/1917	28/04/1917
War Diary	Manin	29/04/1917	30/04/1917
Miscellaneous	63rd Machine Gun Company. Report on recent fighting 9-12 April 1917	15/04/1917	15/04/1917
Miscellaneous	63rd Infantry Brigade. Report on Operation-April 9th-12th 1917	18/04/1917	18/04/1917
Heading	War Diary 63rd Inf. Bde. May 1917. Vol 21.		
War Diary	Manin	01/05/1917	17/05/1917
War Diary	Simencourt	18/05/1917	18/05/1917
War Diary	Dainville	19/05/1917	20/05/1917
War Diary	Achicourt	21/05/1917	27/05/1917
War Diary	Tilloy	28/05/1917	31/05/1917
Miscellaneous	Report on Recent Operation, Covering the Period April 22nd to April 29th.	02/05/1917	02/05/1917
Miscellaneous	Report on the Operation, 22nd-29th April inclusive.	03/05/1917	03/05/1917
Heading	63rd Infantry Brigade 37 War Diary June 1917. Vol 22.		
War Diary	Manin	01/06/1917	04/06/1917
War Diary	Croix	05/06/1917	05/06/1917
Miscellaneous	Anvin	06/06/1917	06/06/1917
War Diary	Fruges	07/06/1917	21/06/1917
War Diary	Ligny-Lez-Aire	21/06/1917	22/06/1917
War Diary	Thiennes	23/06/1917	23/06/1917
War Diary	Caestre	24/06/1917	24/06/1917
War Diary	Scherpenberg Camp	25/06/1917	29/06/1917
War Diary	Trenches	30/06/1917	30/06/1917
Miscellaneous	Nominal Roll of Officers. 63rd Infantry Brigade Headquarters.		
Miscellaneous	Nominal Roll of Officers. 8th Battalion, The Lincolnshire Regiment.		
Miscellaneous	Nominal Roll of Officers. 8th Battalion Somerset Light Infantry.		
Miscellaneous	Nominal Roll of Officers. 4th Battalion, The Middlesex Regiment.		
Miscellaneous	Nominal Roll of Officers. 10th Battalion The York & Lancaster Regiment.		
Miscellaneous	Nominal Roll of Officers. 63rd Machine Gun Company		
Heading	63rd Infantry Brigade War Diary July 1917. Vol 23.		
War Diary	Trenches.	01/07/1916	02/07/1916
War Diary	Kemmel Hill	03/07/1916	11/07/1916
War Diary	Trenches	12/07/1916	19/07/1916

War Diary	Kemmel Hill	20/07/1916	25/07/1916
War Diary	Trenches	26/07/1916	27/07/1916
War Diary	Kemmel Hill	28/07/1916	29/07/1916
War Diary	Trenches	30/07/1916	31/07/1916
Miscellaneous	63rd Infantry Brigade. War Diary July 1917		
Miscellaneous	Report on Operation About Rifle and Beek Farms on July 31st and August 1st, 1917	04/08/1917	04/08/1917
Miscellaneous	Nominal Roll of Officers. Headquarters, 63rd Infantry Brigade.		
Miscellaneous	Nominal Roll of Officers. 8th Battalion, The Lincolnshire Regt.		
Miscellaneous	Nominal Roll of Officers. 6th Battalion, Somerset Light Infantry.		
Miscellaneous	Nominal Roll of Officers. 4th Battalion, The Middlesex Regiment.		
Miscellaneous	Nominal Roll of Officers. 18th Battalion, The York and Lancaster Regiment.		
Miscellaneous	Nominal Roll of Officers. 63rd Machine Gun Company.		
Miscellaneous	Casualties During July 1917		
Miscellaneous	Casualties During Operation 31st July/1st Aug 1917.		
Miscellaneous	63rd Infantry Brigade.		
Miscellaneous	63rd Infantry Brigade. Strength of Units July 31st 1917.		
Heading	63rd Infantry Brigade. War Diary August 1917 Vol 24		
War Diary	Kemmel Hill	01/08/1917	01/08/1917
War Diary	Dranoutre	02/08/1917	06/08/1917
War Diary	Fairy House	08/08/1917	15/08/1917
War Diary	Trenches	16/08/1917	21/08/1917
War Diary	Fairy House	22/08/1917	24/08/1917
War Diary	Locre	26/08/1917	28/08/1917
War Diary	Spoil Bank I.33.c.9880	29/08/1917	31/08/1917
Miscellaneous	63rd Infantry Brigade War Diary		
Miscellaneous	Nominal Roll of Officers. 63rd Infantry Brigade Headquarters.		
Miscellaneous	Nominal Roll of Officers. 8th Battalion, The Lincolnshire Regiment.		
Miscellaneous	Nominal Roll of Officers. 8th Battalion, Somerset Light Infantry.		
Miscellaneous	Nominal Roll of Officers. 4th Battalion, The Middlesex Regiment.		
Miscellaneous	Nominal Roll of Officers. 10th Battalion, The York & Lancaster Regiment.		
Miscellaneous	Nominal Rolls of Officers. 63rd Machine Gun Company.		
Miscellaneous	Casualties During August 1917.		
Miscellaneous	63rd Infantry Brigade. Reinforcements Received During Aug 1917		
Miscellaneous	63rd Infantry Brigade. Strength of Units August 31st 1917		
Heading	63rd Infantry Brigade War Diary September 1917 Vol 25.		
War Diary	Trenches.	01/09/1917	07/09/1917
War Diary	Fairy House	08/09/1917	09/09/1917
War Diary	Mt. Kokereele	10/09/1917	19/09/1917
War Diary	Fairy House	20/09/1917	20/09/1917
War Diary	Mont Kokereele	20/09/1917	27/09/1917
War Diary	Trenches.	28/09/1917	30/09/1917

Miscellaneous	63rd Infantry Brigade. War Diary September, 1917.		
Miscellaneous	63rd Infantry Brigade War Diary October 1917 Vol 26.		
War Diary	Trenches	01/10/1917	05/10/1917
War Diary	Fairy House	06/10/1917	10/10/1917
War Diary	Trenches	11/10/1917	14/10/1917
War Diary	Mont Kokereele	17/10/1917	20/10/1917
War Diary	Merris	21/10/1917	31/10/1917
Miscellaneous	63rd Infantry Brigade.	09/10/1917	09/10/1917
Miscellaneous	Nominal Roll of Officers. 8th Battalion Lincolnshire Regiment.		
Miscellaneous	Nominal Roll of Officers. 8th Battalion Somerset Light Infantry		
Miscellaneous	Nominal Roll of Officers. 4th Battalion Middlesex Regiment.		
Miscellaneous	Nominal Roll of Officers. 10th Battalion York & Lancaster Regt.		
Miscellaneous	Nominal Roll of Officers. 63rd Company, Machine Gun Corps.		
Miscellaneous	Casualties During October 1917		
Miscellaneous	63rd Infantry Brigade Strength of Units, October 31st 1917.		
Heading	63rd Infantry Brigade 37 War Diary November 1917 Vol 27.		
War Diary	Merris	01/11/1917	09/11/1917
War Diary	Kemmel	10/11/1917	16/11/1917
War Diary	La Clytte	17/11/1917	25/11/1917
War Diary	Trenches	26/11/1917	30/11/1917
Miscellaneous	Nominal Roll of Officers. 63rd Infantry Brigade Headquarters.		
Miscellaneous	Nominal Roll of Officers. 8th Battalion, The Lincolnshire Regiment.		
Miscellaneous	Nominal Roll of Officers. 8th Battalion, Somerset Light Infantry.		
Miscellaneous	Nominal Roll of Officers. 10th Battalion, The York & Lancaster Regiment.		
Miscellaneous	Nominal Roll of Officers. 63rd Company, Machine Gun Corps		
Miscellaneous	Nominal Roll of Officers. 4th Battalion, The Middlesex Regiment.		
Miscellaneous	Casualties During November 1917		
Miscellaneous	63rd Infantry Brigade. Reinforcements Received During Nov., 1917.		
Miscellaneous	Explanation		
Miscellaneous	63rd Infantry Brigade Strength of Units November 30th 1917.		
Miscellaneous	63rd Infantry Brigade Reinforcements Received During October, 1917		
Miscellaneous	Officer Other Ranks		
Heading	63rd Infantry Brigade War Diary December 1917. Vol 28.		
War Diary	Trenches.	01/12/1917	05/12/1917
War Diary	Enforden Camp	06/12/1917	13/12/1917
War Diary	La Clytte	14/12/1917	21/12/1917
War Diary	Trenches	22/12/1917	29/12/1917
War Diary	Enforden Camp	30/12/1917	31/12/1917

Miscellaneous	Nominal Roll of Officers. 8th Battalion, The Lincolnshire Regiment.		
Miscellaneous	63rd Infantry Brigade Headquarters.		
Miscellaneous	Nominal Roll of Officers. 8th Battalion, The Somerset Light Infantry		
Miscellaneous	Nominal Roll of Officers 4th Battalion The Middlesex Regiment.		
Miscellaneous	Nominal Roll of Officers. 10th Battalion, The York & Lancaster Regiment.		
Miscellaneous	Nominal Roll of Officers. 63rd Company Machine Gun Corps.		
Miscellaneous	Casualties During December 1917		
Miscellaneous	Reinforcements Received during December 1917.		
Miscellaneous	Strength of Battalions 31st December 1917.		
Heading	63rd Infantry Brigade War Diary January 1918. Vol 29		
War Diary	Enforden Camp	01/01/1918	04/01/1918
War Diary	La Clytte	05/01/1918	10/01/1918
War Diary	Zevecoten	11/01/1918	20/01/1918
War Diary	Balringhem Area C.0.a.9.4	21/01/1918	31/01/1918
Heading	War Diary 63rd Infantry Brigade February 1918 Vol 30		
War Diary	Sercus Area	01/02/1918	13/02/1918
War Diary	La Clytte.	14/02/1918	14/02/1918
War Diary	Bedford House.	15/02/1918	15/02/1918
War Diary	I.26.a.9.3.	16/02/1918	16/02/1918
War Diary	Bedford House	17/02/1918	28/02/1918
Operation(al) Order(s)	63rd Infantry Brigade Order No. 194	27/02/1918	27/02/1918
Miscellaneous	Amendments to 63rd Infantry Brigade Defence Scheme	06/03/1918	06/03/1918
Miscellaneous	63rd Infantry Brigade. 8815	02/03/1918	02/03/1918
Heading	37th Division. B.H.Q. 63rd Infantry Brigade March 1918 List of Appendices follows War Diary.		
Heading	War Diary 63rd Infantry Brigade March 1918. Vol 31.		
War Diary	Tower Hamlets	01/03/1918	27/03/1918
War Diary	Godewaers-Velde	28/03/1918	28/03/1918
War Diary	Pas	29/03/1918	29/03/1918
War Diary	Henu	30/03/1918	31/03/1918
Miscellaneous	63rd Infantry Brigade War Diary		
Miscellaneous	63rd Infantry Brigade. Defence Scheme.	02/03/1918	02/03/1918
Miscellaneous	Appendix "A" Communication.		
Miscellaneous	Appendix 'A' Light Trench Mortars.		
Miscellaneous	Appendix 'C' Machine Guns		
Miscellaneous	Appendix 'D' Artillery Cooperation.		
Miscellaneous	Mutual Support Barrages Southern Group		
Miscellaneous	Appendix (E) Administrative		
Operation(al) Order(s)	63rd Infantry Brigade Order No. 196	04/03/1918	04/03/1918
Miscellaneous	Report on Operations March 8/9th, 1918.	14/03/1918	14/03/1918
Miscellaneous	63rd Infantry Brigade No. A/5	09/03/1918	09/03/1918
Miscellaneous	63rd T.M. Battery	10/03/1918	10/03/1918
Operation(al) Order(s)	63rd Infantry Brigade Order No. 197.	08/03/1918	08/03/1918
Operation(al) Order(s)	63rd Infantry Brigade Order No. 198	13/03/1918	13/03/1918
Miscellaneous	63rd Infantry Brigade No. 9106	15/03/1918	15/03/1918
Miscellaneous	Outline of Project for a Raid		
Miscellaneous	Minor Operation Night March 18/19th 1918		
Miscellaneous	63rd Infantry Brigade No. 9030 March 13th 1918		
Miscellaneous	Operation Orders.		
Miscellaneous	Administrative Instructions.		
Miscellaneous	63rd Infantry Brigade No. 9030/1 March 18th 1918		

Miscellaneous	63rd Infantry Brigade No. 9030/5		
Miscellaneous	63rd Infantry Brigade No. 9030/3	28/03/1918	28/03/1918
Miscellaneous		19/03/1918	19/03/1918
Miscellaneous	63rd Infantry Brigade No. 9030/2	18/03/1918	18/03/1918
Miscellaneous	63rd Infantry Brigade No. 9030/4	18/03/1918	18/03/1918
Operation(al) Order(s)	63rd Infantry Brigade Order No. 199	19/03/1918	19/03/1918
Miscellaneous	Defence Scheme. Front Line Battalion (Right Subsection).		
Miscellaneous			
Operation(al) Order(s)	63rd Infantry Brigade Order No. 200.	24/03/1918	24/03/1918
Operation(al) Order(s)	63rd Infantry Brigade Order No. 201.	25/03/1918	25/03/1918
Operation(al) Order(s)	63rd Infantry Brigade Order No. 203	28/03/1918	28/03/1918
Operation(al) Order(s)	63rd Infantry Brigade Order No. 202	27/03/1918	27/03/1918
Miscellaneous	March Table to accompany 63rd Inf. Bde. Order No. 202 d/27.3.18		
Operation(al) Order(s)	63rd Infantry Brigade Order No. 204	30/03/1918	30/03/1918
Miscellaneous	63rd Infantry Brigade No. 9509	31/03/1918	31/03/1918
Miscellaneous	Table to Accompany 63rd Inf. Bde. Order No. 203 dated 28.3.18		
Miscellaneous	Nominal Roll of Officers. 63rd Infantry Brigade Headquarters.		
Miscellaneous	Nominal Roll of Officers 8th Battalion, The Lincolnshire Regiment.		
Miscellaneous	Nominal Roll of Officers. 8th Battalion, The Somerset Light Infantry.		
Miscellaneous	Nominal Roll of Officers. 4th Battalion, The Middlesex Regiment.		
Miscellaneous	Nominal Roll of Officers. 63rd Trench Mortar Battery.		
Miscellaneous	Casualties During March 1918.		
Miscellaneous	63rd Infantry Brigade.		
Miscellaneous	63rd Infantry Brigade Strength of Units, March 31st, 1918.		
Heading	37th Division. B.H.Q. 63rd Infantry Brigade. April 1918		
Heading	War Diary 63rd Infantry Brigade April 1918 Vol 32		
War Diary	Trenches	01/04/1918	05/04/1918
War Diary	Gommecourt	06/04/1918	08/04/1918
War Diary	Trenches	09/04/1918	15/04/1918
War Diary	Henu	15/04/1918	16/04/1918
War Diary	Authie	16/04/1918	23/04/1918
War Diary	Trenches	23/04/1918	28/04/1918
Miscellaneous	63rd Infantry Brigade War Diary April 1918		
Operation(al) Order(s)	63rd Infantry Brigade Order No. 205.	31/03/1918	31/03/1918
Miscellaneous	March Table to Accompany 63rd Inf. Bde. Order No. 205 dated 31.3.18		
Operation(al) Order(s)	Amendment to 63rd Infantry Brigade Order No. 206		
Operation(al) Order(s)	63rd Infantry Brigade Order No. 206	02/04/1918	02/04/1918
Operation(al) Order(s)	63rd Infantry Brigade Order No. 207	03/04/1918	03/04/1918
Map	Minor Operation of 63rd Inf. Bde. April 5 1918		
Miscellaneous	Communications.		
Miscellaneous	63rd Infantry Brigade No. 119 G.	03/04/1918	03/04/1918
Miscellaneous	63rd Infantry Brigade Instruction No. 1.	04/04/1918	04/04/1918
Miscellaneous	63rd Infantry Brigade Instruction No. 2	04/04/1918	04/04/1918
Miscellaneous	Additional General Instructions.	04/04/1918	04/04/1918
Diagram etc	Diagram Shewing One Battalion Advancing		
Miscellaneous	63rd Infantry Brigade No. 144G	04/04/1918	04/04/1918

Miscellaneous	63rd Infantry Brigade No. 145G.	04/04/1918	04/04/1918
Miscellaneous	63rd Infantry Brigade No. 158 G.	05/04/1918	05/04/1918
Miscellaneous	63rd Infantry Brigade No. 163G	06/04/1918	06/04/1918
Miscellaneous	Report on Operation Carried Out on 5.4.1918.	09/04/1918	09/04/1918
Miscellaneous	Report on Communication of 63rd Infantry Brigade During Operation at Rossignol Wood, April 5th 1918.	09/04/1918	09/04/1918
Miscellaneous	37th Division No. G. 6616	05/04/1918	05/04/1918
Miscellaneous	37th Division No. G. 3603	05/04/1918	05/04/1918
Miscellaneous	IV Corps No. 76/1/2 G.	08/04/1918	08/04/1918
Operation(al) Order(s)	63rd Infantry Brigade Order No. 203	06/04/1918	06/04/1918
Miscellaneous	Table to accompany 63rd Infantry Brigade Order No. 208.		
Operation(al) Order(s)	63rd Infantry Brigade Order No. 209	08/04/1918	08/04/1918
Operation(al) Order(s)	63rd Infantry Brigade Order No. 210.	11/04/1918	11/04/1918
Miscellaneous	Addendum to 63rd Infantry Brigade Defence Arrangements.	14/04/1918	14/04/1918
Miscellaneous	Amendments to 63rd Infantry Brigade Provisional Defensive Arrangements.	14/04/1918	14/04/1918
Miscellaneous	63rd Infantry Brigade Provisional Defensive Arrangements.	12/04/1918	12/04/1918
Operation(al) Order(s)	63rd Infantry Brigade Order No. 211.	14/04/1918	14/04/1918
Operation(al) Order(s)	63rd Infantry Brigade Order No. 212.	13/04/1918	13/04/1918
Miscellaneous	Table to Accompany 63rd Infantry Brigade Order No. 212.	15/04/1918	15/04/1918
Operation(al) Order(s)	63rd Infantry Brigade Order No. 213.	16/04/1918	16/04/1918
Miscellaneous	March Table to accompany 63rd Inf. Bde. Order No. 213 dated 16.4.18.		
Operation(al) Order(s)	63rd Infantry Brigade Order No. 214.	17/04/1918	17/04/1918
Miscellaneous	Communications.	20/04/1918	20/04/1918
Miscellaneous	63rd Infantry Brigade Administrative Instructions.		
Operation(al) Order(s)	63rd Infantry Brigade Order No. 215	21/04/1918	21/04/1918
Operation(al) Order(s)	Amendment to 63rd Inf. Bde. Order No. 215	21/04/1918	21/04/1918
Miscellaneous	March Table to Accompany 63rd Inf. Bde. Order No. 215 21.4.18		
Operation(al) Order(s)	63rd Infantry Brigade Order No. 216.	26/04/1918	26/04/1918
Miscellaneous	63rd Infantry Brigade. Defensive Arrangements.	28/04/1918	28/04/1918
Diagram etc	Light Brigade Communications Less Coys Cons.		
Miscellaneous	63rd Infantry Brigade Defensive Arrangements.		
Miscellaneous	Nominal Roll of Officers. 63rd Infantry Brigade Headquarters.		
Miscellaneous	8th Battalion Lincolnshire Regiment. Nominal Roll of Officers.		
Miscellaneous	8th Battalions Somerset Light Infantry.		
Miscellaneous	4th Battalion Middlesex Regt.		
Miscellaneous	63rd Trench Mortar Battery Nominal Roll of Officers.		
Miscellaneous	Casualties During April 1918.		
Miscellaneous	Particulars of Officers Casualties		
Miscellaneous	63rd Infantry Brigade. Reinforcements Received During April 1918.		
Miscellaneous			
Miscellaneous	63rd Infantry Brigade Strength of Units, April 30th, 1918.		
Heading	War Diary 63rd Infantry Brigade. May 1918. Vol 33.		
War Diary	Bucquoy	01/05/1918	01/05/1918
War Diary	Souastre	02/05/1918	08/05/1918
War Diary	La Brayelle Farm	09/05/1918	15/05/1918

War Diary	St Leger	16/05/1918	23/05/1918
War Diary	Bus-Les-Artois	24/05/1918	29/05/1918
War Diary	Authie	30/05/1918	31/05/1918
Heading	War Diary 63rd Infantry Brigade. June 1918 Vol 34		
War Diary	Authie	01/06/1918	04/06/1918
War Diary	Picquigny Sur-Somme	05/06/1918	09/06/1918
War Diary	Loeuilly	10/06/1918	15/06/1918
War Diary	Rumigny	16/06/1918	19/06/1918
War Diary	Prouzel	19/06/1918	20/06/1918
War Diary	Couin	21/06/1918	24/06/1918
War Diary	La Brayelle Farm	25/06/1918	30/06/1918
Miscellaneous	Artillery Cooperation.		
Heading	War Diary 63rd Infantry Brigade July, 1918 Vol 35.		
War Diary	La Brayelle Farm	01/07/1918	06/07/1918
War Diary	Souastre	07/07/1918	12/07/1918
War Diary	The 'Z'	13/07/1918	25/07/1918
War Diary	Souastre	26/07/1918	31/07/1918
Miscellaneous	Report on Raid Carried Out by 4th Middlesex Regt. on Night 24th/25th July 1918	25/07/1918	25/07/1918
Miscellaneous	Report on Raid Carried Out by 4th Middlesex Regt on Night 24/25th July 1918	25/07/1918	25/07/1918
Map			
Operation(al) Order(s)	63rd Infantry Brigade Order No. 242	22/07/1918	22/07/1918
Miscellaneous	Machine Guns 'A' and 'C' Companies 37th M.G. Battalion. Fire Orders for 'A' 'B' and 'C' Batteries.		
Miscellaneous	3-Inch Stokes Mortars.	22/07/1918	22/07/1918
Miscellaneous	63rd Infantry Brigade No. 1599.G.	22/07/1918	22/07/1918
Miscellaneous	Amendments and Addenda to 63rd Infantry Brigade Order No. 242 dated 22.7.18.	23/07/1918	23/07/1918
Miscellaneous	Amendments to Appendix 'A' 63rd Infantry Brigade Order No. 242 dated 22.7.7.18.	22/07/1918	22/07/1918
Heading	War Diary 63rd Infantry Brigade August 1918 Vol 36.		
War Diary	La Brayelle Farm.	01/08/1918	19/08/1918
War Diary	Bucquoy L.26.a.6.0.	21/08/1918	22/08/1918
War Diary	L.5.a.5.2	23/08/1918	23/08/1918
War Diary	G.3.a.0.5	24/08/1918	24/08/1918
War Diary	Brickworks Achiet Le Grand	25/08/1918	31/08/1918
Miscellaneous	Report on Operations August 21st to 26th (Inclusive).	29/08/1918	29/08/1918
Miscellaneous	63rd Infantry Brigade.		
Map	Sheet 57 D.N.E.		
Map	German Trenches in Blue		
Miscellaneous	Material Captured by 63rd Inf. Bde. During Operation August 21st August 26th 1918.		
Miscellaneous	Nominal Roll of Officers 63rd Trench Mortar Battery.		
Miscellaneous	Nominal Roll of Officers. 4th Battalion, Middlesex Regiment.		
Miscellaneous	Nominal Roll of Officers. 8th Battalion, The Lincolnshire Regiment.		
Miscellaneous	Nominal Roll of Officers. 8th Battalion, Somerset Light Infantry		
Miscellaneous	Casualties During August 1918.		
Heading	War Diary 63rd Infantry Brigade September 1918 Vol 37		
War Diary	Brickworks Achiet Le Grand	01/09/1918	02/09/1918
War Diary	Lebucquiere	03/09/1918	04/09/1918
War Diary	J.32.b.80.80	04/09/1918	05/09/1918

War Diary	Gaika Copse	06/09/1918	07/09/1918
War Diary	P.11.b.0.3	08/09/1918	11/09/1918
War Diary	Lebucquiere	12/09/1918	15/09/1918
War Diary	P.11.b.0.3	16/09/1918	18/09/1918
War Diary	Place Mortmarte	19/09/1918	21/09/1918
War Diary	Thilloy	22/09/1918	29/09/1918
War Diary	Ruyaulcourt	30/09/1918	30/09/1918
Miscellaneous	Report on Operations Carried Out 3rd to 11th September 1918 by 63rd Infantry Brigade.	24/09/1918	24/09/1918
Map	Map to Accompany		
Miscellaneous	O.C. 8th Somersets	13/09/1918.	13/09/1918
Miscellaneous	Report on Operations Carried Out on 21st September 1918 by 63rd Infantry Brigade.		
Heading	War Diary 63rd Infantry Brigade October, 1918 Vol 38		
War Diary	E. of Metz-on Couture	01/10/1918	04/10/1918
War Diary	Gouzeaucourt	05/10/1918	07/10/1918
War Diary	Banteux	08/10/1918	08/10/1918
War Diary	Belleaise Farm	08/10/1918	08/10/1918
War Diary	Brisieux Wood	09/10/1918	09/10/1918
War Diary	Haucourt	10/10/1918	10/10/1918
War Diary	Ligny-en-Cambresis	10/10/1918	10/10/1918
War Diary	Caudry	10/10/1918	10/10/1918
War Diary	Audencourt	10/10/1918	12/10/1918
War Diary	Caudry	13/10/1918	22/10/1918
War Diary	Briastre	23/10/1918	23/10/1918
War Diary	Beaurain	24/10/1918	24/10/1918
War Diary	Salesches Mill	25/10/1918	31/10/1918
Miscellaneous	Report on Operations Sept 30th 1918-Oct 12th 1918.	19/10/1918	19/10/1918
Miscellaneous		19/11/1918	19/11/1918
Map	Sheet 57c		
Map	France		
Miscellaneous	Glossary.		
Map			
Heading	War Diary 63rd Infantry Brigade November, 1918. Vol 39		
War Diary	Salesches Mill	01/11/1918	03/11/1918
War Diary	Chateau, Ghissignies, A.5.c.2.2	04/11/1918	04/11/1918
War Diary	Neuville X.25.b.3.4	05/11/1918	10/11/1918
War Diary	Caudry	11/11/1918	30/11/1918
Miscellaneous	War Diary 63rd Infantry Brigade.		
Miscellaneous	63rd Infantry Brigade.	09/11/1918	09/11/1918
Heading	War Diary 63rd Infantry Brigade December 1918 Vol 40		
War Diary	Haussy	01/12/1918	01/12/1918
War Diary	Villers-Pol	02/12/1918	13/12/1918
War Diary	Sous-Le-Bois	15/12/1918	16/12/1918
War Diary	Grand Reng	17/12/1918	17/12/1918
War Diary	Binche	18/12/1918	18/12/1918
War Diary	Courcelles	19/12/1918	20/12/1918
War Diary	Houtain-Le-Val	21/12/1918	31/12/1918
Heading	War Diary 63rd Infantry Brigade January 1919 Vol 41		
War Diary	Houtain Le Val	02/01/1919	31/01/1919
Miscellaneous	63rd Infantry Brigade War Diary		
Miscellaneous	63rd Infantry Brigade Demobilization.		
Miscellaneous	63rd Infantry Brigade Reinforcements Received During Jan 1919		

Miscellaneous	63rd Infantry Brigade Strength of Units Jan 31st 1919.		
Heading	63rd Infantry Brigade War Diary February 1919 Vol 42		
War Diary	Houtain Le-Val		
Miscellaneous	63rd Infantry Brigade Strength of Units, February 28th 1919.		
Miscellaneous	63rd Infantry Brigade. Reinforcements Received During February 1919		
Miscellaneous	63rd Infantry Brigade Demobilization		
Miscellaneous	63rd Infantry Brigade War Diary February 1919		
Miscellaneous	Ref. G.E. 82 dated 27th Feb., 1919	28/02/1919	28/02/1919
Heading	War Diary 63rd Infantry Brigade March 1919 Vol 43		
War Diary	Jumet Hiegne		
Miscellaneous	War Diary 63rd Infantry Brigade. March 31st, 1919		
Miscellaneous	63rd Infantry Brigade No. 3277	08/03/1919	08/03/1919
Miscellaneous	63rd Infantry Brigade. Reinforcements Received During March, 1919.		
Miscellaneous	63rd Infantry Brigade Strength of Units March 31st 1919.		
Miscellaneous	63rd Infantry Brigade Demobilization.		

WO 95/2528/11

63 INF BDE

HEAD QUARTERS   JULY 1916 – MAR 1919

37TH DIVISION
63RD INFY BDE

BDE HEADQUARTERS.
JLY 1916-MAR 1919

From 21 Div.

37TH DIVISION
63RD INFY BDE

ORIGINAL

37 Lears
63 Inf Bde
63 Inf Bde H Vol II

Bde transferred to 37 Div
2.7.16

63RD INFANTRY BRIGADE.

WAR DIARY

JULY 1916.
--o--

Mar '19

Army Form C. 2118.

WAR DIARY
or
INTELLIGENCE SUMMARY.
(Erase heading not required.)

63RD INFANTRY BRIGADE. JULY 1916.

Instructions regarding War Diaries and Intelligence Summaries are contained in F.S. Regs., Part II. and the Staff Manual respectively. Title pages will be prepared in manuscript.

Place	Date 1916. JULY.	Hour	Summary of Events and Information	Remarks and references to Appendices
ASSEMBLY AREA.	1st	7.30 a.m.	The assault was delivered at 7.30 a.m. Bde. O.O. No.58 and Amendment.	1.
	4th		The fighting continued till 4th (Appendix No.2) on which date the Brigade was relieved by 52nd Infantry Brigade. Brigade Casualties Appendix No.2 a.	2. 2 a.
VAUX	4th		The Brigade entrained at DERNANCOURT about 10 a.m. and proceeded to AILLY - SUR - SOMME from where it marched to VAUX a distance of about 5 miles. Divisional Instructions.	3.
"	5th		The Brigade remain at VAUX. On 5th, 8th Somerset L.I. moved to billets in BERTANGLES owing to overcrowing in VAUX.	
"	6th			
TALMAS.	7th	7.30 p.m.	Brigade marched to TALMAS which was reached at about 7.30 p.m. Brigade O.O. No.62 and Amendment.	4. 4 a.
MONDICOURT	8th	9 a.m.	At 9 a.m. Brigade left TALMAS and started to march to PAS. Brigade O.O. No.63. On this date 63rd Infantry Brigade came under the orders of 37th Division Commanded by Major-General Count Gleichen, and formed part of the above Division. Appendix 5 a. The Brigade was met near THIEVRES, and billets were allotted as under:- Brigade H.Qs. ....MONDICOURT. 8th Lincoln Regiment............-do- 10th York & Lancs Regt..........-do- 8th Somerset L.I...............HALLOY. 4th Middlesex Regiment..........-do- 63rd M.G.Company...............GRENAS. 63rd T.M.Battery................-do- No.3 Coy.Train.................WARLINCOURT.	5. 5 a.
"	9th		Billets were reached between 5 and 6 p.m. after a march of about 16 miles which was found rather a trying one after the fatigue of the fighting between 1st - 4th July. Here the Brigade was joined by the Signal Section of the 110th Brigade, who's place 63rd had now taken in 37th Division. Lieutenant Thorne Brigade Intelligence Officer returned to Command a Company in 8th Somerset Light Infantry, his place being taken by 2nd Lieutenant G.A.HAM, 8th Somerset L.Infantry.	

Army Form C. 2118.

Instructions regarding War Diaries and Intelligence
Summaries are contained in F.S. Regs., Part II.
and the Staff Manual respectively. Title pages
will be prepared in manuscript.

WAR DIARY
or
INTELLIGENCE SUMMARY.
(Erase heading not required.)

63RD INFANTRY BRIGADE.   **JULY 1916.**

Place	Date 1916. JULY.	Hour	Summary of Events and Information	Remarks and references to Appendices
MONDICOURT.	10th		Officers from all units visited the trenches with a view to taking over on the following day. Lieutenant A.J.BOWERMAN Brigade Bombing Officer joined Royal Flying Corps, his place being taken by 2nd Lieutenant F.J.R.SIMPSON 4th Middlesex Regiment.	5
BIENVILLERS	11th		Brigade marched to BIENVILLERS to take over trenches from 138th Brigade vide enclosed maps. A halt was made at HUMBERCAMP for dinners, after which units went independently into the Line. A congratulatory letter received from Major-General Campbell, Commanding 21st Division.	6 Div.O.O.No.25. 7 Bde.O.O.No.64. 8
"	12th		The day passed quietly in the trenches.	
"	13th		No.3 Company Train rejoined 21st Division. No.2 Company 37th Division took their place. The day passed quietly in the trenches. During the Night 13th/14th Gas was discharged from a portion of the trenches held by 63rd Brigade with a view to holding the enemy opposite our front and thus assisting the attack of the Fourth Army on the morning of the 14th. Our Casualties owing to hostile barrage were trivial.	9 37th Div.O.O.No.26.
HUMBERCAMP.	14th		During the evening the 63rd Brigade was relieved by portions of 46th and 56th Divisions(Div.O.O.27) and received orders to join IV Corps, 1st Army. The Brigade billeted the night 14th/15th as follows:- 18th Northumberland Fusiliers (Pioneers) attached and 4th Middlesex Regiment in POMMIER, remainder of the Brigade in HUMBERCAMP.	10. 10a Bde.O.O.No.65. 10b Bde.O.O.No.66.
HOUVIN	15th		Brigade marched at 8.30 a.m. arriving in billets between 3 and 4 p.m.	11 Div.O.O. No.28. 12 ; O.O. No.29. 13 Bde.O.O. No.67.
CHELERS.	16th		Brigade marched at 8.45 a.m. to CHELERS and billeted as follows:- 8th Somersets and 4th Middlesex @ VILLERS BRULIN. 8th Lincolns and 10th York & Lancs @ BAILLEUL-AUX-CORNAILLES. 63rd Machine Gun Company @ GUESTREVILLE. T.M.Battery & Brigade H.Qs. @ CHELERS.	14 Div.O.O. No.30. 15 Bde.O.O. No.68.

Army Form C. 2118.

WAR DIARY
or
INTELLIGENCE SUMMARY.

(Erase heading not required.)

63RD INFANTRY BRIGADE   JULY 1916.

Instructions regarding War Diaries and Intelligence Summaries are contained in F.S. Regs., Part II and the Staff Manual respectively. Title pages will be prepared in manuscript.

Place	Date 1916 JULY.	Hour	Summary of Events and Information	Remarks and references to Appendices
CHELERS.	17th		Brigade rested in Billeting Area.	
CHATEAU DE LA HAIE	18th		Brigade marched at 9.30 a.m. into billets as under:- 8th Lincolns to CAMBLIN L'ABBE 8th Somersets to GOUY - SERVINS 4th Middlesex to MAISNIL BOUCHE 10th Y & Lancs to ESTREE - CAUCHIE 63rd T.M.Batty to GOUY - SERVINS - Brigade H.Q. & 63rd M.G.Coy.to CHATEAU - DE - LA HAIE.	Bde.O.O.No.69 Div.G.689. 16 & 17
"	19th		Brigade rested, training of Specialists (Lewis Gunners, Signallers, Bombers etc)began.	
"	20th		Brigade inspected by Divisional Commander, each unit in own billet.	
"	21st		Brigade remained in billets and continued training.	
"	22nd		- do -	
			The Brigade was placed under orders of 47th Division and at 6 a.m., became Divisional Reserve to above Division. G/1341/9 47th Div. One Section Machine Gun Company was attached to 140th Infantry Bde. 63rd Inf.Bde.No.7244.	18. 19.
"	23rd		Remainder of Machine Gun Company occupied positions in the MAISTRE and BAJOLLE Lines.	
'	24th		Brigade remained in billets.	
VILLA D'AGQ.	25th		During the night 25th/26th the Brigade relieved 140th Infantry Brigade in the BERTHONVAL Section.	47th Div.O.O.No.88 20. 37th : O.O.No.32 21. 63rd Bde.O.O.No.70 22.

Army Form C. 2118.

WAR DIARY
or
INTELLIGENCE SUMMARY.

(Erase heading not required.)

63RD INFANTRY BRIGADE.   JULY 1916.

Instructions regarding War Diaries and Intelligence Summaries are contained in F. S. Regs., Part II and the Staff Manual respectively. Title pages will be prepared in manuscript.

Place	Date 1916. JULY.	Hour	Summary of Events and Information	Remarks and references to Appendices
VILLA D'ACQ	26th	2.45 a.m.	At 2.45 a.m., G.O.C. 63rd Brigade took over command of the line. The relief was completed about 4 a.m.	22a
"	27th		Nothing of interest occurred in the trenches.	
"	28th		-do-	
"	29th		-do-	
"	30th		-do-	
"	31st		The two Front Line Battalions, 4th Middlesex and 10th York & Lancs Regt., by 8th Somerset L.I. and 8th Lincolns respectively. 4th Middlesex Regt., moved into Support Trenches and 10th York & Lancs Regt into Reserve at CAMBLAIN L'ABBE. The relief was completed at 2.15 a.m. on 1st August.	Bde. O.O.No.71. 23.

J.R. Ainsbrighp
Com.g 63'N Inf B
1.8.16.

ORIGINAL
COPY

63RD INFANTRY BRIGADE.
---oOo---

WAR DIARY

AUGUST, 1916.

Army Form C. 2118.

WAR DIARY
or
INTELLIGENCE SUMMARY.
(Erase heading not required.)

Instructions regarding War Diaries and Intelligence Summaries are contained in F.S. Regs., Part II. and the Staff Manual respectively. Title pages will be prepared in manuscript.

Place	Date	Hour	Summary of Events and Information	Remarks and references to Appendices
VILLA d'ACQ.	1916 Aug. 1		Nothing of interest occurred in the trenches.	1
	2		" " " " " " "	
	3		" " " " " " "	
	4		" " " " " " "	
	5		" " " " " " "	
	6		" " " " " " "	
	7		The two front line Battalions, 8th Somerset L.I. and 8th Lincolnshire Regt., Bde. O.O. No. 72 were relieved by 4th Middlesex Regt. and 10th York & Lancs. Regt. respectively. 8th Somerset L.I. moved into support trenches and 8th Lincoln Regt. into reserve at CAMBLAIN L'ABBE. The relief was completed at 4 am on 7th August.	
	7		Nothing of interest occurred in the trenches.	
	8		" " " " " " "	
	9		" " " " " " "	
	10		" " " " " " "	
	11		63rd Machine Gun Company was relieved in trenches by 26th Machine Gun Coy.,(9th Division)	
	12		Working party of 229 was left behind by 8th Lincoln Regt. and attached 176 Tunnelling Coy.	
	12		The remainder of the Brigade was relieved during night 12-13 by 26th Brigade. Div. O.O.No. 33 .... 2 The command of this section of the line was handed over at 2.30 am, 13th, Bde. O.O.No. 73 .... 3 and the Brigade remained in Brigade Reserve Area.	
CHATEAU DE LA HAIE	13		The Brigade marched independently by units to new area via FRESNICOURT, REBREUVE, HOUDAIN, BEUGIN, LA COMTE, and by about 3 am, 14th, all units were in billets. Bde. O.O.No. 74 .... 4 Machine Gun Company and T.M.Battery were billeted in DIEVAL and not as stated in Bde.O.O.No.74.	
CHATEAU du BOIS des MONTS	14		Rest day.	
	15		do.	

Army Form C. 2118.

WAR DIARY
or
INTELLIGENCE SUMMARY.
(Erase heading not required.)

Instructions regarding War Diaries and Intelligence Summaries are contained in F. S. Regs., Part II. and the Staff Manual respectively. Title pages will be prepared in manuscript.

Place	Date	Hour	Summary of Events and Information	Remarks and references to Appendices
CHATEAU du BOIS des MONTS	16		Brigade in billets. Training carried out.	
	17		do.	
	18		do.	
	19		Divisional Commander held a Conference of Brigadiers and Commanding Officers to discuss training. 8th Somerset L.I. furnished party of 12 officers and 300 other ranks for work near CUVIGNY FARM. G 97.	4a
	20		Training and fatigues.	
	21		10th York & Lanc. Regt. furnished a daily working party of 12 officers and 300 other ranks for work near CUVIGNY FARM. Div.O.O. No. 34	5
	21		4th Middlesex Regt. furnished a daily working party of 8 officers and 100 other ranks for work near CUVIGNY FARM.	
	22		Working parties were found by 63rd Brigade in accordance with table. Telegram V G 3 and Div.O.O. No. 35. Bde.O.O. No. 75.	6 7
	23		Brigade moved into new area and came under orders of 9th Division. Bde.O.O. No. 76 8th Lincolnshire Regt. being placed under 26th Bde. in case of emergency	8 9
CHATEAU de la HAIE	24		T.M.Battery moved to LA COMTE to came under orders of 26th Bde., 9th Div. Div.O.O. No. 36	10
	25		Working parties and training	
	26		do.	
	27		do.	
	28		A horse show and driving competition for transport of brigade was held at Brigade H.Q.	
	29		Working parties and training. Change made in the officer personnel of T.M.Battery.	11
	30		200 of 4th Middlesex Regt and 100 of 8th Lincoln Regt. rejoined their units from working parties	
	31		Working parties and training	

John Brig-Gen
Commanding 68th Infy Brigade

63rd INFANTRY BRIGADE.

Account of Operations, July 1st - 4th, 1916.

At 6.25 a.m. on 1st July, the intensive bombardment commenced. The enemy at once opened an accurate but not heavy shell-fire on our front line and close support trenches, the right assaulting Company of 4th Middlesex Regt. suffering a good many casualties. At 5 minutes before zero, i.e. 7.25 a.m., the first lines of the 4th Middlesex attempted to leave their trenches and creep towards the German lines, but came under such heavy machine gun fire from the right that they had to return to their trenches. These leading platoons had by then lost so heavily that they were ordered to advance in one line instead of two. The assault by this Battalion was started one minute before zero and the lines went across without hesitation. O.C. 4th Middlesex states that the machine gun fire against his battalion was very severe and estimates that there were at least six guns, two in the open between EMPRESS SUPPORT and EMPRESS TRENCH and the remainder from the German TAMBOUR and FRICOUR! The direction of the assault was maintained. Battalion H.Q. went over to the German front line with the third Company. On reaching EMPRESS TRENCH the situation was as follows -

The greater part of the remainder of the two leading Companies had advanced towards the SUNKEN ROAD; the third Company had reached EMPRESS TRENCH where it was shortly after joined by the remainder of the fourth. The losses of the Battalion about this time were extremely severe.

The Germans advanced across the open from our right and the O.C. 4th Middlesex decided that the only thing to be done was to hang on to EMPRESS TRENCH and consolidate it. His available strength was then 3 Officers, 100 other ranks, and 2 Lewis Guns. The right of EMPRESS TRENCH and those leading toward the SUNKEN ROAD were then blocked. The enemy made three attempts to bomb up these trenches which were repulsed. About this time, the 50th Brigade on our right was seen to retire from the German front line trenches.

8th Somerset L.I., left assaulting Battalion, crept forward 5 minutes before zero, being at once met by heavy rifle and machine gun fire from both flanks and immediate front. This caused heavy casualties, the C.O. and Adjutant and as far as can be ascertained, all the remaining officers except Lieuts. HALL, KELLETT and ACKERMAN becoming casualties. The leading lines were held up in front of the German tranches by machine gun fire which was eventually silenced by grenades.
In advancing from the German 1st line into the Support line, heavy casualties were suffered and there was considerable bomb fighting before BALL LANE and ARROW LANE were cleared. The advance was then continued up to the junction of LOZENGE ALLEY and SUNKEN ROAD, from where communication with Brigade Headquarters was eventually established.

From the above it will be seen that both leading Battalions lost very heavily in crossing "No-man's-land" and the subsequent fighting in the German trenches. The advance of the leading Battalions resulted in the following.- 4th Middlesex holding EMPRESS TRENCH with their right flank exposed and with parties about the SUNKEN ROAD.
8th Somerset L.I. in SUNKENROAD and LOZENGE ALLEY. This Battalion had become scatteres owing to their Officer casualties.

The supporting Battalions had previously been ordered to start their advance at 8.30 a.m. in order to be in position to pass through the leading Battalions on to the second objective and at the same time follow up the barrage closely. Owing to the opposition met with by the two leading Battalions, these two battalions received orders not to advance until told to do so. Owing to reports of heavy losses of the two leading battalions it seemed not improbable that unless not supported they would be unable to maintain their positions, the supporting Battalions were ordered to advance about 8.40 a.m.

Both supporting Battalions suffered heavily going over the open.

The 10th York & Lancs Regt. advanced through 4th Middlesex and came under heavy machine gun fire from FRICOURT and FRICOURT WOOD; the leading waves got some distance in front of DART LANE and into the SUNKEN ROAD when they were held up by machine gun fire from FRICOURT WOOD; at the same time three large bodies of Germans attempted to bomb their way up all the trenches South of DART LANE and the Battalion Bombers had a hard struggle with a large bombing party in LONELY TRENCH. The Germans had three barricades in this trench which 10th York & Lancs destroyed and then made a barricade at the North end of LONELY TRENCH. A party was sent to ARROW LANE for the protection of their right flank.

8th Lincolnshire Regt. advanced over EMPRESS TRENCH and EMPRESS SUPPORT into the SUNKEN ROAD. The way had to be cleared by bombing down DART LANE, BRANDY TRENCH and LOZENGE ALLEY. The Germans made two bombing attacks up LONELY TRENCH. Owing to the heavy machine gun fire from about FRICOURT, and bombing attacks, 8th Lincolns were compelled to occupy LOZENGE ALLEY in order to protect their right flank. Some parties advanced from the SUNKEN ROAD into CRUCIFIX TRENCH and up the East end of LOZENGE ALLEY. These were compelled to retire owing to lack of bombs. Touch was gained in the SUNKEN ROAD with 64th Brigade on our left.

The Supporting Battalions were now in the following positions -
10th York & Lancs. in SUNKEN ROAD and DART LANE.
8th Lincolns in SUNKEN ROAD and LOZENGE ALLEY (W. from LOZENGE WOOD).

Orders were received from Division about 4.35 p.m. for units of 63rd Brigade to hold the trenches they were then in and reorganise. This was done and the positions then held were as follows:-
4th Middlesex - EMPRESS TRENCH from BALL LANE and EMPRESS SUPPORT. a party of 43 of 4th Middlesex were in the SUNKEN ROAD during the night 1 - 2 July and rejoined their Battalion on the morning of 2nd July.
8th Somerset L.I. in West end of LOZENGE WOOD, SUNKEN ROAD and LOZENGE ALLEY.
10th York & Lancs. - DART LANE
8th Lincolnshire Regt. from DART ALLEY to LOZENGE WOOD.
Battalions remained in those positions during the night 1st - 2nd July.

Next morning I reconnoitred the above positions and had connection established between 10th York & Lancs. and 4th Middlesex, the Brigade then being in a position to repel attacks from the S. and S.E.

Under orders from the Division, 8th Lincoln Regt. sent out patrols on morning of 2nd to RED COTTAGE and FRICOURT FARM. These patrols returned, the first got almost as far as RED COTTAGE where FRICOURT was entered by the troops on our right, the second entered FRICOURT FARM which they reported clear of Germans.

On morning of the 3rd, orders were received to form a subsidiary line from the SUNKEN ROAD along PATCH ALLEY to SOUTH SAUSAGE SUPPORT and there to establish connection with 64th Brigade. This line was occupied by 8th Lincolns on East, 8th Somerset L.I. on West with 4th Middlesex in reserve in LOZENGE ALLEY. The reconnaissance of the line ROUND WOOD ALLEY from ROUND WOOD to its junction with SAUSAGE TRENCH, thence along SODA and SOUTH SAUSAGE SUPPORT was at the same time carried out.

Under orders from the Division, the Brigade Major reconnoitred

ROUND WOOD ALLEY from ROUND WOOD westwards, and conducted 10th York and Lancs. up to ROUND WOOD, where they came under orders of 62nd Brigade. The reconnaissance of ROUND WOOD ALLEY had resulted in finding the above trench strongly held by 34th Division.

The above positions were held and improved until relief by 52nd Brigade during the night 3rd/4th July. The relief was completed about 4 a.m., 4th July.

Action of Machine gun Company and T.M. Battery.

During the last 10 minutes of the intensive bombardment, one section of 63rd Machine Gun Company brought enfilade and oblique fire to bear on the German Front and Support line, also upon FRICOURT FARM and its vicinity; this fire was effective.

One ½-section accompanied 4th Middlesex Regt. with a view to taking up a position in the SUNKEN ROAD from which to deal with a possible counter attack from FRICOURT WOOD, but this party did not succeed in crossing No-man's-land. Another half-section was then sent over and took up a position in BALL LANE in order to cover our right flank. This position was afterwards moved into DART LANE from which KONIG TRENCH was almost enfiladed. These two guns were also able to bring a heavy fire on to Germans advancing from FRICOURT WOOD, over the open, causing many casualties, and they remained with 8th Lincoln Regt. in LOZENGE ALLEY during the night 1/2 July. During 1st July, one additional section was ordered to DART LANE from which position a heavy fire was brought to bear on FRICOURT and FRICOURT WOOD at intervals during the night 1st/2nd. During the 2nd July, these guns were properly dug in in LOZENGE ALLEY and DART LANE. On 3rd, when the Brigade took up its new position, two further guns were placed in position just east of WILLOW PATCH in PATCH ALLEY. The other guns already in position in LOZENGE ALLEY and DART LANE took up new positions when the Brigade changed its position on 3rd July.

The Stokes Guns joined in the Bombardment as arranged. All Officers of the Battery became casualties early on first July, and it is hard to collect any information in consequence. Two guns followed each of the two leading Battalions. Of the two guns which followed 4th Middlesex, one came into action in EMPRESS TRENCH and did good work. Two guns were found very useful by O.C. 8th Lincolns later on in the firing down LONELY TRENCH.

The battery suffered severely during the fighting but succeeded in bringing back all its guns.

The hostile wire was everywhere thoroughly cut by 96th Brigade R.F.A., who throughout the whole operation rendered every possible support to the Infantry.

I consider that throughout these operations all units fought with the utmost gallantry. The opposition was everywhere most determined but the troops pressed on to the limit of their powers and every case maintained the positions they had gained.

July 9th 1916

Brigadier General,
Commanding 63rd Infantry Brigade.

Subject:- Officer Casualties.

37th Division.

Reference your A.331 of to-day. Following is a list of the Officer casualties in this Brigade during the Operations July 1st - 3rd 1916.

8th Lincoln Regiment.

Killed.	2nd Lieut. CRAGG, J.F.
	2nd Lieut. SWIFT, W.
	2nd Lieut. COURTICE, R.L.
	2nd Lieut. PARKINSON, J.H.
Wounded Believed Killed.	Captain JONES, A.C.
Wounded.	Captain DEVONSHIRE, E.R.
	Captain CORDINER, R.G.
	2nd Lieut. MITCHELL, E.G.
	2nd Lieut. ROWCROFT, M.G.
	2nd Lieut. BOADLE, T.S.
	Lieutenant LAFFERTY, G.G.
	2nd Lieut. LILL, A.
	2nd Lieut. HAWARD, H.F.

8th Somerset L.Infantry.

Killed.	2nd Lieut. DALRYMPLE, H.
	2nd Lieut. SCOTT, W.
	2nd Lieut. LEATHLY, W.G.
	2nd Lieut. YOUNG, J.V.
	2nd Lieut. WITHERS, F.D.
	2nd Lieut. LEWIS, J.E.
	2nd Lieut. CHALMERS, J.R.T.
Missing Believed Killed.	Captain WARDEN, W.G.
Missing.	2nd Lieut. DOBSON, S.A.M.
Died of Wounds.	Captain HATT, A.B.
Wounded.	Lieut-Col. SCOTT, J.W.
	Captain SCHLESINGER, G.L.
	2nd Lieut. ROUTH, D.J.L.
	2nd Lieut. ABBOTT, R.C.
	Lieutenant HUSBANDS, R.G.W.
	2nd Lieut. WHITING, W.
	2nd Lieut. BAKER, W.H.
	2nd Lieut. WEBB, A.T.

4th Middlesex Regiment.

   Killed. 2nd Lieut. BRANCH, A.
         2nd Lieut. CHAMBERS, A.G.
         2nd Lieut. CHURCHFIELD, S.P. (T.M.Battery)
         2nd Lieut. JOHNSTON, A.A.H.
         Captain Johnston, O.R.F.
         2nd Lieut. MONEY, G.R.
         2nd Lieut. PAXTON, A.F.C.
         2nd Lieut. PEYTON, R.
         Lieutenant RIDPATH, G.L.C.
         Lieutenant SAPTE, A.
         2nd Lieut. WHITBY, E.V.
         2nd Lieut. WINN-SAMPSON, A.H.
         2nd Lieut. WOOD, W.J.
         2nd Lieut. BARNETT, P.

   Died of Wounds. Captain ROWLEY, D.T.C.

   Wounded. Capt.& Adj. BODEN, T.L.
         2nd Lieut. CARY, R.T.O.
         2nd Lieut. COUMBE, F.E.
         2nd Lieut. LEIGH-PEMBERTON, P.
         2nd Lieut. MARVIN, A.J.

10th York & Lancs Regt.

   Killed. Captain TWENTYMAN, D.C.T.
       Captain MULLINS, R.W.
       Lieutenant ORGAN, H.P.
       2nd Lieut. KINGSFORD, H.J.
       2nd Lieut. GODWIN, C.H.
       2nd Lieut. SYKES, C.
       2nd Lieut. STAINTON, R.M.

   Wounded. Major   WILLIS, A.J.
        Captain BAKER, F.B.
        Lieutenant MEIN, W.H.
        2nd Lieut. DRAKE, D.H.
        2nd Lieut. COCKBURN, E.C.

   Shell Shock. 2nd Lieut. MORTON SMITH, F. (T.M.Battery).

63rd Machine Gun Coy.

   Wounded. 2nd Lieut. BOULTBEE, E.F.

63rd Trench Mortar Batty. Shewn with their Units except:-

   Wounded. Lieutenant JOHNSTONE, R.E. 13th N.F.

                         P.T.O.

The following letter has been received from the G.O.C. 21st Division:-

To/
G.O.C.
63rd Infantry Brigade.

        I cannot allow the 63rd Brigade to leave my command without expressing to all ranks my immense admiration for their splendid behaviour during the recent fighting.

        No troops in the world could have behaved in a more gallant manner.

        I feel sure that the 63rd Brigade will uphold the reputation of the 21st Division in the Division to which they are attached.

        Whilst deeply deploring your heavy losses, I feel that these gallant men have willingly given their lives to vindicate the character of the 21st Division.

        Hoping that our separation may be of short duration only, I wish you Good Luck.

        (sd) DAVID G.M.CAMPBELL, Major-General,
        Commanding 21st Divn.

8th July, 1916.

63rd Infantry Brigade Headquarters.

31st July 1916.

Brigadier General E.R.Hill,   Commanding.
    (Highland L.I.)

Captain W.L.Brodie, V.C.   Brigade Major.
    (Highland L.I.)

Major G.R.Codrington,   Staff Captain.
    (Leicestershire Yeomanry).

2nd Lieut. G.A.Ham,   Intelligence
    (8th Somerset L.I.)   Officer.

2nd Lieut. F.J.R.Simpson,   Brigade Bombing
    (4th Middlesex Regiment).   Officer.

Captain R.A.Ker,   Brigade Transport
    (8th Lincoln Regiment).   Officer.

Lieutenant N.Sizer, R.E.   Brigade Signal
                                           Officer.

Baron H de Courtois   Brigade Interpreter

-----oOOo------

63rd Infantry Brigade.

REINFORCEMENTS ARRIVED DURING JULY 1916.

UNIT.	Officers.		Other Ranks.	Date of arrival.
8th Lincoln Regiment.	1	(a)	Nil.	2nd July 1916.
	-		21.	3rd " "
	3	(b)	Nil.	16th " "
	1	(c)	Nil.	20th " "
	3	(d)	206.	27th " "
	3	(e)	Nil.	29th " "
	11.		227.	
8th Somerset L.Infantry.	-		51.	25th July 1916.
	2	(f)	Nil.	26th " "
	11	(g)	Nil.	28th " "
	-		35.	30th " "
	13.		86.	
4th Middlesex Regiment.	1	(h)	Nil.	15th July 1916.
	15	(i)	Nil.	19th " "
	5	(j)	Nil.	20th " "
	1	(k)	3.	27th " "
	-		45.	28th " "
	22.		48.	
10th York & Lancs Regt.	-		159.	25th July 1916.
	1	(l)	Nil.	28th " "
	1.		159.	
63rd Machine Gun Company.	-		30.	5th July 1916.
	3	(m)	-	7th "
	3.		30.	

TOTAL ARRIVED DURING JULY 1916.   50 Officers and 556 Other Ranks.

(a)	2nd Lieut	H.A.C.Lewis.	8th Lincoln Regiment.
(b)	" "	T.R.Carter.	-do-
	" "	R.G.Godfrey.	-do-
	" "	C.F.Everard.	-do-
(c)	" "	C.F.M.Lilly.	-do-
(d)	" "	E.H.Duke.	-do-
	" "	W.H.Lloyd.	-do-
	" "	D.J.B.Busher.	-do-
(e)	" "	J.Reed.	-do-
	" "	A.F.Forge.	-do-
	" "	W.J.Keeling.	-do-

P.T.O.

- 2 -

```
(f)  2nd Lieut.  T.C.Snow.              8th Somerset L.Infantry.
      :    :     P.C.Hagon.              -do-
(g)  Captain     H.Hussey.               -do-
     2nd Lieut.  L.S.Holmes.             -do-
      :    :     F.H.T.Joscelyne.        -do-
      :    :     E.A.Matthews.           -do-
      :    :     A.Garrad.               -do-
      :    :     W.R.B.Peel.             -do-
      :    :     P.S.Bryant.             -do-
      :    :     J.H.M.Hardyman.         -do-
      :    :     F.H.Baker.              -do-
      :    :     E.H.Morgan.             -do-
      :    :     H.J.Fricker.            -do-

(h)  2nd Lieut.  H.F.Bowser.             4th Middlesex Regiment.
(i)  Lieut.      R.Underhill.            -do-
      :          E.A.H.Fenn.             -do-
     2nd Lieut.  A.C.Terrell.            -do-
      :    :     E.A.M.Williams.         -do-
      :    :     P.M.Curnow.             -do-
      :    :     L.C.Thomspn.            -do-
      :    :     O.N.Martin.             -do-
      :    :     D.C.L.Murray.           -do-
      :    :     O.G.Johnson.            -do-
      :    :     P.W.Smith.              -do-
      :    :     R.M.Hilton.             -do-
      :    :     A.N.MacLeod.            -do-
      :    :     E.A.G.Mitchell.         -do-
      :    :     A.E.Fereman.            -do-
      :    :     W.E.Stockley.           -do-
(j)   :    :     F.W.Scholefield.        -do-
      :    :     A.D.Hooke.              -do-
      :    :     R.G.Williams.           -do-
      :    :     A.D.Trowell.            -do-
      :    :     R.F.T.Irwin.            -do-
(k)  Lieut.      S.W.Melbourne.          -do-

(l)  2nd Lieut.  D.A.Hall.               10th York & Lancs Regiment.

(m)  2nd Lieut.  J.C.Hartley.            63rd Machine Gun Company.
      :    :     D.Crockatt.             -do-
      :    :     A.U.Coulter.            -do-
```

CASUALTIES DURING JULY 1916.

63rd Infantry Brigade.

UNIT.	IN TRENCHES. Officers. Killed.	Wounded.	Missing.	Other Ranks. Killed.	Wounded.	Missing.	TOTAL.	OUT OF TRENCHES. Officers. Killed.	Wounded.	Missing.	Other Ranks. Killed.	Wounded.	Missing.	TOTAL.	Total Casualties In and Out of Trenches.	SICKNESS. Officers.	Other Ranks.	GRAND TOTAL.	REMARKS.
8th Lincoln Regiment.	A 4	B 8	C 1	30	199	12	254	-	-	-	-	-	-	NIL	254	D 1	18	273.	"A" 2/Lieut.W.Swift. 2/Lieut.R.L.Courtice. 2/Lt.J.H.Parkinson. 2/Lt.J.H.Cragg. "B" Capt.E.R.Devonshire. " R.G.Cordiner. Lt. G.G.Lafferty. " M.G.Rowcroft. 2/Lt.E.G.Mitchell. " T.S.Boadle. " A.Lill. " W.F.Haward. "C" Capt.A.C.Jones. "D" 2/Lt.H.C.Baker.
T O T A L.	4	8	1	30	199	12	254	-	-	-	-	-	-	NIL	254	1	18	273.	

63rd Infantry Brigade.

CASUALTIES DURING JULY 1916.

UNIT	IN TRENCHES. Officers.			Other Ranks.				OUT OF TRENCHES. Officers.			Other Ranks.				Total Casualties In and Out of Trenches.	SICKNESS. Officers.	Other Ranks.	GRAND TOTAL.	REMARKS.
	Killed.	Wounded.	Missing.	Killed.	Wounded.	Missing.	TOTAL.	Killed.	Wounded.	Missing.	Killed.	Wounded.	Missing.	TOTAL.					
8th Somerset Light Infantry.	10	8	-	92	318	18	446	-	-	-	-	-	-	NIL	446	2	28	476.	"E" Capt. A.B.Hatt. " W.G.Warden. 2/Lt. F.D.Withers. " J.V.Young. " H.Dalrymple. " W.F.Scott. " W.G.Leathley. " J.G.Lewis. " J.R.T.Chalmers. " W.H.Baker. "F" Lt-Col.J.W.Scott. Lieut.R.G.W.Husbands. 2/Lt. D.J.L.Routh. " S.A.M.Dobson. " W.C.Whiting. " R.G.Abbott. " A.T.Webb Captain G.L.Schlesinger. "G" Major R.H.Huntington, DSO Captain S.Baker.
TOTAL.	10	8	-	92	318	18	446	-	-	-	-	-	-	NIL	446	2	28	476.	

CASUALTIES DURING JULY 1916.

63rd Infantry Brigade.

UNIT	IN TRENCHES - Officers - Killed	Officers - Wounded	Officers - Missing	Other Ranks - Killed	Other Ranks - Wounded	Other Ranks - Missing	TOTAL	OUT OF TRENCHES - Officers - Killed	Officers - Wounded	Officers - Missing	Other Ranks - Killed	Other Ranks - Wounded	Other Ranks - Missing	TOTAL	Total Casualties in and out of Trenches	SICKNESS - Officers	SICKNESS - Other Ranks	GRAND TOTAL	REMARKS
10th York and Lancaster Regiment.	J 7 K 6	6	-	35	247	25	320	-	-	-	-	-	-	NIL	320	1	37	358.	"J" Capt. D.C.T.Twentyman. " R.W.Mullins. Lt. H.P.Organ. 2/Lt. R.J.Kingsford. " C.Sykes. " R.M.Stainton. " C.H.Godwin. "K" Major. A.J.Willis. Capt. F.B.Baker. Lt. W.H.Mein. 2/Lt. E.C.Cockburn. " D.H.Drake. " F.Morton Smith. "L" 2/Lt. R.A.Smith.
TOTAL.	7	6	-	35	247	25	320	-	-	-	-	-	-	NIL	320	1	37	358.	

63rd Infantry Brigade.

CASUALTIES DURING JULY 1916.

UNITS.	IN TRENCHES. Officers.			IN TRENCHES. Other Ranks.				OUT OF TRENCHES. Officers.			OUT OF TRENCHES. Other Ranks.			Total Casualties In and Out of Trenches.	SICKNESS. Officers.	SICKNESS. Other Ranks.	GRAND TOTAL	REMARKS.
	Killed.	Wounded.	Missing.	Killed.	Wounded.	Missing.	TOTAL.	Killed.	Wounded.	Missing.	Killed.	Wounded.	Missing.	TOTAL.				
63rd Machine Gun Company.	-	M 1	-	3	10	-	14	-	-	-	-	-	-	NIL	14	-	6	20.	"M" 2/Lt.E.F.Boultbee.
T O T A L.	-	1	-	3	10	-	14	-	-	-	-	-	-	NIL	14	-	6	20.	
63rd Trench Mortar Battery.	-	N 1	-	4	16	-	21	-	-	-	-	-	-	NIL.	21	-	6	27.	"N" 2/Lt. R.E.Johnstone.
T O T A L.	-	1	-	4	16	-	21	-	-	-	-	-	-	NIL.	21	-	6	27.	

CASUALTIES DURING JULY 1916.

63rd Infantry Brigade.

UNIT	IN TRENCHES. Officers.			Other Ranks.				OUT OF TRENCHES. Officers.			Other Ranks.				Total Casualties In and Out of Trenches.	SICKNESS. Officers	Other Ranks.	GRAND TOTAL.	REMARKS.
	Killed.	Wounded.	Missing.	Killed.	Wounded.	Missing.	TOTAL.	Killed.	Wounded.	Missing.	Killed.	Wounded.	Missing.	TOTAL.					
4th Middlesex Regiment.	15	H 5 I	-	114	314	93	541	-	-	-	@ 4	@ 4	-	8	549	-	4	553.	"H" Capt. D.C.T.Rowley. " O.R.F.Johnson. Lt. A.Sapte. 2/Lt. G.L.C.Ridpath. " A.Branch. " S.P.Churchfield " A.A.H.Johnston. " A.H.Winn-Sampson. " E.V.Whitby. " E.G.Chambers. " G.R.Money. " A.F.C.Paxton. " W.J.Wood. " E.Peyton. " P.Barnett. "I" Capt.& Adjt.T.L.Boden. 2/Lt. R.T.O.Carey. " A.J.Marvin. " F.E.Coumbe. " P.Leigh-Pemberton
TOTAL.	15	5	-	114	314	93	541	-	-	-	4	4	-	8	549	-	4	553.	

@ 8 Other Ranks killed and wounded by Bomb Explosion.

63rd Infantry Brigade.

SUMMARY OF CASUALTIES IN BRIGADE DURING JULY 1916.

UNITS.	IN TRENCHES. Officers. Killed.	Wounded.	Missing.	Other Ranks. Killed.	Wounded.	Missing.	TOTAL.	OUT OF TRENCHES. Officers. Killed.	Wounded.	Missing.	Other Ranks. Killed.	Wounded.	Missing.	TOTAL.	Total Casualties In and out of Trenches.	SICKNESS. Officers.	Other Ranks.	GRAND TOTAL.
8th Lincoln Regiment.	4	8	1	30	199	12	254	-	-	-	-	-	-	NIL	254	1	18	273
8th Somerset L.I.	10	8	-	92	318	18	446	-	-	-	-	-	-	NIL	446	2	28	476
4th Middlesex Regt.	15	5	-	114	314	93	541	-	-	-	4	4	-	8	549	-	4	553
10th York & Lancs Regt.	7	6	-	35	247	25	320	-	-	-	-	-	-	NIL	320	1	37	358
63rd Machine Gun Coy.	-	1	-	3	10	-	14	-	-	-	-	-	-	NIL	14	-	6	20
63rd Trench Mortar Batty	-	1	-	4	16	-	21	-	-	-	-	-	-	NIL	21	-	6	27
TOTALS.	36	29	1	278	1104	148	1596	-	-	-	4	4	-	8	1604	4	99	1707

STRENGTH OF UNITS ON 31ST JULY 1916.

UNIT.	Officers.	Other Ranks.	DETAILS. Officrs.	Other Ranks.
8th Lincoln R.	32.	867.	4.	87.
8th Somerset L.I.	25.	659.	9.	70.
4th Middlesex R.	38.	521.	4.	98.
10th York & Lancs.	26.	885.	5.	100.
63rd M.G. Coy.	12.	215.	2.	15.
63rd T.M. Battery.	3.	42.	-	1.
TOTAL.	136.	3189.	24.	371.

21st DIVISION

Actual casualties among Other ranks are as follows :-

	8th Lincoln Regt.	8th Somerset L.I.	4th Middlesex Regt.	10th York & Lancs.Regt.	Machine Gun Company	TOTAL
KILLED	30	65	102	23	3	223
WOUNDED (including shell shock)	171	281	278	186	10	926
MISSING, BELIEVED KILLED.	-	-	35	-	-	35
MISSING.	34	79	111	71	-	295
T O T A L	235	425	526	280	13	1479

July 6th 1916

Brigadier General,
Commanding 63rd Infantry Brigade.

NOMINAL ROLL OF OFFICERS
OF
8TH LINCOLN REGIMENT.

Rank and Name.	Employment.	Trained.	Arrival in Country.	REMARKS.
Lieut-Colonel.				
R.H.JOHNSTON, D.S.O.	In Command.			
Major.				
H.PATTINSON.	2nd "		10.9.15.	
Captains.				
F.BROWN.	Adjutant.		"	
R.A.KER.	Bde.Tranp O.	Transport.	"	
E.M.HARRISON.	Coy.Cmdr.	Machine Gun.	27.2.16.	
H.B.DAWES.	" "		15.6.16.	
Lieutenants.				
B.J.L.BEARD.	" "	" "	19.11.15.	
F.W.LATHAM.	" "	Grenade wk.	13.10.15.	
C.D.JESSOPP.	Coy Bomb O.	" "	"	
R.A.PRESTON.	Platoon Cmdr.	Lewis Gun.	9.10.15.	
S.FERRY.	" "	Grenade wk.	"	
F.TAYLOR.	Qr.Master.		10.9.15.	
2nd Lieutenants.				
F.W.ALLBONES.	Signal Offcr.	Signalling.	17.2.16.	
F.A.WAUGH.	Bn.Bomb.Off.	Grenade wk.	17.6.16.	
C.W.RHODES.	Platoon Cmdr.	" "	1.11.15.	
E.B.MARKHAM.	" "	T.Mortars.	13.10.15.	
E.A.DUFF.	" "	Lewis Gun.	9.10.15.	
A.J.RAHLES REHBULA.	Transp.Off.	" "	24.3.16.	
C.F.M.LILLY.	Platoon Cmdr.		13.7.16.	
T.R.CARTER.	" "	" "	20.6.16.	
J.READ.			25.7.16.	
R.J.GODFREY.	" "	Grenade wk.	26.6.16.	
A.F.FORGE.	" "		25.7.16.	
W.H.LLOYD.	" "		20.7.16.	
G.H.EVERAD.	" "		26.6.16.	
E.H.DUKES.	" "		27.7.16.	
D.J.B.BUSHER.	" "	T.Mortars.	20.7.16.	
H.A.C.LEWIS.	" "		27.6.16.	
H.J.KEELING.	" "	Lewis Gun.	15.6.16.	
L.D.EDWARDS.	T.M.Batty.	Trench Mtr.		
J.H.C.HENLEY.	Platoon Cmdr.			Hospital.
H.C.BAKER.	" "			"
Lieutenant.				
E.M.CARRE.	Attch R.F.C.			

NOMINAL ROLL OF OFFICERS
OF
8TH SOMERSET L. INFANTRY.

Rank and Name.	Employment.	Trained.	Arrival in Country.	REMARKS.
Majors.				
N.A.H.CAMPBELL.	In Command.		25.6.16.	
R.H.HUNTINGTON,D.S.O.	2nd "	Grenade wk.	10.9.15.	Hospital.
Captains.				
H.HUSSEY.	A/2nd "	" "	28.7.16.	
C.W.GLADE WRIGHT.	Coy.Cmmdr.	" "	9.10.15	
S.BAKER.	" "		5.12.15.	"
Lieutenants.				
W.H.A.THORNE.	" "	Machine Gun	10.9.15.	
J.P.AKERMAN.	L/Gun Offc.	Lewis Gun.	"	
H.PIKE.	Transp.Offc.	Transport.	"	
A.J.BOWERMAN.		Grenade wk.	"	Att R.F.C.
2nd Lieutenants.				
T.F.WALLIS.	Coy.Cmmdr.		9.10.15.	
M.F.F.SAUNDERS.	Platoon Cmdr.	" "	"	Hospital.
F.G.ADLAM.	Bomb.Offcr.	" "	5.1.16.	
A.P.MORGAN.	Platoon Cmdr.	" "	9.10.15.	"
G.A.HAM.	Bde.Bmth.Off.		24.3.16.	
J.R.MELLOR.	Platoon Cmdr.		"	
C.KELLETT.	" "	Physical T.	14.4.16.	Attdg Course
M.W.MAURICE.	" "		24.4.16.	
F.G.HINTON.	" "	Grenade wk.	23.5.16.	
H.P.V.BARKER.	A/L.Gun Off.	Lewis Gun,	17.6.16.	
H.EMMS.	Platoon Cmdr.	T.Mortars.	19.6.16.	
P.C.HAGON.	" "	Grenade wk.	26.7.16.	
T.C.SNOW.	" "	R.Finding.	26.7.16.	
L.S.HOLMES.	" "	Transport.	28.7.16.	
F.H.T.JOSCELYNE.	" "	R.Finding.	"	
E.A.MATTHEWS.	" "	Sniping.	"	
A.GARRAD.	" "	Grenade wk.	"	
W.R.B.PEEL.	" "	Machine Gun.	"	
P.S.BRYANT.	" "	Lewis Gun.	"	
J.H.M.HARDYMAN.	" "	Staff Work.	"	
H.J.FRICKER.	" "	Grenade wk.	"	
A.H.HALL.	A/Adjutant.	Signalling.	10.9.15.	
F.H.BAKER.	Platoon Cmdr.	Grenade wk.	28.7.16.	
Captain.				
A.W.PHILLIPS.			"	att 2/Army.
J.E.UNDERWOOD.R.A.M.C.	Medical Off.		11.6.15.	
L.GREEN.	Chaplain.		10.9.15.	
Lieut & Qr.Mr.				
J.SCHOOLING.	Quartermaster.		10.9.15.	
2nd Lieutenant.				
E.H.MORGAN.	Platoon Cmdr.		28.7.16.	

NOMINAL ROLL OF OFFICERS
of
4th MIDDLESEX REGIMENT.

Rank and Name.	Employment.	Trained.	Date of Arrival Country.	REMARKS.
Lieut-Colonel.				
H.P.F.BICKNELL, D.S.O.	In Command.		7.11.14.	
Captains.				
S.A.WILLIS.	Coy.Cmmdr.	Grenade wk.	4.10.15.	
H.L.G.FRY.	" "	" "	22.6.15.	
Lieutenants.				
E.A.H.FENN.	Platoon Cmdr.	Engineering.	13.7.16.	
R.UNDERHILL.	" "		"	
S.W.MELBOURNE.	" "		"	
2nd Lieutenants.				
H.F.BOWSER.	" "		1.2.15.	
A.C.TERRELL.	" "	Grenade wk.	13.7.16.	
W.K.MAITLAND.	Coy.Cmmdr.	" "	4.5.16.	
E.A.M.WILLIAMS.	Grenade wk.	" "	13.7.16.	
A.A.BURCH.	Platoon Cmdr.	Physical T.	29.5.16.	
F.J.R.SIMPSON.	Bde.Bomb Off.	Grenade wk.	19.11.15.	
R.E.TAYLOR.	Bde.H.Qs.		29.5.16.	
P.W.SMITH.	Platoon Cmdr.		13.7.16.	
W.E.STOCKLEY.	" "		"	
S.MIRIAMS.	" "	Range Find.	5.6.16.	
D.CUTBUSH.	Coy.Cmmdr.	T.Warfare.	2.10.15.	
R.M.HILTON.	L/Gun Offc.	Lewis Gun.	13.7.16.	
M.W.S.HARRIS.	Platoon Cmdr.		29.5.16.	
R.F.T.IRWIN.	" "		13.7.16.	
O.G.JOHNSON.	" "	Physical T.	"	
F.W.SCHOLEFIELD.	" "		15.7.16.	
E.A.G.MITCHELL.	" "		13.7.16.	
P.M.CURNOW.	" "	Grenade wk.	"	
L.C.THOMPSON.	" "	Physical T.	"	
D.C.L.MURRAY.	" "		"	
H.E.HEFFER.	A/Adjutant.	" "	5.11.14.	
O.N.MARTIN.	Platoon Cmdr.	" "	13.7.16.	
A.E.FEREMAN.	" "		"	
A.F.MAC LEOD.	" "	Signalling.	"	
A.D.TROWELL.	" "	"	15.7.16.	
F.LOFTS.	" "	Grenade wk.	26.1.16.	
H.M.WILLIAMS.	" "	Physical T.	24.1.16.	
R.G.WILLIAMS.	" "		15.7.16.	
A.D.HOOKE.	" "		"	
J.H.HODGSON.	Transp.Offc.	Grenade wk.	28.4.16.	
G.S.SUTHERLAND.	Signal "	Signalling.	4.5.15.	
Lieut & Qr.Mr.				
E.H.AMOR.	Quartermaster		18.10.15.	
Captains.				
A.D.SHARP., R.A.M.C. c	Medical Offcr.			
R.W.DUGDALE.	Chaplain.			

NOMINAL ROLL OF OFFICERS
OF
10th YORK & LANCS REGIMENT.

Rank and Name.	Employment.	Trained.	Arrival in Country.	REMARKS.
Lieut-Colonel.				
J.H.RIDGWAY.	In Command.		1.9.14.	
Major.				
J.B.O.TRIMBLE.	2nd :		13.6.16.	
Captains.				
C.D.ST G. McCLELLAN.			5.6.16.	
R.H.FITTS.	Coy.Commdr.	Grenade wk.	11.9.15.	
C.F.AIREY.	Transp.Off.	Transport.	:	
W.B.DRYNAN.	Coy.Commdr.	Grenade wk.	:	
E.G.J.FAIRNIE	: :		19.11.15.	
Lieutenants.				
J.H.RAMSDEN.	: :	: :	10.10.15.	
S.J.S.GROVES.	Platoon Cmdr.		17.3.15.	
L.A.ELSWORTH.	Bn.Intell Off.	Sniping.	11.9.15.	
H.BROADBENT.	Adjutant.	Signalling.	:	
2nd Lieutenants.				
D.A.HALL.	Platoon Cmdr.	Grenade wk.	25.7.16.	
C.A.J.NICHOLSON.	: :	: :	6.1.16.	
J.A.HEALD.	Ant- Gas Off. 21st Divn.	Chemistry.	26.10.15.	
R.M.WILKINSON.	Staff Duties.	Grenade wk.	9.10.15.	
F.E.KNOWLES.	Platoon Cmdr.	: :	:	
R.J.MITCHELL.	: :	: :	19.11.15.	
C.BAINES.	R.F.C. attchd.	: :	9.10.15.	
A.L.QUANCE.	Platoon Cmdr.	Range Find.	10.3.16.	
F.AYRES.	L.Gun Off.	Lewis Gun.	10.11.15.	
F.E.PAYNE.	Bomb Offcr.	Grenade wk.	11.10.15.	
D.D.HAWLEY.	Platoon Cmdr.	Musketry.	29.5.16.	
E.SAMUELS.	Signal Offcr.	Signalling.	25.1.16.	
J.DOUGLAS.	Platoon Cmdr.	Gunnery.	16.6.16.	
A.HOCKLY.	: :	Signalling.	15.6.16.	
A.W.LAMOND.	A/Qr.Mr.	Grenade.	6.12.14.	
Lieutenant.				
G.R.PLAISTER.	Medical Offcr.		11.9.15.	

NOMINAL ROLL OF OFFICERS
of
63RD MACHINE GUN COMPANY.

Rank and Name.	Employment.	Trained.	Arrival in Country.	REMARKS.
Major.				
W.G.A.COLDWELL.	In Command.	Machine Gun.	4.11.14.	
2nd Lieutenants.				
W.A.WEBB.	A/Adjutant.	: :	25.2.15.	
E.TALL.	2nd Command.	: :	:	
G.E.R.CROAGER.	Section Off.	: :	:	
C.F.LARN.	: L	: :	:	
A.B.HAYWARD.	: :	: :	:	
N.F.HAWES.	Transp.Offc.	: :	25.6.16.	
R.HAY.	103.Inf.Bde.	: :	26.6.16.	
I.C.HARTLEY.	Section Off.	: :	1.7.16.	
D.CROCKATT.	: :	: :	2.7.16.	
C.W.THOMPSON.	: :	: :	4.6.16.	
A.V.COULTER.	103 Inf.Bde.	: :	1.7.16.	

NOMINAL ROLL OF OFFICERS

of

63RD TRENCH MORTAR BATTERY.

2nd Lieut. L.D. EDWARDS.   8th Lincoln Regt.

2nd Lieut. G.H. SIMS.   8th Somerset L.I.

2nd Lieut. L.W. ANDREAE.   4th Middlesex Regt.

NOMINAL ROLL OF OFFICERS.

4th Battalion Middlesex Regiment.

Rank and Name		Present Employment	Trained in	Embarked
Lt.-Col.	H.P.F.BICKNELL, D.S.O.	Commanding(Leave U.K.)		7.11.14
Major	J.D.MAYHEW	Commanding		
Captain	A.G.DAWSON	2nd in Command		24.12.16
,,	T.L.BODEN	Adjutant		14.11.16
,,	P.GROVE WHITE	Coy. Comdr.		26.10.16
,,	E.J.DONALDSON	,,		4.12.16
,,	S.A.WILLIS	,,	Bombing	4.10.15
,,	H.E.HEFFER	,,		5.10.14
Lieut.	E.A.H.FENN	Town Major	Engineer	13.7.16
,,	B.P.JONES	Plat. Comdr.		6.9.16
2nd Lieut.	H.F.BOWSER	Bde.Sniping Off.	Sniping	1.2.15
,,	A.C.TERRELL	a/Adjutant	Bombing	13.7.16
,,	E.A.M.WILLIAMS		Bombing	13.7.16
,,	F.J.R.SIMPSON	Bde. Bombing Off.	Bombing	19.11.15
,,	R.E.TAYLOR	a/D.A.D.O.S.		29.5.16
,,	SMITH P.W.	Platoon Comdr.		13.7.16
,,	W.E.STOCKLEY	,,	Trench Warfare	13.7.16
,,	S.MIRAMS			5.6.16
,,	D.CUTBUSH	Lewis Gun Offr.	Co. Offs. Crse.	2.10.16
,,	R.M.HILTON	Plat. Comdr.	Lewis Gun	13.7.16
,,	GROGAN E.G.			4.12.16
,,	M.W.S.HARRIS	Attd.63rd T.M.B.	Trench Mortar	29.5.16
,,	R.F.T.IRWIN	Platoon Comdr.	Mining (Listening)	13.7.16
,,	SCHOLEFIELD F.W.	Sniping Offr.	Sniping	15.7.16
,,	A.G.MITCHELL			13.7.16
,,	L.C.THOMSON	Plat. Comdr.	P.T.& B.F.	13.7.16
,,	O.N.MARTIN	Div. Sal. Off.	P.T.& B.F.	13.7.16
,,	L.W.ANDREAE	Plat. Comdr.	Trench Mortar	12.6.15
,,	A.D.TROWELL	T.M.Course	Signalling	15.7.16
,,	H.M.WILLIAMS	A/Bombing Offr.	Bombing	24.1.16
,,	R.G.WILLIAMS	Attd. 63rd Bde. HQ	P.T. & B.F.	15.7.16
,,	A.D.HOOKE	Plat. Comdr.	Gas Course	15.7.16
,,	J.K.GRAYSON	,,		4.12.16
,,	H.S.WHITLOCK	a/Transport Off.		10.9.16
,,	J.H.HODGSON		Transport	28.4.16
,,	G.S.SUTHERLAND	Signalling Off.		4.5.15
,,	J.C.LYAL	Transport Offr.		12.12.16
,,	D.F.HURR	Course, 37th Div. School		6.9.16
,,	H.M.MONK	Course, 5th ,,		4.12.16
Lieut.	E.H.AMOR	Quartermaster		18.10.15
Captain	A.D.SHARP, R.A.M.C.	Medical Officer		
Captain	W.G.LARGIE, C.F.,	Chaplain.		

NOMINAL ROLL OF OFFICERS

8th (Service) Battalion Lincolnshire Regiment.

Rank	Name	Present Employment	How Trained	Arrived in Country
Lt-Col.	JOHNSTON R.H., D.S.O.	Commanding		
Major	PATTINSON H.	2nd in Command	Musketry, Hythe	11.9.15
Captain	BROWN F.	Adjutant		11.9.15
:	CAMERON E.A.	XX.X.XX		25.8.16
:	KER R.A.	Bde. Transport Officer		11.9.15
:	CORDINER R.G., M.C.	Coy. Comdr.	Lewis & Vickers Guns	11.9.15
:	DAWES H.B.	: :		17.6.16
:	HARRISON E.M.	On leave		10.3.16
:	BEARD B.J.L.	Attd. 63 Bde HQ	Lewis & Vickers Guns	2.10.15
Lieut.	JESSOPP C.D.	Temp.Co. Cdr.	Grenade, Lewis Gun	13.10.16
:	FERRY S.	Sick	do. do.	2.10.15
:	HALDWELL F.H.G.	Att.112 Bde. HQ	Musketry	21.8.16
2nd Lieut.	ALLBONES F.W.	Signal Officer	Signalling	12.2.16
:	WAUGH F.A.	Bn. Bomb. Offr.	Bombing	19.6.16
:	RAHLES RAHBULA A.J.	Transport Off.	Transport duties	4.4.16
:	DUKES E.H.	Asst. do.		27.7.16
:	READ J.	Attd. 37th Div.		28.7.16
:	LILLY C.F.M.	do.		20.7.16
:	KEELING W.J.	Coy. Cdr.	Bombing	30.7.16
:	POSNER P.E.	Plat. Comdr.	Sniping	26.7.16
:	HODGSON D.C.	do.	Bombing	28.7.16
:	LEWIS H.A.C.	Bn. L.G.Offr.	Lewis Gun	27.6.16
:	BRADES H.C.		Bombing, Lewis Gun	16.9.16
:	GODFREY R.G.	Att.I.B.D. CALAIS	Bombing, Lewis Gun	20.6.16
:	DUFF E.A.	Sick	Bombinh, Lewis Gun	6.10.15
:	MARKHAM E.B.	63 T.M.B.	Bombing	13.10.15
:	FORGE A.F.	Plat. Comdr.	XXXX.Bombing	25.7.16
:	MOLYNEUX A.W.	XXXXX do.	Bombing Lewis Gun	26.7.16
:	HARVEY M.	Plat. Comdr.		10.11.16
:	WHITE A.	do.	Bombinh, Lewis Gun	25.7.16
:	BUSHER D.J.B.	do.	Bombing, Lewis Gun	20.7.16
Lieut.	TAYLOR F.	Quartermaster		11.9.15

NOMINAL ROLL OF OFFICERS.

8th (S) Battalion Somerset Light Infantry.

Rank	Name	Present Employment	How Trained	Arrivee in Country
Lt.-Col.	SCOTT J.W., D.S.O.	Commanding		8.10.16
Captain	WATTS R.A.P.B.	Att.37th Div.		14.8.16
:	GLADE WRIGHT C.W.	Coy. Comdr.	Army School Instrn.	9.10.15
:	AKERMAN J.P.	O.C.63 T.M.B.	T.M. and machine gun	10.9.15
Lieut.	PIKE H.	Transport Off.		10.9.15
2nd Lieut.	MATTHEWS A.E.	Intell. Off.	Sniping, Signalling	28.7.16
:	BAKER H.G.	Signal Off.	Bombing	14.9.16
:	SAUNDERS M.K.F.	Coy. Comdr.	Trench Warfare	9.10.15
:	HAM G.A.		Physical Training	24.3.16
:	HARDYMAN J.H.M.		Bde.& Div.Staff Crse.	28.7.16
:	HINTON F.G.	Coy. Comdr.	Grenade	23.5.16
:	SNOW T.C.	Lewis Gun Off.	Adjts.Course, L.G.	26.7.16
:	HAGON P.C.	A/Adjt.	P.T. & B.F. Musketry	26.7.16
:	BRYANT P.S.	Coy. Comdr.	Musketry, Trench W're	26.7.16
:	PEEL W.R.B.		Machine Gun	28.7.16
:	MORGAN A.P.		Grenade	9.10.15
:	BAKER F.H.		Grenade, Gas	28.7.16
:	ADLAM F.G.		Trench Warfare	5.1.16
:	TUBBS C.B.	Bomb. Off.	Bombing	11.10.16
:	WILLATT V.G.		Sniping Course	3.8.16
:	GARRAD A.		Bombing & Phys.Tr.	28.7.16
:	CROCKER E.G.M.		Gas	5.8.16
:	MORGAN E.H.			
:	MELLOR J.R.		Trench Warfare	24.3.16
:	HOOPER P.F.M.	Coy. Comdr.		7.11.16
:	KING KING K.E.			8.11.16
:	SARGEANT R.L.			14.11.16
:	GEGG J.H.B.			14.11.16
:	GIBBS G.F.			23.11.16
:	LLEWELLYN A.H.			24.11.16
Lieut.	SCHOOLING A.H.	Quartermaster		10.9.15
Major	DAVIES EVANS	2nd in Command	Attd. from Pembroke Yeo.	10.11.16
Captain	GREEN L.C.F.	R.C.Chaplain		10.9.15
Lieut.	RUSSELL G.H.H.	Medical Officer		2.10.16

NOMINAL ROLL OF OFFICERS.

4th Battalion Middlesex Regiment.

Rank	Name	Present Employment	How Trained	Arrived in Country
Lt.-Col.	BICKNELL H.P.F., D.S.O.	Commanding		7.11.14
Captain	GROVE WHITE P.	2nd in Command		26.10.16
:	T.L.BODEN	Adjutant		14.11.16
:	H.G.ELLIS	Coy. Comdr.		27.7.16
:	S.A.WILLIS	do.	Bombing	4.10.15
Lieut.	E.A.H.FENN	Plat. Comdr.	P.T. & B.F.	13.7.16
:	B.P.JONES	do.	Bombing	6.9.16
2nd Lieut.	H.F.BOWSER	SNIPING Off.	Sniping	1.2.15
:	A.C.TERRELL	Plat. Off.	P.T. & B.F.	13.7.16
:	E.A.M.WILLIAMS	Bombing Off.	Bombing	13.7.16
:	F.J.R.SIMPSON	Bde. Bomb.Off.	Bombing	19.11.15
:	R.E.TAYLOR	Plat. Offr.		24.5.16
:	P.W.SMITH	do.	P.T. & B.F.	13.7.16
:	W.E.STOCKLEY	do.	Lewis Gun	13.7.16
:	S.MIRAMS	do.		5.6.16
:	D.CUTBUSH	On Leave	Lewis Gun	2.10.15
:	R.M.HILTON	Temp.L.G.Off.	Lewis Gun	13.7.16
:	R.F.T.IRWIN	Plat. Off.	Lewis Gun	16.5.16
:	F.W.SCHOLEFIELD	do.	Bombing	15.7.16
:	A.G.MITCHELL	Sick	-	13.7.16
:	L.C.THOMSON	Coy. Comdr.	Bombing	13.7.16
:	D.C.L.MURRAY	Hospital	Trench Warfare	13.7.16
:	H.E.HEFFER	Coy. Comdr.		5.10.14
:	O.N.MARTIN	Plat. Offr.	Lewis Gun	13.7.16
:	L.W.ANDREAE	do.	Trench Mortar	12.6.15
:	A.E.FEREMAN	Course, 5 Army	Lewis Gun	13.7.16
:	A.D.TROWELL	Plat. Off.	Signalling	15.7.16
:	H.M.WILLIAMS	do.	Bombing	24.1.16
:	R.G.WILLIAMS	Div.Sal.Off.		15.7.16
:	A.D.HOOKE	Plat. Off.	Gas	15.7.16
:	H.S.WHITLOCK	Transport Off.		6.9.16
:	J.H.HODGSON	Transport Course	Bombing	28.1.16
:	G.S.SUTHERLAND	Sig. & Intell.O.		4.5.15
:	D.F.HURR	Plat. Off.	ø.	6.9.16
Lieut.	E.H.AMOR	Quartermaster		18.10.15
Captain	A.D.SHARP, R.A.M.C.	Medical Officer.		

NOMINAL ROLL OF OFFICERS.

10th (S) Battalion York & Lancaster Regiment.

Rank	Name	Present Employment	How Trained	Arrived in Country
Lt.-Col.	RIDGWAY, J.H.	Commanding		1.9.14
Captain	AIREY C.F.	Sick	Transport	11.9.15
:	DRYNAN W.B.	2nd in Command	Vickers & LG.	11.9.15
:	ELSWORTH L.A.	Adjutant	Sniping	11.9.15
:	BROADBENT H.	Coy. Comdr.	Signalling	11.9.15
Lieut.	O'BRIEN W.B.S.		Transport	26.8.16
:	GROVES S.J.S.			17.3.16
:	HALL D.A.		Gas.	25.7.16
:	ROBINSON A.R.			4.10.16
:	WILKINSON R.M.	Coy. Comdr.	R.X.X. Grenades	9.10.15
:	QUANCE A.L.	P.T.	P.T. & B.F.	10.3.16
2nd Lieut.	NICHOLSON C.A.J.		Grenades	6.1.16
:	KNOWLES F.E.	Transport Off.	Transport	9.10.15
:	MITCHELL R.J.	Plat. Comdr.	Vickers	19.11.15
:	AYRES F.	Coy. Comdr.	Vickers	10.11.15
;	PAYNE F.E.	Bombing Off.	Grenade	11.10.15
:	HAWLEY D.D.	Lewis Gun Off.	Musketry Lewis Gun	29.5.16
:	SAMBELS, E.	Signal Officer	Signalling	25.5.16
:	CHAMBERS E.S.		Range F'd'g	21.7.16
:	LAMOND A.W.		Signalling	21.12.14
:	CARTER H.W.		Sniping	3.9.16
:	STROTHER J.M.	Coy. Comdr.	Sniping	3.9.16
:	WALNE H.A.		L.T.M.	16.9.16
:	HILL J.E.	Plat. Comdr.	Gas	16.9.16
:	OAKLEY M.H.	do.	P.T.& B.F.	4.9.16
:	MAGEE J.F.		Range F'd'g	28.10.16
Lieut.	JAMIESON A	Quartermaster		31.10.16
Captain	PLAISTER J.R.	Medical Officer		11.9.15

NOMINAL ROLL OF OFFICERS.

63rd Machine Gun Company.

Major	COLDWELL W.G.A.	Commanding
Lieut.	WEBB W.A.	2nd in command
2nd Lieut.	MACRAE D.A.	
:	SQUIBB C.H.	
:	HAWES N.F.	
:	GRAY R.E.	
:	HARTLEY I.C.	
:	THOMPSON C.W.	
:	HEMSOLL E.	
:	SCOTT F.E.B.	

63rd Trench Mortar Battery.

Captain	AKERMAN J.P.	8th Somerset L.I.	Commanding
2nd Lieut.	SIMS G.H.	do.	
:	MARKHAM E.B.	8th Lincolnshire Regt.	
:	HARRIS M.W.S.	4th Middlesex Regt.	

NOMINAL ROLL OF OFFICERS.

63rd Infantry Brigade Headquarters.

Brigadier General E.R.HILL,   Commanding
    (H.L.I.)

Captain W.L.BRODIE, V.C.   Brigade Major.
    (H.L.I.)

Major G.R.CODRINGTON,   Staff Captain
    (Leicester Yeomanry)

2nd Lieut. F.J.R.SIMPSON   Brigade Bombing
    (4th Middlesex Regt.)   Officer

Lieut. W.J.COOKSON, R.E.   Brigade Signal
                                                Officer.

Baron H. De COURTOIS   Brigade Interpreter.

CASUALTIES DURING NOVEMBER, 1916.

UNIT	IN TRENCHES							OUT OF TRENCHES							TOTAL CASUALTIES IN AND OUT OF TRENCHES	SICK		GRAND TOTAL	REMARKS
	Officers			O.Ranks				Officers			O.Ranks					Off.	OR		
	Killed	Wounded	Missing	Killed	Wounded	Missing	Total	Killed	Wounded	Missing	Killed	Wounded	Missing	Total					
8th Lincolnshire Regt.	-	2[a]	1[b]	14	112	8	137	-	-	-	-	-	-	-	137	1[c]	49	50	187	[a]Capt.J.T.Preston 2/Lt.A.B.Wiggins [b]2/Lt.L.D.Edwards
8th Somerset L.I.	4[d]	5[e]	-	17	84	13	123	-	-	-	-	-	-	-	123	5[f]	57	62	185	[c]2/Lt.F.W.Latham [d]Capt.A.H.Hall Lt.F.H.Joscelyne 2/Lt.B.T.Chippendall
4th Middlesex Regt.	2[g]	3[h]	-	27	105	9	144	-	-	-	-	-	-	-	144	3[i]	112	115	259	Lt.L.Fitzmaurice [e]2/Lt.King King K.E. 2/Lt.J.R.Mellor
10th York & Lanc. Regt.	1[j]	5[k]	-	30	164	2	202	-	-	-	-	-	-	-	202	6[l]	104	110	312	2/Lt.J.H.T.Hardyman 2/Lt.W.R.B.Peel
63rd Machine Gun Company	-	3[m]	-	5	12	2	22	-	-	-	-	-	-	-	22	1[n]	17	18	40	[f]2/Lt.Crocker E.G.M. 2/Lt.C.B.Tubbs 2/Lts.F.G.Adlam,F.G.Hinton 2/Lt.F.H.Baker,A.P.Morgan
63rd T.M.Battery	-	-	-	-	-	-	-	-	-	-	-	-	-	-	-	-	-	-	-	[g]Lt.R.Underhill 2/Lt.W.K.Maitland
TOTAL	7	19	1	93	477	34	628	-	-	-	-	-	-	-	628	16	339	355	983	[h]2/Lts.F.Lofts,A.A.Burch, A.F.MacLeod. [i]2/Lts,A.G.Mitchell,D.C.F. Murray,Capt.S.A.Willis.

[j]2/Lt.R.Fisher(S.Staffs) [k]Lts.A.L.Quance,S.J.S.Groves,W.B.S.O'Brien,2/Lts H.W.Carter,J.F.Magee.
[l]Capts.J.H.Ramsden,C.F.Airey,Lt.D.A.Hall,2/Lts.E.S.Chambers,R.J.Mitchell,H.A.Walne.[m]2/Lts.C.F.Larn,D.Crockatt,R.E.Gray. C.H Squibb

63rd Infantry Brigade.

REINFORCEMENTS RECEIVED DURING NOVEMBER, 1916.

	Officers	Other Ranks	Date
8th Lincolnshire Regt.	-	4	3.11.16
	-	4	13.11.16
	-	13	20.11.16
	1 a	9	21.11.16
	-	59	28.11.16
	1	89	
8th Somerset Light Infantry	-	8	4.11.16
	1 b	-	7.11.16
	1 c	-	8.11.16
	-	8	9.11.16
	1 d	-	10.11.16
	2 e	-	14.11.16
	-	15	17.11.16
	1 f	5	23.11.16
	-	93	20.11.16
	1 g	-	24.11.16
	-	5	28.11.16
	7	134	
4th Middlesex Regt.	1 h	-	16.11.16
	-	6	8.11.16
	-	3	19.11.16
	-	6	25.11.16
	1	15	
10th York & Lancaster Regt.	1 i	-	2.11.16
	1 j	-	6.11.16
	-	9	8.11.16
	-	4	16.11.16
	-	6	18.11.16
	-	3	24.11.16
	2	22	
63rd Machine Gun Company.	1 k	-	23.11.16
	1 l	-	29.11.16
	-	1	
	2	1	

Total Reinforcements arrived during Nov.: 13 Officers.
                                           261 Other Ranks.

```
a Captain R.G.Cordiner, M.C.           8th Lincolnshire Regt.
b 2nd Lt. P.F.M.Hooper                 8th Somerset L.I.
c   ,,    K.E.King King                    ,,
d Major   D.Davies Evans (Pembroke Yeo.)   ,,
e 2nd Lt. R.L.Sargeant                     ,,
    ,,    H.H.B.Gegg                       ,,
f   ,,    G.F.Gibbs                        ,,
g   ,,    A.H.Llewellyn                    ,,
h Capt. & Adjt. T.L.Boden              4th Middlesex Regt.
i Lt.&Q.M.A.Jamieson                   10th York & Lanc. Regt.
j 2nd Lt. J.F.Magee
k   ,,    E.Hemsoll                    63rd Machine Gun Coy.
l   ,,    F.E.B.Scott                      ,,
```

63rd Infantry Brigade.

STRENGTH OF UNITS

November 30th, 16.

Unit	Officers	O.Ranks	Details Officers	Details O.Ranks
8th Lincolnshire Regt.	32	798	9	106
8th Somerset L.I.	34	794	6	32
4th Middlesex Regt.	36	772	2	90
10th York & Lanc. Regt.	21	642	4	18
63rd Machine Gun Company	9	152		22
63rd T.M.Battery	4	41		
TOTAL	136	3199	21	268

	8 Lincs.	8 Som L.I.	4 Middx.	10 Y & L.	M.G.C.	13 N.F.	TOTAL
Killed and Died of Wounds.	4.	8.	15.	7.			34.
Wounded.	9.	6.	5.	6.	1.	1.	28.
Missing.		4.					4.
	13.	18.	20.	13.	1.	1.	66.

ORIGINAL
COPY

WAR DIARY

63rd Infantry Brigade

DECEMBER 1916

Army Form C. 2118.

WAR DIARY
or
INTELLIGENCE SUMMARY

(Erase heading not required.)

Instructions regarding War Diaries and Intelligence Summaries are contained in F.S. Regs., Part II. and the Staff Manual respectively. Title pages will be prepared in manuscript.

Place	Date	Hour	Summary of Events and Information	Remarks and references to Appendices
BEAUQUESNE	Dec. 1st		The Brigade was disposed in billets as follows:- Brigade H.Q. and 8th Somerset L.I. in BEAUQUESNE, 4th Middlesex in RAINCHEVAL, 8th Lincolns in SARTON, 10th York & Lancs., Machine Gun Coy. and T.M.Battery in TERRAMESNIL.	
	2nd		Training in vicinity of billets. Working parties found for construction of ranged and bombing grounds.	
	3rd		Church Parades	
	4th		Training and usual working parties. 4th Middlesex Regt. moved to BEAUVAL. B.M.3........1 The following Brigade Schools were started, the personnel being attached to Brigade H.Q.:- Brigade Bombing School under Brigade Bombing Officer and 2/Lt. W.J.KEELING, 8th Lincoln Regt., the course to last one week, 20 men from Battalions to be trained at a time. Brigade Lewis Gun School under 2/Lt. AYRES, 10th York & Lanc. Regt. also for one week course, 16 men from Battalions. Brigade Signalling School under Brigade Signal Officer, to last an indefinite period, 21 men from all units of of the Brigade. Brigade School for Sergeants or acting sergts. under R.S.M. CAMPBELL, 8th Somerset L.I., for an indefinite period - 4 N.C.Os from each Battalion.	
.	5th		G.O.C. and LT.-COL. XXX BICKNELL proceeded on leave to England for one month; Lt.-Col. SCOTT, 8th Somerset L.I. took over command of Brigade temporarily.	
	6th		Lt.-Col. CHESTER-MASTER took over command of Brigade from Lt.-Col. SCOTT. A 353........2 Training and working parties.	
	7th		Training and working parties. Major MAYHEW, Denbighshire Hussars, took over temporarily command of 4th Middlesex.	
	8th		Training and Working parties.	
	9th		The Brigade was inspected by the Corps Commander (Special order re Corps Commander's Inspection)......3 Lt.-Col. JOHNSTON, D.S.O., proceeded on leave to England before taking up an appointment at home. Captain CAMERON appointed temporary Major and took over command of 8th Lincoln Regt.	
	10th		Church Parades	
	11th		Training. Brigade was ordered to be ready to move at short notice.	
	12th		Training	

Army Form C. 2118.

WAR DIARY
or
INTELLIGENCE SUMMARY

(Erase heading not required.)

Instructions regarding War Diaries and Intelligence Summaries are contained in F. S. Regs., Part II. and the Staff Manual respectively. Title pages will be prepared in manuscript.

Place	Date	Hour	Summary of Events and Information	Remarks and references to Appendices
BEAUQUESNE	Dec. 13		4th Middlesex Regt. moved in accordance with Div.O.O. 54 and Bde. O.O. 98. 9th N.Staffs (P) and 152nd Field Co. R.E. joined the Brigade Group.	4, 5
REMAISNIL	14		The Brigade marched in accordance with Brigade O.O.No. 99 and Div.O.O.55.	6, 7
BOUBERS	15		" " Brigade O.O.NO. 100.	8, 9
VALHUON	16		" " Div.O.O.56 and Bde.O.O.101.	10
			The following alterations were made in the billetingarrangements:- 10th York & Lancs. were billeted in FLEURY and CONTEVILLE and 8th Lincolns in HUCLIER, & BRITEL and 49th Fd. Ambulance in BRYAS.	
FONTAINES-LEZ-HERMANS	17		The Brigade marxxx marched in accordance with Bde. O.O. No. 102.	11
BUSNES	18		The Brigade marched in accordance with Div. O. 57 andBde. O.O.103.	12
	19		Resting and cleaning up, etc.	13
	20		" "	
	21		" " Conference of Commanding Officers at Brigade H.Q., 2.30 pm	
VIEILLE CHAPELLE	22		The Brigade marched in accordance with Div. O. 58 and Bde. O.O. 104. On arrival the Brigade became Divisional Reserve. Conference of Battalion Commanders at Brigade H.Q. at 2.30 pm. Training.	14, 15
	23		Training and working parties	
	24		" "	
	25		" "	
	24		" "	
	26		" "	
	27		" "	
	28		" " Major-General SIMPSON, C.B., Colonel of The Lincolnshire Regiment inspected 8th Lincolnshire Regt. and 4th Middlesex Regt.	
	29		" " Officers from Battalions, Machine Gun Company and T.M.Battery reconnoitred the NEUVE CHAPELLE Section.	
	30		" "	
	31		Divisional Commander attended Church Parade of 8th Lincolnshire Regt. and in the afternoon held a conference at Brigade Headquarters. The following attended:- C.O's and 2nds in command, of Battalions and Os.C Machine Gun Company and T.M.Battery	

R.Westr-Martin/Lt/Col.
Comm.g. 63 Inf Bde.

WAR DIARY

63rd Infantry Brigade.

	Appendix No.
B.M.3	1
A 353	2
Corps Commander's Inspection	3
Div.O.O. 54	4
Bde. O.O.98	5
Div. O.55	6
Bde.O.O.99	7
Bde.O.O.100	8
Div.O.O.56	9
Bde.O.O.101	10
Bde. O.O.102	11
Div.O.O.57	12
Bde.O.O.103	13
Div.O.O.58	14
Bde.O.O.104	15
Nominal roll of officers	16
Casualties during December	17
Reinforcements during December	18
Strength, Dec. 31st 1916.	19

NOMINAL ROLL OF OFFICERS.

63rd Infantry Brigade Headquarters.

Lieutenant-Colonel R. CHESTERMASTER,   Commanding.
  (13th King's Royal Rifle Corps)

Captain W.L. BRODIE, V.C.   Brigade Major
  (Highland Light Infantry)

Major G.R. CODRINGTON,   Staff Captain.
  (Leicestershire Yeomanry)

2nd Lieut. F.J.R. SIMPSON,   Brigade Bombing Officer
  (4th Middlesex Regt.)

Lieut. W.J. COOKSON, R.E.   Brigade Signal Officer

Baron H. De COURTOIS   Brigade Interpreter.

NOMINAL ROLLS OF OFFICERS.

8th Battalion Lincolnshire Regiment.

Rank and Name		Present Employment	Trained in	Arrived in Country
Lt.-Col.	CAMERON E.A.	Commanding		25.8.16
Major	PATTINSON H.	2nd in Command		11.9.15
Captain	BROWN F.	Adjutant		11.9.15
,,	KER R.A.	Bde. Transpobt Off.		11.9.15
,,	CORDINER R.G., M.C.	Coy. Comdr.	Lewis & Vickers	11.9.15
,,	HARRISON E.M.	,,		10.3.16
,,	BEARD B.J.L.	Attd.112th Bde. HQ.	Lewis & Vickers	24.11.15
Lieut.	TAYLOR F.	Quartermaster		11.9.15
,,	JESSOPP C.B.		Lewis Gun	13.10.15
,,	HLADWELL F.H.G.	~~Musketry~~ Sick	Musketry	21.8.16
2nd Lieut.	ALLBONES F.W.	Bn. Signal Off.	Signalling	17.2.16
,,	WAUGH F.A.	Bn. Bombing Off. Asst. Adjutant.	Bombing	19.6.16
,,	RAHLES RAHBULA A.J.	Coy. Comdr.	Lewis Gun	4.4.16
,,	DUKES E.H.	Transport Offr.		27.7.16
,,	READ J.	Attd. 37th Div.		28.7.16
,,	LILLY C.F.M.	Attd. V Corps HQ		20.7.16
,,	KEELING		Bombing	30.7.16
,,	POSNER P.E.	Plat. Comdr.	Sniping	26.7.16
,,	HODGSON B.C.	On Crse. Instrn.	Bombing	28.7.16
,,	LEWIS H.A.C.	Platoon Comdr.	Lewis Gun	27.6.16
,,	BRADER H.C.	Coy. Comdr.	Lewis Gun	16.9.16
,,	GODFREY P.G.	I.B.D.,Calais	Lewis Gun	20.6.16
,,	DUFF E.A.	,,	,, & Vickers	6.10.15
,,	MARKHAM E.B.	Att. 63rd T.M.B.	Bombing	13.10.15
,,	FORGE H.F.		Bombing	25.7.16
,,	MOLYNEAUX A.W.		Lewis Gun	26.7.16
,,	TOMLINSON H.	Plat. Comdr.		13.12.16
,,	GREGORY B.W.	,,		13.12.1916
,,	BROWN A.	,,		13.12.16
,,	HARVEY M.	On Crse. Instrn.		10.11.15
,,	WHITE A.	Sniping Course	Lewis Gun	25.7.16
,,	BUSHER D.J.B.	,,	,,	20.3.16

NOMINAL ROLL OF OFFICERS.

8th Battalion Somerset Light Infantry.

Name and Rank		Present Employment	Trained in	Arrived in Country
Lt.-Col.	SCOTT J.W.	Commanding		8.10.16
Major	DAVIES EVANS D.W.C.	2nd in Command		10.11.16
Captain	WATTS R.A.B.P.	Attd. 37th Div.		14.8.16
,,	GLADE WRIGHT C.W., M.C.	Coy. Comdr.	Grenade Work	9.10.15
,,	AKERMAN J.P.	O.C. 63rd T.M.B.	Machine Gun	10.9.15
Lieut.	PIKE H.	Transport Off.		10.9.15
2nd Lieut.	MATTHEWS A.E.	Intelligence Off.	Sniping, Signal.	14.9.16
,,	BAKER H.G.	Signalling Offr.	Bombing	14.9.16
,,	SAUNDERS M.K.F.	Coy. Comdr.	Trench Warfare	9.10.15
,,	HAM G.A.		Phys. Training	24.3.16
,,	HINTON F.G.		Grenade Work	23.5.16
,,	SNOW T.C.	Lewis Gun Off.	Adjt's Course.	26.7.16
,,	HAGON P.C.	A/Adjutant	P.T. & B.F.	26.7.16
,,	BRYANT P.S.		Musketry, T. W'fare.	26.7.16
,,	BAKER F.H.		Gas Course	28.7.16
,,	ADLAM F.G.		Trench W'fare	5.1.16
,,	TUBBS C.B.	Bombing Off.	Bombing	11.10.16
,,	WILLATT V.G.		Sniping	3.8.16
,,	GARRAD A,	On Course	Phys. Training	28.7.16
,,	MORGAN E.H.			28.7.16
,,	HOOPER P.F.M.	Coy. Comdr.		7.11.16
,,	Sargeant R.L.			14.11.16
,,	GEGG T.H.B.	On Course		14.11.16
,,	GIBBS G.F.	Bombing Off.		23.11.16
,,	LLEWELLYN A.H.			24.11.16
,,	HEAL R.W.	On Course		22.12.16
,,	BULLIVANT R.W.		Signalling	23.12.16
,,	ROWLAND E.J.	On Course	Phys. Training	22.12.16
,,	CLARK F.J.			24.12.16
,,	COOKSLEY F.R.		Transport Duty	24.12.16
Lieut.	SCHOOLING J.J.	Quartermaster		10.9.15
Captain	GREEN L, C.F.	R.C. Chaplain		10.9.15
Lieut.	RUSSELL G.H.	Medical Officer		2.10.16

NOMINAL ROLL OF OFFICERS.

10th Battalion York & Lancaster Regiment.

Rank & Name		Present Employment	Trained In	Embarked
Lt.-Col.	RIDGWAY J.H.	Commanding(Sick)		1.9.14
Major	WELSH D.T.	Commanding	Hythe	8.12.16
Captain	DRYNAN W.B.	Coy. Comdr.	Vickers & Lewis	11.8.15
,,	ELSWORTH L.A.	Adjutant	Sniping	11.9.15
,,	LUCAS S.			4.12.16
,,	BROADBENT H.		Signalling	11.9.15
Lieut.	ROBINSON A.R.	Coy. Comdr.	Gas.	4.10.16
,,	WILKINSON R.M.	,,	Grenades	9.10.15
,,	F.E.KNOWLES	Transport Offr.	Transport	9.10.15
2nd Lieut.	NICHOLSON C.A.J.		Grenades	6.1.16
,,	MITCHELL R.J.	Plat. Comdr.	Lewis & Vickers	19.11.15
,,	AYRES F.	Brigade School	Lewis Gun	10.11.15
,,	PAYNE F.E.	Bombing Offr.	Grenade	11.10.15
,,	HAWLEY D.D.	Lewis Gun Offr.	Musketry, Gas	29.5.16
,,	SAMUELS E.	Signalling Offr.	Grenades	25.1.16
,,	LAMOND A.W.	Coy. Comdr.	Signalling	21.12.14
,,	STROTHER J.M.	Inteel. Offr.	Sniping	3.9.16
,,	HILL J.E.	Plat.-Comdr.	P.T. & B.F.	16.9.16
,,	OAKLEY M.H.	Crse. Instrn.	P.T. & B.F.	4.9.16
,,	CORBAN J.		Gymnastics	12.8.14
,,	FAIRBAIRN H.J.W.	Plat. Comdr.	Musketry	15.12.16
,,	JACKSON F.C.	Crse.	XX.XX.XX	15.12.16
,,	WILKS E.L.	Plat. Comdr.		15.12.16
,,	GAUNT B.W.	,,		15.12.16
,,	TAYLOR J.B.	,,	Musketry	15.12.16
,,	SUMNER W.G.	,,	Machine Gun	16.7.16
,,	TOPPING E.	,,		15.12.16
,,	HORSFALL J.R.	,,		15.12.16
,,	WOODMANSEY K.G.	,,		15.12.16
,,	LUPTON F.	Course	Musketry	15.12.16
Lieut.	JAMIESON A.	Quartermaster		31.10.15
Captain	PLAISTER G.R.	Medical Officer		11.9.15

NOMINAL ROLL OF OFFICERS

63rd Machine Gun Company.

Rank and Name		Employment	Trained in	Arrived in Country
Major	W.G.A.COLDWELL	Commanding	Machine Gun	24.2.16
Lieut.	W.A.WEBB	2nd in command	,,	24.2.16
2nd Lieut.	N.F.HAWES	Transport Offr.	Transport duties	24.5.16
,,	I.C.HARTLEY	Section Officer	Machine Gun	1.7.16
,,	C.W.THOMPSON	,,	,,	4.6.16
,,	D.A.MACRAE	,,	,,	16.10.16
,,	R.E.GRAY	,,	,,	,,
,,	E.HEMSOLL	,,	,,	18.11.16
,,	F.E.B.SCOTT	,,	,,	19.11.16
,,	H.R.HIPWELL	,,	,,	,,

63rd Trench Mortar Battery.

Captain J.P.AKERMAN, Commanding   8th Somerset L.I.
2/Lieut. E.B.MARKHAM,   8th Lincoln Regt.
2/Lieut. M.W.S.HARRIS,   4th Middlesex Regt.
2/Lieut. G.H.SIMS,   8th Somerset L.I.

CASUALTIES DURING DECEMBER, 1916.

UNIT	IN TRENCHES — Officers						IN TRENCHES — Other Ranks				OUT OF TRENCHES — Officers			OUT OF TRENCHES — Other Ranks			Total Casualties in and out of trenches.	SICK Officers	SICK Other Rks.	SICK Total	GRAND TOTAL	REMARKS
	Killed	Wounded	Missing	Killed	Wounded	Missing	Total				Killed	Wounded	Missing	Killed	Wounded	Missing	Total					
8th Lincolnshire Regt.	-	-	-	-	-	-	-				-	-	-	-	-	-	-	1a	46	47	47	a Lt. F.H.G. HALDWELL
8th Somerset L.I.	-	-	-	-	-	-	-				-	-	-	-	-	-	-	1b	55	56	56	b 2/Lt. G.A. HAM
4th Middlesex Regt.	-	-	-	-	-	-	-				-	-	-	-	-	-	-	2c	87	89	89	c Capt. H.C. ELLIS / 2/Lt. R.F.T. IRWIN
10th York & Lanc. Regt.	-	-	-	-	-	-	-				-	-	-	-	-	-	-	1d	49	50	50	d Capt. S. LUCAS
63rd Machine Gun Company	-	-	-	-	-	-	-				-	-	-	-	-	-	-	-	5	5	5	
63rd Trench Mortar Battery	-	-	-	-	-	-	-				-	-	-	-	-	-	-	1e	7	8	8	e Capt. J.P. AKERMAN
TOTAL	-	-	-	-	-	-	-				-	-	-	-	-	-	-	6	249	255	255	

REINFORCEMENTS
RECEIVED
DURING
DECEMBER, 1916

	Officers	Other Rks.	Date
8th Lincolnshire Regt.	-	36	1.12.16
	-	23	2.12.16
	-	3	7.12.16
	-	164	11.12.16
	3 a	-	20.12.16
	-	26	26.12.16
	3	252	
8th Somerset L.I.	-	6	1.12.16
	-	21	4.12.16
	-	63	10.12.16
	-	106	11.12.16
	-	15	13.12.16
	2 b	-	22.12.16
	1 c	26	23.12.16
	2 d	-	24.12.16
	-	9	30.12.16
	5	246	
4th Middlesex Regt.	-	7	3.12.16
	1 e	-	6.12.16
	4 d¹	-	7.12.16
	-	4	8.12.16
	-	15	9.12.16
	-	249	12.12.16
	-	9	15.12.16
	1 f	-	20.12.16
	-	10	22.12.16
	-	6	23.12.16
	-	11	25.12.16
	-	6	27.12.16
	1 g	-	30.12.16
	7	317	
10th York & Lanc. Regt.	-	5	2.12.16
	1 h	-	4.12.16
	1 i	16	9.12.16
	-	2	11.12.16
	-	5	13.12.16
	-	9	15.12.16
	9 j	5	20.12.16
	2 k	-	22.12.16
	1 l	-	27.12.16
	14	42	
63rd Machine Gun Company.	-	15	5.12.16
	-	9	11.12.16
	1 m	1	20.12.16
	-	5	28.12.16
	1	30	

Total Reinforcements arrived during December, 1916:
        30 Officers, 887 O.R.

Over.

a	2nd Lieut.	H. Tomlinson	8th Lincolnshire Regt.
	,,	B.W.Gregory	,,
	,,	Brown A.	,,
b	2nd Lieut.	R.W.Heal	8th Somerset Light Inf.
	,,	E.J.Rowlands	,,
c	,,	R.W.Bullivant	,,
d	,,	F.J.CLARK	,,
	,,	F.R.Cooksley	,,
e	Major	J.D.Mayhew (joined from 3/1 Denbigh Hussars)	4th Middlesex Regt.
d[1]	Captain	E.J.Donaldson	,,
	2nd Lieut.	C.K.Grayson	,,
	,,	C.G.Grogan	,,
	,,	H.M.Monk	,,
f	,,	J.C.Lyal	,,
g	Captain	A.G.Dawson	,,
h	2nd Lieut	J.Corban	10th York & Lanc. Regt.
i	Major	D.T.Welsh	,,
j	2nd Lieut.	J.J.W.Fairbairn	,,
	,,	F.C.Jackson	,,
	,,	E.L.Wilks	,,
	,,	B.W.Gaunt	,,
	,,	J.B.Taylor	,,
	,,	E.Topping	,,
	,,	J.R.Horsfall	,,
	,,	K.G.Woodmansey	,,
	,,	F.Lupton	,,
k	Captain	S.W.Wicks	,,
	2nd Lieut.	W.G.Sumner	,,
l	Captain	S.Lucas	,,
m	2nd Lt.	H.R.Hipwell	63rd Machine Gun Company.

STRENGTH, DECEMBER, 1916.

Unit	Strength		Details	
	Officers	O.R.	Officers	O.R.
8th Lincolnshire Regt.	32	1014	9	130
8th Somerset Light Infantry	33	980	10	222
4th Middlesex Regt.	40	997	10	114
10th York & Lanc. Regt.	31	652	4	111
63rd Machine Gun Company	10	172	1	18
63rd Trench Mortar Battery	4	63	-	6
Total	150	3878	34	601

ORIGINAL COPY.

Vol 17

WAR DIARY.
63RD INFANTRY BRIGADE.
JANUARY 1917.

Army Form C. 2118.

WAR DIARY
or
~~INTELLIGENCE SUMMARY~~
(Erase heading not required.)

Instructions regarding War Diaries and Intelligence Summaries are contained in F.S. Regs., Part II. and the Staff Manual respectively. Title pages will be prepared in manuscript.

Place	Date	Hour	Summary of Events and Information	Remarks and references to Appendices
VIEILLE CHAPELLE	Jan. 1		Training and working parties. A new reserve area taken up.	Div.O.O.60......... 1
NEUVE CHAPELLE	2		The Brigade relieved 111th Inf. Bde. in the NEUVE CHAPELLE Section 2/Lt. H.F.BOWSER, 4th Middlesex, joined Brigade Staff as Brigade Sniping Officer. Quiet day in trenches.	Div.O.O.61......... 2 Bde.O.O.105....... 3
	3		,,	
	4		,,	
	5		,,	
	6		,,	
	7		,,	
	8		Front line Battalions were relieved. The Corps Commander presented medal ribbons to men of the Brigade at MERVILLE. A representative detachment from units of the Brigade attended.	Bde.O.O.106........ 4
	9		Quiet day in trenches.	
	10		,,	
	11		,,	
	12.		Captain W.L.BRODIE, V.C., M.C., Brigade Major, went to England for a month's leave. The duties of Acting Brigade Major were taken over by Captain R.A.B.F.WATTS, 8th Somerset L.I.	
	13		Quiet day in trenches. Issued Bde.O.107 for relief by 111th Inf. Bde. on the 15th.............	5
	14		Foggy day. In the morning, at 10 o'c. Lt.-Col.E.A.CAMERON, taking advantage of the fog tried to reconnoitre the enemy wire. He discovered a gap but while investigating it was shot by an enemy sniper sentry and wounded in the shoulder. He was able to return to our trenches assisted by Major PATTINSON.	

Army Form C. 2118.

WAR DIARY
or
INTELLIGENCE SUMMARY.
(Erase heading not required.)

Instructions regarding War Diaries and Intelligence Summaries are contained in F.S. Regs. Part II. and the Staff Manual respectively. Title pages will be prepared in manuscript.

Place	Date	Hour	Summary of Events and Information	Remarks and references to Appendices
NEUVE CHAPELLE.	Jan. 15		Brigade was relieved in daylight by 111th Inf. Bde. and returned to Reserve Bde. Area. Cleaning up after return from the trenches.	Div. O. 62......6
	16		,,	
	17		,,	
	18		Training and working parties.	
	19		,,	
	20		,,	
	21		Lecture at Divisional Headquarters for Sniping Officers by Major HESKETH PRITCHARD.	
	22		Inspection by Divisional Commander of 10th York & Lanc. Regt., 8th Somerset L.I. and 63rd Machine Gun Company in the morning.	
	23		Inspection by Divisional Commander of 4th Middlesex Regt., 8th Lincolnshire Regt. and 63rd T.M.Battery.	
	24		Training continued in Battalions. Brigade Commander visited 1st Army Workshops.	
	25		,, Brigade Commander held conference of Commanding Officers.	
	26		Brigade less 10th York & Lanc. Regt., 63rd Machine Gun Company and 63rd T.M.Battery was exercised in an aeroplane contact scheme with flares, a machine of 'A' Flight, 10th Squadron, R.F.C. taking part. Brigade Commander inspected 10th York & Lanc. Regt., 63rd Machine Gun Company & 63rd T.M.Battery in the afternoon.	
	27		8th Somerset L.I. and 8th Lincolnshire Regt. moved up into support billets, FERME DU BOIS Section.	Bde. O.108......5
FERME DU BOIS Sect.	28		Brigade H.Q. moved to CENSE DU RAUX. 8th Somerset L.I. & 8th Lincolnshire Regt. moved to front line in relief of 112th Inf. Bde. Patrols sent out this night to search for men of 10th Loyal North Lancs. Regt. reported missing after MINOR Operation by 112th Inf. Bde. No one found. Div.O.63.......6	Div.O.49.O......7

Army Form C. 2118.

WAR DIARY
or
~~INTELLIGENCE SUMMARY~~
(Erase heading not required.)

Instructions regarding War Diaries and Intelligence Summaries are contained in F. S. Regs., Part II. and the Staff Manual respectively. Title pages will be prepared in manuscript.

Place	Date	Hour	Summary of Events and Information	Remarks and references to Appendices
FERME DU BOIS Section	Jan. 29		Quiet in front line. Some shelling of left battalion back area. 10th York & Lanc. Regt. and 4th Middlesex Regt. moved into support billets.	
	30		Frost continued hard. White patrolling suits were used and found most necessary.	
	31st		Quiet day. Prepared to assist a minor operation planned by 111th Inf. Bde. for the next night.	

R.A.B. Loveto Caplan
for Brigadier General,
Commdg. 63rd Infantry Brigade.

63rd Infantry Brigade.

NOMINAL ROLL OF OFFICERS

8th (S) Bn. Somerset L.I.

Rank and Name	Present employment	How Trained	Arrived in Country.
Lt.-Col. SCOTT J.W., D.S.O.	Commanding		8.10.16
Captain WATTS R.A.B.P.	Attd. 63rd Inf. Bde HQ		14.8.16
,, HUSSEY H.		C.O's Course	9.1.17
,, GLADE WRIGHT C.W., M.C.	Coy. Comdr.	Bombing	9.10.15
,, AKERMAN J.P.	63rd T.M.B.	T.M. & M.G.	10.9.15
,, ROWLAND P.		Musketry	15.1.17
,, SAUNDERS M.K.F.	Coy. Comdr.	Trench Warfare	9.10.15
,, HOOPER P.F.M.	Coy. Comdr.	School/Instruction	7.11.16
Lieut. PIKE H.	Transport Off.		10.9.15
,, SCHOOLING J.J.	Quartermaster		10.9.15
2nd Lt. MATTHEWS A.E.	Intelligence Off.	Sniping, Signal.	14.9.16
,, BAKER H.G.	Signal Officer	Signalling	14.9.16
,, HINTON F.G.		Bombing	23.5.16
,, SNOW T.C.	Lewis Gun Off.	Adjts. Course	26.7.16
,, HAGON P.C.	A/Adjutant	P.T. & B.F.	26.7.16
,, BRYANT P.S.	Plat. Comdr.	Musketry	26.7.16
,, Baker F.H.	,,	Gas	28.7.16
,, ADLAM F.G.	Att. 63rd Inf. Bde.	Trench Warfare	5.1.16
,, TUBBS C.B., M.C.	xxxx	Bombing	11.10.16
,, WILLATT V.G.	Plat. Comdr.	Sniping	3.8.16
,, GARRAD A.	,,	P.T. & B.F.	28.7.16
,, MORGAN.E.H.	,,		28.7.16.
,, SARGEANT.R.L.			14.11.16.
,, GEGG.J.H.B.			14.11.16.
,, GIBBS.G.F.	Bombing Off.	Bombing.	23.11.16.
,, LLEWELLYN.A.H.			24.11.16.
,, HEAL.R.W.		Lewis Gun.	22.11.16.
,, BULLIVANT.R.W.		Signalling.	23.12.16.
,, ROWLAND.E.J.		P.T.&B.F.	22.12.16.
,, CLARK.F.J.		?	24.12.16.
,, COOKSLEY.F.R.		Transport.	24.12.16.
,, THORNTON.C.H.			2.1.17.
,, FROST.H.C.			,,
,, BAIRDC.A.			15.1.17.
,, BOUCHER.H.M.		Trench Warfare.	19.1.17.
,, GOODMAN.S.		Gas	15.1.17.
,, GORDON.C.C.B.			20.1.17.
,, OWEN.A.C.			24.1.17.
Capt. GREEN.L. C.F.	R.C. Chaplain.		10.9.15.
Lieut. ALFORD.E.F.	Medical Officer.		10.1.17.

63rd. INFANTRY BRIGADE.

NOMINAL ROLL OF OFFICERS.

4th. Bn. Middlesex Regiment.

Rank & Name.	Present Employment.	How Trained.	Arrived in Country.
Lt.-Col. BICKNELL.H.P.F. D.S.O.	Commanding		27.11.14.
Captain. DAWSON.A.G.	Second in Command.		24.12.16.
,, BODEN.T.L.,M.C.	Adjutant.		13.18.14.
,, DONALDSON.E.J.			4.12.16.
,, MORAN.C.G.	Attd.C/124 Bty.R.F.A.	C.O!sCourse.	24.8.16
,, WILLIS.S.A.	Coy.Comdr.	Bombing.	15.10.15.
,, HEFFER.H.E.	C ,,		5.10.14.
Lieut. FENN.A.E.H.	Town Major VIEILLE CHAPELLE.		13.7.16.
,, JONES.B.P.	37th.Div.School	Bombing.	6.9.16.
2/lieut. BOWSER.R.F.	Bde.Sniping.OFF.	Sniping.	1.2.15.
,, TERRELL.A.C.	Coy.Comdr.	Bombing.	13.7.16.
,, WILLIAMS.E.A.M.	Bombing Officer.	,,	,,
,, SIMPSON.F.J.R.	Bde. ,, ,,	,,	19.11.15.
,, TAYLOR.R.E.	37th.Div."Q"		29.5.16.
,, SMITH.P.W.	A/Quartermaster	Lewis Gun½	13.7.16.
,, STOCKLEY.W.E.		Gas Course.	,,
,, GROGAN.E.G.	Bde.Training Depot.		4.12.16.
,, MIRIAMS.S.	Plat.Comdr.	Lewis Gun.	5.6.16.
,, CUTBUSH.D. ,M.C.	Lewis Gun Off.	,,	14.10.15.
,, HILTON.R.M.		,,	13.7.16.
,, IRWIN.R.F.T.	Plat.Comdr.	Bombing.	16.5.16.
,, SCHOLEFIELD.F.W.		Sniping.	15.7.16.
,, MITCHELL.A.G.		Bombing.	13.7.16.
,, THOMSON.L.C.	A/Adjt.	P.T.& B.F.	
,, MARTIN.O.N.	37th.Div.Sal.Off.	L.T.M.	13.7.16.
,, ANDREAE.L.W.	Plat.Comdr.	,,	12.6.15.
,, TROWELL.A.D?	,,	Signalling.	15.7.16.
,, WILLIAMS.H.M.	A/Sniping Off.	Bombing.	24.1.16.
,, WILLIAMS.R.G.	Plat.Comdr.		15.7.16.
,, HOOKE.A.D.	Coy.Comdr.	Gas.	,,
,, GRAYSON.J.K.	Plat.Comdr.	Gas.	4.12.16.
,, WHITLOCK.H.S.	37th.Div.Train.	Bombing.	6.9.16.
,, HODGSON.J.H.	Plat.Comdr.	Transport.	28.4.16.
,, SUTHERLAND.G.S.	Signalling Off.		4.5.15.
,, LYAL.J.C.	Plat.Comdr.		12.12.16.
,, HURR.D.F.	,,	37th.Div.School.	6.9.16.
,, MONK.H.M.	,,	5th.School.	4.12.16.
Lieut. AMOR.E.H.	Quartermaster.		18.10.15.
Capt. SHARP.A.D.	Medical Officer.		-
,, LARGIE.W.G. C.F.	Chaplain.		

83rd Infantry Brigade.

NOMINAL ROLL OF OFFICERS

10th (S) Bn. York & Lancaster Regiment.

Rank and Name		Present Employment	How Trained	Arrived in Country
Lt.-Col.	RIDGWAY J.H.	Commanding		1.9.14
Major	WELSH D.T.	O.C. Bde. Depot	Hythe	8.12.16
,,	DRYNAN W.B.	2nd in command	Lewis & Vickers	11.9.15
Captain	FAIRNIE E.G.J.	Coy. Comdr.	Bombing	5.1.17
,,	ELSWORTH L.A.	Adjutant	Grenades, Sniping	11.9.15
,,	LUCAS S.			4.12.16
,,	BROADBENT H.	Coy. Comdr.	Signalling	11.9.15
Lieut.	ROBINSON A.R.	Coy. Comdr.	Lewis Gun, Gas	4.10.16
,,	WILKINSON R.M.	Course Instruction	Grenades	9.10.15
,,	KNOWLES F.E.	Plat. Comdr.	Grenades	9.10.15
2nd Lt.	NICHOLSON C.A.J.	Plat. Comdr.	Grenades	6.11.16
,,	MITCHELL R.J.	,,	Vickers & Lewis	10.11.15
,,	AYRES F.	Bde. School	,,	10.11.15
,,	DRAKE D.H.	Bombing Offr.	Grenades	17.1.17
,,	PAYNE F.E?	Bde. Bombing School	Grenades	11.10.15
,,	HAWLEY D.D.	Lewis Gun Officer	Vickers & Lewis	29/5/16
,,	SAMUELS E.	Signal Officer	Signalling	25.1.16
,,	LAMOND A.W.	Bde. Depot	Signalling	21.12.14
,,	STROTHER J.M.		Sniping	3.9.16
,,	HILL J.E.	Coy. Comdr.	P.T. & B.F. Gas	16.9.16
,,	OAKLEY M.H.	Plat. Comdr.	P.T. & B.F.	4.9.16
,,	CORBAN J.	A/Adjutant	P.T. & B.F.	12.8.14
,,	FAIRBAIRN J.J.W.	Plat. Comdr.	Grenades, musketry	15.12.16
,,	JACKSON F.C.	,,	Sniping	15.12.16
,,	WILKS E.L.	Course of Instruction		15.12.16
,,	GAUNT B.W.	Plat. Comdr.	XXXXXXX	15.12.16
,,	TAYLOR J.B.	,,	Musketry	15.12.16
,,	SUMNER W.G.	Bde. Depot	Machine Gun	16.7.16
,,	TOPPING E.	Plat. Comdr.		15.12.16
,,	HORSFALL J.R.	,,		,,
,,	WOODMANSEY K.G.	Course of Instruction		,,
,,	LUPTON F.	Plat. Comdr.	Musketry	,,
Lieut.	JAMIESON A	Quartermaster		11.9.16
Captain	PLAISTER G.R.	Medical Officer		11.9.15

NOMINAL ROLL OF OFFICERS.

63rd Machine Gun Company.

Major	COLDWELL W.G.A.	Commanding
Lieut.	WEBB W.A.	Adjutant
2/Lt.	HIPWELL H.R.	
,,	MACRAE D.A.	
,,	HAWES N.F.	Transport Officer
,,	GRAY R.E.	
,,	HARTLET I.C.	
,,	THOMPSON C.W.	
,,	HEMPSOLL E.	
,,	SCOTT F.E.B.	

63rd Trench Mortar Battery

Captain AKERMAN J.P. (8th Somerset L.I.) Commanding

2/Lieut. SIMS G.H. (8th Somerset L.I.)
  ,, MARKHAM E.B. (8th Lincoln Regt)
  ,, HARRIS M.W.S. (4th Middlesex Regt.)

ORIGINAL COPY.

WAR DIARY.

63rd Infantry Brigade.

FEBRUARY, 1917.

Army Form C. 2118.

WAR DIARY
or
~~INTELLIGENCE SUMMARY~~
(Erase heading not required.)

Instructions regarding War Diaries and Intelligence Summaries are contained in F. S. Regs., Part II. and the Staff Manual respectively. Title pages will be prepared in manuscript.

Place	Date	Hour	Summary of Events and Information	Remarks and references to Appendices
FERME DU BOIS	Feb. 1		Brigade relieved by 15th Infantry Brigade and moved to BETHUNE area	Div.O.O.No.66....... 1
	2			Bde.O.O.No.67....... 2
BETHUNE				Bde.O.O.No.109...... 3
	3		Training	
	4		"	
	5		"	
	6		"	
	7		" 8th Somerset L.I. practised in the new French Organisation for the attack. Div.O.O.No.68...... received.	4
	8		Reconnaissance of 14 BIS Section - All C.Os, 6 officers per front line Bn. 2 per support Bn.	
	9		Training	
	10		"	
	11		" Major G.R.Codrington, Staff Captain, appointed D.A.Q.M.G. XI Corps, Capt. F.M.Gillmore, 13th Royal Fusiliers, taking over his duties.	
	12		Brigade moved in accordance with Div. O.O.69 and Amendment Bde.O.O.No.111.and Amendments......	5, 6.
MAZIN-GARBE	13		63rd Bde. relieved 17th Inf. Bde. and 7 pm G.O.G. 63rd Inf. Bde. took over command of the 14 BIS Section.	
	14		Normal day in trenches.	
	15		" "	
	16 ⎱ 17 ⎰		" " A Divisional Conference was held at 5.30 pm for Brigade Commanders at 63rd Inf." Bde. H.Q." " 8th Somerset L.I. furnished a Guard of Honour of 3 offs. & 100 O.R. for General NIVELLE on arrival at CHOCQUES Station at 9.30 am............	7

Army Form C. 2118.

WAR DIARY
or
~~INTELLIGENCE SUMMARY~~

(Erase heading not required.)

Instructions regarding War Diaries and Intelligence Summaries are contained in F. S. Regs., Part II and the Staff Manual respectively. Title pages will be prepared in manuscript.

Place	Date	Hour	Summary of Events and Information	Remarks and references to Appendices
MAZINGARBE	18		Normal day in trenches.	
	19		Relief of front line battalions took place.	Bde.O.O.No.112......8
	20		Normal day intrenches.	
	21		,, ,, ,,	
	22		,, ,, ,, Divisional Conference at 63rd Bde. H.Q. at 5.30 pm for Bde. Commanders.	
	23		Normal day in trenches.	
	24		,, ,, ,,	
	25		Reliefs carried out of front line battalions, Bde. O.O. 114........	9
	26		Normal day in trenches	
	27		A dummy raid was carried out at 10 pm, Bde. Order No. 115....... report of dummy raid.......	10 11
	28		Normal day in trenches.	

E.B. ffrench
Brigadier General,
Commdg. 63rd Infantry Brigade.

REPORT ON DUMMY RAID CARRIED OUT ON THE
NIGHT OF 27/28th. FEBRUARY 1917.
OBSERVED FROM 'MAN TRAP' O.P., G 26 c.1.7.

ZERO - 10 p.m.

At 10 pm. Guns opened. The enemy immediately sent up a large number of Very Lights on our front and on our right and left.

At Zero plus 1, single red lights were fired. These were also fired in salvoes of three. This continued till zero plus 40 Six green lights were sent up, fired in pairs at intervals.

During the quiet period, there was no retaliation from artillery but some from Trench Mortars, little machine gun fire but considerable rifle fire. There was no appreciable increase in rifle and machine gun fire on our firing a 'golden rain' light during the quiet period. This points to the fact that the parapet was manned. It is therefore hoped that casualties were inflicted on the resumption of our Stokes bombardment.

At zero plus 15, numerous white lights were fired which burst into a single red and a single green. These continued until zero plus 40.

German Artillery opened at about Zero plus 12. No flashes could be observed, but all batteries firing appeared to be 7.7's. There was considerable retaliation at about zero plus 25, especially on our right Battalion. This principally consisted of heavy and light T.M's. This continued until about zero plus 40.

                      (sd) E.R.HILL   Brigadier General.
Feb. 28th.1917.   Commdg. 63rd. Infantry Brigade.

NOMINAL ROLL OF OFFICERS.

63rd Infantry Brigade Headquarters.

Brigadier General E.R. Hill,   Commanding.
  (H.L.I.)

Captain W.L. Brodie, V.C., M.C.   Brigade Major.
  (H.L.I.)

Captain F.M. Gillmore   Staff Captain.
  (13th R.Fus.)

2nd Lieut. F.J.R. SImpson   Brigade Bombing
  (4th Middlesex Regt.)   Officer.

Baron H. de Courtois.   Brigade Interpreter.

NOMINAL ROLL OF OFFICERS.

8th Battalion (S) Lincolnshire Regiment.

Rank and Name	Present Employment	How Trained	Embarked
Lt.-Col. CUBITT, T.A., C.M.G., D.S.O.	Commanding		
Major PATTINSON H.	On Course		11.9.15
Captain HUSSEY H. (Attd. from 8th Som.L.I.)	2nd in command		
Captain BROWN F.	Adjutant		11.9.15
,, KER R.A.	Bde. Transport Off.		11.9.15
,, CORDINER R.G., M.C.	Coy. Comdr.	Lewis & Vickers	11.9.15
,, HARRISON E.M.	,,		10.3.16
,, RAHLES RAHBULA A.J.	,,	Lewis Gun	4.4.16
Lieut. TAYLOR F.	Quartermaster		11.9.15
,, ALLBONES F.W.	Signal Offr.	Signalling	17.2.16
,, WAUGH F.A.	Coy. Comdr.	Bombing	19.6.16
,, BRADER H.C.	Coy. 2nd in Comd.	Lewis Gun	27.6.16
,, READ J.	Transport Off.		28.8.16
2/Lieut. MOLYNEUX	Plat. Comdr.	Lewis Gun	26.7.17
,, DUKES E.H.	Plat. Comdr.		27.7.16
,, POSNER P.E.	,,	Sniping	26.7.16
Lieut. KEELING W.J.	Sick	Bombing	29.7.16
2/Lieut. HODGSON D.C.	Plat. Comdr.	Bombing	28.7.16
2/Lieut. LEWIS H.A.C.	Coy. 2nd in Comd.	Lewis Gun	27.6.16
,, GODFREY R.J.		Lewis Gun	26.6.16
,, MARKHAM E.B.	63rd T.M.B.	Bombing, L.T.M.	13.10.15
,, FORGE A.F.	Plat. Comdr.	Bombing	25.7.16
,, TOMLINSON H.	Plat. Comdr.	Lewis Gun	20.7.16
,, BROWN A.	Plat. Comdr.	Gas	20.12.16
,, HARVEY M.	Plat. Comdr.		10.11.16
,, WHITE A.	Sniping Offr.	Sniping, Lewis G.	27.7.16
,, BUSHER D.J.B.	Plat. Comdr.	Bombing L. Gun	20.7.16
,, WILKINSON L.H.	On course		14.1.17
,, JEVONS J.B.	173 Tun.Co. RE.		9.1.17
,, WARNER C.W.	Platl Comdr.		9.1.17
,, KNIGHT S.G.	152 Fd.Co. RE.		22.1.17
,, GREGORY B.W.	Asst. Adjt.		20.12.16
,, TEDDER O.S.	Plat. Comdr.	Sniping	9.1.17
,, SMITH O.F.	Plat. Comdr.		3.2.17
,, DICKENSON S.	Plat. Comdr.		25.2.17
,, HANSELL	Plat. Comdr.		25.2.17
,, TOLHURST G.	Plat. Comdr.		3.2.17

NOMINAL ROLL OF OFFICERS.

8th (S) Battalion, Somerset Light Infantry.

Rank and Name		Present Employment	How Trained	Embarked
Lt.-Col.	SCOTT J.W., D.S.O.	Commanding		8.10.16
Major	DAVIES EVANS, D.W.C.	2nd in Command		10.11.16
Captain	WATTS R.A.B.P.	Att. 63rd Inf.Bde.		14.8.16
,,	HUSSEY H	Attd. 8/Lincs.	C.O.s Course	9.1.17
,,	GLADE WRIGHT C.W.	Coy. Comdr.	Grenades	9.10.15
,,	BOUCHER H.M.	Coy. Comdr.	P.T. & B.F.	19.1.17
,,	AKERMAN J.P.	Att. 63rd T.M.B.	T.M. & M.G.	9.10.15
,,	ROWLAND P.	152 Fd.Co.RE	Musketry	15.1.17
,,	SAUNDERS M.K.F.	Coy. Comdr.	Trench Warfare	9.10.15
Lieut.	PIKE H.	Transport Officer		10.9.15
,,	BAKER F.H.	Coy. Comdr.	Bombing, Gas	28.7.16
2/Lieut.	MATTHEWS N.A.	Intelligence Offr.	Sniping, Signals.	14.9.16
,,	BAKER H.G.	Att. Divl.Sigs.	Bombing, Signals.	14.9.16
,,	HINTON F.G.		Grenade Work	23.5.16
,,	HAGON P.C.	A/Adjutant	P.T. & B.F.	26.7.16
,,	BRYANT P.S.	Plat. Comdr.	Musketry, L.Gun.	26.7.16
,,	ADLAM F.G.	Att. 63rd Inf.Bde.	Trench Warfare	5.1.16
,,	WILLATT V.G.		Sniping	3.8.16
,,	MORGAN E.H.			,,
,,	SARGEANT R.L.			14.11.16
,,	GEGG J.H.B.			14.11.16
,,	GIBBS G.F.	Bombing Offr.		23.11.16
,,	LLEWELLYN A.H.	Plat. Comdr.		24.11.16
,,	HEAL R.W.	Lewis Gun Offr.	Lewis Gun	22.11.16
,,	BULLIVANT R.W.		Signalling	23.12.16
,,	HOOPER P.F.M.		1st Army School	7.11.16
,,	ROWLANDS E.J.		P.T. & B.F.	22.12.16
,,	CLARK F.J.			24.12.16
,,	COOKSLEY F.R.	On Course	Transport duties	
,,	THORNTON C.H.	,,	Sniping	2.1.17
,,	FROST H.C.		Course, Divl.Schl.	,,
,,	BAIRD C.A.			15.1.17
,,	GOODMAN S.			15.1.17
,,	GORDON C.C.B.		Gas	20.1.17
,,	OWEN A.C.			24.1.17
,,	WHITING W.C.		Bombing	6.2.17
,,	SWAIN A.G.		P.T., Bombing	6.2.17
,,	SMITH H.B.		Bombing	6.2.17
,,	GARDNER A.CJ			6.2.17
,,	WARD H.			14.2.17
,,	VAUGHAN L.H.			28.2.17
Lieut.	SCHOOLING J.J.	Quartermaster		10.9.15
Capt.	GREEN L., C.F.	R.CChaplain.	10.9.15	
Lieut.	ALFORD E.F.	Medical Officer		10.1.17
Major	SKAE E.T.	Attached		20.2.17

NOMINAL ROLL OF OFFICERS.

4th Battalion Middlesex Regiment.

Rank and Name	Present Employment	How Trained	Embarked
Lt.-Col. H.P.F. BICKNELL, D.S.O.	Commanding		7.11.14
Captain A.G. DAWSON	2nd in Command		24.12.16
,, T.L. BODEN, M.C.	Adjutant		13.8.14
,, E.J. DONALDSON			4.12.16
,, C.G. MORAN	Coy. Comdr.	C.Os Course	1.8.16
,, S.A. WILLIS	,,	Bombing	13.8.14
,, H.E. HEFFER	,,		13.8.14
Lieut. E.A.H. FENN	Town Major, VIEILLE CHAPELLE	XX.X.XX	13.7.16
Lieut. B.P. JONES		Divnl. School	6.9.16
2/Lieut. H.F. BOWSER	Brigade Sniping Off.	Sniping	1.2.15
,, A.C. TERRELL	On Course	Bombing	13.7.16
,, E.A.M. WILLIAMS	Bombing Officer		13.7.16
,, F.J.R. SIMPSON	Bde. Bombing Offr.	Bombing	19.11.15
,, R.E. TAYLOR	Attd. 37th Div.	Staff Duties	29.5.16
,, B.W. SMITH	Plat. Comdr.	Lewis Gun	13.7.16
,, W.E. STOCKLEY	,,	Bombing	13.7.16
,, E.G. GROGAN	Divnl. Gas Course	Lewis Gun	4.12.16
,, S. MIRAMS	Coy. Comdr.	Lewis Gun	5.6.16
,, D. CUTBUSH, M.C.	Lewis Gun Officer	Lewis Gun	2.10.15
,, R.M. HILTON	Plat. Comdr.	Lewis Gun	13.7.16
,, R.F.T. IRWIN	a/Signal Officer	Signalling	16.5.16
,, F.W. SCHOLEFIELD	Div. Camouflage Offr.	Sniping	15.7.16
,, A.G. MITCHELL		Bombing	13.7.16
,, L.G. THOMSON	a/Adjutant		13.7.16
,, O.N. MARTIN	Div. Salvage Offr.		13.7.16
,, L.W. ANDREAE	On Course	Light T.M.	12.6.15
,, A.D. TROWELL	Plat. Comdr.	Signalling	15.7.16
,, H.M. WILLIAMS	,,	Sniping	24.1.16
,, R.G. WILLIAMS	,,	Staff duties	15.7.16
,, A.D. HOOKE	,,	Gas	15.7.16
,, J.K. GRAYSON	On Course	Gas	4.12.16
,, H.S. WHITLOCK	Transport Officer	Transport	6.9.16
,, J.H. HODGSON	Plat. Comdr.	Bombing	28.4.16
,, G.S. SUTHERLAND	,,	Signalling	4.5.15
,, J.C. LYAL	On Course		12.12.16
,, D.F. HURR	Plat. Comdr.	Div. School	6.9.16
,, H.M. MONK	152 Fd.Co.R.E.	Div. School.	4.12.16
,, L. BARTLETT	Platoon Offr.		29.1.17
,, E. SLADE	,,		29.1.17
Lieut. A.H. AMOR	Quartermaster		18.10.15
Captain A.D. CHARP	Medical Officer		
Revd. W.G. LARGIE C.F.	Chaplain.		

NOMINAL ROLL OF OFFICERS.

10th (S) Battalion, York & Lancaster Regiment.

Rank and Name		Present Employment	How Trained	Embarked
Lt.-Col.	RIDGWAY J.H.	Commanding		1.9.14
Major	WELSH D.T.	2nd in command	Hythe	8.12.16
,,	DRYNAN W.B.	Coy. Comdr.	Vickers _ L.Guns	11.9.15
Captain	LUCAS S.	Coy. Comdr.		4.12.16
,,	FAIRNIE E.G.J.	Coy. Comdr.	Bombing, L. Gun	5.1.17
,,	ELSWORTH L.A.	Coy. Comdr.	Sniping	11.9.15
Lieut.	ROBINSON A.R.	Staff Learner	Lewis Gun, Gas	4.10.16
,,	WILKINSON R.M.	Plat. Comdr.	Grenades	9.10.15
,,	KNOWLES F.E.	On Course	,,	,,
2/Lieut.	NICHOLSON, C.A.J.	Plat. Comdr.	Grenades	6.1.16
,,	MITCHELL R.J.	Att.152.Fd.Co.RE.	Vickers & LewisG.	10.11.15
,,	AYRES F.	Lewis Gun Officer	Vickers & Lewis G.	10.11.15
,,	PAYNE F.E.	Plat. Comdr.	Grenades	11.9.15
,,	DRAKE D.H.	Bombing Offr.	Grenades	17.1.17
,,	HAWLEY D.D.	Plat. Comdr.	V & L Guns	29.5.16
,,	SAMUELS E.	Signal Offr.	Signalling	25.1.16
,,	LAMOND A.W.	Plat. Comdr.	Signalling	21.12.14
,,	HILL J.E.	Plat. Comdr.	P.T. & B.F., Gas	16.9.16
,,	WALNE H.A.	Asst.Transport Off.	Lt.T.M., Gas	6.2.17
,,	TAYLOR J.B.	Plat. Comdr.	Musketry Gas	15.12.16
,,	STROTHER J.M., M.C.	Intelligence Off.	Sniping	3.9.16
,,	OAKLEY M.H.		P.T. & B.F.	4.9.16
,,	GAUNT B.W.	63rd T.M.B.		15.12.16
,,	TOPPING E.	On Course		15.12.16
,,	HORSFALL J.R.	Plat. Comdr.		15.12.16
,,	WILKS E.L.	i/c Bde.Dump		15.12.16
,,	Jackson F.C.	Plat. Comdr.	Sniping	15.12.16
,,	FAIRBAIRN J.J.W.	Plat. Comdr.	Musketry	15.12.16
,,	LUPTON F.	Plat. Comdr.	Musketry	15.12.16
,,	WOODMANSEY K.G.	Plat. Comdr.	Lewis Gun	15.12.16
,,	CORBAN J.	Adjutant	Gym, P.T. & B.F.	12.8.14
,,	SUMNER W.G.	Plat. Comdr.	Machine Gun	10.7.16
Lieut.	JAMIESON A.	Quartermaster		11.10.16
Captain	PLAISTER G.R.	Medical Officer		11.9.15

NOMINAL ROLL OF OFFICERS.

63rd Machine Gun Company.

Rank and Name	Present Employment	How Trained	Embarked.
Major COLDWELL W.G.A.	Commanding	Vickers Gun	24.2.16
Lieut. WEBB W.A.	2nd in Command	,,	24.2.16
,, MACRAE D.A.		,,	16.10.16
2/Lt. HIPWELL H.R.		,,	19.11.16
,, HAWES N.F.		,,	25.6.16
,, GRAY R.E.		,,	16.10.16
,, HARTLET I.C.		,,	1.7.16
,, THOMPSON C.W.		,,	4.6.16
,, HEMSOLL E		,,	18.11.16
,, SCOTT F.E.B.		,,	19.11.16

63rd Trench Mortar Battery.

Captain AKERMAN J.P. (8th Somerset L.I.)   Commanding

2/Lieut. SIMS G.H.   (8th Somerset L.I.)   2nd in command

2/Lieut. MARKHAM E.B. (8th Lincoln Regt.)
2/Lieut. HARRIS M.W.S. (4th Middlesex Regt.)
2/Lieut. GAUNT B.W. (10th York & Lanc. Regt.)

CASUALTIES DURING FEBRUARY, 1917.

Unit	Casualties In Trenches								Casualties Out Of Trenches								Total Casualties in and out of trenches	Sick			Grand Total	Remarks
	Officers			Other Ranks					Officers			Other Ranks						Offrs.	O.R.	Total		
	Killed	Wounded	Missing	Killed	Wounded	Missing	Total		Killed	Wounded	Missing	Killed	Wounded	Missing	Total							
8th Lincolnshire Regt.	-	-	-	1	6	-	7		-	-	-	-	-	-	-		7	1	38	39	45	1 Lt. B.P. Jones Capt. E.J. Donaldson
4th Middlesex Regt.	-	-	-	3	6	-	9		-	-	-	-	-	-	-		9	2	64	66	75	1 Capt. C.W.G. Wright
8th Somerset Light Infantry	-	-	-	-	5	-	5		-	-	-	-	-	-	-		5	2	39	41	46	2/Lt. A.C.J. Gardner
10th York & Lancaster Regt.	1	1	-	3	9	-	13		-	-	-	-	-	-	-		13	-	36	36	49	1 Capt. H. Broadbent.
65rd Machine Gun Company	-	-	-	-	-	-	-		-	-	-	-	-	-	-		-	-	8	8	8	
63rd Trench Mortar Battery	-	-	-	1	1	-	2		-	-	-	-	-	-	-		2	-	8	8	10	
TOTAL	1	-	-	8	27	-	36		-	-	-	-	-	-	-		36	4	193	197	233	

ORIGINAL COPY

63rd INFANTRY BRIGADE
WAR DIARY
MARCH
1917

Army Form C. 2118.

WAR DIARY
or
INTELLIGENCE SUMMARY

(Erase heading not required.)

Instructions regarding War Diaries and Intelligence Summaries are contained in F.S. Regs., Part II. and the Staff Manual respectively. Title pages will be prepared in manuscript.

Place	Date	Hour	Summary of Events and Information	Remarks and references to Appendices
MAZINGARBE	1.3.17		Quiet day in trenches. 63rd M.G.Coy. and 63rd T.M.Battery relieved in trenches. (Div. O.O. 72....	1
	2.3.17		Quiet day in trenches. 8th Lincoln Regt. in reserve moved to BETHUNE. (Amendment	
BETHUNE	3.3.17		Reliefs took place in accordance will Bde. O.O. 116 & Amendment.............	2
ROBECQ	4.3.17		The Brigade marched in accordance with Bde. O.O. 116 and Amendment.	
RELY	5.3.17		"	
	6.3.17		"	
	7.3.17		Training	
	8.3.17		"	
	9.3.17		The Brigade marched in accordance with Div. O.O. 75 and Bde. O.O. 117............Div. O.O. 75....	3
LA THIEULOYE			Brigade Headquarters at LA THIEULOYE and not as stated in Bde. Orders. Bde. O.O.117.....	4
HOUVIN-HOUVIGNEUL	10.3.17		The Brigade marched into the HOUVIN-HOUVIGNEUL Area. 63rd M.G.Coy. and 63rd T.M.Battery were billeted in GOUY-EN-TERNOIS and not as stated in Bde Orders.	
	11.3.17		Training.	
	12.3.17		Training. Lt.-Col. BICKNELL, D.S.O., 4th Middlesex Regt., proceeded to England to an Officers' Training School. Major F.W.GREATWOOD joined 8th Lincolnshire Regt.	
	13.3.17		Training.	
	14.3.17		Training.	
	15.3.17		Brigade Route March.	
	16.3.17		Training. Brig.-Gen. E.R.HILL handed over command of the Brigade to Brig-Gen. E.L.CHALLENOR, D.S.O.	
	17.3.17		Training. Lt.-Col. W.I.WEBB-BOWEN took over command of 4th Middlesex Regt.	
	18.3.17		Church Parades.	
	19.3.17		Training.	
	20.3.17		Training	
	21.3.17		Training	
	22.3.17		Training	
	23.3.17		Training	
	24.3.17		Training	
	25.3.17		Church Parades.	
	26.3.17		Training. Capt. COULON, Superintendent, Physical Training and Bayonet Fighting, lectured to officers and N.C.Os of the Brigade on Bayonet fighting. The G.O.C., Brigade Major and Battalion Commanders attended a Corps Conference at NOYELLE-VION at 5.30 pm.	
	27.3.17		Training.	
	28.3.17		Training.	
	29.3.17		Training.	

Army Form C. 2118.

WAR DIARY
or
~~INTELLIGENCE SUMMARY~~
(Erase heading not required.)

Instructions regarding War Diaries and Intelligence Summaries are contained in F. S. Regs., Part II. and the Staff Manual respectively. Title pages will be prepared in manuscript.

Place	Date	Hour	Summary of Events and Information	Remarks and references to Appendices
HOUVIN-HOUVIGNEUL	30.3.17		Training.	
	31.3.17		do 20 Officers of the Brigade attended a demonstration at the Divisional School FOUFFLIN-RICAMETZ of a Platoon in the attack and afterwards attended a lecture on Tanks at HOUVIN-HOUVIGNEUL.	

N Challenor. Brigadier-General,
Commdg. 63rd Infantry Brigade.

WAR DIARY
or
INTELLIGENCE SUMMARY

(Erase heading not required.)

Army Form C. 2118.

Place	Date 1917	Hour	Summary of Events and Information	Remarks and references to Appendices
HOUVIN- HOUVIGNEUL	April 1		Church Parades.	
	2		Training	
	3		Training	
	4		Training	
MANIN	5		The Brigade and attached troops marched in accordance with Div. O.O. 77 & amendment and Bde O.O.118. Conference of C.Os at Bde. H.Q. at 5.30 pm. Lt.-Col. CUBITT, C.M.G., D.S.O. on promotion handed over command of 8th Lincolnshire Regt. to Major GREATWOOD	1 2
	6		The Brigade did not march as directed by Brigade O.O. 119. Training was carried out instead.	
LATTRE St. QUENTIN	7		The Brigade Group marched in accordance with Brigade O.O. 119	3
DUISANS	8			
	9		The Brigade Group marched in accordance with Brigade O.O. 120	4
	10		The Brigade took part in the operations east of ARRAS. Brigade Instructions No. 1	5
	11		'Div. O.O. No. 78 ',',' No. 2	6 6A
	12		Brigade Instructions No. 3 & Amendment	7 8
ARRAS			For account of these operations see appendix No. 3. On 12th the Brigade less 10th York & Lancs. and 8th Lincolns was relieved and was billeted in ARRAS.	
DUISANS	13		Brigade Billeted in ARRAS, 8th Lincolns and 10th York & Lancs. arriving about 5.30 am. Brigade Group less 10th York & Lancs. and 8th Lincolns marched in accordance with Bde. O.O. 120A	9
AGNEZ LEZ DUISANS	14		Brigade Group marched in accordance with Div. O.O. 79, Bde O.O. 121, 8th Lincolns and 10th York & Lancs. rejoining.	10, 11
MANIN	15		Brigade Group marched in accordance with Brigade O.O. No. 122	12
	16		Resting and Refitting	
	17		Resting and Refitting	
	18		Resting and Refitting	
MONTENES- COURT	19		Brigade Group marched in accordance with Div. O.O. 80 and Bde. O.O. No. 123	13, 14
" "	20		Brigade Group moved by motor bus in accordance with Div O.O. 81 and Bde. O.O. No. 124 and took over the line held by 10th Inf. Bde. the relief being completed at 4.30 am, 21st.	15 16
Trenches	21		After dark half the Brigade front was taken over by 111th Inf. Bde. Bde. O.O. 125	17
	22			
	23		Brigade carried out operations, orders for which were issued in Div O. 82 & Bde. O.O. 126.	18 19

Army Form C. 2118.

WAR DIARY
or
INTELLIGENCE SUMMARY

(Erase heading not required.)

Instructions regarding War Diaries and Intelligence Summaries are contained in F. S. Regs., Part II. and the Staff Manual respectively. Title pages will be prepared in manuscript.

Place	Date	Hour	Summary of Events and Information	Remarks and references to Appendices
Trenches	24			
	25		Div. O.O. No. 83 and Bde. O.O. No. 127	20
	26			21
	27		Appendix 22 gives an account of these operations on 23rd - 28th	22
	28			
	29		By 4 am the Brigade less 63rd Machine Gun Coy. had been withdrawn to the vicinity of POINT DU JOUR and embussed at POINT ROND, ARRAS in accordance with Div O.O. 84 and Bde. O.O. 128	23
			and moved to the LIGNEREUIL Area. 63rd M.G.Company rejoined.	24
MANIN	30		Resting, re-organising and washing.	

M[illegible].
Brigadier General,
Commdg. 63rd Infantry Brigade.

63rd Machine Gun Company.

Report on recent fighting 9 - 12 April 1917.

April 15th 1917.

About mid-day April 9th the 63rd Machine Gun Company took up a position in the assembly trenches.

At 1:15 p.m. I reported to Brigade Headquarters for orders and was informed that the BLUE Line had been captured, and that groups Nos. 7 & 8 were to advance in rear of the 111th Brigade to their barrage positions on ORANGE HILL.

I accordingly despatched No. 3 & 4 Sections to take up their positions preparatory to give barrage fire for the 112th Brigade when it should advance. Nos. 3 & 4 sections advanced, but on reaching about H.27.d.5.5. came under hostile M.G. fire from the German trenches running through H.34.a. there being no sign of our own Infantry in front. The two sections accordingly withdrew to about H.27.a.2.3. until such time as it would be possible to take up their barrage positions on Orange Hill. Meanwhile on receipt of orders from Brigade Headquarters that the 63rd Infantry Brigade was to leave assembly trenches and move to BATTERY VALLEY I issued orders to my remaining two sections (Nos 1 & 2) to advance to BATTERY VALLEY, No, 1 Section being in support and No.2 section being split up - 2 guns with 8th Lincolnshire Regiment and 2 guns with 8th Somerset L.I..

About 7:30 p.m. orders were issued for the 8th Somerset L.I. and 8th Lincolnshire Regt to move forward ~~with the 8th Lincolns echeloned~~ through H.28.- the 8th Somersets on the right with the 8th Lincolns echeloned to their left and rear.

The 4 guns of No. 2 Section - 2 guns with each Regiment - moved with these Regiments.

By 9:0 p.m. the position of the sections was asfollowws :- No. 1 Section in reserve in BATTERY VALLEY. Nos.3 & 4 Sections about H.33.a.9.9. waiting for the line on ORANGE HILL to be established so that they could advance to their barrage positions. No.2 section ~~with 8th Lincolns~~ 2 guns with 8th Lincolns and 2 with 8th Somerset L.I. about H.28.b & d respectively

By 12 m.n. the situation was unchanged except that No 2 Section guns had advanced a little further forward.

At about 11 a.m. on the 10th 8th Somerset L.I. reported to Brigade H.Q. that they had reached the Valley running through H.30 b and c and were pushing on.

I accordingly issued orders for Nos. 3 and 4 sections (groups 8 & 9) to move to their barrage positions on ORANGE HILL. During the afternoon these guns were able to fire on small direct targets on or about the high ground WEST of MONCHY-LE-PREUX, though most of the damage being done to our own troops came from Machine guns in MONCHY, which could not possibly be spotted.

At about 4:30 pm. on the afternoon of the 10th Sgt HUGHES i/c the two guns of No.2 section attached 8th Lincolns saw a considerable number of Germans apparently massing just North of the river in H.25.a. He at once opened rapid fire on them obtaining good observation and undoubtedly inflicting casualties.

The two guns of No 2 Section with 8th S.L.I. fired on one or two direct targets but were unable to do much firing owing to the fact that they were short of ammunition on account of casualties, so wisely decided to hold their fire in case of hostile counter-attack. By 12 mid-night on the 10th the guns were in the following positions :-

No. 1 Section in reserve in BATTERY VALLEY.
No. 3 & 4 sections (groups 8 & 9) on ORANGE HILL.
No.2 section 2 guns approx. H.30c.8.8. with 8th Lincolns
     2 ,, ,, H.36.a.3.8. with 8th Somerset L.I.

Shortly after mid-night orders were issued that the green line was to be attacked at 5 a.m. on the morning of the 11th by the 15th Division and that the 37th Division was to pass through it with the 63rd Brigade in support. Accordingly No. 7 and 8 groups opened fire at 5 a.m. as per barrage programme but were unable to fire the prescribed number of rounds owing to the rapidity of the advance.

Meanwhile No. 1 section advanced to H.28.c.3.7. where orders were given by G.O.C. 63rd Infantry Brigade for it to halt pending further instructions. As the advance seemed to be going well I ordered this section to advance and picking up No. 9 group (No 3 section) these two sections advanced to H.35.b.3.5., No. 4 section remaining in r reserve at H.35.a.2.1.

About 3 p.m. I received orders that the river and its north bank in H.25.a. and b. must be carefully watched. I accordingly despatched No. 3 section to guard this ground, taking up a position by 4 p.m. about H.30.c.7.3. Meanwhile No. 4 section in reserve at H.35.a.2.1. was given orders to be prepared to sweep the high ground in N.6,a, in case of a successful counter-attack, the 4 guns of No 2 section being respectively in pairs about H.36.c.5.5. and H.36.b.8.2. No 1 section coming into immediate support and being prepared to advance with 8th Somerset L.I. if ordered to do so from H.36.a.5.4.

At 6 a.m. April 12th I received orders to withdraw my company to FEUCHY CHAPEL REDOUBT. This move was completed by mid-day.

    sgd. W.G.A.COLDWELL
     O.C. 63rd ?.G.Coy.

April 15th 1917.

63rd Infantry Brigade.

REPORT ON OPERATIONS - APRIL 9th - 12th 1917.

April 9th. The Brigade Group left the vicinity of PORTE BAUDIMONT about 9.30 am and marched through ARRAS to its assembly trenches. The only casualties during this approach march was from the explosion of an ammunition dump under the railway bridge. This explosion occurred just as the rear of the 10th York & Lanc. Regt. had passed the bridge and the head of the 4th Middlesex Regt. was approaching, causing about 20 casualties in all.

The Brigade was assembled in the trenches by 11.30 am.

At 3.35 pm the Brigade advanced to BATTERY VALLEY and by 6 pm was assembled in H 26 b. During the advance to BATTERY VALLEY it had been anticipated that touch would have been gained with 111th Infantry Brigade which had started in front, but its position was not ascertained till about 7.30 pm.

At 7.35 pm I ordered 8th Somerset Light Infantry and 8th Lincolnshire Regt. and 1 section 63rd Machine Gun Company to advance and occupy ORANGE HILL, 4th Middlesex Regt. to move in support and 10th York & Lancaster Regt. to remain in reserve in BATTERY VALLEY. On arrival at the BROWN LINE, O.C. 8th Somerset L.I. reported as follows:- "8th Somerset L.I., 2 companies digging in on ORANGE HILL, the right turned back to join H.L.I. (15th Div.) in BROWN LINE about H 34 central; one company in support about H 34 b 5.3 and 1 company in reserve in BROWN LINE about H 28 c 8.0 with a post pushed down south in the BROWN LINE from H 34 central in touch with the enemy". 8th Lincolnshire Regt prolonged the left of 8th Somerset L.I. in H 29 c; 4th Middlesex Regt. was in support of these two battalions at H 27 d along the track running south from BROKEN MILL in H 27 b. 10th York & Lanc. Regt. in reserve BATTERY VALLEY in reserve with Brigade Headquarters.

At 10.15 pm a report was received from 8th Somerset L.I. that he had not gained touch with 111th Inf. Bde. and that there appeared to be a very large gap on his right. At midnight, April 9/10th, I ordered up 4th Middlesex Regt. to prolong the left of 8th Lincolnshire Regt. along the SUNKEN ROAD about H 29 b and informed 10th York & Lanc. Regt. to be ready to prolong left of 4th Middlesex Regt. when the two Battalions of 111th Infantry Brigade should arrive in support.

April 10th. An officers' patrol sent out from 8th Somerset L.I. reported 111th Inf. Bde. on road in H 33 d.

At 2 am on the 10th, a message was received from 111th Inf. Bde. that two battalions were on their way and I ordered 10th York & Lanc. Regt. to move forward to prolong the left of 4th Middlesex in the SUNKEN ROAD in H 23 d to gain touch with the Corps Mounted troops in FAMPOUX and push patrols along the valley.

About 10 am on the 10th, 8th Somerset L.I. sent forward two Companies to make good LONE COPSE VALLEY, and the remainder of the Battalion followed, and about noon their position was as follows:- One company about H 36 c 3.4, one company about H 36 a 7.4 and two companies in LONE COPSE VALLEY. The advance from ORANGE HILL to this position was carried out by dribbling small parties from shell-hole to shell-hole as there was heavy machine gun fire from the low ground about ROEUX and north of the river, MOUNT PLEASANT WOOD in enfilade. 8th Lincolnshire Regt. moved forward echeloned in rear of 8th Somerset L.I. and experienced the same difficulty from enemy enfilade fire into LONE COPSE VALLEY. 4th Middlesex Regt. pushed forward in the same way from the SUNKEN ROAD in H 29 b.

10th York & Lanc. Regt. were also ordered to advance to LONE COPSE VALLEY but immediately their advance commenced, their leading companies suffered heavily from Machine gun fire in the direction of MOUNT PLEASANT WOOD; they were unable to get forward and remained dug in in their previous position.

The 10th..........

About noon, 1 company of 8th Somerset L.I. from LONE COPSE VALLEY was ordered to advance on to the crest in H 36 b and make good the trenches in H 36 d N.E. This company came under very heavy fire and could not get on; they were supported by 8th Lincolnshire Regt. who sent one company on to the ridge about H 36 central, from where it could get no further. Soon after noon, when the attack of 111th Infantry Brigade was seen advancing towards to MONCHY-LE-PREUX, two companies, 8th Somerset L.I. were directed to attack the enclosures west of MONCHY about H 36 c. They got up to the hedges where they were stopped by machine gun and rifle fire, and the 111th Inf. Bde appeared to have stopped in the right rear of these two companies. 8th Lincolnshire Regt., trying to move to their support, found it impossible to get on owing to the heavy enfilade machine gun fire in LONE COPSE VALLEY and the ridge in H 36 b, and the situation remained the same until dusk, 7.30 pm.

During the afternoon of the 10th, LONE COPSE VALLEY and positions in the vicinity were heavily barraged by the enemy's guns from the N.E. As soon as it was dusk, 10th York & Lanc. Regt. were ordered to move forward to LONE COPSE VALLEY, which they did, and occupied the position in H 33 d, dug into the bank with their right immediately north on LONE COPSE.

At 4.55 pm, orders were sent to 8th Somerset L.I. and 8th Lincolnshire Regt., and 4th Middlesex Regt. to advance at 7.30 pm to their final objective, 10th York & Lanc. Regt. to be in reserve in LONE COPSE VALLEY. These Battalions advanced a short distance but were stopped by very heavy fire from the trenches in H 36 d and by machine gun fire from MONCHY and their left flank, and apparently 111th Inf. Bde. only got as far as the enclosures in H 36 c and N 6 a. The enemy were holding the western outskirts of MONCHY and the trenches in H 36 d., and the ridge in I 31 d. A patrol reported that the 111th Inf. Bde. were similarly held up on our right about the enclosures and the Battalions consolidated along LONE COPSE VALLEY.

April 11th. At 5 am on the 11th, the attack of 111th Inf. Bde. and 15th Division developed, one battalion of 15th Division passing through 8th Somerset L.I. and capturing the trenches in H 36 d. The Brigade was assembled along the bank in LONE COPSE VALLEY as owing to the barrage it was impossible to move then on the high ground in H 35 d as this was in full view and subjected to heavy shelling.

At 10.30 am a message was received from 37th Division that 15th Division were on the line KEELING COPSE - PELVES, and orders were at once issued for the Brigade to move to the high ground O 2 d and BOIS DES AUBEPINES. 10th York & Lanc. Regt. were ordered to cover the advance. At 11 am this battalion, on crossing the ridge running through H 36 b at once came under enfilade machine gun fire from the direction of ROEUX and from the N.E., and it became evident that the line KEELING COPSE - PELVES was not in our possession and that 10th York & Lanc. Regt. were held up about the trenches in H 36 d. Shortly after this instructions were received to reinforce 111th Inf. Bde. in MONCHY.

4th Middlesex and 8th Lincolnshire Regt. were ordered to move into MONCHY, moving south of 10th York & Lanc. Regt. to avoid the enemy's enfilade machine gun fire as much as possible. 4th Middlesex arrived and got into touch with 111th Inf. Bde. and on being asked for assistance by the Cavalry Brigade on the S.E. part of the village, detached a platoon and two Lewis guns.

They established posts on a line approximately on the line of the road running North through O 1 a with Lewis Gun posts in the wood O 1 b and O 1 c 24. At this time the village was being heavily bombarded and the remainder of this battalion were kept in cellars in the village about O 1 a O.3, ready to reinforce any of these posts. The posts were consolidated. 8th Lincolnshire Regt., advancing to the village in rear of 4th Middlesex also came under heavy machine gun and barrage fire and were hung up S.E. of the trenches H 36 d, in N 6 b and O 1 a.

8th Somerset L.I. were kept in LONE COPSE VALLEY.
The position remained the same during the afternoon.
At 5.25 pm we received orders from 37th Division that this

Brigade would be relieved by 37th Infantry Brigade. The two Battalions of 37th Inf. Bde. relieved 111th Inf. Bde. and 4th Middlesex Regt., relief being completed about 11 pm, and 4th Middlesex proceeded to BATTERY VALLEY.

The other three battalions remained in their positions during the night, as the relief of 15th Division in whose area we were was obscure. The night was quiet and at dawn 8th Somerset L.I. were ordered to withdraw to FEUCHY CHAPEL. 8th Lincolnshire Regt. and 10th York & Lanc. Regt. were ordered to remain during the day as it was impossible to extricate them in daylight without casualties.

At 8.30 pm, these two Battalions withdrew to ARRAS.

The action of 8th Somerset Light Infantry in their advance from ORANGE HILL to LONE COPSE VALLEY was executed with great skill and with a minimum of losses considering the heavy fire. The advance of all battalions from ORANGE HILL to SUNKEN ROAD in H 29 b and H 23 d line presented great difficulties owing to enfilade fire and the bare slopes and valleys running down to the river SCARPE.

Action of Machine Gun Company attached.

Brigadier General,
Commdg. 63rd Infantry Brigade.

April 18th 1917

ORIGINAL COPY

WAR DIARY

63rd Inf.,Bde.

MAY, 1917

Army Form C. 2118.

WAR DIARY
or
INTELLIGENCE SUMMARY.
(Erase heading not required.)

Instructions regarding War Diaries and Intelligence Summaries are contained in F.S. Regs., Part II. and the Staff Manual respectively. Title pages will be prepared in manuscript.

Place	Date	Hour	Summary of Events and Information	Remarks and references to Appendices
MANIN.	1917 May 1		Bathing and reorganising.	
	2		Training; a conference was held at Brigade H.Q. and recent operations were discussed with C.Os.	
	3		Training.	
	4		Training.	
	5		Training.	
	6		Church Parades; a Memorial Service was held at the Church of England Parade.	
	7		Training.	
	8		Training; the Army Commander visited Battalions at training.	
	9		Training; 4th Middlesex competed in a Divisional Field Firing Competition, each Brigade being represented by a Battalion team.	
	10		Training.	
	11		Training; a team from 4th Middlesex won a Divisional Rapid Wiring Competition, one team representing each Brigade.	
	12		Training; The Divisional Commander visited units at training.	
	13		Church Parades.	
	14		Training.	
	15		Training.	
	16		Training. at Div. H.Q. in the afternoon.)	
	17		Training; the Corps Commander visited units at training, & lectured to officerson recent operations/)	
SIMENCOURT	18		The Brigade Group marched in accordance with Div. Order No. 85 and Bde. O.O. No. 129	1, 2
DAINVILLE	19		The Brigade Group marched in accordance with Div. Order No. 86 and Bde. O.O. No. 130 & amendment.	3, 4
	20		Church Parades and training.	
ACHICOURT	21		Moves took place in accordance with Brigade O.O. No. 131.	5
	22		Training; officers from units went forward to reconnoitre front line.	
	23		Training.	
	24		Training.	
	25		Training; officers reconnoitred front line; a congratulatory message received from Lieut.-General Sir Charles Fergusson, commanding XVII Corps.	6
	26		Training	
	27		Training and Church Parades. Div. O. No. 89 and Div. M.G.Scheme received, requiring one section... 63rd M.G.Company to co-operate in a small attack on night 29/30. Letter 9037 sent to 63rd M.G.Coy.	7, 8 9

Army Form C. 2118.

WAR DIARY

or

INTELLIGENCE SUMMARY.

(Erase heading not required.)

Instructions regarding War Diaries and Intelligence Summaries are contained in F. S. Regs., Part II. and the Staff Manual respectively. Title pages will be prepared in manuscript.

Place	Date	Hour	Summary of Events and Information	Remarks and references to Appendices
TILLOY	May 28		The Brigade less 8th Lincolnshire Regt., relieved 111th Inf. Bde. in support in and around TILLOY. Div. O.O. 88 and Bde. O.O. No. 132	10, 11
	29		The Brigade in support; training as far as possible carried out. The operation arranged for night 29/30 postponed till Night 30/31. Div. Order No. 92	12
	30			
	31		The Brigade relieved by 184th Inf. Bde. and marched to billets in ARRAS. Div. O. No. 90 Bde. O.O. No. 133	13 14

R. Chumm

Brigadier General,
Commdg. 63rd Infantry Brigade.

REPORT ON RECENT OPERATIONS, COVERING THE PERIOD APRIL 22nd to APRIL 29th.

63rd MACHINE GUN COMPANY.

On April 22nd I received the following orders for operations commencing 4.45 am 23rd inst :-
1 section of 3 guns to be attached to 8th Somerset L.I.
1   ,,   ,,   ,,   ,,   8th Lincolns.
2   ,,   ,,   to do barrage fire under orders of D.M.G.C

At 12.45 am 2/Lt. HIPWELL reported with 3 guns to O.C. 8th S.L.I. and took up position in the assembly trenches.

2/Lt. GRAY with 3 guns reported to O.C. 8th Lincolns at 1.45 am and proceeded to the assembly trenches.

At 2 am 6 guns under 2/Lt. SCOTT and 2/Lt. HAWES were in position for barrage fire in H 10 d 2.9 and HERON Trench, H 11 a, 3 in each position. At 4.45 am barrage fire was opened by these guns on the targets selected. Fire ceased at 5.40 am Rounds fired, 11,750. At 8 am 2/Lt. GRAY reported at Brigade Headquarters that he was out of touch with Lincolns. He was ordered to take his guns to cross roads in I 7 a. 2/Lt. HIPWELL, following S.L.I. suffered heavy casualties on the way through HYDERABAD REDOUBT about 6 am. The remnants of his section were gathered together in CLYDE Trench about 500 yards E. of REDOUBT. This officer went forward to reconnoitre, but never reappeared. 7 men and 2 guns of his section reported at Brigade H.Q. at 9 pm on 23rd and were placed in the RAVINE in H 15 b.

At 8.15 am barrage guns were ready to move and I reported to G.O.C. 63rd Inf. Bde. that they were at his disposal. About 9 am I received orders to take these six guns towards GREENLAND HILL to assist the advance of infantry. By 10 am I had both sections assembled in HERON Trench and ordered them to proceed in echelon of gun teams with half an hour interval between sections to a position 200 yards west of cross roads in I 7 a. Two guns were ordered to have a field of fire to the S.E. covering our right flank.

At 12 noon teams were resting in and east of Black Line in H 22 b. Two teams of Lt. GRAY'S Section were absorbed under my command. I reconnoitred our right flank from FAMPOUX to Cross Roads in I 7 a and noticed enemy activity behind ridge as if preparing for counter attack.

By 1.30 pm 8 guns were in position along line selected just west of cross roads and in touch with O.C. Lincolns and O.C. S.L.I. About 1.30 pm the first enemy counter attack commenced and advancing in three waves from I 8 b and I 9 c. Fire was opened and the attack broken. Almost immediately a second attack developed in closer formation, about 12 lines of 50 each line. My guns completely smashed this attack. According to reports from prisoners enemy losses from artillery during this phase were nil, from machine guns 30% (XVII Corps Summary No. 104)

Under cover of our fire, some Somersets and Lincolns had advanced to Sunken Road in I 7 a.

Some Lewis Guns took part in firing but infantry kept their heads down to allow our fire to clear them.

All afternoon till dusk, small groups of Germans dribbled back from crest to positions about always half way down slope in I 7 b, I 7 d and I 8 c. Our guns fired as targets presented themselves and accounted for a number of enemy. We were subjected to shellfire from 2 pm - 7.30 pm, had two guns knocked out of action and a number of casualties. At 8 pm I changed positions of teams and by midnight had 4 guns under 2/Lt. HAWES and 2/Lt. HOFMEYER in CLASP Trench, two near BRICKSTACKS and two near I 7 c. This was the line to which the attack of 112th Bde. had advanced.

Rounds fired between 1.30 and 7.30 pm, 3,000.

Two guns were in support with the Lincolns, one at H 12 b 9.3 and one at H 12 b 7.6. These guns covered effevtually teh ground in I 2 c, I 8 a and I 8 b.

24th passed quietly; 4,000 rounds were fired by guns in CLASP Trench at batches of enemy who all day dribbled down slope in I 2 c, I 8 c, I 8 a and I 14 a.

9 pm, Company withdrawn to HERON Trench.

On the evening of the 26th I was informed that further operations would commence on the 28th. 63rd Inf. Bde. was to advance from CUBA Trench to the Black Line.

Two Vickers Guns were to advance with 8th S.L.I. on the right and two with 8th Lincolns on the left.

Four Vickers and 4 Lewis Guns (latter from 9th N. Staffs Rgt) were placed under my command to be used according to the tactical situation.

At 9 pm on the 27th, Sgt. CROSS with two guns, left HERON TRENCH with the 8th S.L.I. At 10 pm he arrived in position on the tape line and reported to the O.C. D Coy. of the Somersets when the latter arrived, about midnight.

At 10 pm, Sgt. COLEMAN, with 2 guns, reported to the O.C. Lincolns in Sunken Road, H 11 a, and followed the Battalion to CUBA Trench. He arrived on the Tape line at 2.30 am on the 28th. At 4.25 am the whole Brigade moved forward, endeavouring to keep between the German barrage and our own. The four Vickers guns followed in rear of the leading battalions. The advance continued straight away for 350 yards to CUTHBERT Trench. Very few Germans were found in this trench as the enemy had evacuated all the ground in front to beyond the crest immediately our barrage opened.

My two Vickers on the right followed the infantry over CUTHBERT Trench and took up positions in shell holes some 50 yards behind the infantry. the latter had dropped into shell holes about 100 yards beyond CUTHBERT Trench. As no observation or field of fire was possible for these two guns, they fell back to I 7 b 9.0 - I 7 b 7.4. Casualties had been suffered from machine gun and shell fire and snipers (machine guns & snipers were active on right flank) The two left guns took up a position just behind trench from about I 1 d 6.1 - I 7 b 7.8. The Sgt. in charge was killed while reconnoitring forward. None of the four teams could get into action to the front because of enemy fire from I 14 b 8.9, I 8 d 2.1, I 8 d 8.½. They could not fire to the right flank because the position of our own troops was not known.

During the two counter-attacks by the enemy about 1 pm and between 8 and 9, fire was opened by my two guns in CHILI Trench (v. below). All day, from the moment our barrage ceased and the enemy saw that our attack was not being pushed, Germans dribbled back down the slope to the shell holes near our own troops.

A considerable amount of reconnoitring was done by Sergt. CROSS during the afternoon of the 28th and after cessation of the German barrage about 9 o'clock, he withdrew his teams to a short trench in front of CUBA. When the infantry were relieved at night, he brought 3 guns and the remains of 4 gun teams back to HERON Trench.

The 4 Vickers and 4 Lewis Guns I placed in position between H 12 b 9.3 and H 12 b 7.6. Time 3.30 am on the 28th inst. Officers in charge of guns, Lt. D.A.MACRAE and 2/Lt. HAWES. During the counter attacks between 12.20 and 1.30 and 8 and 9 pm, three of these guns fired a total of 3000 rounds at the enemy. The right gun was knocked out and its team buried by a salvo of 5 big shells immediately it opened fire. Sergt. HUGHES did excellent work in observing fire effect and in passing the information to the nearest gun. A number of the enemy were hit in I 2 c, I 8 a and I.8 b.

About 6 pm, I arranged with O.C. 26th M.G.Company for relief on the night of 29/30th.

The four Lewis Guns of the N. Staffs. were placed under the orders of 4th Middlesex at 8.45 pm on 28th.

29.4.17. Intermittent shelling of CHILI Trench. At 12.30 am on the 30th, gun teams were withdrawn and taken with 13 guns to transport lines, ST. NICHOLAS.

(sd) W.A.WEBB, Lieut.,
Acting O.C. 63rd M.G.Company.

2.5.17

REPORT ON THE OPERATIONS, 22nd - 29th APRIL inclusive.

On 22nd April, 63rd Infantry Brigade held the front of 37th Division as follows :-

4th Middlesex, line of posts from H 12 c 7.8 to H 11 b 6.8 (junction of HONEY and HUSSAR Trenches) in touch with 51st Division on their right; 10th York & Lancs. the line of posts from H 11 b 6.8 to H 5 b 4.6, in touch with 63rd Division on their left; 8th Lincolnshire Regt. in support about HERON, LUCID and HAGGARD Trenches; 8th Somerset L.I. in reserve south of POINT DU JOUR; 63rd T.M. Batty. in SUNKEN ROAD, H 11 a 5.3, with 2 guns in action in HUDSON and HAZARD Trenches south of HONEY Trench; 63rd Machine Gun Company with 2 sections about HERON and H 4 d 5.0, the remainder in reserve and in anti-aircraft positions south of POINT DU JOUR.

During the night 22/23rd April, the front held by 10th York & Lanc. Regt. was taken over by 111th Inf. Bde. and 63rd Inf. Bde. was disposed as follows in preparation for the attack at 4.45 am on 23rd :-

4th Middlesex   from H 12 c 7.8 to H 12 a 0.3
10th York & Lanc.   from H 12 a 0.3 to H 11 b 6.8
8th Somerset L.I. in support of 4th Middlesex in HALO and HOARY trenches; 8th Lincolns in support of 10th York & Lancs. in HUDSON and HAZARD Trenches. 1 section 63rd Machine Gun Company accompanied each of the two supporting battalions and the remainder of the company was in position for barrage fire in H 10 d 2.9, HERON TRENCH.

2 guns 63rd T.M. Battery, from their positions in HUDSON and HAZARD trenches fired on the following points at zero hour:- H 6 c 0.2 and H 12 a 1.9.

At zero hour, 4.45 am, Battalions moved forward, 10th York and Lancs. on the left meeting with heavy front and enfilade machine gun fire from H 6 c, and on the right 4th Middlesex met with considerable fire from all directions but followed the barrage up to the road in X I 7 a and c, south of cross roads, but was unable to get further forward than a line about 200 yards east of the road, owing to enfilade machine gun fire from the right. The delay apparently caused the barrage to move away from 10th York & Lanc. Regt.. The opposition met with by 10th York & Lancs. caused 8th Lincolns to pass through this battalion at an early stage. The advance was then continued by 8th Lincolnshire Regt. towards CHILI Trench, but further progress was impossible as part of CHILI Trench about H 12 b 3.8 was occupied by some 50 or 60 Germans. One company of 8th Lincolns was directed to turn the right flank of these from the North, which it succeeded in doing between 10 and 11 am. The battalion then occupied the southern end of CANDIA and CHILI Trench. 8th Somerset L.I. in support of 4th Middlesex Regt. reached the road south of cross roads immediately in rear of 4th Middlesex. By 12 noon 10th York & Lancs. and 8th Lincolns had advanced towards the road and established a line between CHILI Trench and the road. About this time a German counter-attack came over the western slopes of GREENLAND HILL and was broken by rifle and machine gun fire, the latter being in the same line as 10th York & Lancs. and 8th Lincolns.

At about this time, noon, 6th Bedford Regt. passed through 10th York & Lancs. and 8th Lincolns and reached a line 200 yards east of the INN and CROSS ROADS.

At this time, the enemy's shrapnel barrage was very heavy between CHILI TRENCH and the road and this ground was also swept by enemy machine gun fire. The advance of 8th Lincolns and 10th York & Lancs. was continued by small parties moving from shell hole to shell hole until these two battalions reached a position 50 yards east of the road between the INN and the CROSS ROADS between 2 and 3 pm, where they dug in.

During the afternoon the machine guns in CHILI Trench successfully engaged small parties of Germans advancing over GREENLAND HILL.

2.....

At 7.30 pm the Brigade was in line about the road from the INN to I 7 c 8.8, in the following order from North to South:- 10th York & Lanc. Regt, 8th Lincolns, 8th Somerset L.I., 4th Middlesex, with 6th Bedfordshire Regt. on the left of 10th York & Lanc. Regt. After dark touch was gained with some scattered parties of 51st Division about 300 yards south of 4th Middlesex.

The attack of the remaining three battalions of 112th Inf. Bde. reached the line of this Brigade about 8.30 pm after which 10th York & Lancs. and 8th Lincolns were withdrawn to CHILI and CANDIA trenches in support.

About 9 pm, 4th Middlesex, after relief by 112th Inf. Bde., withdrew to the road immediately west of the position it had been holding.

The Brigade remained in these positions until after dark on 24th when it was relieved by 112th Inf. Bde. and withdrew to positions in H 11 c and H 10 d in Divisional Reserve. During this period the trenches were intermittently shelled and certain number of casualties were sustained. The Battalions were re-organized and formed into 4 platoons each. The average strength of the Battalions was then about 220.

Orders having been received for a further attack on 28th inst., units moved forward and occupied positions detailed in Addendum No. 2 to 63rd Inf. Bde. Order No. 127.

At zero hour, 4.25 am, all battalions moved forward and were east of the line INN - cross roads soon afterwards, with the exception of ½ battalion 4th Middlesex in Brigade Reserve in CHILI Trench. A very heavy barrage was placed on the line of the road a few minutes after zero.

Owing to the darkness and smoke from the barrage, units undoubtedly lost direction and the majority went too much to the left. This probably accounts for the fact that CUTHBERT Trench was missed and the first check took place about WHIP Trench which was mistaken for the former. Only a small party of 8th Somerset L.I. remained in CUTHBERT Trench. As far as can be ascertained, the majority of all battalions pushed on through WHIP past WEAK and WHY trenches, nearly up to RAILWAY COPSE, some parties reaching WICK Trench. During their advance, they took prisoners, and 3 or 4 batches of prisoners were sent back but were recaptured by the enemy probably about WEED Trench and southern portion of WHIP Trench. Parties from all battalions, finding that they were too far advanced, worked back to WHIP Trench and some to a position about 300 yards east of CUTHBERT Trench, where they dug in and remained throughout the day. This was the position at 6.30 am.

Between 6.30 am and 12 noon, parties continued to work back to WHIP Trench and to a line east of CUTHBERT Trench. The remainder who had not become casualties did not apparently succeed in getting back from the advanced position until after dark.

Numerous patrols had been sent out during the day from the Brigade Reserve to find out the situation and whether a continuous line was established on the objective. A report was received from 111th Inf. Bde. that some Germans were also in CUTHBERT Trench. As soon as it was dark, the Brigade Reserve (½ battalion 4th Middlesex) accompanied by Battalion Liaison officers was sent forward with instructions to clear CUTHBERT Trench of any Germans there and establish touch with 111th Inf. Bde. about cross roads I 2 c and fill any gaps in our line, whose right had been reported in touch with 112th Inf. Bde. This party was held up by machine gun fire about I 7 b 4.8 and did not reach CUTHBERT Trench. About 11 pm information was received that 112th Inf. Bde. had withdrawn to their jumping off trenches. From then onwards, all efforts were concentrated on bringing in the remainder of the Brigade to the original front line and in withdrawing 3 companies 9th N. Staffs Regt. and 152nd Field Co. R.E., which had gone out to dig a communication trench through CUTHBERT up to WHIP Trench. 111th Inf. Bde. was also asked to assist in bringing back parties of our men on their right. Meanwhile two companies 7th Seaforth Highlanders were on their way to occupy our old front line trenches and 9th N. Staffs Regt. were given orders to occupy our front line until the arrival of the former. By 4 am, 29th inst., the Brigade, except isolated parties which continued to come in for 24 hours had been withdrawn behind out original front line.

During the operations on 23rd and 28th April, the very greatest difficulty was experienced in getting back information from units. Telephone lines were cut, runners become casualties and visual signalling was not feasible. On the 23rd the advance of the supporting battalions was rendered extremely difficult owing to the wire round HYDERABAD REDOUBT, which necessitated companies making wide detours to get round it.

On the morning of 28th inst., units were formed up correctly in their assembly areas, CUBA Trench, and a tape line for the leading battalions. Compass bearings were taken and the direction was given to officers and N.C.Os. The loss of direction was apparently due to the following reasons (a) lack of officers owing to casualties. (b) the heavy hostile barrage which followed up our men and apparently urged them forward even through our own barrage, (c) darkness.

As regards (c) the consensus of opinion of officers who took part in this attack is that it would have been an advantage to have the zero hour later. At the time of starting, O.C. 8th Lincolns states that at about 20 yards distance it was impossible to distinguish between our own men and the Germans. The difficulties of a night attack were more or less experienced by battalions and it must be remembered that the officer casualties had been heavy and that the men were tired.

If the objective had been on some actual line, easily recognizable by the men, there seems every reason to believe that the majority of the Brigade would have reached the Black Line.

Throughout these operations and more particularly on 28th inst., most useful work was accomplished by 63rd Machine Gun Coy. The report of the acting C.O. of the company is attached.

May 3rd 1917

Brigadier General,
Commdg. 63rd Infantry Brigade.

ORIGINAL COPY

SECRET

63rd INFANTRY BRIGADE
WAR DIARY
JUNE 1917

Army Form C. 2118.

WAR DIARY
or
INTELLIGENCE SUMMARY.

(Erase heading not required.)

Instructions regarding War Diaries and Intelligence Summaries are contained in F. S. Regs., Part II. and the Staff Manual respectively. Title pages will be prepared in manuscript.

Place	Date	Hour	Summary of Events and Information	Remarks and references to Appendices
MANIN	June 1 1917		The Brigade moved to the MANIN - BEAUFORT Area in accordance with Div. O. No. 90 and Bde. O.O. No. 133 (See War Diary, May 1917.)	
,,	2		Training	
,,	3.		Church Parades	
,,	4.		Training	
CROIX	5		The Brigade moved in accordance with Div. O. No. 93 and Bde. O.O. 134	1, 2
ANVIN	6		The Brigade moved in accordance with Bde. O.O. No. 135	3
FRUGES	7		The Brigade moved in accordance with Bde. O.O. No. 136	4
,,	8		Training and settling into billets	
,,	9		Training; readjustments in billeting area - Brigade letter No. 9274	5
,,			Owing to the arrival of reinforcements, more accommodation was required in FRUGES	
,,	10		Church Parades.	
,,	11		Training.	
,,	12		Training.	
,,	13		Training.	
,,	14		Training. The Brigade Major went on leave, Major R.A.B.P.WATTS, 8th Somerset L.I. acting for him	
,,	15.		Training was continued; owing to the untrained condition of the last drafts, no Brigade days were possible and all training was done within the Battalions.	
,,	16		Training as above.	
,,	17		Training	
,,	18		Training } The Range at HEZECQUES was allotted to Battalions in turn	
,,	19		Training } for a complete day.	
,,	20		Training	
,,	21		A medal presentation parade was held in the Square at 4 pm. The First Army commander giving medals to 204 recipients of the 37th Division, of which 39 belonged to 63rd Infantry Brigade.	
LIGNY-LEZ-AIRE	22		These awards covered the operations from and including the ANCRE to and including GREENLAND HILL. The Brigade Group, including B Echelon D.A.C. marched to the LIGNY-LEZ-AIRE Area in accordance with Div. O. No. 95 and Brigade O.O. No. 137	6, 7
THIENNES	23		Continued the march to the STEENBECQUE Area - Bde. O.O. 138	8
CAESTRE	24		Continued the march to the CAESTRE Area and Camp. Div. O. 97 and Bde. O.O. 139	9,10
SCHERPENBERG	25		Continued the march to the SCHERPENBERG Area and Camps VI and VIII. Second Army Commander inspected the Brigade on the march in METEREN. Div. O. No. 97 & G 1552/20 and Bde. O. 140	11,12
CAMP			Brigade Major returned from leave.	

Army Form C. 2118.

WAR DIARY
or
INTELLIGENCE SUMMARY.
(Erase heading not required.)

Instructions regarding War Diaries and Intelligence Summaries are contained in F. S. Regs., Part II. and the Staff Manual respectively. Title pages will be prepared in manuscript.

Place	Date	Hour	Summary of Events and Information	Remarks and references to Appendices
SCHERPENBERG CAMP	June 26		Div. O.O. No. 99 received	13
	27		G.O.C. and Brigade Major went to Bde. H.Q., 109th Inf. Bde. to discuss taking over of trenches	
	28		G.O.C. reconnoitred the line.	
	29		Relief of 109th Inf. Bde. commenced after dark - Bde. O.O. No. 141	14
			Relief of 109th Inf. Bde. continued.	
Trenches	30		G.O.C. assumed command of the line from G.O.C. 109th Inf. Bde. Maps showing line	15

N Chaunn.

Brigadier General,
Commdg. 63rd Infantry Brigade,

NOMINAL ROLL OF OFFICERS.

63rd Infantry Brigade Headquarters.

Brigadier-General E.L.CHALLENOR, D.S.O.   Commanding
   (Leicestershire Regiment)

Captain W.L.BRODIE, V.C., M.C.   Brigade Major.
   (Highland Light Infantry)

Captain F.M.GILLMORE   Staff Captain
   (Royal Fusiliers)

2nd Lieut. F.J.R.SIMPSON   Brigade Bombing Officer.
   (4th Middlesex Regiment)

Lieut. W.J.COOKSON, M.C.   Brigade Signal Officer
   (Royal Engineers)

Baron H. De COURTOIS   Brigade Interpreter.

NOMINAL ROLL OF OFFICERS.

8th Battalion, The Lincolnshire Regiment.

Rank and Name		Present Employment	How Trained	Embarked
Lt.-Col.	Davies Evans D.	Commanding		
Major	Hussey H.	2nd in command		
Captain	Ker R.A.	Transport Officer		11.9.15
,,	Waugh F.A., MC	Coy. Comdr.	Bombing	19.6.16
Lieut.	Keeling W.J. MC	Sick	Bombing	30.7.16
,,	Rowcroft M.G.	Adjutant		11.9.15
,,	Latham F.W.	Coy. Comdr.		11.9.15
,,	Read J.	Att. 37 Div. HQ		25.7.16
2nd Lt.	Hansell F.J.	Coy. Comdr.	XX.X.XX	30.1.17
,,	Moss W.	Coy. Comdr.		19.4.17
,,	White A.	Sniping & Int. Offr.	Bombing, Sniping & Lewis Gun	27.7.16
,,	Dukes E.H.	On leave		27.7.16
,,	Hunter W.S.			14.3.17
,,	Robilliard F.H.J.	Plat. Comdr.	Lewis Gun	16.4.17
,,	Cain J.M.	Plat. Comdr.		16.4.17
,,	Hine S.T.	Signalling Offr.	Signalling	25.7.16
,,	Brown F.W.A.	Plat. Comdr.		30.4.17
,,	Wells Cole W.H.	Plat. Comdr.		16.4.17
,,	Westoby R.H.	Plat. Comdr.		15.6.17
,,	Stuart-Menteth M.	On course		17.6.16
,,	Sutcliffe J.G.	Plat. Comdr.		28.3.17
,,	Linton A.	Plat. Comdr.		25.7.16
,,	Copeman W.H.	Plat. Comdr.		21.5.17
,,	Timpson N	Bombing Offr.	Bombing	25.5.17
,,	Askey C.H.L.	Lewis Gun Offr.	Lewis Gun	21.5.17
,,	Beales F.C.	Plat. Comdr.	XXX.X.XX	21.5.17
,,	Major W.H.	Plat. Comdr.		21.5.17
,,	Lee H.	Plat. Comdr.		27.5.17
,,	Stones H.	Plat. Comdr.		26.6.17
,,	Williams J.R.	A/Transport Offr.		17.6.15
,,	McDonnell J.M.	A/Adjutant		2½.6.17
Lieut.	Taylor F.	Quartermaster		11.9.15
Capt.	Smart D., MC	Medical Officer		

NOMINAL ROLL OF OFFICERS.

8th Battalion Somerset Light Infantry.

Rank and Name		Present Employment	How Trained	Embarked
Lt.-Col.	H.K.Umfreville DSO	Commanding		16.4.17
Major	J.G.Underwood	2nd in command		
Captain	R.H.E.Bennett	Brigade School		
,,	J.H.M.Hardyman MC	Coy. Comdr.	Staff duties	24.2.17
Lieut.	H.Pike	Transport Officer	Transport	10.9.15
,,	A.H.Llewellyn	Coy. Comdr.	3rd Army School	4.11.16
,,	F.R.Cooksley MC	Coy. Comdr.		10.12.16
2nd Lt.	E.A.Matthews	Signalling Offr.	Sniping Signalling	20.7.16
,,	H.G.Baker	Coy. Comdr.	Signalling	8.9.16
,,	P.C.Hagon	A/Adjutant	P.T. & B.F.	4.7.16
,,	P.S.Bryant	Plat. Comdr.	Musketry, L.Gun.	20.7.16
,,	F.G.Adlam	Att. 63rd Bde. HQ	Trench Warfare	1.1.16
,,	V.G.Willatt	Plat. Comdr.	Sniping	1.8.16
,,	C.A.Baird	Sick		3.1.17
,,	S.Goodman	Lewis Gun Offr.	Course Divl. Sch.	3.1.17
,,	A.G.Swain	Sick	P.T. & Bombing	14.1.17
,,	H.B.Smith	Bombing Offr.	Bombing	14.1.17
,,	H Ward		Divl. School	14.2.17
,,	H.O.Pring	A/Adjutant		15.2.17
,,	H.R.Kirk	Plat. Comdr.	Bombing	23.4.17
,,	C.D.Hagon	Plat. Comdr.	Corps School	23.4.17
,,	L.J.H.White	Plat. Comdr.	M.G. Bombing Musk.	8.5.17
,,	H.J.Hunt	Plat. Comdr.		8.5.17
,,	E.W.R.Blake	Plat. Comdr.		5.5.17
,,	W.Wood	8.		8.5.17
,,	L.C.Bodey			2.5.17
,,	A.J.Crease			2.5.17
,,	R.W.Adams			8.5.17
,,	G.Durston			24.5.17
,,	H.A.de F. Ford		Bombing	24.5.17
,,	R.P.Braund		P.T.	24.5.16
,,	F.Channing		Pioneer Work	29.5.17
,,	C.O.Finlay	On course	A.	4.6.17
,,	W.R.Worsley		M.G. Bombing	4.6.17
Lieut.	J.J.Schooling	Quartermaster		10.9.15
,,	E.F.Alford	Medical Officer.		

NOMINAL ROLL OF OFFICERS.

4th Battalion, The Middlesex Regiment.

Rank and Name	Present Employment	How Trained	Embarked
Lt.-Col. G.A. Bridgman	Commanding		25.4.17
Major M.C.G. Miers	2nd in command		11.4.17
Major C.R. Hay			28.6.17
Captain B.R. Newman	Coy. Comdr.		28.4.17
,, E. Belfield	,,		13.5.17
,, M.D. FitzGibbon	,,		3.5.17
,, P.W. Smith M.C.	,,	1st Army School	13.7.16
Lieut. E.A.H. Fenn	Plat. Comdr.	Bombing	13.7.16
,, L.C. Thomson	,,	3rd Army School	13.7.16
,, P.W. Farr	,,	Bombing	27.5.17
,, A.G. Mitchell	Bombing Officer	Bombing	13.7.16
2nd Lt. H.F. Bowser	Plat. Comdr.	Sniping	1.2.15
,, H.R. Odling	,,	Signals	19.4.17
,, F.J.R. Simpson	Bde. Bombing Offr.	Bombing	19.11.15
,, R.E. Taylor	Att. 37th Div.	Staff duties	29.5.16
,, S. Mirams	A/Adjutant		5.6.16
,, E.G. Grogan	Hospital	Lewis Gun	4.12.16
,, R.F.T. Irwin	Plat. Comdr.	,,	17.5.16
,, F.E. Beauchamp	,,		1.6.17
,, F.W. Scholefield	Intelligence & Sniping	Sniping	15.7.16
,, O.N. Martin	Divl. Salvage Offr.		13.7.16
,, L.W. Andreae	Bde. Sniping Offr.	Sniping	12.6.15
,, R.G. Williams	On leave	Bombing	15.7.16
,, H.S. Whitlock	Transport Officer.	Transport	6.9.16
,, J.H. Hodgson	Plat. Comdr.	Transport	28.4.16
,, G.S. Sutherland	Signalling Officer	Signalling	4.5.15
,, J.C. Lyal, M.C.	Plat. Comdr.	1st Army School	12.12.16
,, F.I. Rogers	Plat. Comdr. Sick		31.5.17
,, A.V. Weller	Plat. Comdr.	Bombing	19.4.17
,, D.F. Hurr	,,	Divl. School	6.9.16
,, T. De Val	,,	Gas	10.5.17
,, H.M. Monk	152 Fd. Co. R.E.		4.12.16
,, P.H. Steele	Plat. Comdr.	Div. Sch.	24.2.17
,, J.P. Jamieson	Lewis Gun Officer	Lewis Gun	27.4.17
,, J.H. Woods	Sick		19.4.17
,, A.D. Reid	6th Corps School		11.5.17
,, H. McDonnell	Plat. Officer		2.6.17
,, A.C. Coombs	Sick	Corps School	21.4.16
,, H.F. Backhouse	Plat. Comdr.	,,	21.4.16
,, S.W. Wridgway	Plat. Officer		31.5.17
Lieut. E.H. Amor	Quartermaster		18.10.15
Lieut. G.H. Ensing	Medical Officer		
Captain W.G. Largie C.F.	Chaplain.		

NOMINAL ROLL OF OFFICERS.

10th Battalion, The York & Lancaster Regiment.

Rank and Name	Present Employment	How Trained	Embarked.
Lt.-Col. Layton A.B.	Commanding		
Major Richardson H.S.C.	2nd in command		3.5.17
Major Watts R.A.B.P.	Att. 63rd Bde. HQ		
Captain Ellwood C.F.	Coy. Comdr.		22.4.17
,, Fairnie E.G.J.	,,	Bombing, M.G. & L.G.	16.11.15
,, Jarrard W.J.	A/Adjutant		23.5.17
,, Elsworth L.A.	Leave	Sniping	10.9.15
,, Boss J.G.	Plat. Comdr.	Musketry, Tactics	2.5.17
Lieut. Robinson A.R.	Coy. Comdr.	Lewis Gun	4.10.16
,, Wilkinson R.M.	Bombing Offr.	Bombing	5.10.15
,, Sutcliffe E.H.	Course		1.5.17
,, Corban J.	Plat. Comdr.	Gym. P.T. & B.F.	12.8.14
,, Loamond A.W.	Coy. Comdr.	Signalling	30.12.14
,, Ayres F.	Lewis Gun Officer	Lewis & V. Guns	10.11.15
2nd Lt. Mitchell R.J.	Fd. Co. R.E.	Vickers & Lewis G.	10.11.15
,, Rockley W.L.	Intelligence Offr.	Sniping	6.4.17
,, Horsfall J.R.	O i/c Wiring	Sanitation	15.12.16
,, Gaunt B.W.	Att. 63rd T.M.B.	L.T.M.	15.12.16
,, Walne H.A.	Transport Offr.	Gas	16.9.16
,, Woodmansey K.G.	Plat. Comdr.	XX.XX.XX Lewis Gun	15.12.16
,, Cameron H.	Plat. Comdr.		17.4.17
,, Williams S.	Instr. Base	Musketry	17.4.17
,, Kaplan I.	Army Rest Camp		16.4.17
,, Parry W.	Plat. Comdr.	XX.XX1XX	16.4.17
,, Hughes H.D.	Plat. Comdr.	Signalling	16.4.17
,, Jackson A.H.	Plat. Comdr.		16.4.17
,, Sykes T.P.	Course	Veterinary	11.5.17
,, Gladman A.F.	Plat. Comdr.	P.T. Lewis Gun	11.5.17
,, Holt W.L.	Plat. Comdr.		11.5.17
,, Teasdale S.B.	Plat. Comdr.		11.5.17
,, Byrne J.	Plat. Comdr.	Musketry, Maxim	28.2.17
,, Revill A.	Plat. Comdr.	Lewis Gun, Bombing	11.5.17
,, Forrest R.A.	Bde. School		11.5.17
,, Snowden H.	Plat. Comdr.	Signalling	31.5.17
,, Tune G.E.	Bde. Salvage Offr.		4.6.17
,, Marshall H.W.H.	Plat. Comdr.	Gas. Signals	2½.5.17
,, Knight J.W.	Plat. Comdr.	Musketry	2.6.17
,, Dawson G.C.	Course of Instruction		12.6.17
,, Lea W.C.	Plat. Comdr.		12.6.17
Lieut. Jamieson A.	Quartermaster		31.10.16
Lieut. Grellet H.R.	Medical Officer		31.10.16
Captain Thomas H.G., C.F	Chaplain		

NOMINAL ROLLS OF OFFICERS.

63rd Machine Gun Company.

Major	Coldwell W.G.A.	Commanding
Lieut.	W.A.Webb	2nd in command
Lieut.	D.A.Macrae	Section officer.
,,	I.C.Hartley	a/Transport Officer.
,,	N.F.Hawes	Section Officer.
2nd Lt.	W.S.Maclean	,, ,,
,,	T.A.Richards	,, ,,
,,	F.Denning	Sub-section Officer
,,	F.Laughton	,, ,,
,,	R.J.Ramsay	,, ,,
,,	G.B.Henderson	,, ,,

63rd Trench Mortar Battery

				Embarked
Captain	Akerman J.P.	Somerset L.I.	Commanding.	9/9/15
Lieut.	Sims G.H.	Somerset L.I.	2nd in command	9/9/15
Lieut.	Harris M.W.S.	Middlesex Regt.		23/5/16
Lieut.	Markham E.B.	Lincolnshire Regt.		5/10/15
2/Lt.	Gaunt B.W.	10th York & Lanc. Rgt.		13.12.16

63rd INFANTRY BRIGADE
WAR DIARY
JULY
1917

Army Form C. 2118.

WAR DIARY
or
INTELLIGENCE SUMMARY.
(Erase heading not required.)

Instructions regarding War Diaries and Intelligence Summaries are contained in F. S. Regs., Part II. and the Staff Manual respectively. Title pages will be prepared in manuscript.

Place	Date	Hour	Summary of Events and Information	Remarks and references to Appendices
Trenches	1.7.16		A small readjustment of line carried out during the night. Our patrols active during night 30 June/1st July. Bde. O. 142, Div. Os. 100 & 101	1, 2, 3
KEMMEL HILL	2nd		Relief according to above Div. Orders and Bde. O. No. 143	#. 3a
	3rd		Relief completed (except 63rd M.G.Coy) by 2 am, at which hour command of the line passed to G.O.C. 57th Inf. Bde. Units billeted in camps west of KEMMEL HILL	
xxx			Parties, strength 635 detailed from 8th Lincolns and 8th Somerset L.I. for work on trenches. 63rd Machine Gun Company placed at disposal of 111th Inf. Bde. from night 3/4th	#. 4.
,,	4th		The Divisional Commander addressed a party of 10th Y & L. Regt. regarding successful patrol work	5
,,			Large fatigue parties employed in front line. 63rd M.G.Coy. returned to billets after relief.	#. #.
,,	5th		Officers from Battalions reconnoitred RIDGE Defences. Fatigue parties found. One section 63rd M.G.Coy. lent tp 111th Inf. Bde.	
,,	6th		Large fatigue parties found.	
,,	7th		Large fatigue parties found.	
,,	8th		Large fatigue parties found. Section of 63rd M.G.Coy. lent to 111th Inf. Bde. returned to its company.	
,,	9th		Large fatigue parties found. Div. O. No. 103 received - Bde. O. No. 144 issued	6, 7.
,,	10th		16 men per battalion joined 63rd M.G.Coy. to bring its strength up to 10 men per gun.	
,,	11th		Relief of 111th Inf. Bde. commenced.	
Trenches	12th		Relief of 111th Inf. Bde. continued.	
,,	13th		At 10 am G.O.C. 63rd Inf. Bde. took over command of the line from G.O.C. 111th Inf. Bde. Considerable hostile shelling during night 13/14th. 10th York & Lancs. secured a prisoner of 84th R.I.R. Work on front line and outpost line carried out.	
,,	14th		A successful patrol carried out by 2nd Lt. H.G.BAKER, 8th Som. L.I. and a prisoner taken belonging to 86th R.I.R. Considerable hostile shelling during night 14/15th.	
,,	15th		Work of improving trenches continued. Heavy artillery bombarded certain points in enemy's line.	
,,	16th		Work of improving trenches continued.	
,,	17th		Work of improving trenches continued.	
,,	18th		Work of improving trenches continued.	
,,	19th		Brigade less M.G.Coy. and T.M.Battery relieved by 112th Inf. Bde. Div. O. No. 104, Bde. O.146	8, 9.
KEMMEL HILL	20th		G.O.C. handed over command of the line at 10 am to G.O.C. 112th Inf. Bde. 63rd M.G.Coy. relieved during night by 112th M.G.Coy.	
,,	21st		Washing and refitting.	
22	22nd		Washing and refitting.	

Army Form C. 2118.

WAR DIARY
or
INTELLIGENCE SUMMARY.
(Erase heading not required.)

Instructions regarding War Diaries and Intelligence Summaries are contained in F.S. Regs., Part II. and the Staff Manual respectively. Title pages will be prepared in manuscript.

Place	Date	Hour	Summary of Events and Information	Remarks and references to Appendices
KEMMEL HILL	23rd		The Brigade practised in operations to be carried out, see Bde. O. No. 147	...10.
	24th		The Brigade practised in operations to be carried out.	
"	25th		63rd Inf. Bde. relieved 112th Bde. in the line. Div. O. No. 106 & Bde. O. No. 148	...11, 12.
Trenches	26th		G.O.C. assumed command of the line at 10 am.	
"	27th		63rd Inf. Bde. relieved during night 26/27th by 111th Inf. Bde. Div. O. 107 & Bde. O. No. 149	...13, 14.
KEMMEL HILL	28th		G.O.C. 63rd Inf. Bde. handed over command to G.O.C. 111th Inf. Bde. at 10 am) Training. A conference of C.Os held at Brigade H.Q. at 6 pm.	
"	29th		63rd Inf. Bde. relieved 111th Inf. Bde. in the line. Bde. O. No. 150, Div. O. No. 110	...16, 15.
Trenches	30th		G.O.C. 63rd Inf. Bde. took over command of line at 10 am.	
"	31st		63rd Inf. Bde. carried out operations as directed in Div. O. No. 109 & Bde. O. No. 147	...17, 10.
			For account of operations see appendix No. 18	...18.

August 5th 1917

E.J. Challenor.
Brigadier General,
Commdg. 63rd Infantry Brigade.

63rd Infantry Brigade.

W A R   D I A R Y.

JULY, 1917.

LIST OF APPENDICES.   NO. OF APPENDIX.

63rd Inf. Bde. O. No. 142	1
37th Div. O. No. 100	2
37th Div. O. No. 101	3
63rd Inf. Bde. O. No. 143	3a
37th Div. No. G. 1763	4
37th Div. No. G. 1766	5
37th Div. O. No. 103	6
63rd Inf. Bde. O. No. 144	7
37th Div. O. No. 104	8
63rd Inf. Bde. O. No. 146	9
63rd Inf. Bde. O. No. 147	10
37th Div. O. No. 106	11
63rd Inf. Bde. O. No. 148	12
37th Div. O. No. 107	13
63rd Inf. Bde. O. No. 149	14
37th Div. O. No. 110	15
63rd Inf. Bde. O. No. 150	16
37th Div. O. No. 109	17
Account of Operations, July 31st/Aug. 1st ...	18
Nominal roll of officers	19
Casualties during July, 1917 (excluding operations)	20
Casualties incurred during operations	20a
Reinforcements during July, 1917	21
Strength of Units, July 31st 1917, ...	22

REPORT ON OPERATIONS ABOUT RIFLE AND BEEK FARMS ON JULY 31st AND AUGUST 1st, 1917.

I.   In conjunction with operations on a larger scale farther North, the Division attacked the enemy holding the line BEEK FARM - Road junction, O.23.b.2.4, on the morning of the 31st July, in co-operation with the 19th Division on the left.

In accordance with order the attack was carried out in two phases.

II. FIRST PHASE.

1. For the First Phase, the 63rd Infantry Brigade, less two battalions, and the 37th Divisional Artillery were placed under the orders of the G.O.C. 19th Division, a call being retained on certain batteries in case the 37th Divisional Front was attacked further south during the operation.

2. At 3.50 am, 4th Middlesex Regt., prolonging the right of 19th Division, advanced under an artillery barrage to its objective, JULY FARM and RIFLE FARM, while one company of 8th Lincolnshire Regt. moved forward to protect the Right of 4th Middlesex and form a defensive flank facing S.E., with its left on JULY FARM.

3. During the advance, soon after Zero, the left Company 4th Middlesex lost touch in the dark for a short time with the right Company of 7th Kings Own Royal Lancaster Regt., the latter having moved rather northwards, but regained it very soon afterwards just West of BEE FARM.

4. At Zero plus 40 minutes, the 7th K.O.R.Lanc. Regt. moved through BEE FARM and took up their position east of that Farm. The left Company 4th Middlesex was in touch with them, with their left slightly in rear of the right of 7th K.O.R.Lanc. Regt.

This company 4th Middlesex had about 20 casualties during their advance and remained in position on the right of 7th K.O.R.Lanc. Rgt. till the latter were heavily attacked from the direction of WASP FARM about 1.30 pm and driven out of that farm. This exposed their left flank and they also had some 25 casualties during the morning and so they fell back to the original front line in front of WALL FARM in the 19th Divisional Area.

5. The right Company 4th Middlesex Regt. advanced and gained its objective and at 4.30 am the 2 platoons of the supporting Company went through them to reconnoitre and clear BAB FARM.

These two platoons became heavily engaged just west of BAB FARM and the right front company of 4th Middlesex, instead of holding on to their objective, went to the support of the platoons at BAB FARM. The leading platoon of 8th Lincolnshire Regt. forming the defensive flank were also drawn into this fight.

Severe fighting took place at close quarters in front of of BAB FARM and all accounts point to very severe casualties having been inflicted on the enemy.

Owing to the ground in front of RIFLE FARM and BAB FARM being exposed to fire from north and south, the runners who were sent back with messages did not get through, and the runners sent forward from the reserve company also failed to get through.

This party fought it out where they were, until they were all either killed or wounded.

6. The fourth Company 4th Middlesex were engaged in dealing with a pocket of the enemy about MAY FARM which had been missed by the moppers up in the dark.

7. All messages from O.P. and from Aeroplane reports stated that 4th Middlesex were on the objective and they were known to have been there at Zero plus 40; no information of the fighting at BAB FARM was received till about 1.30 pm, when 4th Middlesex were at once reinforced by the 8th East Lancashire Regt. from Reserve.

II. SECOND PHASE......

(2)

III. SECOND PHASE.

1. At 7.50 am the 2nd phase of the Operation commenced. In accordance with orders, the advance to the line BEEK FARM - JULY FARM was made under an artillery barrage. 8th Somerset L.I. on the right, two companies 8th Lincolnshire Regt. on the left, with the WAMBEEK as dividing line.

The objectives were gained and heavy casualties were inflicted on the enemy and BEEK FARM enclosures cleared. Some 40 prisoners were sent back, many of whom were killed or wounded on the way back, as the approaches to the shell-hole line were exposed to enemy machine gun fire and snipers.

Heavy casualties were also inflicted by Lewis Guns on the enemy retiring from the enclosures to the trench running south from CODE FARM to the BEEK Enclosures.

At about 8 am, both battalions began consolidating the line 80 yards west of WAM and BEEK FARMS, with posts at both these places. Owing th action on the left, however it was found necessary to throw back the left of 8th Lincolns to JUNE FARM.

The artillery also engaged the trench running south from CODE FARM and inflicted heavy casualties on the enemy in this trench.

The enemy sniping was very consistent throughout the day from O.29.b. and d. and the work of consolidating was rendered very difficult.

2. During this phase, the 3rd Australian Division protected our right flank, firing a most effective 18 pdr. smoke barrage on OTIRA Trench and CINEMA Road opposite our right flank, and by bombarding the ruins in the neighbourhood of ARROW FARM with 4.5" howitzers.

The 19th Divnl. Artillery also cooperated by bringing enfilade fire to bear on the WARNETON LINE in front of LAKE FARM.

IV. Throughout the first and second phases, the 6" howitzers of the 9th Corps H.A. fired on selected points in the WARNETON LINE and just behind it. The counter battery guns and the heavy howitzers were engaged in neutralising the enemy's heavy artillery and preventing it from firing against the flank of the main attack further north.

V.

1. As soon as definite information was received that RIFLE FARM was no longer in our hands, it was decided to employ the 8th East Lancs. Regt. and a company of the 19th Division onits left to re-establish the line.

2. The advance of the three companies 8th East Lancs. Regt. (the 4th in support) was carried out at 8 pm and was supported by a standing 18-pounder barrage on a north and south line about 200 yards east of RIFLE FARM and by a portion of the IX Corps Heavy Artillery. The artillery of 3rd Australian Division also assisted on their original target.

The objective was gained and a few prisoners taken.

3. During the advance, however, touch was lost with the 19th Division and the three companies 8th East Lancs. found themselves with their left flank in the air.

Owing to this and the fact that many rifles and Lewis Guns had been rendered unserviceable for firing by men falling on the wet and slippery ground, the three companies retired back to their original line, being heavily fired on from their left and front. They fell back to the Shell Hole Line.

In transpired that a company of 19th Division came under heavy rifle fire soon after the attack commenced and was held up.

VI. During the night our troops dugin on the line O.29.c.55.00 - O.29.c.55.20 - O.29.a.95.65 (with a post at O.29.b.05.65) - O.23.c.75.12 (with a post near BEEK FARM) - JUNE FARM, thence to O.23.a.70.30, where touch was again established with 19th Division.

VII. All reports point to the enemy's casualties having been very severe and the 63rd Inf. Bde. Snipers claim 25 hits.

In addition to the casualties inflicted by the Infantry, the artillery and machine guns found many favourable targets and caused the enemy much loss.

OVER.

(3)

One officer and 50 O.R. of the 31st R.I.R. and 86th R.I.R. were sent back. Of this number 1 officer and 34 O.R. reached the Cage, the others having become casualties on the way down.

VIII. The 63rd Infantry Brigade had the following casualties :- 27 officers and 594 other ranks. - 8th East Lancs. Regt., 5 officers and 94 other ranks.

August 4th, 1917.

Brigadier General,
Commdg. 63rd Infantry Brigade.

NOMINAL ROLL OF OFFICERS.

Headquarters, 63rd Infantry Brigade.

Brigadier General E.L.Challenor, D.S.O.   Commanding.
    (Leicester Regiment)

Captain W.L.Brodie, V.C., M.C.   Brigade Major.
    (Highland Light Infantry)

Captain F.M.Gillmore   Staff Captain.
    (Royal Fusiliers)

Lieut. W.J.Cookson, M.C., R.E.   Signal Officer

2nd Lieut. F.J.R.Simpson,   Brigade Bombing
    (4th Middlesex Regt.)   & Intelligence Officer.

Baron H. de Courtois   Brigade Interpreter.

NOMINAL ROLL OF OFFICERS.

8th Battalion, The Lincolnshire Regt.

Rank and Name		Present employment	How trained	Embarked
Lt.-Col.	Davies Evans D.	Commanding		
Major	Hussey H.	2nd in command		
Captain	Ker R.A.	Sick		11.9.15
,,	Waugh F.A., M.C.	Coy. Comdr.		19.6.16
,,	Gordiner R.G., MC	,,		11.7.17
,,	Latham F.W.	,,		7.4.17
,,	Moss W.	,,		19.4.17
Lieut.	Keeling W.J., MC.	Sick		30.7.16
,,	Rowcroft M.C.	Adjutant		11.9.15
2nd Lieut.	Hansell F.J.	2nd i/c Coy.		30.1.17
,,	White A.	On course	Sniping, Lewis Gun	27.7.16
,,	Dukes E.H.	2nd i/c Coy.		27.7.16
,,	Hunter W.S.	Plat. Comdr.		14.3.17
,,	Robilliard F.H.J.	Att. 63rd Bde. School.	Lewis Gun	16.4.17
,,	Cain J.M.	Plat. Comdr.		16.4.17
,,	Hine S.T.	Signal Officer	Signalling	25.7.16
,,	Weals Cole W.	Plat. Comdr.		15.6.17
,,	Westoby R.H.	2nd Army Rest Cp.		15.6.17
,,	Stuart Menteth M.	Plat. Comdr.		17.8.15
,,	Sutcliffe J.G.	,,		28.3.17
,,	Linton A.	,,		25.7.15
,,	Copeman W.H.	On Course		21.5.17
,,	Timpson N.	Bombing Offr.	Bombing	25.5.17
,,	Askey C.H.L.	Lewis Gun Offr.	Lewis Gun	21.5.17
,,	Beales F.C.	On course.		21.5.17
,,	Major W.H.	Plat. Comdr.		21.5.17
,,	Lee H.	,,		27.5.17
,,	Stones H.	,,		26.6.17
,,	Wiggins A.B.	2nd i/c Coy.		29.6.17
,,	Williams J.R. MC	Transport Offr.		17.6.15
,,	McDonnell J.R.	A/Adjutant		2.6.17
,,	Mulcuck J.	Plat. Comdr.		29.6.17
,,	Tunney F.	,,		29.6.17
Captain	Billiat J.J.	Att. Div. HQ		26.4.17
Lieut.	Taylor F.	Quartermaster		11.9.15

NOMINAL ROLL OF OFFICERS.

6th Battalion, Somerset Light Infantry.

Rank and Name		Present employment	How Trained	Embarked
Lt.Col.	Richardson H.S.C.	Commanding		
Major	Hardyman J.H.M.	2nd in command	Staff	24.2.17
Captain	Humphreys F.C.			14.7.17
,,	Baker F.	Coy. Comdr.	Bombing, Gas.	3.7.17
,,	Hunt H.J.	,,		8.3.17
,,	Baker H.G.	,,	Signalling	8.9.16
Lieut.	Pike H.	Transport Offr.		10.9.15
,,	Cooksley F.R. MC		Transport	10.12.16
,,	Morgan A.P.			14.7.17
,,	Hinton F.G.		Bombing	9.7.17
,,	Hagon P.C.	Adjutant	P.T. & B.F.	4.7.16
2nd Lt.	Matthews E.A	Sig. & Int. Off.	Sniping & Signlg.	10.7.16
,,	Bryant F.S		Musketry Lewis Gun	20.7.16
,,	Adlam F.G.	Att. 63rd Bde HQ	Trench Warfare	1.1.16
,,	Willatt V.G.	Plat. Comdr.	Sniping	1.8.16
,,	Goodman W		Course Div.School	3.1.17
,,	Ward H.		,,	
,,	Pring H.O.	Asst. Adjutant		15.2.17
,,	Kirk H.R.	Plat. Comdr.	MG, Bombing, Musk.	23.4.17
,,	White L.J.H.	,,	,, ,,	8.5.17
,,	Blake E.W.R.			5.5.17
,,	Wood W.			8.5.17
,,	Bodey L.C.		Sniping	2.5.17
,,	Adams R.W.		MG, Bombing	8.5.17
,,	Findlay C.O.		,, ,,	4.6.17
,,	Worsley W.R.			4.6.17
,,	Pople H.K.		LG, Bombing Musky.	18.6.17
,,	Cox D.H.	Coy. Comdr. Bombing Officer		16.6.17
Lieut.	Donne S.	Coy. Comdr.	Gas	5.6.17
Lieut.	Schooling J.J.	Quartermaster		10.9.15
Lieut.	Alford E.F.	Medical Officer.		

NOMINAL ROLL OF OFFICERS.

4th Battalion, The Middlesex Regiment.

Rank and Name	Present Employment	How Trained	Embarked
Lt.-Col. G.A.Bridgman	Commanding		25.4.17
Major C.R.Hay	O.C. Bde. School		28.6.17
Captain B.R.Newman			28.4/17.
,, E.Belfield	Coy. Comdr.		5.5.17
,, M.D.FitzGibbon			3.5.17
,, P.W.Smith, M.C.	Coy. Comdr.	1st Army School	13.7.16
Lieut. E.A.H.Fenn			13.7.16
,, P.W.Farr	T/Coy. Comdr.	Bombing	27.5.17
,, A.G.Mitchell	On Course	Bombing	13.7.16
,, L.C.Thomson	T/Coy. Comdr.	1st Army School	13.7.16
2nd Lieut. H.F.Bowser	On course	Sniping	1.2.15
,, H.R.Odling	On course	Signalling	19.4.17
,, F.J.R.Simpson	Bde. Bombing Offr.	Bombing	19.11.15
,, R.E.Taylor	Att. 37th Div.	'Q' duties	29.5.16
,, S.Mirams	A/Adjutant		5.6.16
,, E.G.Grogan	Sick	Lewis Gun	4.12.16
,, R.F.T.Irwin		Signalling	17.5.16
,, F.E.Beauchamp	Plat. Comdr.		1.6.17
,, F.W.Scholefield	Intelligence Offr.	Sniping	15.7.16
,, O.N.Martin	Div.Salvage Offr.		13.7.16
,, L.W.Andreae	Bde. Sniping Offr.	Sniping	12.6.15
,, R.G.Williams	Bde. School	Bombing	15.7.16
,, S.J.Bear	Plat. Comdr.	Transport	16.7.17
,, H.S.Whitlock	,,	,,	6.9.16
,, J.H.Hodgson	Transport Offr.	,,	28.4.16
,, G.S.Sutherland	On course	Signalling	4.5.15
,, J.C.Lyal, M.C.	Plat. Comdr.	1st Army School	12.12.16
,, A.V.Weller	,,	Bombing	19.4.17
,, D.F.Hurr	On leave		6.9.16
,, T. De Val	2nd Army Rest Camp	Gen. Course	10.5.17
,, H.M.Monk	Att. 152 Fd. Co. RE		4.12.16
,, P.H.Steele	On course		24.2.17
,, J.P.Jamieson	Lewis Gun Officer	Lewis Gun	24.4.17
,, J.H.Woods	Sick		19.4.17
,, A.D.Reid	Plat. Comdr.		11.5.17
,, H.McDonnell			2.6.17
,, H.F.Backhouse	On Course		21.4.16
,, C.W.Wridgway	Plat. Comdr.		31.5.17
Lieut. E.H.Amor	Quartermaster		18.10.15
Lieut. G.H.Ensing RAMC	Medical Officer		
Captain L.G.Largie, C.F.	Chaplain.		

NOMINAL ROLL OF OFFICERS.

10th Battalion, The York and Lancaster Regiment.

Rank and Name		Present Employment	How Trained	Embarked.
Lt.-Col.	Layton A.B.	Commanding		
Major	Fairnie E.G.J.	Sick	Bombing, M.G., L.G.	16.11.15
Captain	Watts R.A.B.P.	Bde. School		
"	Eldworth L.A.	Adjutant	Sniping, Bombing	10.9.15
"	Ellwood C.F.	Coy. Comdr.		22.4.17
"	Jarrard W.J.	,,		23.5.17
"	Boss J.G.	,,	Musketry, Bombing	2.5.17
"	Wilkinson R.M.	A/Adjutant	Bombing & General	5.10.15
"	Robinson A.R.	On Course	Lewis Gun	4.10.16
"	White R.C.	A/Q.M.	Musketry, Bombing	25.6.17
Lieut.	Sutcliffe E.H.	Bde. Salvage Off.		1.5.17
"	Ayres F.	Lewis Gun Offr.	Lewis Gun Bombing	10.11.15
"	Lamond A.W.	Sick	Signalling, Bombing	30.12.14
2/Lieut.	Rockley W.L.	Int. and Sniping Offr.	Sniping	6.4.17
"	Mitchell R.J.	Att. 152 Fd.Co. RE	V & L. Guns	10.11.15
"	Horsfall J.R.		General & Sanitation	15.12.16
"	Gaunt B.W.	Att. 63rd T.M.B.	L.T.M.	15.12.16
"	Walne H.A.		Transport, Gas	16.9.16
"	Woodmansey N.G.	Course	Lewis Gun	15.12.16
"	Cameron H.	Plat. Comdr.		17.4.17
"	Williams S.	Instr. Base	Musketry	17.4.17
"	Kaplan I.	On Course		16.4.17
"	Parry W.	Plat. Comdr.	Bombing, Gas	16.4.17
"	Hughes H.D.	Signal Offr.	Signalling	16.4.17
"	Jackson A.H.	Plat. Comdr.	Lewis Gun	16.4.17
"	Sykes T.P.	Plat. Comdr.	Veterinary Course	11.5.17
"	Gladman A.F.	Plat. Comdr.	P.T.	11.5.17
"	Holt W.L.	On Course		11.5.17
"	Teasdale S.B.	Plat. Comdr.		11.5.17
"	Byrne J.	Plat. Comdr.	Musketry, M.G.	28.2.17
"	Forrest R.A.	Plat. Comdr.		11.5.17
"	Snowden H.	On Course	Signalling Gen.	31.5.17
"	Tune G.E.	Plat. Comdr.		4.6.17
"	Marshall J.W.H.	Course	Signalling, Gas	2.6.17
"	Knight J.W.	Coy. Comdr.	Musketry, General	2.6.17
"	Dawson G.C.	Plat. Comdr.	General	12.6.17
"	Lea W.G.	Plat. Comdr.	General	12.6.17
"	Cleveland H.A.	Plat. Comdr.		11.5.17
Lieut.	Jamieson A.	Quartermaster		31.10.16
Lieut.	McConnell W.G.	Medical Officer		13.3.17
Captain	Thomas X.K.H.G.	Chaplain.		

NOMINAL ROLL OF OFFICERS.

63rd Machine Gun Company.

Major	Coldwell W.G.A.	Commanding.
Lieut.	Webb W.A.	On leave - 2nd i/c
,,	Macrae D.A.	Sick.
,,	Hartley I.C.	Transport Officer
,,	Hawes N.F.	Acting Adjutant
2nd Lieut.	MacLean W.S.	Section Officer
,,	Ramsay R.J.	Sick
,,	Richards T.A.	Section Officer
,,	Laughton F.	Section Officer
,,	Henderson G.B.	Section Officer
,,	Denning F.	On Course.

63rd Trench Mortar Battery

Captain	Akerman J.P.	Commanding	Light T.M.	9.9.15
Lieut.	G.H.Sims	2nd i/c	,,	9.9.15
Lieut.	M.W.S.Harris		,,	28.5.16
Lieut.	E.B.Markham		,,	5.10.15
2/Lieut.	B.W.Gaunt		,,	13.12.16

CASUALTIES DURING JULY, 1917

UNIT	IN TRENCHES						OUT OF TRENCHES						TOTAL CASUALTIES IN AND OUT OF TRENCHES.	SICK			REMARKS.
	Officers			Other Rks.			Officers			Other Rks.				Officers	Other Ranks	Total	
	Killed	Wounded	Missing	Killed	Wounded	Missing	Total	Killed	Wounded	Missing	Killed	Wounded	Missing	Total					
8th Lincolnshire Rgt.	-	3[a]	-	1	39	2	45	-	-	-	-	-	-	-	45	1[b]	25	26	71
8th Somerset L.I.	1[b]	1[c]	-	14	35	1	52	-	-	-	-	-	-	-	52	1[c]	57	58	117
4th Middlesex Regt.	-	-	-	7	30	-	37	-	-	-	-	-	-	-	37	-	5	5	42
10th York & Lanc. Rgt.	1[f]	2[g]	-	18	88	-	109	-	-	-	-	1	-	1	110	3[h]	20	23	133
63rd Machine Gun Co.	-	-	-	-	-	-	-	-	-	-	-	-	-	-	-	2[i]	6	8	8
63rd T.M.Battery	-	-	-	1	1	-	2	-	-	-	-	-	-	-	2	-	15	15	17
TOTAL	2	13	-	41	193	3	252	-	-	-	-	1	-	1	253	7	128	135	388

Remarks:
a Capt. H.D.Smart
   2/Lt. H.W.A.Brown
   2/Lt. R.H.Westoby.
b Capt. R.A.Ker
c 2/Lt. H.B.Smith
d Lt.Col. M.C.G.Miers
   Major J.G.Underwood
   Lieut.A.H.Llewellyn
   2/Lt. C.D.Hagon
   2/Lt. A.J.Grease
   2/Lt. G.Darston
   2/Lt. H.A.deF.Ford
   2/Lt. F.Channing
e 2/Lt. R.P.Braund
f Lieut.J.Corban
g 2/Lt. A.Revill
   2/Lt. W.L.Holt
h Capt. A.W.Lamond
   2/Lt. H.Snowden
   Major E.G.J.Fairnie

i Lieut. D.A.Macrae
   2/Lt. R.J.Ramsay

CASUALTIES DURING OPERATIONS 31st JULY/1st AUG. 1917.

UNIT	IN TRENCHES Officers Killed	Wounded	Missing	Other Rks. Killed	Wounded	Missing	Total	OUT OF TRENCHES Officers Killed	Wounded	Missing	Other Rks. Killed	Wounded	Missing	Total	SICK Officers	Other Ranks	Total	TOTAL CASUALTIES IN AND OUT OF TRENCHES. GRAND TOTAL	REMARKS
8th Lincolnshire Regt.	2 a	2 b	3 c	8	44	105	162												a/ 2Lt.Hunter W.S.; Lee.H.
8th Somerset L.I.	3 d	4 e	-	35	74	42	158												b/ 2Lts. Stone H. Linton.A.
4th Middlesex Regt.	3 f	1 g	4 h	16	72	116	212												c/ 2Lts. Wells-Cole W. Cain J.M. Timson M.
10th York & Lanc: Regt.	1 i	4 j	-	20	57	4	86												d/ 2Lts. Worsley W.R. Kirk H.R., Blake E.W.R.
63rd Machine Gun Company					3		3												e/ A/Cap.Hunt H.J. Cap. F.H.Baker Lt. S.Donne
63rd T.M.Battery				1	1		1												2Lt. Adams R.W.
TOTAL	9	11	7	79	251	265	622											622	f/ 2Lt. Thompson L.C. Simpson F.J.R? ; McDonnell H.

g/ 2Lt Reid A.D?
h/ Capt. E.Belfield Lt. Farr.P.W. 2Lt. Beauchamp F.E. ; Bear S.J.
i/ 2Lt. Teasdale S.B.
j/ 2Lt. Dawson G.C. ; Sykes T.P. ; Knight J.W.

63rd Infantry Brigade.

REINFORCEMENTS RECEIVED DURING JULY, 1917.

	Officers	Other Ranks	Arrived
8th Lincolnshire Regt.	3 a	6	30.6.17
	-	8	7.7.17
	1 b	5	11.7.17
	-	7	20.7.17
	-	1	24.7.17
	-	7	28.7.17
	4	34	
8th Somerset L.I.	1 c	-	2.7.17
	1 d	-	3.7.17
	1 e	-	13.7.17
	1 f	6	15.7.17
	1 g	16	18.7.17
	1 h	9	24.7.17
	2 i	-	26.7.17
	3 j	-	29.7.17
	11	31	
4th Middlesex Regt.	-	4	4.7.17
	-	11	19.7.17
	1 k	-	21.7.17
	-	1	24.7.17
	1	16	
10th York & Lanc. Regt.	-	6	2.7.17
	1 l	9	3.7.17
	-	3	19.7.17
	1 m	-	20.7.17
	1 n	-	21.7.17
	3	18	
63rd Machine Gun Company	-	1	1.7.17
	-	1	6.7.17
	-	6	7.7.17
	-	7	11.7.17
	-	6	18.7.17
	-	1	20.7.17
		22	

TOTAL REINFORCEMENTS RECEIVED DURING JULY, 1917:-

18 officers, 121 other ranks.

OVER.

EXPLANATION.

```
a 2nd Lieut. A.B.Wiggins              8th Lincolnshire Regt.
    ,,       J.Mulcuck                        ,,
    ,,       T.Tunney                         ,,
b Captain    R.G.Cordiner, M.C.                ,,

c 2nd Lieut. D.H.Cox                  8th Somerset Light Infantry
d   Lieut.   S.Donne                           ,,
e Lt.-Col.   H.S.C.Richardson                  ,,
f Captain    F.H.Baker                         ,,
g 2nd Lieut. H.K.Pople                         ,,
h Captain    F.C.Humphreys                     ,,
i   Lieut.   F.G.Hinton                        ,,
             A.P.Morgan                        ,,
j 2nd Lieut. W.V.Glanville                     ,,
    ,,       F.J.Pickard                       ,,
    ,,       W.H.Pickard                       ,,

k 2nd Lieut. S.J.Bear                 4th Middlesex Regt.

l Captain    R.C.White                10th York & Lancaster Regt.
m 2nd Lieut. W.L.Holt                          ,,
n   ,,       H.A.Cleveland                     ,,
```

63rd Infantry Brigade.

STRENGTH OF UNITS

JULY 31ST,

1917.

UNIT	STRENGTH		DETAILS INCLUDED	
	Officers	Other Ranks	Officers	Other Ranks
8th Lincolnshire Regt.	35	924	5	173
8th Somerset Light Infantry	34	869	4	150
4th Middlesex Regiment	39	848	18	210
10th York & Lanc. Regt.	39	891	11	131
63rd Machine Gun Company	11	175	3	10
63rd Trench Mortar Battery	5	64	1	6
TOTAL	163	3771	42	680

ORIGINAL COPY

63rd INFANTRY BRIGADE

WAR DIARY

AUGUST

1917

Army Form C. 2118.

WAR DIARY
or
INTELLIGENCE SUMMARY.
(Erase heading not required.)

Instructions regarding War Diaries and Intelligence Summaries are contained in F. S. Regs., Part II. and the Staff Manual respectively. Title pages will be prepared in manuscript.

Place	Date	Hour	Summary of Events and Information	Remarks and references to Appendices
KEMMEL HILL	August 1st		Bad weather prevented consolidation or further operations; 7.30 pm a patrol of 8th E. Lancs. sent out to RIFLE FARM to find out if occupied by us; no sign of our troops found in it. 63rd Infantry Brigade relieved by 111th Inf. Bde. 1h line.	
			37th Div. Order No. 111	1.
			63rd Bde. Order No. 151	2.
DRANOUTRE	2nd		Relief complete 5 am; 63rd Bde. back in KEMMEL Support area. 112th Bde. (less 8th E.Lancs) took over KEMMEL Support area; 63rd Bde. (less 10th York & Lancs.) moved to DRANOUTRE Reserve Area.	
			37th Div. Order No. 112	3.
			63rd Bde. Order No. 152	4.
			63rd Bde. Order No. 153	5.
	3rd		10th York & Lanc. Regt. moved to DRANOUTRE Warning order received regarding proposed relief of 19th Division by 37th Div. G 2411/1	6.
	4th		Reorganising and washing	
	5th		Church parades; 2 sections of 63rd M.G.Co. relieved 111th M.G.Co. in line. M.Gs in line came under orders of O.C. 63rd M.G.Co. on completion of relief. Div. O. No. 114	7.
			Bde. O. No. 153A	8.
	6th		Conference of C.Os at which training, recent operations and lessons learnt were discussed. Working parties, strength about 400 sent up to trenches for work. Major RIDEAL, D.S.O. took over command of 63rd M.G.Coy. from Major COLDWELL. Div. Order. 115 received.	9.
	7th		10th York & Lancs. sent party of 2 officers and 50 O.R. as guard over Prisoners Cage, BAILLEUL. Training and working parties. Div. Order. 116 and G. 2499 received; Bde. O. 154 issued	10, 11.
FAIRY HOUSE	8th		Brigade moved in accordance with Brigade Order 154.	
	9th		Working parties sent up for work in forward area. G.O.C. attended conference at Div. HQ, 5 pm.	
	10th		Conference at Bde. H.Q. when points raised at Div. Conference were discussed. G.O.C. proceeded on leave; Lt.-Col. BRIDGMAN 4th Middlesex, assumed command.	
	11th		G.2564 re relief of M.Gs of 63rd M.G.Coy. received	12.
	12th		Working parties	
	13th		Working parties. Div. O. 118 received and Bde. Order 155 issued	13, 14.
	14th		Reconnaissance of the line carried out.	
	15th		Reconnaissance of the line carried out. 63rd Bde. relieved 112th Bde. in the line.	
	16th		G.O.C. 63rd Bde. assumed command of the line at 10 am. Lt.-Col. Chester-Master, D.S.O. took over command of 63rd Bde from Lt.-Col. Bridgman.	
Trenches	17th		In conjunction with the operations further north, our artillery bombardment was carried out. Considerable hostile artillery retaliation, consequently a certain number of casualties. 37th Div. Order. 119	15.

Army Form C. 2118.

WAR DIARY
or
INTELLIGENCE SUMMARY
(Erase heading not required.)

Instructions regarding War Diaries and Intelligence Summaries are contained in F. S. Regs., Part II. and the Staff Manual respectively. Title pages will be prepared in manuscript.

Place	Date	Hour	Summary of Events and Information	Remarks and references to Appendices
Trenches	Aug. 17th		Nothing unusual in trenches	
	18th		,, ,, ,, ,,	
	19th		,, ,, ,, ,,	
	20th		,, ,, ,, ,,	
	21st		63rd Bde. relieved by 112th Bde. during night. Div. Order 121, Bde. Order 156	16, 17.
FAIRY HOUSE	22nd		G.O.C. 112th Bde. assumed command of the line at 10 am. Brig.-Gen. Challenor D.S.O. took over command of Brigade on return from leave.	
	23rd		Working parties.	
	24th		,, ,,	
	25th		,, ,,	
	26th		The Brigade moved into reserve Brigade area from support Bde. area. Div. O. 123	18.
				Bde. O. 157 ... 19.
	27th		Owing to reduced strength of battalions, companies organised in 2 platoons, surplus men in any forming nucleus of a third platoon. G.2804.	20.
	28th		Units carried out reconnaissance of line to be taken over from, FORRET FARM to the YPRES - COMINES CANAL, inclusive.	
SPOIL BANK I.33.c.9880	29th		Relief of 117th Inf. Bde. by 63rd Bde. commenced. Div. Order 124 & Bde. Order 158	21, 22
	30th		Relief completed by 12.45 am at which hour G.O.C. 63rd Inf. Bde. took over command of the line.	
	31st		Quiet day in trenches.	

August 31st 1917

[signature]
Brigadier General,
Commdg. 63rd Infantry Brigade.

63rd Infantry Brigade

WAR DIARY

LIST OF APPENDICES	NO. OF APPENDIX
37th Division Order No. 111	1
63rd Inf. Bde. Order No. 151	2
37th Division Order No. 112	3
63rd Inf. Bde. Order No. 152	4
63rd Inf. Bde. Order No. 153	5
37th Division No. G 2411/1	6
37th Division Order No. 114	7
63rd Inf. Bde. Order No. 153A	8
37th Division Order No. 115	9
37th Division Order 116 and G.2499	10
63rd Inf. Bde. Order No. 154	11
37th Division No. G.2564	12
37th Division Order No. 118	13
63rd Inf. Bde. Order. No. 155	14
37th Division Order No. 119	15
37th Division Order No. 121	16
63rd Inf. Bde. Order No. 156	17
37th Division Order No. 123	18
63rd Inf. Bde. Order No. 157	19
37th Division No. G.2804	20
37th Division Order No. 124	21
63rd Inf. Bde. Order No. 158	22
Nominal Rolls of Officers	23
Casualties during August 1917	24
Reinforcements received during August 1917	25
Strength of units, Aug. 31st 1917	26

NOMINAL ROLL OF OFFICERS.

63rd Infantry Brigade Headquarters

Brigadier General E.L.CHALLENOR, D.S.O. (Leicestershire Regt.)	Commanding
Captain W.L.BRODIE, V.C., M.C. (Highland Light Infantry)	Brigade Major
Captain F.MacS. GILLMORE (Royal Fusiliers)	Staff Captain
Lieut. W.J.COOKSON, M.C., R.E.	Brigade Signal Officer
2nd Lieut. F.G.ADLAM, (8th Somerset L.I.)	Brigade Intelligence Officer
Baron H. DE COURTOIS	Brigade Interpreter

NOMINAL ROLL OF OFFICERS

8th Battalion, The Lincolnshire Regiment.

Rank and Name	Present Employment	How Trained	Embarked.
Lt.Col. D.W.C.Davies Evans	Commanding		
Major H. Hussey	On Course		
Captain Waugh F.A., M.C.	2nd in command	Bombing	19.6.16
,, Cordiner R.G., M.C.	Coy. Comdr.		11.7.17
,, Latham F.W.	,,		7.4.17
,, Moss W.	,,		19.4.17
,, Billiatt J.J.	Attd.63rd Nde. HQ		26.4.17
Lieut. Rowcroft M	Adjutant		11.9.15
,, Dukes E.H.	Coy. Comdr		27.7.16
,, Hansell F.J.	2nd i/c Coy.		30.1.17
,, Keeling W.J., M.C.	Sick	Bombing	30.7.16
2/Lt. White A.	Intelligence Off.	Sniping, L.G.	27.7.16
,, Robilliard F.H.J.	Plat. Comdr.	Lewis Gun	16.4.17
,, Hine S.T.	Signal Officer	Signalling	25.7.16
,, Westoby R.H.	Plat. Comdr.	Lewis-Gun	15.6.17
,, Stuart Menteth M, MC	,,		17.6.15
,, Sutcliffe J.G.	2nd Army Rest Camp	Bombing	28.3.17
,, Copeman W.M.	On course		21.5.17
,, Askey C.H.L.	Sick	Lewis Gun	21.5.17
,, Beales F.C.	Plat. Comdr.		21.5.17
,, Wiggins A.B.	On course		29.6.17
,, Williams J.R., M.C.	Transport Officer		17.6.15
,, McDonnell J.M.	Asst. Adjt.		2.6.17
,, Mulcuck J.	Plat. Comdr.		29.6.17
,, Tunney F.	,,		29.6.17
,, Draper P.	,,		1.8.17
,, Farrow F.	,,		1.8.17
,, Christie E.J.A.	,,		2.8.17
,, Gibson W.R.	,,		20.8.17
,, Kneen H.E.	,,		20.8.17
,, Mitchell A.F.	,,		21.8.17
,, Moody F.H.	,,		20.8.17
Lieut. Taylor F.	Quartermaster		11.9.15
Captain Hardy T.B., C.F.	Chaplain		

NOMINAL ROLL OF OFFICERS.

8th Battalion, Somerset Light Infantry

Rank and Name	Present Employment	How Trained	Embarked
Lt-Col. Richardson H.S.C.	Commanding		3.5.17
Major Hon. R.T.St. John	2nd in command		
,, Hardyman J.H.M.	Coy. Comdr.	Staff duties	24.2.17
Captain Humphreys F.C.	,,	Lewis Gun	14.7.17
,, Baker H.G., M.C.	,,	Signalling	8.9.16
,, Hagon P.C.	Adjutant	P.T.& B.F.	11.7.16
Lieut. Pike H.	Transport Officer	Transport	10.9.15
,, Cooksley F.R., MC		General	10.12.16
,, Morgan A.P.		Bombing, General	14.7.17
,, Hinton F.G.	Coy. Comdr.	,, ,,	9.7.17
,, Pring H.O.	A/Adjutant		15.2.17
2/Lt. F.G.Adlam	Bde. Intelligence O.	Trench warfare	26.12.15
,, Willatt V.G.	Signal Officer	Sniping, Signalling	20.7.16
,, Goodman S.		Div.School, L.G.	8.1.17
,, Ward H.	Plat. Comdr.		
,, White L.J.H.	Lewis Gun Offr.	M.G., Bombing Musketry, Corps School	8.5.17
,, Wood W.		IX Corps School	8.5.17
,, Bodey L.C.			2.5.17
,, Findlay C.O.	Bde. School	M.G., Bombing	4.6.17
,, Pople H.K., M.C.		L.G., Musketry	18.6.17
,, Cox D.H.	Bombing Officer	Bombing	16.6.17
,, Glanville W.V.		2nd Army School	
,, Bickard W.H.	Plat. Comdr.	Musketry, L.G.	14.7.17
,, Pickard F.J.	,,	Musketry	14.7.17
,, Cunningham H.J.			26.7.17
,, Ham G.A.	Coy. Comdr.	P.T. & B.F.	24.7.17
,, Bennett P.H.R.			26.7.17
,, Plant V.H.			26.7.17
,, Radford J.A.		Gas	,,
,, Eskell E.N.		IX Corps School P.T. & B.F.	,,
,, Ward W.L.		IX Corps School	5.8.17
,, Madden C.H.		M.G.	31.7.17
,, Austin H.K.		Signalling Bombing	11.8.17
,, Stone H.G.		Signalling	,,
,, Smith H.J.			,,
,, Hearder G.H.			,,
,, Friend H.J.			,,
,, Crees N.H.			,,
,, Hill D.A.		Signalling, Musky.	,,
,, Brown C.B.			,,
,, Doman L.P.B.		Lewis Gun	,,
,, Pfaff E.			,,
Lieut. Schooling J.J.	Quartermaster		10.9.15
Lieut. Taunton T.J.	Medical Officer		

NOMINAL ROLL OF OFFICERS.

4th Battalion, The Middlesex Regiment.

Rank and Name	Present Employment	How Trained	Embarked
Lt.-Col. G.A. Bridgman	On leave		25.4.17
Major C.R. Hay	Commandant Bde. School		28.6.17
Captain B.R. Newman	Commanding		28.4.17
,, M.D. FitzGibbon	Coy. Comdr.		3.5.17
,, P.W. Smith M.C.	Leave	1st Army School	13.7.16
Lieut. Fenn E.A.H.	2nd Army School	Bombing	13.7.16
,, Mitchell A.G.	Bombing Officer	Bombing	13.7.16
2/Lt. Bowser H.F.	Brigade School	Sniping	1.2.15
,, Odling H.R.		Signals	19.4.17
,, Taylor R.E.	Att. 37th Div. Q		29.5.16
,, Mirams S.	A/Adjutant		5.6.16
,, Irwin R.F.T.	Brigade School	Signals	17.7.16
,, Scholefield F.W.	Intelligence & Sniping	Sniping	15.7.16
,, Martin O.N.	Div. Salvage Offr.		13.7.16
,, Andreae L.W.	Platoon Commander	Sniping	12.6.15
,, Williams R.G.	Coy. Comdr.	Bombing	15.7.16
,, Whitlock H.S	9th Corps School	Transport	6.9.16
,, Hodgson J.H.	Transport Officer	Transport	28.4.16
,, Sutherland G.S?	Signalling Officer	Signals.	4.5.15
,, Lyal J.C., M.C.	Plat. Comdr.		12.12.16
,, Weller A.V.	Sick	Bombing	19.4.17
,, Hurr. D.F.	9th Corps School	Bombing Div.Sch.	6.9.16
,, De Val T.	Brigade School	Corps School	10.5.17
,, Monk H.M.	152nd Fd. Co. RE		4.12.16
,, Steele P.H.	Brigade School	Bombing	24.2.17
,, Halley K.B.	Brigade School		30.7.17
,, Jamieson J.P.	L/C.Bn. details	Lewis Gun	27.4.17
,, Backhouse H.F.	Plat. Comdr.	Stokes Gun	21.4.16
,, Wridgway C.W.	Brigade School L.G.O.	Lewis Gun	31.5.17
,, Stanley M.T.	9th Corps Signal Schl.		30.7.17
,, Swallow E.H.	Plat. Comdr.		30.7.17
,, Klaiber A.J.	Brigade School		11.8.17
,, Yates A.S.	Brigade School		11.8.17
,, Batty D.H.	Plat. Comdr.		11.8.17
,, Andrews A.G.	Plat. Comdr.		11.8.17
,, Chaundy H.M.			11.8.17
,, Felgate H.	Plat. Comdr.		11.8.17
,, Gates H.A.	Brigade School		11.8.17
,, Heath D.W.	Plat. Comdr.		11.8.17
Lieut. Amor E.H.	Quartermaster		18.10.15
Lieut. Ensing G.H.	Medical Officer		
Captain Largie W.G., C.F.	Chaplain.		

NOMINAL ROLL OF OFFICERS.

10th Battalion, The York & Lancaster Regiment.

Rank and Name	Prsent Employment	How Trained	Embarked
Lt.Col. Layton A.B.	On leave		
Major Austin F.C.	Commanding		31.7.15
,, Fairnie E.G.J.	Sick	Bombing, Tactics	16.11.15
Captain Watts R.A.B.P.	Sick		
,, Bozs J.G.	Coy. Comdr.	Musketry, Bombing	2.5.17
,, White R.C.	,,	Musketry, Bombing	25.6.17
,, Jarrard W.J.	,,		23.5.17
,, Elsworth L.A.	Adjutant	Sniping, Bombing	10.9.15
,, Robinson A.R.	Coy. Comdr.		4.10.16
,, Wilkinson R.M.	Army Rest Camp	Bombing	5.10.15
Lieut. Ayres F.	Lewis Gun Offr.	Lewis Gun, Bombing	10.11.15
,, Dixon G.B.	Plat. Comdr.		14.8.17
,, Sansom C.P.	,,	Lewis Gun, Bombing	19.8.17
2/Lt. Rockley W.L.	Intelligence Offr.	Sniping	6.4.17
,, Walne H.A.	Transport Officer	Transport, Gas	16.9.16
,, Gaunt B.W.	Att. 63rd T.M.B.	Trench Mortar	15.12.16
,, Horsfall J.R.	Plat. Comdr.	Sanitation	15.12.16
,, Snowden H.	Sick	Signalling	31.5.17
,, Cameron H.	Plat.Comdr.	Bombing	17.4.17
,, Woodmansey K.G.	Bde. School	Lewis Gun	15.12.16
,, Mitchell R.J.	Att. 152 Fd. Co.RE	Lewis Gun	10.11.15
,, Sutcliffe E.H.	Bde. Salvage Offr.		1.5.17
,, Williams S.	Sick	Musketry	17.4.17
,, Jackson A.H.	Course	Lewis Gun	16.4.17
,, Parry W.	Course	Bombing and Gas	16.4.17
,, Hughes H.D.	Course	Signalling	16.4.17
,, Forrest R.A.	Sick		11.5.17
,, Marshall J.W.H.	Course	Signalling, Gas	2.6.17
,, Tune G.E.	Sick		4.6.17
,, Kaplan I.	Plat. Comdr.	L.T.M., Bombing	16.4.17
,, Byrne J.	Course	Musketry, M.G.	28.2.17
,, Lea W.G.	Plat.Comdr.	General	12.6.17
,, Gladman A.F.	,,	Lewis Gun & P.T.	11.5.17
,, Holt W.L.	,,	General	11.5.17
,, Hardwick A.	,,		19.8.17
,, Lyon F.J.W.	,,	Lewis Gun	19.8.17
,, McNally T.P.	Brigade School	Musketry, Bombing	19.8.17
Lieut. Jamieson A.	Quartermaster		31.10.16
Lieut. McConnel W.G.	Medical Officer		13.3.17
Captain Thomas H.G., C.F.	Chaplain.		

NOMINAL ROLLS OF OFFICERS.

63rd Machine Gun Company

Major	J.G.E. Rideal, D.S.O.	Acting Divnl. M.G. Officer	
Lieut.	W.A. Webb, M.C.	Commanding	24.2.16
Lieut.	N.F. Hawes	A/2nd in command	25.5.16
Lieut.	I.C. Hartley	Transport Officer	1.7.16
Lieut.	T. Thomson	Section Officer	4.8.17
2/Lt.	W.S. MacLean	On Leave	9.4.17
2/Lt.	R.J. Ramsay	Section Officer	23.4.17
2/Lt.	F. Denning	,,	13.5.17
2/Lt.	F. Laughton	,,	23.4.17
2/Lt.	F.H. Weatherill	Sub-section officer	9.8.17

63rd Trench Mortar Battery

Captain	J.P. Akerman	Commanding	8.9.15
Lieut.	G.H. Sims, M.C.	2nd in command	8.9.15
Lieut.	M.W.S. Harris		28.5.16
Lieut.	E.B. Markham		5.10.15
2nd Lt.	B.W. Gaunt		15.12.16

CASUALTIES DURING AUGUST, 1917.

	IN TRENCHES						OUT OF TRENCHES						TOTAL CASUALTIES IN AND OUT OF TRENCHES.	SICK			GRAND TOTAL	REMARKS
	Officers			Other Rks			Officers			Other Rks				Officers	O.R.	Total		
	Killed	Wounded	Missing	Killed	Wounded	Missing	Killed	Wounded	Missing	Killed	Wounded	Missing	Total					
8th Lincolnshire Regt.		a 1		9	37	2			-	NIL			49	1	44	45	94	a 2/Lt. Bowden H.J. b 2/Lt. Askey C.H.L.
8th Somerset L.I.				8	27				-	NIL			35	c 1	66	67	102	c 2/Lt. Goodman S.
4th Middlesex Regt.				2	1				-	NIL			3	d 1	16	17	20	d 2/Lt. Weller A.V.
10th York & Lanc. Regt.				11	12	1			-	NIL			24	e 4	25	29	53	e 2/Lt. Tune G.E. 2/Lt. Forrest R.A. 2/Lt. Williams S. 2/Lt. Snowden H.
63rd Machine Gun Coy.		f 1		3	21				-	NIL			25	g 1	7	8	33	f 2/Lt. Henderson G.B. g 2/Lt. Richards T.A.
63rd Trench Mortar Battery				2	1				-	NIL			3	1	7	7	10	
T O T A L		2		35	99	3			-	NIL			139	8	165	173	312	

63rd Infantry Brigade.

REINFORCEMENTS RECEIVED DURING AUG. 1917.

	Officers		Other Ranks	Date.
8th Lincolnshire Regt.	3	a	6	7.8.17
	-		4	11.8.17
	1	b	9	21.8.17
	4	c	10	28.8.17
	8		29	
8th Somerset Light Infantry	1	d	4	3.8.17
	1	e	-	6.8.17
	1	f	-	8.8.17
	1	g	-	9.8.17
	1	h	22	11.8.17
	2	i	-	12.8.17
	1	j	31	21.8.17
	1	k	-	24.8.17
	1	l	-	26.8.17
	8	m	23	27.8.17
	1	n	-	29.8.17
	19		80	
4th Middlesex Regt.	3	o	-	7.8.17
	3	p	-	17.8.17
	5	q	4	18.8.17
	-		6	28.8.17
	11		10	
10th York & Lanc. Regt.	-		4	4.8.17
	-		9	11.8.17
	-		4	14.8.17
	1	r	-	16.8.17
	5	s	-	19.8.17
	-		5	23.8.17
	-		14	28.8.17
	6		36	
63rd Machine Gun Company	1	t	-	4.8.17
	-		20	6.8.17
	-		2	14.8.17
	1	u	9	18.8.17
	1	v	-	27.8.17
	-		1	29.8.17
	3		32	
63rd Trench Mortar Battery	-		1	21.8.17
	-		2	24.8.17
	-		1	28.8.17
			4	

TOTAL REINFORCEMENTS RECEIVED DURING AUGUST: 47 officers, 191 O.R.

EXPLANATION.

a	2nd Lieut.	Draper P.	8th Lincolnshire Regt.
	,,	Farrow F.	,,
	,,	Bowden H.J.	,,
b	,,	Christie E.J.A.	,,
c	,,	Gibson W.R.	,,
	,,	Kneen H.E.	,,
	,,	Mitchell A.T.	,,
	,,	Moody F.H.	,,
d	Major	Hon. St.John, R.T.	8th Somerset L.Infantry
e	2nd Lieut.	Cunningham H.J.	8th Somerset L.Infantry
f	,,	Ham G.A.	,,
g	,,	Bennett P.H.R.	,,
h	,,	Plant V.L.	,,
i	,,	Radford J.A.	,,
	,,	Eskell E.N.	,,
	,,	Ward W.L.	,,
j	,,	Madden C.H.	,,
k	,,	Austin H.K.	,,
l	,,	Stone H.G.	,,
m	,,	Smith H.J.	,,
	,,	Hearder G.H.	,,
	,,	Friend H.J.	,,
	,,	Crees N.H.	,,
	,,	Hill D.A.	,,
	,,	Brown C.B.	,,
	,,	Doman D.P.B.	,,
n	,,	Pfaff E.	
o	2nd Lieut.	Halley K.B.	4th Middlesex Regt.
	,,	Stanlet M.T.	,,
	,,	Swallow E.H.	,,
p	,,	Klaiber A.J.	,,
	,,	Yates A.S.	,,
	,,	Batty D.H.	,,
q	,,	Andrews A.G.	,,
	,,	Chaundy H.M.	,,
	,,	Felgate H.	,,
	,,	Gates H.A.	,,
	,,	Heath D.W.	,,
r	~~2nd Lieut.~~		
r	Major	Austin F.C.	10th York & Lanc. Regt.
s	Lieut.	C.B.	,,
	,,	Sansom P.C.	,,
	2nd Lieut.	Hardwick A.	,,
	,,	Lyons F.J.W.	,,
	,,	McNalty T.P.	,,
t	Major	Rideal, J.G.E., D.S.O.	63rd Machine Gun Company
u	2nd Lieut.	Weatherill T.H.	,,
v	Lieut.	Thomson T.	,,

63rd Infantry Brigade.

STRENGTH OF UNITS,
AUGUST 31ST 1917

	Strength		Details included	
	Officers	O.R.	Officers	O.R.
8th Lincolnshire Regt.	33	739	8	179
8th Somerset L.I.	43 ~~40~~	715	4	147
4th Middlesex Regt.	40	633	7	57
10th York & Lanc. Regt.	37	800	12	79
63rd Machine Gun Company	10	181	1	20
63rd Trench Mortar Battery	5	60	-	-
Total	168 ~~173~~	3128	32	482

ORIGINAL COPY

63rd INFANTRY BRIGADE

WAR DIARY

SEPTEMBER

1917

Army Form C. 2118.

WAR DIARY
or
INTELLIGENCE SUMMARY.
(Erase heading not required.)

Instructions regarding War Diaries and Intelligence Summaries are contained in F. S. Regs., Part II. and the Staff Manual respectively. Title pages will be prepared in manuscript.

Place	Date	Hour	Summary of Events and Information	Remarks and references to Appendices
Trenches	1.9.17		Quiet day intrenches. The following work was carried out :- Wiring the front line and support line was commenced also a communication trench.	1
do	2.9.17		ditto During the night an inter-battalion relief was carried out Brigade Order No. 127 and addendum received	2
do	3.9.17		Clearer weather. Slightly increased shelling.	
do	4.9.17		Quiet day. A Divisional Conference of Brigadiers C.R.E. & C.R.A. held at 3rd Infantry Brigade Headquarters at 4.30.pm.	
do	5.9.17		Quiet Day. Divisional Order No. 128 received	3
do	6.9.17		do Brigade Order No. 160	4
do	7.9.17		do. Reliefs carried out.	
FAIRY HOUSE	8.9.17		G.O.C. 63rd Infantry Brigade handed over Command of the line to G.O.C. 111th Infantry Brigade at 10.0.am.	
do	9.9.17		Large working parties found. Divisional Order No. 129 received............	5
Mt. KOKEREELE	10th		63rd Infantry Brigade marched in accordance with Brigade Order No.161............	6
do	11.9.17		Large working parties found. Individual training	
do	12.9.17		do do do	
do	13.9.17		do do do	
do	14.9.17		do do do	

(Continued)

Army Form C. 2118.

WAR DIARY
or
INTELLIGENCE SUMMARY.
(Erase heading not required.)

Instructions regarding War Diaries and Intelligence Summaries are contained in F. S. Regs., Part II. and the Staff Manual respectively. Title pages will be prepared in manuscript.

Place	Date	Hour	Summary of Events and Information	Remarks and references to Appendices
MONT KOKEREELE	15.9.17		Large working parties found. Individual training	
	16.9.17		do.	
	17.9.17		Individual training	
	18.9.17		"Cooperation with aeroplane" practice. Battalions were represented by skeleton platoons.	7
	19.9.17		The Brigade marched to the FAIRY HOUSE Area in accordance with Div. O.O. 131 and Bde. O.O. 162.	8
FAIRY HOUSE	20.9.17		The move was completed by 1.30 am on morning of 20th.	
MONT KOKEREELE	21.9.17		The Brigade moved back to the MONT KOKEREELE Area - 37th Div. G.360 & Bde. O. 163.	9 10
	22.9.17		Training	
	23.9.17		,,	
	24.9.17		,,	
	25.9.17		,,	
	26.9.17		,,	
	27.9.17		63rd Inf. Bde. relieved 118th Inf. Bde. in the line - Div. O. 134, Bde. O. 164	11
Trenches	28.9.17		G.O.C. 63rd Inf. Bde. assumed command of the line at 7 am. Relief of 118th M.G.Coy. by 63rd Inf. Bde. completed at 10 pm. Improvement of the line commenced.	12
	29.9.17		Improvement of the line continued.	
	30.9.17		do.	

N. Mawun
Brigadier General,
Commdg. 63rd Infantry Brigade.

63rd Infantry Brigade.

W A R   D I A R Y

SEPTEMBER, 1917.

List of Appendices.	No. of Appendix.
37th Div. Order No. 127 & Addendum............	1
63rd Bde. Order No. 159.......................	2
37th Div. Order No. 128.......................	3
63rd Bde. Order No. 160.......................	4
37th Div. Order No. 129.......................	5
63rd Bde. Order No. 161.......................	6
37th Div. Order No. 131.......................	7
63rd Bde. Order No. 162.......................	8
37th Div. Wire No. G 360......................	9
63rd Bde. Order No. 163.......................	10
37th Div. Order No. 134.......................	11
63rd Bde. Order No. 164.......................	12
Nominal rolls of officers.....................	13
Casualties during September, 1917.............	14
Reinforcements received during Sept.1917......	15
Strength of Units, September 30th, 1917.......	16

ORIGINAL COPY

63rd INFANTRY BRIGADE

WAR DIARY

OCTOBER

1917

Army Form C. 2118.

WAR DIARY

or

INTELLIGENCE SUMMARY

(Erase heading not required.)

Instructions regarding War Diaries and Intelligence Summaries are contained in F. S. Regs., Part II. and the Staff Manual respectively. Title pages will be prepared in manuscript.

Place	Date	Hour	Summary of Events and Information	Remarks and references to Appendices
Trenches	1.10.17		Relief of front line battalions carried out as directed by Bde. Order.165.	1
	2.10.17		Conference of Commanding Officers at which forthcoming operations were discussed.	
	3.10.17		Bde. Order.166 issued.	2
	4.10.17		Operations undertaken - see separate account.	3
			During night, units were reinforced and reorganised and attempts made to push out posts on the front of our line. No. 2686 and 2688. Div. O. 139	4 & 5
	5.10.17		The Brigade was relieved by 112th Inf. Bde. in the Line.	6
FAIRY	6.10.17		G.O.C. 63rd Bde. handed over command of the line to G.O.C. 112th Bde. at 7 am Bde. O. 167	7
HOUSE			During the night relief of 63rd M.G.Coy. and T.M.Battery carried out.. (Div. O. 140.	8
			G.O.C. & O.C. 8th Lincs. and 8th Som. L.I. attended conference at (Bde. NO. 2123.	9
	7.10.17		Div. HQ. at 2.30 pm at which the Army Commander was present.	
	7.10.17		10th York & Lancs. relieved in the line by 13th R.B. Div. O. 141, Bde. O. 168.	10 & 11
	8.10.17		Div. Order 142 received. Bde. 169 issued.	12 & 13
	9.10.17		The Brigade remained in camp. Lt.-Col. Davies-Evans proceeded to England for 6 months, Major St.John, from 8th Som. L.I., assumed temporary command of 8th Lincolns.	
	10.10.17		In accordance with Div. O. 143 and Bde. O. 170 63rd Inf. Bde. relieved 112th Inf. Bde.	14 & 15
			Major Ostle, Artists' Rifles, joined 10th York & Lancs. as second in command.	
Trenches	11.10.17		At 9 am G.O.C. 63rd Inf. Bde. assumed command of the line. The relief was carried out with difficulty owing to the state of the ground and complete darkness. Considerable hostile shelling. Relief of 112th M.G.Coy. and T.M.Battery by 63rd M.G.Coy. and T.M.Battery carried out during night.	
Trenches	12.10.17		Enemy artillery active.	
	13.10.17		Enemy artillery active.	
	14.10.17		Enemy artillery active. At 10.55 pm a post held by 8th Som. L.I. was raided by the enemy. (see Appendix.	16
	15.10.17		63rd Inf.Bde. relieved by 116th Inf. Bde. in the line. Div. O. 145 & Amendment,Bde. O. 171.	17 & 18
MONT	16.10.17		G.O.C. 116th Inf. Bde. assumed command of the line at 7 am	
KOKEREELE	17.10.17		Resting, washing and reorganising. Staff Captain proceeded on leave. Capt. J.J.Billiat, 8th Lincolns, took over duties of Staff Captain.	
	18.10.17		Training.	
	20.10.17		Training.	
	21.10.17		Owing to the very wet state of the camps occupied by units, of the Brigade marched to billets in the MERRIS Area. Div. O. 146 and Bde. O. 172	19 & 20
MERRIS	22.10.17		Training.	
	23.10.17		Training.	
	24.10.17		Training.	

Army Form C. 2118.

WAR DIARY
or
INTELLIGENCE SUMMARY.

(Erase heading not required.)

Instructions regarding War Diaries and Intelligence Summaries are contained in F. S. Regs., Part II. and the Staff Manual respectively. Title pages will be prepared in manuscript.

Place	Date	Hour	Summary of Events and Information	Remarks and references to Appendices
MORRIS	25.10.17		Training.	
	26.10.17		Training.	
	27.10.17		Training.	
	28.10.17		Training.	
	29.10.17		Working party, 1,000 strong, detailed by 63rd Inf. Bde. relieved similar party of 111th Inf. Bde. for work on roads east of YPRES under Canadian Corps. Div. No. 3577/4. Bde. O. 173...21 & 22 Captain W.L.Brodie, V.C., M.C., Brigade Major, proceeded on leave. Major M.Cuthbertson took over duties of Brigade Major.	
	30.10.17		Training. Captain F.M.Gillmore, Staff Captain, returned from leave.	
	31.10.17		Bombs dropped by enemy aircraft during afternoon on camps of working party in I.3.b. 5.O.R. slightly wounded	

October 31st 1917

R Challenor.
Brigadier General,
Comdg. 63rd Infantry Brigade.

63rd INFANTRY BRIGADE.

REPORT on OPERATIONS South of the YPRES – MENIN Road 4th October 1917 and previous days.

PRELIMINARY.

During the night 27th – 28th September, 63rd Brigade relieved 118th Infantry Brigade in the line, from about J.26.d.7.9. to J.21.c.2.1. The relief was carried out very hurriedly on account of the short notice given. It was understood from the outgoing Unit that the general line held, was the line of the Road running North and South through JUTE COTTS. This was subsequently found to be not the case, the general line running about 150 yards West of the road and in places even more. Owing to the previous heavy shelling of this area, the road was no longer a land-mark, which would easily account for the mistake made by the outgoing Brigade and for the subsequent difficulty experienced by this Brigade in determining its exact position, no movement being possible by day.

PREPARATION. As soon as it was known that offensive operations had to be undertaken, posts were pushed out and the result of reconnaisance showed that the road line was the German post line, with strong points behind.

At the same time, preparations for attack were made, assembly trenches were dug with the assistance of one Company Pioneers.

During the period up to 4th October, preparations were difficult for the following reasons :-

(a) The ground was unusually difficult to work on, both on account of the shell holes, and also of the difficulty of locating places due to the absence of landmarks.

(b) Communications up to the front line was only possible by night, by day even individual runners being shot at from the time of leaving Headquarters of Battalions in the line. The country across the BASSEVILLE BEEK was exceptionally difficult. It was only owing to the fact that the weather was excellent and that there was a moon that movement was not made far more difficult.

(c) The shelling was very heavy from the direction of COMINES particularly on the 3rd October and during the night of assembly 3/4th October. There was also constant and very heavy flank Machine Gun fire from the South.

ASSEMBLY. The assembly was carried out without any incident. According to his custom of late, the enemy put down a heavy barrage behind our front line for about an hour before Zero, causing some casualties.

The attacking troops were necessarily rather crowded for the following reasons :-

1. It was impossible to reinforce the attacking troops by day, therefore all the necessary reserves had to be East of the BASSEVILLE BEEK before daylight and in assembly trenches.

2. Assembly trenches were limited owing to the hurried preparations and the wet nature of the ground.

It was at first intended to have only one objective, but owing to the lie of the ground and the forward posts of the enemy on the high ground just East of the road through JUTE COTTS, it was impossible to reconnoitre BERRY COTTS and the Trench North and South of it and they could not be observed from our Front Line or forward posts. It was also thought that the final objective might be strongly wired. It was therefore decided to gain the high ground first.

By 5 a.m. the assembly had been completed and all troops for the attack were in psoition. The forward posts were withdrawn at 5:30 a.m. to allow the barrage to come down on the line of the first objective.

ATTACK. At Zero the barrage came down and appeared very thin. The leading wave advanced under it. The enemy on the right, opposite the 8th Somersets, were found occupying a series of strong points North and South of the strong point at J.27.a.05.05.

This line was just East of the high ground which was our objective and was practically on the same level. Immediately the Companies appeared on the crest level, they were received by Machine Gun and Rifle fire.

They reached their objective by sectional rushes and attempted to consolidate under intense Machine Gun fire from J.27.c.05.05 and 3 Machine Guns in JAGER TRENCH about 450 yards away on the right flank at J.27.c.central.

It was hoped that the Artillery barrage would keep these guns under, remaining on this line, but this was not the case. Moreover the barrage seemed thin and ineffective.

Immediately the leading Companies reached their objective they were swept by Machine Gun fire and met local bombing counter-attacks by the enemy. The Right Company of the 8th Somersets was fully employed trying to keep down the fire of the three enemy Machine Guns at J.27.c. central and could therefore not assist the two Companies on their left. These two Companies tried hard to overcome the Machine Gun at J.27.a.05.05 but were almost annihilated in trying to do so. Losses here caused a gap between 8th Somersets and 8th Lincolns on left and a Lewis gun team was at once sent to cover the gap and the objective line reinforced.

Another effort was made against J.27.a.05.05 but this also proved costly and unsuccessful.

Meanwhile, on the left, the 8th Lincolns advanced, and after going about 100 yards, came under fire of several Machine Guns which swept the slope. Two of these appeared to be between the road and JOIST TRENCH and another at BERRY COTTS. These guns inflicted very heavy casualties on the leading Companies.

The enemy about 100 strong were occupying the trench about 50 yards East of the JUTE COTTS ROAD and were reinforced from JOIST TRENCH.

The enemy also made local counter-attacks, but it was entirely due to the Machine Gun fire that the attack was held up here.

Owing to the whole plateau being swept by these Machine Guns and also by the Machine Guns from the South, it was decided that the attack could not get over the ground and owing to casualties the original line was occupied.

The 8th Somersets on right, after setting aside sufficient men from their Support and Reserve to hold the original Front line made another very gallant attack on J.27.a.05.05, but this attack also failed.

On the Right flank a strong post was dug in advance of the posts previously held by the Right Company. This was successfully held against repeated bombing attacks. On the Left and centre 2nd Lieut. PICKARD, 8th Somersets, who had been sent up with reinforcements, withdrew the only three remaining unwounded. The situation on the whole front was therefore the same as we originally started from.

It was impossible to send up reinforcements from the Reserve owing to the approaches to the Front being visible to the enemy and under Machine Gun fire in addition to the heavy enemy barrage. Arrangements were however made to reinforce the front line as soon as it was dark and the remaining three Companies of 10th York & Lancs were sent up as soon as it was possible.

The 8th Lincolns were in touch with 111th Brigade at Zero hour, but after advancing, touch was lost and only regained when the original line was straigthened out after dark.

During the action there were very many complaints that some of our Guns were shooting short, and after sifting all the evidence I am satisfied that this was the case. In each case the artillery were asked to lengthen.

The road through JUTE COTTS is absolutely obliterated.

TO SUM UP.

The strong point at J.27.a.05.05 made the objective line untenable, while the Machine Gun at J.27.c. central rendered Flank attacks on J.27.a.05.05 impossible.

The plateau in front of the 8th Lincolns was swept by Machine Gun fire.

The artillery barrage was far too thin.

The following were losses in the Brigade during the action :-

Officers.   Killed 6.   Wounded 10.   Missing 3 (believed killed or wounded)

Other Ranks.   ,,   66   ,,   258   ,,   57

The large number of missing occurred on the left of the line which came under very heavy Machine Gun fire as soon as it got on to the high ground and they were probably all casualties.

I attach :-

    1 Copy of Orders.

    2. Map showing positions of attacking troops at Zero and furthest positions reached.

    3. Map showing objectives.

Sd E.L. Challener
Brigadier General.
Commdg. 63rd Inf. Brigade.

9/10/17.

NOMINAL ROLL OF OFFICERS.

8th Battalion Lincolnshire Regiment.

Rank.	Name.	Present Employment.	How Trained.	Embarked.
Lt.-Col.	Hon. R.T.St.John	Commanding.		
Captain	Waugh F.A., M.C.	2nd in command	Bombing	19.6.16
"	Latham F.W.	Coy. Comdr.		7.4.17
"	Moss W.	"		19.4.17
"	Wiggins A.B.	"	Bombing	29.6.17
"	Hansell F.J.	"	Lewis Gun	30.1.17
"	Rowcroft M.	Adjutant		11.9.15
"	Billiatt J.J.	Att. 63rd Bde. HQ		26.4.17
Lieut.	Christie E.J.H.	Asst. Adjutant		2.8.17
"	Williams J.R., M.C.	Transport Officer		17.6.15
"	Hine S.T.	Signal Officer	Signalling	25.6.16
"	White A.	Intelligence Off.	Bombing, L.G., Sniping	27.7.16
"	Stuart Menteth M, MC	On prob. R.F.C. HQ		17.6.15
2nd Lt.	Askey C.H.L.	Plat. Comdr.	Lewis Gun	21.5.17
"	McDonnell J.R.	IX Corps Reinf'm't Camp.		2.6.17
"	Copeman W.H.		Signalling	21.5.17
"	Draper P.	2nd i/c Coy.		1.8.17
"	Peadon P.H.	Plat. Comdr.		12.10.17
"	Mills F.	"		17.10.17
"	Woollatt J.L.	"		12.10.17
"	Plant J.S.	"		17.10.17
"	Anker A.G.	2nd i/c Coy.		27.6.17
"	Hamilton C.G.H.	Plat. Comdr.		6.10.17
"	Owen C.J.	Bombing Offr.	Bombing	12.10.17
"	Wilcockson R.R.	Plat. Comdr.		11.10.17
"	Jones J.R.	"		17.10.17
"	Brown F.	"		17.10.17
"	Beales F.C.	Asst. Transport Off.		21.5.17
"	Sutcliffe J.G.	2nd i/c Coy.	Bombing	28.5.17
"	Mitchell A.T.	Plat. Comdr.	Lewis Gun	21.8.17
"	Watson J.	On Course		27.6.17
"	Tunney J.	Plat. Comdr.		28.6.17
"	Moody H.F.	2nd i/c Coy.		20.8.17
"	Smalley H.	Plat. Comdr.		17.10.17
"	Gray J.H.	63rd Bde. School		12.10.17
"	Lowe C.			17.10.17
"	Bousfield W.R.			17.10.17
"	Naylor T.			17.10.17
Lieut.	Taylor F.	Quartermaster		11.9.15

NOMINAL ROLL OF OFFICERS.

8th Battalion Somerset Light Infantry

Rank	Name	Present employment	How trained	Embarked
Lt.Col.	H.S.C.Richardson	Commanding		3.5.17
Major	J.H.M.Hardyman, M.C.	2nd in command	Staff duties	24.2.17
Captain	H.G.Baker, M.C.	Coy. Commander	Signalling	8.9.16
,,	A.P.MORGAN	,,	Bombing, Gen. Course	14.7.17
,,	L.J.H.White		M.G., Bombing Musky., L.gun.	8.5.17
,,	P.C.Hagon	Adjutant	P.T. & B.F.	11.7.16
Lieut.	H.Pike	Transport Offr.	Transport	10.9.15
,,	F.R.Cooksley, M.C.	IX Corps Camp	Gen. Course	10.12.16
,,	H.O.Pring	Asst. Adjutant		15.2.17
,,	H.J.Cunningham			26.7.17
,,	F.G.Adlam	Att. 63rd Bde.HQ	Trench W'fare	26.12.15
,,	V.G.Willatt	Signal Offr.	Sniping, Sig.	20.7.16
,,	V.L.Plant	Musketry Off.	Musketry	26.7.17
,,	D.H.Cox	Bombing Offr.	Bombing	16.6.17
2nd Lt.	W.Wood		IX Corps Gen. Course	8.5.17
,,	L.C.Bodey		Gen. Course	2.5.17
,,	H.K.Pople, M.C.		L.Gun, Musky.	18.6.17
,,	F.J.Pickard		Musky.,IX Corps Infy.School	14.7.17
,,	P.H.R.Bennett		Gas, IX Corps Infy. School	26.7.17
,,	J.A.Radford		Gas Course	26.7.17
,,	W.L.Ward		IX Corps Gen., Bombing	5.8.17
,,	C.H.Madden		M.G., Lewis G.	31.7.17
,,	H.K.Austin		Bombing	11.8.17
,,	H.G.Stone		Signalling	11.8.17
,,	G.H.Hearder		Gen. Course & IX Corps Inf. School	11.8.17
,,	N.H.Crees	Coy. Comdr.	Bombing	11.8.17
,,	E.Pfaff		Transport	11.8.17
,,	W.Deeming			-
Lieut.	J.J.Schooling	Quartermaster		10.9.15
Captain	T.Taunton	Medical Officer		

NOMINAL ROLL OF OFFICERS.

4th Battalion Middlesex Regiment.

Rank.	Name.	Present Employment.	How Trained.	Embarked.
Lt.-Col.	Bridgman G.A.	Commanding		25.4.17
Major	Hay C.R.	O.C. Bde School		28.6.17
Captain	Newman B.R.	Coy. Comdr.		28.4.17
"	Smith P.W., M.C.	"	1st Army School	13.7.16
"	Mirams S.	A/Adjutant	Musketry	5.6.16
"	Scholefield F.W.	Sniping & Int. Off.	Sniping	15.7.16
"	Jamieson J.P.	On course	Lewis Gun	27.4.17
"	Fenn E.A.H.	Coy. Comdr.	Bombing	13.7.16
Lieut.	Mitchell A.G.	Bombing Offr.	Bombing	13.7.16
"	Bowser H.F.	IX Corps Reinf'm't Camp	Sniping	1.2.15
"	Moryoseph E.C.	On Course		17.9.17
"	Odling H.R.	Bde. School	Signalling	19.4.17
"	Taylor R.E.	Att. 37th Div. HQ	Staff duties	29.5.16
"	Irwin R.F.T.	Plat. Comdr.	Lewis Gun	17.5.16
"	Martin O.N.	Div. Salvage Off.	Lewis gun	13.7.16
"	Andreae L.W.	Plat. Comdr.	Sniping	12.6.15
"	Williams R.G.	Plat. Comdr.	Bombing	15.7.16
"	Whitlock H.S.	Plat. Comdr.	Transport	6.9.16
"	Hodgson J.H.	Transport Offr.	Transport	28.4.16
2nd Lt.	Sutherland G.S.	A/Adjutant and Signal Offr.	Signalling	4.5.15
"	Lyal J.C., M.C.	Plat. Comdr.	Lewis Gun	12.12.16
"	De Val T.	Plat. Comdr.	Corps School	10.5.17
"	Monk H.M.	152 Fd. Co. RE		4.12.16
"	Steele P.H.	On Course	Lewis Gun	24.2.17
"	Halley K.B.	Plat. Comdr.	Corps School	30.7.17
"	Backhouse H.F.	"	Stokes Gun	21.4.16
"	Stanley M.T.	"	Signalling	30.7.17
"	Klaiber A.J.	"	Corps School	11.8.17
"	Yates A.S.	Bde. School	Bombing	11.8.17
"	Batty D.H.		Lewis Gun	11.8.17
"	Andrews A.G.	Lewis Gun Offr.	Lewis Gun	11.8.17
"	Chaundy H.M.		Stokes Gun	11.8.17
"	Felgate H.	Plat. Comdr.	Corps School	11.8.17
"	Gates H.A.			11.8.17
"	Heath D.W.	Plat. Comdr.		11.8.17
"	Elmore E.	"		17.9.17
"	Stuart R.A.K.	Coy. Comdr.		23.9.17
Captain	Amor E.H.	Quartermaster		18.10.15
Captain	Largie W.G., C.F.	Chaplain		
Lieut.	Fletcher J. RAMC	Medical Officer		

NOMINAL ROLL OF OFFICERS.

10th Battalion York & Lancaster Regt.

Rank	Name	Present Employment	How Trained	Embarked
Lt-Col.	Layton A.B.	Commanding		
Major	Ostle H.K.E.	2nd in command	Chelsea Course, Sen. Officers' Course, Staff Course	2.10.17
"	Boss J.G.	Coy. Comdr.	Bombing, Musky. Tactics	2.5.17
Captain	White R.C.	Plat. Comdr.	Musky, Bombing	25.6.17
"	Robinson A.R.	Coy. Comdr.	General, Lewis gun	4.10.16
"	Wilkinson R.M.	"	Bombing, General	5.10.15
"	Willis C.H.S.	a/Adjutant	Adjutant's duties	2.10.17
Lieut.	Ayres F.	On Course	V & L Guns, Bombing	10.11.15
"	Dixon C.B.	Plat. Comdr.	Tactics	14.8.17
"	Sansom C.P.	Sick	Bombing, Lewis gun	19.8.17
"	Mitchell R.J.	152 Fd.Co.RE	V & L Guns	10.11.15
"	Sutcliffe E.H.	Sick		1.5.17
2nd Lt.	Walne H.A.	Transport Offr.	Transport, Gas	16.9.16
"	Woodmansey K.G.	Bde. School	Lewis Gun	15.12.16
"	Horsfall J.R	On Course	Bombing, Sanitation, General	15.12.16
"	Parry W.	Coy. Comdr.	Bombing, Gas. Gen'l	16.4.17
"	Hughes H.D.		Signalling	16.4.17
"	Forrest R.A.	Plat. Comdr.		16.4.17
"	Marshall J.W.H.	"	Signalling, Gas	2.6.17
"	Lea W.G.	"	General	12.6.17
"	Kaplan I.	"	T.M., Bombing	16.4.17
"	Byrne J.	On Course	M.G., Musketry	28.2.17
"	Holt W.L.	Plat. Comdr.	General	11.5.17
"	Cameron H.	"	Bombing	17.4.17
"	Stops T.S.	"		20.10.17
"	Mansfield H.	"		20.10.17
"	Stears S.G.	"		11.10.17
"	Mills H.	"		20.10.17
"	Hastings W.B.	"		21.10.17
"	Moorhouse S.H.	"		11.10.17
"	Brierley S.	Bde. School		20.10.17
"	Ransom H.	Plat. Comdr.		20.10.17
"	Darricptt H.H.	"		20.10.17
"	Lyons F.J.W.	Sick	Lewis Gun	19.8.17
Lieut.	Jamieson A.	Quartermaster		31.10.16
Lieut.	Scott W.F. (U.S.A., R.C.)	Medical Officer		9.9.17

NOMINAL ROLL OF OFFICERS.

63rd Company, Machine Gun Corps.

Rank	Name	Present Employment	How trained	Embarked
Major	Rideal J.G.E., D.S.O.	Commanding	M.G.	30.7.17
Lieut.	Hartley I.C.	Transport Offr.	M.G.	1.7.17
"	Thomson T.	Section Officer	M.G.	4.8.17
"	Denning F.	" "	M.G.	13.5.17
2nd Lt.	MacLean W.S.	Section Officer	M.G.	9.4.17
"	Laughton F.	Subsection Offr.	M.G.	23.4.17
"	Weatherill T.H.	Section Officer	M.G.	9.8.17
"	Faulkner R.A.	Subsection offr.	M.G.	26.9.17
"	Thornton G.H.	Subsection Offr.	M.G.	22.10.17
"	Forrest W.	Subsection Offr.	M.G.	10.10.17

63rd Trench Mortar Battery.

Rank	Name	Present Employment	How trained	Embarked
Captain	Akerman J.P.	Commanding	Light T.M.	8.9.15
Lieut.	Harris M.W.S.		Light T.M.	28.5.16
2nd Lt.	Gaunt E.W.		Light T.M.	13.12.16

CASUALTIES DURING OCTOBER, 1917.

	IN TRENCHES							OUT OF TRENCHES						TOTAL CASUALTIES IN AND OUT OF TRENCHES	SICK			GRAND TOTAL	REMARKS
	Officers			Other Rks				Officers			Other Rks								
	Killed	Wounded	Missing	Killed	Wounded	Missing	Total	Killed	Wounded	Missing	Killed	Wounded	Missing	Total		Officers	O.R.	Total	
8th Lincolnshire Regt.	3[a]	3[b]	3[c]	26	142	55	232								232	1[d]	40	41	273	Capt. R.G. Cordiner M.C.[a] 2/Lt. A.F. Forge—[b] 2/Lt. D. Mulcuck [a] 2/Lt. H.E. Kneen.— Lt. E.H. Dukes.—[c] 2/Lt. O.F. Farrar.[c] 2/Lt. R.H. Westoby— 2/Lt. F.H.J. Robilliard[d]
8th Somerset L.I.	3[e]	6[f]	.	31	92	15	147								147	1[g]	80	81	228	2/Lt. W.R. Gibson[e] 2/Lt. W Copeman, 2/Lt. H.J. Smith — 3/Lt. H.S. Friend[f] Capt. F.C. Humphreys.[g]
4th Middlesex Regt.	2[h]	.	.	16	33	5	56								56	3[i]	135	138	194	Lt. F.G. Hinton - 3/Lt. W.H. Pickard.[h] 2/Lt. W.V. Glanville.- 2/Lt. E.M. Eskell[i]
10th York & Lanc. Regt.	1[j]	2[k]	.	29	59	1	92								92	1[m]	49	50	142	2/Lt. L.P.D. Doman 2/Lt. C.O. Finlay[j] 2/Lt. G.B. Brown. 2/Lt. E.M. Swallow- 2/Lt. A.W. Bays[k] 2/Lt. H.M. Chaundy - 2/Lt. D.M. Barry[l]
63rd Machine Gun Coy.	.	.	.	.	16	1	17								17	1[m]	17	18	35	2/Lt. M. S. Gates[l] Lt/Lt. L. Rockley[m]
63rd Trench Mortar Battery	.	.	.	1	2	.	3								3	.	29	29	32	Capt. W.J. Jarrard. - 2/Lt. H Cameron Lt. Sansom 2/Lt. S. Johnson[n]
TOTAL	9	11	3	104	344	76	547								547	7	350	357	904	

63rd Infantry Brigade

STRENGTH OF UNITS, OCTOBER 31st 1917.

UNIT	STRENGTH		DETAILS INCLUDED	
	Officers	Other Ranks	Officers	Other Ranks
8th Lincolnshire Regt.	39	574	7	140
8th Somerset L.I.	30	815	5	64
4th Middlesex Regt.	38	619	8	62
10th York & Lanc. Regt.	34	619	7	103
63rd Machine Gun Company	10	156	-	15
63rd Trench Mortar Battery	3	65	-	-
TOTAL	154	2848	27	384

Original Copy.

63rd. INFANTRY BRIGADE
WAR DIARY
NOVEMBER
1917

Army Form C. 2118.

WAR DIARY
or
INTELLIGENCE SUMMARY.
(Erase heading not required.)

Instructions regarding War Diaries and Intelligence Summaries are contained in F. S. Regs., Part II. and the Staff Manual respectively. Title pages will be prepared in manuscript.

Place	Date	Hour	Summary of Events and Information	Remarks and references to Appendices
MERRIS	NOV. 1st.17.		Training	
	2		do	
	3		do	
	4		do	
	5		do	
	6		Two composite Battalions working on forward roads under Canadian Corps relieved. Bde. Order No.174	1
	7		Divisional Yukon Pack competition held. Won by 8th Lincolns and 63rd T.M.Bty. (Tie)	
	8		Divisional Transport Competion. No events. Won by 63rd Inf. Bde.	
	9		Baths and general cleaning up.	
	10		Brigade moved to LOGRE. Div. Order No.148. Brigade Order No. 175.	2 & 3
KEMMEL			Brigade moved to BOIS Area. Headquarters at KEMMEL CHATEAU. Bde.Order No. 177	4
	11		37th Division took over line from 19th Division.	
			Brig. Gen. E.L.CHALLONER, D.S.O.,proceeded to ENGLAND for Machine Gun Course at GRANTHAM. During his absence, Lt-Col. H.S.C.RICHARDSON, 8th Somerset L.I. commanded the Brigade.	
			Daily working parties supplied by the Brigade. 500 in number.	
	11/12		63rd M.G.Coy. (less 2 sections) relieved the 247th M.G.Coy. (less 2 sections). Bde.Order No.176	5
	12		Working parties.	
	13		do	
	14		do Captain W.L.BRODIE, V.C.,M.C.,Brigade Major, returned from leave	
	15		do	
	16		do	
LA CLYTTE	17		Brigade moved into the Reserve Brigade Area. Div.Order No.150. Bde. Order No.179 and amendt.	6 & 7
	18		Training in Reserve Area	
	19		G.O.C. returned from Machine Gun Course GRANTHAM	
	20		Training and working on Camps	
	21		do	
	22		do	
	23		do	
	24		do	
	25		63rd Brigade less M.G.Coy, relieved the 111th Inf. Bde. in the line. Div Order No.151	8
			Bde. Order No. 180	9

(CONTINUED)

Army Form C. 2118.

WAR DIARY
or
INTELLIGENCE SUMMARY.

(Erase heading not required.)

Instructions regarding War Diaries and Intelligence Summaries are contained in F.S. Regs., Part II. and the Staff Manual respectively. Title pages will be prepared in manuscript.

Place	Date	Hour	Summary of Events and Information	Remarks and references to Appendices
TRENCHES	NOV.26th,1917		(CONTINUED)	
	27		At 10.0 am the G.O.C.63rd Inf. Bde. assumed the Command of the Line. Situation quiet.	
	28		Situation quiet. At about 10.pm. a joint post manned by 8th Somerset L.I. and 4th Middlesex Regt. was raided by the enemy. 1 N.C.O. and 4 men of 8th Som.L.I. and 1 man 4th Mdlx. Regt. being reported missing.	
	29		Situation quiet.	
	30		About 5.30 am, a post manned by the 8th Somerset L.I. and with 2 Machine Guns of the 111th Machine Gun Company was raided. Fire was opened on the enemy who retired. Three men of 8th Som. L.I. and three men of M.G.Coy. were wounded by bombs.	

N Cullum
Brigadier General,
Commdg. 63rd. Inf.Brigade.

NOMINAL ROLL OF OFFICERS

63rd Infantry Brigade Headquarters.

Brigadier General E.L.CHALLENOR, D.S.O.   Commanding
    (Leicestershire Regiment)

Captain W.L.BRODIE, V.C., M.C.   Brigade Major.
    (Highland Light Infantry)

Captain F.M.GILLMORE   Staff Captain.
    (Royal Fusiliers)

Lieut. F.G.ADLAM   Intelligence
    (8th Somerset L.I.)   Officer

Lieut. W.J.COOKSON, R.E., M.C.   Signal Officer.

Baron H. de COURTOIS   Interpreter.

NOMINAL ROLL OF OFFICERS.

8th Battalion, The Lincolnshire Regiment.

Rank	Name	Present Employment	How Trained	Embarked
Lt.-Col.	Hon. R.T.ST.JOHN	Commanding		
Major	Phelips R.M.	2nd in command		
Captain	Waugh F.A., M.C.		Bombing	19.6.16
"	Latham F.W.	Coy. Comdr.		7.4.17
"	Moss W.	Coy. Comdr.		19.4.17
"	Wiggins A.B.	Coy. Comdr.	29.6.1	29.6.17
"	Hansell F.J.	Coy. Comdr.	Lewis Gun	30.1.17
"	Rowcroft M.	Adjutant		11.9.15
"	Hine S.T.	Course	Signalling	25.6.16
"	Billiat J.J.	Att. 63rd Bde. HQ		26.4.17
Lieut.	Christie E.J.A.	A/Adjutant		2.8.17
"	Williams J.R., M.C.	Transport Officer		17.6.15
"	White A.	Intelligence Off.	Bombing, Sniping Lewis Gun	27.7.16
2nd Lieut.	Askey C.H.L.	Attd. 63rd Bde. Schl.	Lewis Gun	21.5.17
" "	McDonnel J.R.	37th Div. Wing, IX Corps Reinf't Camp		2.6.17
" "	Draper P.	Plat. Comdr.		1.8.17
" "	Peadon P.H.	Plat. Comdr.		12.10.17
" "	Mills F.	Course		17.10.17
" "	Woollatt F.L.	Plat. Comdr.		12.10.17
" "	Plant J.S.	Plat. Comdr.		17.10.17
" "	Anker A.G.	Plat. Comdr.		27.6.17
" "	Hamilton C.G.H.	Signal Officer		6.10.17
" "	Owen E.J.	Bombing Officer	Bombing	12.10.17
" "	Wilcockson R.R.	Course		11.10.17
" "	Jones G.P.			17.10.17
" "	Brown F.	Att. 63rd T.M.B.		17.10.17
" "	Beales F.C.	153 Fd.Co. R.E.		21.5.17
" "	Sutcliffe J.G.	Sub-Area Commdt.		8.5.17
" "	Mitchell A.T.	Course	Lewis Gun	21.8.17
" "	Watson J.	Plat. Comdr.	P.& B.T.	22.6.17
" "	Tunney J.	Plat. Comdr.		28.6.17
" "	Moody H.F.	Plat. Comdr.		20.8.17
" "	Smalley H.	Course		17.10.17
" "	Gray J.H.	Plat. Comdr.		12.10.17
" "	Lowe C.	Course		17.10.17
" "	Bousfield W.R.	Course		17.10.17
" "	Naylor T.	Plat. Comdr.		17.10.17
" "	Wood R.H.	Plat. Comdr.		29.10.17
" "	Hartley R.W.	Plat. Comdr.		28.10.17
Lieut.	Taylor F.	Quartermaster	✗✗.∅.✗	11.9.15
Capt.	Thomas G.	Medical Officer		
Capt. Rev.	Hardy T.B., D.S.O., M.C., C.F.	Chaplain		

NOMINAL ROLL OF OFFICERS.

8th Battalion, Somerset Light Infantry.

Rank	Name	Present Employment	How Trained	Embarked
Lt.-Col.	Richardson H.S.C.	Commanding		3.5.17
Major	Hardyman J.H.M., MC	2nd in Command	Staff duties	24.2.17
Captain	Baker H.G., MC	Coy. Comdr.	Signalling & 2nd Army School	8.9.16
"	Morgan A.P.	Att. P.of.W.Coy.	Bombing & General Course	14.7.17
"	White L.J.H.	Coy. Comdr.	M.G., L.G. Bombing Musketry	8.5.17
"	Crees N.H.	Coy. Comdr.	Bombing	11.8.17
"	Hagon P.C.	Adjutant	P & B.T.	11.7.16
Lieut.	Pike H.	Bde. Transport Off.	Transport	10.9.15
"	Cooksley F.R., MC	IX Corps Reinf't Camp	General Course	10.12.16
"	Pring H.O.	A/Adjutant		15.2.17
"	Cuningham H.J.	Plat. Comdr.		26.7.17
"	Adlam F.G.	63rd Bde. H.Q.	Trench Warfare	26.12.15
"	Willatt V.G.	Bde. Signal School	Signalling	20.7.16
"	Plant V.L.	Musketry Off.	Musketry	26.7.17
"	Cox D.H.	Bombing Offr.	Bombing	16.6.17
"	Bennett P.H.R.	Plat. Comdr.	General Course	26.7.17
2nd Lieut.	Bodey L.C.	Plat. Comdr.	General Course	2.5.17
"	Pople H.K., MC	Coy. Comdr.	L.G., Musketry	18.6.17
"	Pickard F.J.	Plat. Comdr.	Musketry, IX Corps School	14.7.17
"	Radford J.A.	Plat. Comdr.	Gas Course	26.7.17
"	Ward W.L.	Plat. Comdr.	General Course, IX Corps School, Bombing	5.8.17
"	Madden C.H.	Plat. Comdr.	M.G., L.G., Gas	31.7.17
"	Austin H.K.	Sick	Bombing	11.8.17
"	Stone H.G.	Signal Officer	Signalling	11.8.17
"	Hearder G.H.	Plat. Comdr.	Gen. Course, IX Corps School	11.8.17
"	Pfaff E.	Transport Off.	Transport	11.8.17
"	Deeming W.	Plat. Comdr.	Intelligence Crse	
"	Hucker W.T.	Plat. Comdr.		9.11.17
Lieut.	Schooling J.J.	Quartermaster		10.9.15
Captain	Taunton T.	Medical Officer		

NOMINAL ROLL OF OFFICERS.

10th Battalion, The York & Lancaster Regiment.

Rank	Name	Present Employment	How Trained	Embarked
Lt.-Col.	Ostle H.K.E. MC	Commanding	Chelsea & Senior Officers Course. Staff Course	2.10.17
Major	Boss J.G., M.	Bde. School	Bombing, Musketry	2.5.17
Captain	White R.C.	Coy. Comdr.	Musketry, General	25.6.17
"	Robinson A.R.	Coy. Comdr.	L.G., General	4.10.16
"	Wilkinson R.M.	Sick	Bombing, General	5.10.15
"	Willis C.H.S.	Adjutant	General, Senior Officers Course	2.10.17
"	Parry W.	Coy. Comdr.	Bombing, Gas, Gen.	16.4.17
Lieut.	Ayres F.	Coy. Comdr.	M.G., L.G., Gen. Bombing	10.11.15
"	Dixon C.B.	Course	Tactics, General	14.8.17
"	Mitchell R.J.	152 Fd. Co. RE	MG and LG	10.11.15
"	Magee J.F.	Plat. Comdr.		7.11.17
2nd Lieut.	Walne H.A., MC	Transport Offr.	Transport, Gas	16.9.16
"	Woodmansey K.G.	Bde. School	Lewis Gun	15.12.16
"	Thompson Horsfall J.R.	Town Major LA CLYTTE	Bombing, General	15.12.16
"	Hughes H.D.	Signalling Offr.	Signalling	16.4.17
"	Firrest R.A.	Intelligence Offr.		16.4.17
"	Marshall J.W.H.	Plat. Comdr.	Signalling, Gas	2.6.17
"	Lea W.G.	Plat. Comdr.	L.G., General	12.6.17
"	Kaplan I.	Course	T.M., Bombing	16.4.17
"	Byrne J.	Course	M.G., Musketry	28.2.17
"	Holt W.L.	Leave	General	11.5.17
"	Cameron H.	Bombing Offr.	Bombing	17.4.17
"	Lyons F.J.W.	Plat. Comdr.	Lewis Gun	19.8.17
"	Stops T.S.	Plat. Comdr.		20.10.17
"	Mansfield H.	Course		20.10.17
"	Stears S.G.	Plat. Comdr.	xxxxxxx	11.10.17
"	Moorhouse S.H.	Bde. School	xx	11.10.17
"	Mills H.	Plat. Comdr.		20.10.17
"	Hastings W.H.	Course	xxxxxxx	21.10.17
"	Brierley S.	Plat. Comdr.	Lewis Gun	20.10.17
"	Ranson H.S.	Plat. Comdr.	xxxxx.	20.10.17
"	Darricott H.H.	Plat. Comdr.		20.10.17
"	Wright C.H.	Employed Forward Area		4.11.17
"	Nolan B.	Plat. Comdr.		4.11.17
"	Sedgwick L.E.S.	Plat. Comdr.	xxxxxxx	4.11.17
Lieut.	Jamieson A.	Quartermaster		31.10.16
Lieut.	Scott W.F.	Medical Officer		9.9.17
Captain	Thomas H.G., C.F.	Chaplain.		

NOMINAL ROLLS OF OFFICERS.

63rd Company, Machine Gun Corps.

Rank	Name	Present Employment	Embarked
Major	Rideal J.G.E., DSO	Commanding	30.7.17
Lieut.	Thomson T	A/2nd in command	4.8.17
Lieut.	Hartley I.C.	Transport Officer	1.8.16
Lieut.	Denning F.	Section Officer	13.5.17
2nd Lieut.	MacLean W.S.	Section Officer	9.4.17
2nd Lieut.	Laughton F.	Section Officer	23.4.17
2nd Lieut.	Weatherill T.H.	Section Officer	9.8.17
2nd Lieut.	Faulkner R.A.		26.9.17
2nd Lieut.	Thornton G.H.		22.10.17
2nd Lieut.	Forrest W.		10.10.17

63rd Trench Mortar Battery

Rank	Name	Present Employment	Embarked
Captain	Akerman J.P.	Commanding	8.9.15
Lieut.	Harris M.W.S.		28.5.16
2nd Lieut.	Gaunt B.W.		13.12.16
2nd Lieut.	Brown F.		17.10.17

NOMINAL ROLL OF OFFICERS.

4th Battalion, The Middlesex Regiment.

Rank	Name	Present Employment	How Trained	Embarked.
Lt.-Col.	Hanley H.A.O. MC	Commanding		4.11.14
Lt.-Col.	Bridgman G.S.	Base (Sick)		25.4.17
Major	Hay C.R.	Cdg. 63rd Bde. School		28.6.17
Captain	Newman B.R.	A/2nd in Command		28.4.17
"	Smith P.W. MC	Coy. Comdr.	13.7.	13.7.16
"	Mirams S.	A/Adjutant		5.6.16
"	Scholefield F.W.	Intelligence Off.	Sniping	15.7.16
"	Jamieson J.P.	Coy. Comdr.	Lewis Gun	27.4.17
"	Fenn E.A.H.	Coy. Comdr.	2nd Army School	13.7.16
Lieut.	Mitchell A.G.	Bombing Officer	Bombing	13.7.16
"	Bowser H.F.	Instr. IX Corps Schl.	Sniping	1.2.15
"	Moryoseph E.C.	Plat. Officer	Lewis Gun	17.9.17
"	Odling H.R.	A/Adjt. Bde. School	Signalling	19.4.17
"	Taylor R.E.	Att. 37th Div. HQ		29.5.16
"	Irwin R.F.T.	Asst. Signal Offr.	L.G., Signalling	17.5.16
"	Martin O.N.	Div. Salvage Offr.	Lewis Gun	13.7.16
"	Andreae L.W.	Coy. Comdr.	Trench Warfare	12.6.15
"	Williams R.G.	Plat. Officer.	IX Corps School	15.7.16
"	Whitlock H.S.	Plat. Officer	IX Corps School	6.9.16
"	Hodgson J.H.	Transport Officer	Bombing	28.4.16
2nd Lieut.	Sutherland G.S.	Signal Officer	Signalling	4.5.15
"	Lyal J.C., MC	Plat. Officer	Lewis Gun	12.12.16
"	De Val T.	Plat. Officer	9th Corps School	10.5.17
"	Monk H.M.	Sick	R.E.	4.12.16
"	Steele P.H.	Plat. Officer	Signalling	24.2.17
"	Halley K.B.	Plat. Officer		30.7.17
"	Bakchouse H.F.	Plat. Officer	Trench Mortar	21.4.16
"	Klaiber A.J.	No. 2 Can.Tun.Coy.		11.8.17
"	Yates A.S.	Instr. Bde. School	Bombing	11.8.17
"	Andrews A.G.	Lewis Gun Offr.	Lewis Gun	11.8.17
"	Chaundy H.M.	Plat. Officer	Stokes Mortar	11.8.17
"	Felgate H.	Sick	IX Corps School	11.8.17
"	Elmore E.	Plat. Officer	IX Corps School	17.9.17
"	Stuart R.A.K.	Plat. Officer	2nd Army School	23.9.17
"	Bloy H.A.	Plat. Officer		9.11.17
"	F.F. Marshall	Plat. Officer		9.11.17
"	Millican R.I.	Plat. Officer		9.11.17
"	Franklin J.	Plat. Officer		19.11.17
"	Pierce G.A.	Plat. Officer		19.11.17
Captain	Amor E.H.	Quartermaster		18.10.15
Captain	T?Martin	Medical Officer		
Captain	Largie W.G., C.F.	Chaplain.		

CASUALTIES DURING NOVEMBER, 1917.

UNIT	IN TRENCHES							OUT OF TRENCHES							Total Casualties in and out of trenches.	SICK			Grand Total	REMARKS
	Officers			O.Ranks			Total	Officers			O.Ranks			Total		Officers	O.Ranks	Total		
	Killed	Wounded	Missing	Killed	Wounded	Missing		Killed	Wounded	Missing	Killed	Wounded	Missing							
8th Lincolns					1		1								1		27	27	28	
8th Somersets						5	5				1			1	6	1ᵃ	66	67	73	a 2/Lt. H.K.Austin
4th Middlesex					1	1	2					4		4	6	4ᵇ	32	36	42	b Lt.Col. G.A.Bridgman
10th York & Lancs.				2	4		6					7		7	13	2ᶜ	41	43	56	2/Lt. D.W.Heath
63rd Machine Gun Coy.					1		1								1	2ᵈ	5	7	8	2/Lt. H.M.Monk
63rd T.M.Battery																	10	10	10	2/Lt. H.Felgate
TOTAL				2	7	6	15				1	11		12	27	9	181	190	217	c Lt. C.P.Sansom

d Lt. B.H.Sutcliffe
Lt. Denning
2/Lt. Thornton G.H.

63rd Infantry Brigade.

REINFORCEMENTS RECEIVED DURING NOV., 1917.

Unit	Officers	Other Ranks	Date
8th Lincolnshire Regt.	-	4	2.11.17
	1 a	2	3.11.17
	1 b	1	5.11.17
	-	8	7.11.17
	-	1	8.11.17
	-	1	12.11.17
	-	1	16.11.17
	1 c	-	19.11.17
	-	14	21.11.17
	3	32	
8th Somerset Light Infantry	1 d	-	16.11.17
	-	19	21.11.17
	1	19	
4th Middlesex Regiment.	-	5	1.11.17
	-	2	3.11.17
	-	1	5.11.17
	-	1	6.11.17
	-	6	7.11.17
	-	1	8.11.17
	-	3	9.11.17
	1 e	1	11.11.17
	-	1	14.11.17
	3 f	-	18.11.17
	-	18	21.11.17
	2 g	-	23.11.17
	1 h	8	26.11.17
	7	47	
--10th York & Lancaster Regt.	-	1	3.11.17
	-	2	4.11.17
	-	6	7.11.17
	-	3	16.11.17
	4 i	-	18.11.17
	-	14	21.11.17
	-	2	26.11.17
	4	28	
63rd Machine Gun Company	-	5	16.11.17

TOTAL REINFORCEMENTS
RECEIVED DURING NOVEMBER, 1917: 15 officers, 131 other ranks.

Explanation over.

EXPLANATION.

a   2nd Lieut. Hartley R.W.   8th Lincolnshire Regt.
b   Major R.M. Phelips   "
c   2nd Lieut. Wood R.H.   "

d   2nd Lieut. Hucker W.T.   8th Somerset Light Infantry

e   Major   Grove White P.   4th Middlesex Regt.
f   2nd Lieut. Bloy W.A.   "
    2nd Lieut. Marshall F.F.   "
    2nd Lieut. Millican R.I.   "
g   2nd Lieut. Franklin J.   "
    2nd Lieut. Pierce G.A.   "
h   Lt.-Col.   Hanley H.A.O., M.C.   "

i   Lieut.   Magee J.F.   10th York & Lancaster Regiment
    2nd Lieut. Wright C.H.   "
    2nd Lieut. Sedgwick L.E.S.   "
    2nd Lieut. Nolan B.

63rd Infantry Brigade.

STRENGTH OF UNITS, NOVEMBER 30TH, 1917.

UNIT	STRENGTH		DETAILS INCLUDED	
	Officers	Other Ranks	Officers	Other Ranks
8th Lincolnshire Regt.	40	547	14	134
8th Somerset L.I.	29	798	6	193
4th Middlesex Regt.	40	644	12	97
10th York & Lancs. Regt.	36	584	9	71
63rd Machine Gun Company	10	172	4	22
63rd T.M. Battery	4	63	-	6
TOTAL	159	2808	45	523

63rd Infantry Brigade

REINFORCEMENTS RECEIVED DURING OCTOBER, 1917.

Unit.	Officers	Other Ranks	Date.
8th Lincolnshire Regiment.		2	4.10.17
		2	7.10.17
		7	8.10.17
		52	9.10.17
		3	10.10.17
		2	14.10.17
	1 a		14.10.17
	4 b		17.10.17
		4	18.10.17
		12	19.10.17
		2	22.10.17
	9 c		22.10.17
		20	24.10.17
	1 d	4	26.10.17
		1	29.10.17
		1	30.10.17
	15	112	
8th Somerset Light Infantry		106	4.10.17
		58	19.10.17
	1 e	6	24.10.17
		4	26.10.17
	1	174	
4th Middlesex Regiment		50	5.10.17
		33	7.10.17
		16	8.10.17
	1 f		13.10.17
		5	19.10.17
		32	24.10.17
		26	26.10.17
		8	29.10.17
	1	170	
10th York & Lancaster Regt.		26	4.10.17
		40	7.10.17
		8	9.10.17
	1 g		11.10.17
	1 h	7	12.10.17
	2 i		16.10.17
	1 j		17.10.17
		3	19.10.17
		1	21.10.17
	6 k	8	24.10.17
	1 l		25.10.17
		2	26.10.17
		1	28.10.17
		3	29.10.17
	12	99	

OVER.

EXPLANATION ATTACHED.

	Officers	Other Ranks	Date
63rd Machine Gun Company	1 m		6.10.17
	1 n		10.10.17
		24	20.10.17
	1 o		28.10.17
	3	24	

Total reinforcements received during October:-

32 Officers, 579 other ranks.

EXPLANATION.

a	2nd Lt.	Hamilton C.G.H.	8th Lincolnshire Regt.
b	"	Owen E.J.	"
	"	Peadon P.H.	"
	"	Gray J.H.	"
	"	Wilcockson R.R.	"
c	"	Mills F.	"
	"	Lowe C.	"
	"	Lockyear H.	"
	"	Woollatt F.L.	"
	"	Jones G.P.	"
	"	Brown F.	"
	"	Bousfield W.R.	"
	"	Smalley H	"
	"	Plant J.S.	"
d	"	Naylor T.	
e	2nd Lt.	Deeming W.	8th Somerset Light Infantry
f	2nd Lt.	Moryoseph E.C.	4th Middlesex Regt.
g	Major	Ostle H.K.E.	10th York & Lancaster Regt.
h	2nd Lt.	Forrest R.A.	"
i	"	Cameron H.	"
	"	Spears S.C.	"
j	"	Moorhouse S.H.	"
k	"	Stops T.S.	"
	"	Mansfield H.	"
	"	Mills H.	"
	"	Brierley S.	"
	"	Ransom H.	"
	"	Darricott H.H.	"
l	Captain	Willis C.H.S.	
m	2nd Lt.	Johnston S.	63rd Machine Gun Company
n	"	Forrest W.	"
o	"	Thornton G.H.	

Original Copy

63rd INFANTRY BRIGADE
WAR DIARY
DECEMBER
1917

Army Form C. 2118.

WAR DIARY

~~INTELLIGENCE SUMMARY~~

(Erase heading not required.)

Instructions regarding War Diaries and Intelligence
Summaries are contained in F. S. Regs., Part II.
and the Staff Manual respectively. Title pages
will be prepared in manuscript.

Place	Date	Hour	Summary of Events and Information	Remarks and references to Appendices
Trenches	Dec. 1st		Situation quiet	
	2nd		Reorganising of shell-hole line commenced, posts being grouped together.	
	3rd		Situation quiet	
	4th		do	
	5th		63rd Bde. relieved in the line by 112th Infantry Brigade. Brigade Order No.181...........1 At 9.50 am relief reported complete and G.O.C. 112th Inf. Bde assumed command of the line.	
ENFORDEN CAMP	6th		Working parties furnished for night work	
	7th		Large day and night working parties furnished for Corps. Improvement of line etc. G.O.C. 63rd Infantry Brigade proceeded to ENGLAND on one months leave. Lt-Col. H.S.C.RICHARDSON 8th Somerset L.I. assumed temporary command of the Brigade	
	8th		Large working parties found.	
	9th		do	
	10th		do Captain W.L.BRODIE, V.C.,M.C. Brigade Major, left the Brigade to take Command of the 2nd/10th Liverpool Scottish Regiment. Lieut. F.G.ADLAM carried out the duties of Brigade Major.	
	11th		Large Working parties found.	
	12th		do Captain R.D.CROSBY, M.C., Lincolnshire Regiment, reported for attachment to Brigade Headquarters as Staff learner.	
	13th		Working parties. Battalions moved to Reserve Areas in relief of 111th Infantry Brigade Brigade Order No.182......2	
LA CLYTTE	14th		do Brigade H.Q. moved to Reserve Area. Captain C.J.de B.SHERINGHAM, Cameron Highlanders, took over the duties of Brigade Major.	
	15th		Working Parties.	
	16th		Small working parties and training. Improvement of camps	
	17th		do	
	18th		Training. Attack demonstration at Brigade School.	
	19th		do	
	20th		do	
	21st		Brigade relieved the 111th Infantry Brigade in the line Brigade Order No.183...........3	

(CONTINUED)

Army Form C. 2118.

WAR DIARY
or
INTELLIGENCE SUMMARY.
(Erase heading not required.)

Instructions regarding War Diaries and Intelligence Summaries are contained in F. S. Regs., Part II. and the Staff Manual respectively. Title pages will be prepared in manuscript.

Place	Date	Hour	Summary of Events and Information	Remarks and references to Appendices
			(CONTINUED)	
Trenches	Dec. 22nd		Brigade H.Q. moved to line. Lt-Col. H.S.C.RICHARDSON, 8th Somerset L.I. assumed command of the line at 10.0 am.	
	23rd		Situation quiet. 8th Somerset L.I. captured 1 prisoner.(3rd Coy. 1st.Bn. 3rd Bav. R.I.R.) in O.6.c. (HOLLEBEKE)	
	24th		Situation quiet. Enemy attempted a raid on 4th Middlesex Regiment and were driven off.	
	25th		do Heavy fall of snow.	
	26th		do	
	27th		do Practice alarm at 4.0 pm	
	28th		do	
	29th		do Brigade relieved by 112th Infantry Brigade, and moved to ENFORDEN CAMP Brigade Order No. 184.....4	
ENFORDEN Camp	30th		Baths	
	31st		Working parties.	

[signature]
Lieutenant Colonel,
Comdg, 63rd Infantry Brigade.

NOMINAL ROLL OF OFFICERS

8TH Battalion, The Lincolnshire Regiment.

Rank and Name		Present Employment	How Trained	Arrived
Lt.-Col.	The Hon. R.T.St.John	Commanding		
Major	Phelips R.M.	2nd in command		
Captain	Waugh F.A., M.C.		Bombing	19.6.16
"	Latham F.W.	Coy. Comdr		7.4.17
A/Capt.	Moss W.	Coy. Comdr		19.4.17
"	Wiggins A.B.		Bombing	19.6.17
"	Hansell F.J.	On Course	Lewis Gun	30.1.17
Captain	Rowcroft M.G.	Adjutant		11.9.15
A/Capt.	Hine S.T.		Signalling	25.6.16
Lieut.	Christie E.J.A.	Asst. Adjt.		2.8.17
"	Williams J.R., MC	Transport Officer		17.6.15
"	White A.	On Course	Bombing, L.G.	27.7.16
"	Gooseman F.L.	Plat. Comdr.		17.12.17
2/Lieut.	Askey C.H.L.	On leave	L.G.	21.5.17
"	McDonnell J.R.	IX Corps School		2.6.17
"	Draper P.	On Course		1.8.17
"	Peadon P.A.	On Course		12.10.17
"	Mills F.	Plat. Comdr.		17.10.17
"	Woollatt F.L.	Asst. Transport Off.		12.10.17
"	Plant J.S.	Plat. Comdr.		17.10.17
"	Anker A.G.	Plat. Comdr.		27.6.17
"	Hamilton C.G.H.	Signal Officer	Signalling	6.10.17
"	Owen E.J.	Plat. Comdr.	Bombing	10.12.17
"	Jones F.P.	On Course		17.10.17
"	Brown F.	Attd. T.M.B.		17.10.17
"	Beales F.C.	Attd. 152 Fd. Co. RE		21.5.17
"	Sutcliffe J.G.	Sub-area Comdt.		8.5.17
"	Mitchell A.T.	Plat. Comdr.	L.G.	21.8.17
"	Watson J.	Plat. Comdr.	P.T. & B.F.	22.6.17
"	Tunney J.	Plat. Comdr.		28.6.17
"	Moody H.E.	Plat. Comdr.		28.8.17
"	Smalley H.	Plat. Comdr.		17.10.17
"	Gray J.H.	On Course		12.10.17
"	Lowe C.	On Course		17.10.17
"	Bousfield W.R.	Plat. Comdr.		17.10.17
"	Naylor T.	Plat. Comdr.		17.10.17
"	Wood R.H.	Plat. Comdr.		29.10.17
"	Ingham F.T.	Plat. Comdr.		17.12.17
Lieut.	Taylor F.	Quartermaster		11.9.15
Captain	Thomas, R.A.M.C.	Medical Officer		

63rd Infantry Brigade Headquarters.

Brigadier-General E.L.Challenor, C.M.G., D.S.O.   Commanding
  (Leicestershire Regiment)

Captain C.J. de B. Sheringham   Brigade Major
  (Cameron Highlanders)

Captain F. MacS. Gillmore   Staff Captain
  (Royal Fusiliers)

Lieut. F.G. Adlam   Intelligence Officer
  (8th Somerset Light Infantry)

Baron H. De Courtois   Interpreter

NOMINAL ROLL OF OFFICERS.

8th Battalion, The Somerset Light Infantry.

Rank and Name		Present Employment	How Trained	Arrived
Lt.-Col.	Richardson H.S.C.	Commanding 63 Bde.		3.5.17
Lt.-Col.	Henkyns S.S.	Commanding		
Major	Hardyman J.H.M. MC	37th Divn.	Staff duties	24.2.17
Captain	Baker H.G., MC	A/2nd in command	Signalling	8.9.16
"	Morgan A.P.	Coy. Comdr.	Bombing, General	14.7.17
"	White L.J.H.	Coy. Comdr.	M.G., L.G. Bombing Musketry	8.5.17
"	Crees N.H.	Coy. Comdr.	Bombing	11.8.17
"	Peard C.J.	Coy. Comdr.		17.12.17
"	Hagon P.C.	Adjutant	P.F. & B.T.	11.7.16
Lieut.	Pike H.	Brigade Transport Off.	Transport duties	10.9.15
"	Cooksley F.R. MC	IX Corps Reinforcement Camp	General	10.12.16
"	Pring H.O.	Asst. Adjutant		15.2.17
"	Cunningham H.J.	Plat. Comdr.	Musketry	26.7.17
"	Adlam F.G.	Att. 63rd Inf. Bde. HQ	Trench Warfare	26.12.15
"	Willatt V.G.	Att. Bde. HQ	Sniping, Signals	20.7.16
"	Plant V.L.	Musketry Offr.	Musketry	26.7.17
"	Cox D.H.	63rd Bde. School	Bombing	16.6.17
"	Bennett P.H.R.	Plat. Comdr.	General	26.7.17
2/Lieut.	Bodey L.C.	Plat. Comdr.	General	2.5.17
"	H.K. POPLE	A/Coy. do	Lewis Gun	8.6.17
"	F.H. PICKARD	Plat. Comdr.	Gas	14.7.17
"	J.A. RADFORD	do do	Gas	26.7.17
"	C.H. MADDEN	do do	Machine Gun	31.7.17
"	H.G. STONE	Signal Officer	Signalling	11.8.17
"	G.H. HEARDER	Plat. Comdr.	General	do
"	E. PFAFF	Transport	Transport	do
"	W. DEEMING	Plat. Comdr	Intelligence	24.10.17
Lieut	H.K. AUSTIN	do	Bombing	do
2/Lieut	J.P. HEWITT	do		15.12.17
"	R.H. BUTTON	do		do
Lt.& Qr.M	J.J. SCHOOLING	Qr.Mr.		10.9.15
Lieut.	S.R. MAXEINER	M.O.R.C.		

NOMINAL ROLL OF OFFICERS

4th Battalion, The Middlesex Regiment.

Rank and Name		Present Employment	How Trained	Arrived
Lt.-Col.	Hanley H.A.O., MC	Commanding		4.11.14
Major	Hay C.R.	IX Corps School		28.6.17
Major	Grove White P.	Second in Command	Sen. Offrs. Crse	26.10.17
Captain	Newman B.R.	Company Commander		28.4.17
"	Smith P.W., MC	" "		13.7.16
"	Mirams S.	Acting Adjutant		5.6.16
"	Scholefield F.W.	On Course	Sniping	15.7.16
"	Jamieson J.P.	Company Commander	Lewis Gun	27.4.17
"	E.A.H. Fenn			13.7.16
Lieut.	Mitchell A.G.	Bombing Officer		13.7.16
"	Moorat F.F.	Plat. Officer	Gas	3.12.17
"	Bowser H.F.	IX Corps School	Sniping	1.2.16
"	Moryoseph E.C.	Divnl. Road Company		17.9.17
"	Odling H.R.	Brigade School	Signalling	19.4.17
"	Taylor R.E.	Attd. 37th Divn.	Staff duties	29.5.16
"	Irwin R.F.T.	Signalling Officer	Signalling	17.5.16
"	Martin O.N.	Divnl. Salvage Offr.		13.7.16
"	Andreae L.W.	IX Corps School	Light T.M.	12.6.15
"	Whitlock H.S.	Sick	Transport	6.9.16
"	Hodgson J.H.	Transport Officer	Transport	38.4.16
"	Sutherland G.S.	On Course		4.5.15
2/Lieut.	Lyal J.C., M.C.	Plat. Comdr.	Lewis Gun	12.12.16
"	De. Val T.	" "		10.5.17
"	Viner G.N.	Asst. Adjutant		
"	Backhouse H.F.	On leave	T.M.	21.4.16
"	Klaiber A.J.	On leave		11.8.17
"	Yates A.S.	On leave	Bombing	11.8.17
"	Andrews A.G.	On leave	Lewis Gun	11.8.17
"	Chaundy H.M.	On leave	Power Buzzer	11.8.17
"	Elmore E.	Plat. Commander		17.9.17
"	Stuart R.A.K.	" "	2nd Army School	23.9.17
"	Bloy W.A.	On Course		9.11.17
"	Marshall F.F.	Plat. Commander		9.11.17
"	Millican R.I.	On Course		9.11.17
"	Selfe J.L.	Plat. Commander		2.12.17
"	Elliott F.W.	" "		2.12.17
"	Benda P.	Plat. Officer		19.12.17
"	Pierce G.A.	" "		19.11.17
Captain	Douglas P.S., C.F.	Chaplain		
Captain	Amor E.H.	Quartermaster		

NOMINAL ROLL OF OFFICERS

10th Battalion, The York & Lancaster Regiment.

Rank and Name	Employment
Lt.-Col. Ostle H.K.E., MC	Commanding
Major Boss J.G.E.	Attd. Brigade School
Captain Willis C.F.	Adjutant
" Robinson A.R.	Company Commander
" Wilkinson K.R.M.	On leave
" White R.C.	On leave
Lieut. Magee J.F.	
" Kaye G.H.C.	On Course
" Dixon C.B.	Attd. 152nd Fd. Co. RE
" Mitchell R.J.	Sick
" Ayres F.	Company Commander
2/Lieut. Walne H.A., MC	On leave
" Hughes D.H.	Signalling Officer
" Forrest R.A.	Intelligence Officer
" Marshall J.W.H.	Assistant Adjutant
" Lea W.G.	On leave
" Kaplan I.	
" Byrne J.	Attd. Brigade School
" Mansfield H.	
" Stops T.S.	
" Forster T.	
" Goad A.E.	
" Hastings W.B.	
" Mills A.	
" Wild J.	
" Hall A.	
" Parry W.	Company Commander
" Cameron H.	Company Commander
" Lyons F.J.W.	On Course
" Moorhouse S.A.	
" Brierley S.	
" Nolan B.	On Course
" Dickinson C.G.	
" Darricott H.H.	On Course
" Wright C.H.	Employed in Forward Area
" Ranson H.S.	
" Pugh H.H.	Course of Instruction
" Merrall E.	
" Whitehead M.J.	
" Woodmansey K.G.	Attd. Brigade School
" Horsfall J.R.	Town Major, LA CLYTTE
" Sedgwick L.E.S.	Transport Officer.

NOMINAL ROLL OF OFFICERS.

63rd Company, Machine Gun Corps.

Rank and Name		How employed	Arrived
Major	Rideal J.G.E. D.S.O.	Commanding, Acting D.M.G.O.	30.7.17
Lieut.	Hartley I.C.		~~XX.X.XX~~ 1.7.16
Lieut.	Thomson T.	Section Officer	4.8.17
Lieut.	Chater S.W., M.C.	Second in command A/C.O.	14.2.17
Lieut.	Beaumont W.E. M.C.		-
2/Lieut.	Maclean W.S	Section Officer	9.4.17
"	Laughton F.	Sub section officer	23.4.17
"	Weatherill T.H.	Section Officer	9.8.17
"	Faulkner R.A.	Section Officer	26.9.17
"	Forrest W.	Sub-section officer	10.10.17
"	Oliver H.D.	Sub-section Officer	8.3.17
"	Thornton G.H.	Wounded - -	24.12.17

63rd Trench Mortar Battery.

Rank	Name	How employed	Arrived
Captain	Akerman J.P.	Commanding	8.9.15
Lieut.	Harris M.W.S.		28.5.16
2/Lieut.	Gaunt B.W.		13.12.16
"	Brown F.		17.10.17
"	Stears S.G.		11.10.17

CASUALTIES DURING DECEMBER, 1917.

	IN TRENCHES						OUT OF TRENCHES						TOTAL CASUALTIES IN AND OUT OF TRENCHES	SICK			GRAND TOTAL	REMARKS
	Officers			Other Rks			Officers			Other Rks				Officers	O.R.	Total		
	Killed	Wounded	Missing	Killed	Wounded	Missing	Total	Killed	Wounded	Missing	Killed	Wounded	Missing	Total					
8th Lincolnshire Regt.				2	16		18								18	5	20	25	43
6th Somerset L.I.				2	5		9								9		121	121	130
4th Middlesex Regt.		3		3	10		16								16	4	52	56	72
10th York & Lanc. Regt.	1	1		5	7		13								13	—	12	12	25
63rd Machine Gun Coy.					1		2								2		5	5	7
65rd Trench Mortar Battery				1			1								1		27	27	28
TOTAL	3	4		13	39		59								59	9	237	246	305

Reinforcements received during DECEMBER 1917

8th Lincoln Regt,

			Joined
2 Lt. F.T.INGHAM	O.R.	1.	17.12.17
	;	1	1.12.17
Lt. GOOSEMAN F.L.			17.12.17
	;	72	10.12.17
	,	48	18.12.17
Capt. G.L.WATKINS (RAMC)			19.12.17
	,	32	20.12.17
	,	32	30.12.17.

8th Somerset L.I.

	O.R.	10	10.12.17.
	,	5	18.12.17
	,	10	20.12.17
Capt.C.J.PEARD	,	3)	
2/Lt. R.H.BUTTON		)	30.12.17
; J.P.HEWITT		)	

4th Middlesex Regt.

Major. P.GROVE-WHITE			3.12.17
Lieut. F.F.MOORAT			9.12.17
2 Lt. J.L.SELFE			7.12.17
2 Lt. F.W.ELLIOTT			7.12.17
	O.R.	7	10.12.17
2 Lt. G.N.VINER			12.12.17
	;	11	18.12.17
	,	26	20.12.17
2 Lt. P.BENDA			30.12.17

10th York & Lancs Regt,

	O.R.	4	1.12.17
	;	2	8.12.17
Lieut.G.H.L.KAYE	;		6.12.17
2 Lt. J.WILD			9.12.17
	;	1	10.12.17
2.Lt. T.FORSTER			9.12.17
; A.N.PUGH			do
; G.C.DICKINSON			do
; A.E.GOAD			do
; E.MERRALL			do
	O.R.	73	10.12.17
; M.J.WHITEHEAD			11.12.17
; A.HALL			do
	O.R.	7	14.12.17
	;	6	20.12.17
Lieut BRIGGS			21.12.17
	O.R.	1	26.12.17
	;	21	30.12.17

63rd Machine Gun Coy.

Lieut. S.W.CHATER M.C.	O.R.	1.	3.12.17
2.Lt. H.D.OLIVER			6.12.17
	;	4	7.12.17
	;	2	9.12.17
	;	3	13.12.17
	;	1	23.12.17
Lieut W.E.BEAUMONT			30.12.17

63rd Trench Mortar Bty

2.Lt.S.G. STEARS	O.R.	1	12.12.17
	;	1	15.12.17

Grand Total   Officers 26   Other Ranks 386

STRENGTH OF BATTALIONS 31st. DECEMBER, 1917

UNIT	OFFICERS	OTHER RANKS	DETAILS OFFICERS	DETAILS OTHER RANKS
8th Lincoln Regt	39	701	18	162
8th Somerset L.I.	30	719	10	219
4th Middlesex Regt	38	636	14	137
10th York & Lancaster Regt.	44	654	13	93
63rd Machine Gun Coy	12	172	4	23
63rd Trench Mortar Bty.	5	58	1	7
	168	2930	60	641

Original Copy

63rd Infantry Brigade
War Diary
January
1918

Army Form C. 2118.

WAR DIARY
or
INTELLIGENCE SUMMARY
(Erase heading not required.)

Instructions regarding War Diaries and Intelligence Summaries are contained in F. S. Regs., Part II. and the Staff Manual respectively. Title pages will be prepared in manuscript.

Place	Date	Hour	Summary of Events and Information	Remarks and references to Appendices
ENFORDEN CAMP	1.1.1918		Large working parties	Fine and cold
	2nd.		do	do
	3rd		do	do
	4th		do	Snow
LA CLYTTE	5th		Brigade Major proceeded to CAMIERS on Course Brigade Order No.185............	do 1
	6th		Brigade moved to LA CLYTTE (Reserve Area)	do
	7th		Working parties and training Brigade Major returned from Course.	do
			Brigade Commander returned from one months leave. Thaw followed by snow.	
	8th		Brigade Commander and Brigade Major proceeded to 6th Squadron, R.F.C. for special course.	
	9th		Working parties and training	
	10th		Large wiring party supplied to wire the front line (350 men)	
	11th		Brigade relieved by 4th Australian Brigade and moved to ZEVECOTEN Area for work in Army Battle Zone under the 20th Division. Brigade Order No. 186 & 187 and amendment............2 & 3	
ZEVECOTEN	12th		Working parties	
	13th		Brigade Commander and Brigade Major returned from Special Squadron R.F.C. Fine. Order No.188.....4	
	14th		Working parties	Fine
	15th		- do -	Rain
	16th		Somerset L.I. and York & Lancaster moved from BURGOMASTER FARM and DICKEBUSCH to camps shewn in Order No. 188. Working parties supplied.	Fine
	17th		Working parties	Wet
	18th		- do -	Fair
	19th		- do -	do
	20th		- do - Transport moved to STRAZEELE en route for Corps Reserve Area.	
BLARINGHEM AREA	21st		Brigade moved by train to Corps Reserve Area, BLARINGHEM. Brigade H.Q. at C.4.a.9.4. Sheet 36 A N.W. Brigade Order No. 189 and No.6478 5	
C.0.a.9,4,	22nd		G.O.C. visited the Battalions, Machine Gun Coy. and Trench Mortar Battery. Bathing. Fine.	
	23rd		Baths and inspections within Battalions. Machine Gun Coy and Trench Mortar Bty. moved in accordance with Brigade Order No. 190................................6	
	24th		Baths and inspections within Battalions.	Fine

(CONTINUED)

Army Form C. 2118.

WAR DIARY
INTELLIGENCE SUMMARY.
(Erase heading not required)

Place	Date	Hour	Summary of Events and Information	Remarks and references to Appendices
			(CONTINUED)	
BLARINGHEM AREA C.4.a.9.4.	25.1.1918		Presentation of medals by Fourth Army Commander, General Sir H.S.RAWLINSON to recipients of 37th Division (37 of 63rd Infantry Brigade) for period July 31st to October 4th and half Yearly Honours. Orders issued for Tactical move of Brigade to Forward Area. Brigade No.6428...................	7
	26th		Brigadier inspected the 10th York & Lancaster Regt. and 8th Somerset L.I. The Divisional Commander arrived whilst the inspection was in progress and inspected. Meeting of Recreation Committee to decide the dates etc. for competitions.	
	27th		Brigadier addressed the 8th Somerset L.I. after Church Parade.	
	28th		Divisional Commander inspected the 4th Middlesex Regt., 8th Lincolnshire Regt., and 10th York & Lancaster Regt.	
	29th		Training carried on. Shooting on range commenced. Recreation in afternoon. Brigade Commander selected a site for Contact Aeroplane Scheme.	
	30th		Information received from 37th Division that the 10th.Battalion York & Lancaster Regiment is to be disbanded. Training continued in morning, recreation in afternoon.	
	31st		Ground reconnoitred with Officer of Units for Contact Aeroplane Scheme to be held on February 1st. Brigade Major 37th Divisional Artillery and observer and pilot of 53rd Squadron R.F.C. present. Training continued. Recreation in afternoon.	

E. Challenor.
Brigadier General,
Commdg, 63rd Infantry Brigade.

ORIGINAL COPY.

WAR DIARY

63rd Infantry Brigade

FEBRUARY, 1918

Army Form C. 2118.

WAR DIARY
or
INTELLIGENCE SUMMARY.

(Erase heading not required.)

Instructions regarding War Diaries and Intelligence Summaries are contained in F. S. Regs., Part II. and the Staff Manual respectively. Title pages will be prepared in manuscript.

Place	Date	Hour	Summary of Events and Information	Remarks and references to Appendices
SERCUS Area	Feb. 1		Training and shooting. Aeroplane scheme postponed on account of ground mist.	
	2.		Training and shooting.	
	3.		Church parades.	
	4.		Brigade Commander proceeded to WISQUES for demonstration. 1st round Brigade inter-platoon football played off. Transport turn-out competition - won by 4th Middlesex Regt.	
	5.		Training continued. Brigade Scout competition won by 8th Somerset L.I. and Brigade Driving competition, won by 8th Somerset L.I. Bde. Commander went to demonstration at WISQUES.	
	6.		Contact aeroplane scheme again postponed on account of low clouds. Brigade "Guard Turn Out" Competition, won by 8th Lincolns.	
	7.		Training continued. Signalling competition commenced. Inter-platoon football semi-finals played off.	
	8.		Signalling competition completed. Won by 8th Somerset L.I. Brigade Commander visited 20th Division re relief. Afterwards attended lecture on "Cambrai" by the Army Commander at H.Q., XXII Corps.	
	9.		Trench Mortar Competition held in afternoon, won by section of 4th Middlesex. Lewis Gun Competition held in morning, won by 8th Somerset L.I. Boxing tournament held. Aeroplane scheme again postponed on account of weather. C.Os conference on relief of 20th Division in line.	
	10.		Church Parades. Final of inter-platoon football played off in afternoon, won by 8th Lincolns.	
	11.		Os.C. 8th Lincolns, 8th Somersets and Brigade Intelligence Officer visited 20th Divn. and 61st Infe. Bde. in line to reconnoitre. Brigade Commander and Divnl. Staff attended memorial service in BLARINGHEM Church to "those fallen during the war".	
	12.		Orders received for relief of 20th Division.	
	13.		Brigade Commander and Brigade Major visited 61st Inf. Bde. to discuss relief. 63rd Inf. Bde. Order No. 190 re move to forward area issued. .... 1 Transport of Brigade, and Instructional Cadre and students of Brigade School marched from BLARINGHEM Area, staging the night at STRAZEELE.	1
	14.		Left BLARINGHEM Area as per Order No. 190. Brigade H.Q. re-opened at LA CLYTTE CAMP. Weather fair.	
LA CLYTTE. BEDFORD HOUSE I.26.a.9.3	15		Relieved 61st Inf. Bde. in the line, TOWER HAMLETS - MENIN ROAD Sector. Liaison with right and left established.	
	16		Very active patrolling all along front after dark. Located enemy much nearer our front line N. of MENIN Road than was reported by 61st Inf. Bde. Wire put out along front.	

Army Form C. 2118.

WAR DIARY
or
INTELLIGENCE SUMMARY.
(Erase heading not required.)

Instructions regarding War Diaries and Intelligence Summaries are contained in F. S. Regs., Part II. and the Staff Manual respectively. Title pages will be prepared in manuscript.

Place	Date	Hour	Summary of Events and Information	Remarks and references to Appendices
BEDFORD HOUSE	17		Patrolling carried out on, and posts in enemy line definitely located, both north and south of MENIN Road. Wiring continued. KILLICK Trench continued and trench towards POLDERHOEK system begun.	
	18.		Further definite information obtained of enemy front system. Further wiring and commenced carrying T.M. ammunition on to TOWER HAMLETS Ridge by mules. Brigade Defensive arrangements (Provisional) issued, 63rd Inf. Bde. No. S148.	2
	19		Great patrolling activity and wiring. AMBROSE Trench connected. 63rd Bde. Order No. 191.	3
	20		4th Middlesex Regt. relieved 8th Somerset L.I. in line, who withdrew into support. The Brigade from now onwards will be on a one-battalion front, with one battalion in support in CANADA TUNNELS and 1 battalion in reserve in SCOTTISH WOOD CAMP.	
	21		8th Lincolnshire Regt. relieved by 1st Essex Regt. Upon relief, 8th Lincolns moved into reserve at SCOTTISH WOOD CAMP, H.35.c. A good deal of rain fell. 63rd Inf. Bde. Order No. 192 confirming order No. 191 issued.	4
	22		Order No. 193 issued.	5
	23		Wiring and other work carried on - many stores carried up. 8th Somersets withdrew into reserve and 8th Lincolns moved into support. Good daylight patrol and observation carried out.	
	24		Work and wiring and preparation of T.M. emplacements carried on. Very light night.	
	25th		8th Lincolns moved into front line in relief of 4th Middlesex Regt. who withdrew into Reserve, 8th Somersets moving into support as per 63rd Inf. Bde. Order No. 193. No patrolling done owing to brightness of night. Some gas shelling by enemy.	
	26		Our Stokes Mortars inflicted considerable casualties on an enemy working party which was fired on at night. Deserter to 111th Inf. Bde. reported attack contemplated by enemy on POLDERHOEK Sector on 28th.	
	27		Protective patrols pushed out at night along whole front. 63 rd Bde Order 195 issued	6
	28		Counter preparation 4.15 am - 4.30 am. 5 patrols carried out.	

March 12th 1918

NChalmers

Brigadier General,
Comdg. 63rd Infantry Brigade.

SECRET.   Copy No. 1

63rd Infantry Brigade Order No. 194

Reference Sheet: Feb. 27th 1918.
28, 1:40,000.

1. (a) On the night March 1/2nd, 8th Somerset L.I. will relieve 8th Lincolnshire Regt. in the line; 8th Lincolns will, upon relief, withdraw into Reserve at SCOTTISH WOOD CAMP, N.35.c.

   (b) 4th Middlesex Regt. will move into support about CANADA TUNNELS.

2. The first platoon of 4th Middlesex will pass I.29.a.55.55 (intersection of KNOLL ROAD and MORLAND AVENUE) at 5.45 pm.
   No troops will move forward of the MOUNT SORREL - TORR TOP RIDGE before 6 pm.

3. All details of the above reliefs will be arranged between Commanding Officers concerned.

4. No post, trench or strong point will be vacated until relieved.

5. Completion of reliefs will be notified to this office in B.A.B. Code.

                                          C.R.B. Sheringham
                                              Captain,
                                           Brigade Major,
Issued at 5 pm   63rd Infantry Brigade.

Distribution	Copy No.		Copy No.
War Diary & File	1 - 3	C.R.E.	21
Brigade Staff	4 - 8	B.G.R.A.	22
8th Lincolns	9	111th Inf. Bde.	23
8th Somerset L.I.	10	112th Inf. Bde.	24
4th Middlesex	11	13th Aust. Inf. Bde.	25
63rd Machine Gun Coy.	12	Brigade Gas Officer	26
63rd T.M. Battery	13	Brigade Transport Offr.	27
154th Fd. Co. R.E.	14	Brigade Supply Officer	28
No. 2 Coy. Train	15	37th M.G. Battalion	29
50th Fd. Ambulance	16	Area Commandant,	30
Southern Group, Arty.	17	KRUISSTRAATHOEK Area	
Centre Group, Arty.	18	Brigade School	31
37th Division	19 - 20		

63rd Infantry Brigade No.8615/1.

AMENDMENTS TO 63rd INFANTRY BRIGADE DEFENCE SCHEME

PAGE 6.   Section 5.   ACTION IN CASE OF ATTACK.

    Para. 2 (a). 10th line :- After the word "forward" delete "or back".

PAGE 7.   6th line :- After the word "post" delete "P".

                                                    C.J.de B.Sheringham, Captain.
                                                         Brigade Major.
6.3.18.   63rd Infantry Brigade.

SECRET.   63rd Infantry Brigade No. 8615.

1.   Herewith copy No. 7/0 of 63rd Infantry Brigade
Defence Scheme for the TOWER HAMLETS Subsector.

2.   The map will only be issued to units marked @

3.   Please acknowledge receipt.

                                        Captain,
                                        Brigade Major,
2.3.18   63rd Infantry Brigade.

Distribution.   Copy No.

G.O.C.   1   @
Brigade Major   2   @
Staff Captain   3
8th Linc Lnshire Regt.   4   @
8th Somerset L.I.   5   @
4th Middlesex Regt.   6   @
63rd Machine Gun   7   @
63rd T.M.Battery   8   @
37th Division 'G'   9   @
37th Division 'Q'   10
B.G.R.A.   11   @
C.R.E.   12
111th Infantry Brigade   13
112th Infantry Brigade   14   @
1st Aust. Infantry Brigade   15   @
37th L.G.Battalion   16
Southern Group, Artillery   17   @
 or Diary & File   18 - 20

37th Division.

B. H. Q.

63rd INFANTRY BRIGADE

MARCH 1 9 1 8

List of Appendices follows War Diary.

ORIGINAL COPY.

WAR DIARY

63rd Infantry Brigade

MARCH, 1918

Army Form C. 2118.

WAR DIARY
or
INTELLIGENCE SUMMARY.
(Erase heading not required.)

Instructions regarding War Diaries and Intelligence Summaries are contained in F. S. Regs., Part II. and the Staff Manual respectively. Title pages will be prepared in manuscript.

Place	Date	Hour	Summary of Events and Information	Remarks and references to Appendices
TOWER HAMLETS	March 1		8th Somerset L.I. relieved 8th Lincolnshire Regt. in line, 4th Middlesex Regt. moving into Support as per O. 194.	1
	2		Counter preparation carried out at 21.10 hrs. Defence Scheme issued, 63rd Inf. Bde. No. 8615.	2
	3		Counter preparation shoot at 4.10 am. Shoot by Heavy Artillery on BERRY COTTS at 4.15 pm. Strong enemy patrol approached No. 5 post of our Centre Company and threw two stick grenades. Garrison opened fire with rifles and Lewis guns. Casualties were inflicted but in spite of search, no enemy dead were found.	3
	4		6" Newton T.Ms carried out shoot on defensive works in neighbourhood of GENERAL'S DUGOUT. Order No. 196 issued.	
	5		Relief of 8th Somerset L.I. by 4th Middlesex Regt., 8th Somerset L.I. withdrawing to Support.	
	6		Counter preparation shoot on S.O.S. lines at 1.5 am. Two enemy captured by patrol of 4th Middlesex led by 2/Lt. R.A.K.STUART.	
	7		Counter preparation shoot at 5 am till 5.15 am. Unsuccessful enemy attack astride MENIN ROAD - see special report, 63rd Inf. Bde. No. 8952	4
				A/5 5
				8924 6
	8			
	9	5.30pm	8th Lincolns relieved 4th Middlesex in line, 8th Somersets withdrawing into reserve at SCOTTISH WOOD, Order No. 197. 11 pm Summer Time came into force, clocks being put on to 12 midnight.	7
	10	6 am	Counter preparation shoot on S.O.S. lines.	
	11	5.15 am	and 7.15 pm counter preparation shoots on S.O.S. lines.	
	12	4.45 am	Counter preparation shoot on S.O.S. lines.	
	13		Field Artillery carried out harassing fire on enemy dugouts and tracks. 9.20 pm, Counter preparation on S.O.S. lines.	
	14	5.45 am	Counter preparation shoot on S.O.S. lines. 1.40 pm LEWIS HOUSE bombarded by Heavies.	
		9.10 pm	Brigade on left carried out raid immediately S. of MENIN Road. Southern Group Artillery cooperated, as also did 63rd M.G.Company and 63rd T.M.Battery. A dummy attack was launched against LEWIS HOUSE, canvas figures being used by 8th Lincolns for the purpose.	
	15	4.25 am	Enemy barrage put down on our front system. At 4.20 am a hostile raiding party approached our No. 2 post and threw bombs, but was dispersed by our Lewis gun fire. All quiet at 4.50 am Our trenches sustained some damage during the bombardment. Casualties, 6 killed, 10 wounded. 63rd Inf. Bde. No. 9106 issued.	8
			8th Lincolns relieved in front line by 8th Somerset L.I. 4th Middlesex moved to reserve at SCOTTISH WOOD, O. 198.	9

Army Form C. 2118.

WAR DIARY
or
INTELLIGENCE SUMMARY.
(Erase heading not required.)

Instructions regarding War Diaries and Intelligence Summaries are contained in F.S. Regs., Part II. and the Staff Manual respectively. Title pages will be prepared in manuscript.

Place	Date	Hour	Summary of Events and Information	Remarks and references to Appendices
TOWER HAMLETS	17	10 pm	Our Battery positions and back areas of Brigade on right were heavily shelled with gas.	
	18	4 am	Counper preparation shoot. Our battery areas heavily engaged all day with H.E. and gas.	10
	19	2.30am	2 officers and 57 O.R., 8th Somerset L.I. carried out on GENERAL'S DUGOUT under cover of Field artillery and T.M. bombardment. Everything worked well and in accordance with programme but the enemy had evacuated the position. The dugout was entered and found to be in a state of disrepair and apparently not used. Tree near dugout was blown down by R.E. Casualties to raiding party, 1 O.R. slightly wounded. 63rd Inf. Bde. No. 9030, etc...	
	20		Hostile shelling of our back areas with H.V. guns continues.	11
	21		8th Somerset L.I. relieved in front line by 4th Middlesex. 8th Lincolns relieved in support by 8th Somersets and moved into reserve at SCOTTISH WOOD. Relief carried out without incident. 63rd Inf. Bde. Order. No. 199... Battalion Defence Scheme issued	12
	22		Battle in south commenced. Simultaneously hostile artillery showed great activity on our front, much gas shell used, chiefly counter battery work.	
	23		Marked decrease in hostile artillery activity.	
	24		Another comparatively quiet day.	
	25		10.30 pm, Brigade H.Q. shelled with 15 cm shell, otherwise quiet on whole sector. Brigade took over ground S. of BASSEVILLEBEEK to NORTH FARM (inclusive). 8th Lincolns relieved 8th Aust. Inf. Battalion (1st Aust. Inf. Bde.) In this sector after dark. Relief completed without incident by 11.5 pm. Order No. 200 Dispositions now as follows - Left, (TOWER HAMLETS) Subsector, 4th Middlesex; right subsector 8th Lincolnshire Regt. In support, CANADA TUNNELS and vicinity, 8th Somerset L.I. Order No. 201 issued	13
	26		Quiet day. Prisoner of 93rd R.I.R. captured by 8th Lincolnshire Regt.	14
	27	11 pm	Warning order received from Division of relief to be carried out on 27th. O. 201 cancelled and O. 202 issued Brigade relieved by 1 Bn. 49th Division (left subsector) and composite Bn. (XXII Corps troops) right subsector as per O. 202. Command passed to G.O.C. 148th Inf. Bde. at 12 midnight. Brigade moved on relief by light railway and lorry to BOESCHEPE and GODEWAERSVELDE Areas.	15
GODEWAERS- VELDE	28		Brigade Headquarters at GODEWAERSVELDE.	
	29		Brigade rested in billets.	
PAS			Brigade entrained at CAESTRE and HOPOUTRE (4th Middlesex Regt.) as per O. No. 203 Detrained at MONDICOURT and BOUQUEMAISON (4th Middlesex). Brigade H.Q. at PAS. Battns. billeted in vicinity of detraining stations.	16

Army Form C. 2118.

WAR DIARY
or
INTELLIGENCE SUMMARY.
(Erase heading not required.)

Place	Date	Hour	Summary of Events and Information	Remarks and references to Appendices
HENU	30		37th Division transferred to IV Corps, Third Army. Brigade H.Q. and 4th Middlesex moved to HENU. Order No. 204 issued	17
	31		8th Lincolns and 8thvSomersets proceeded by march route to HENU. The three Battalions of the Brigade now concentrated in billets in the village. Reconnoitring parties proceeded to front line. 63rd Inf. Bde. No. 9509 issued	18

April 4th 1918.

N Callum
Brigadier General,
Comdg. 63rd Infantry Brigade.

63rd Infantry Brigade

WAR DIARY

March, 1918.

List of Appendices.   No. of Appendix

63rd Inf. Bde. Order No. 194   1
Defence Scheme, 63rd Inf. Bde. No. 8515   2
63rd Inf. Bde. Order No. 196   3
Report on Hostile Attack -
    63rd Inf. Bde. No. 8952   4
    63rd Inf. Bde. No. A/5   5
    63rd Inf. Bde. No. 8924   6
63rd Inf. Bde. Order No. 197   7
63rd Inf. Bde. No. 9106...   8
63rd Inf. Bde. Order No. 198   9
63rd Inf. Bde. No. 9030, etc....   10
63rd Inf. Bde. Order No. 199 11
Battalion Defence Scheme   12
63rd Inf. Bde. Order No. 200 13
63rd Inf. Bde. Order No. 201 14
63rd Inf. Bde. Order No. 202 15
63rd Inf. Bde. Order No. 203 16
63rd Inf. Bde. Order No. 204 17
63rd Inf. Bde. No. 9509... 18
Nominal Rolls of Officers   19
Casualties during March, 1918...   20
Reinforcements during March, 1918   21
Strength od Units, March 31st, 1918...   22

SECRET.   Mar. 2nd 1918

63rd Infantry Brigade.

DEFENCE SCHEME.

Reference Maps:
Sheet 2 & 8, 1:40,000
ZILLEBEKE, N.1., 1:10,000

I. DESCRIPTION OF BRIGADE AREA.

(a) FRONT.

The front held by 63rd Infantry Brigade extends from the BASSEVILLEBEEK at J.26.d.4.9 on the RIGHT to J.21.c.70.65 on the LEFT. It is the RIGHT Subsector of the 37th Divisional Front and is about 1,200 yards long. The CENTRE Subsector, astride the MENIN Road is held by 112th Infantry Brigade and the left subsector up to the POLYGONEBEEK, by the 111th Infantry Brigade. The 1st Australian Brigade is on the RIGHT of 63rd Infantry Brigade southwards from the BASSEVILLEBEEK.

(b) BOUNDARIES.

(i) BRIGADE BOUNDARY ON SOUTH.

Front line at J.26.d.40.90 - along the BASSEVILLE BEEK to J.26.b.30.40 - LOWER STAR POST, J.25.b.22.10 - I.30.d.00.70 - Railway Crossing at I.28.b.80.30 - LOCK 8. Present RIGHT POST at J.26.b.60.50.

(ii) BRIGADE BOUNDARY ON NORTH.

Front line at J.21.c.70.65 - J.20.d.25.90 - J.20 a.20.30 - J.19.b.42.25 - I.24.b.70.45 - I.24.a.80.35 - thence due west to ZILLEBEKE - HELLFIRE CORNER Rd.
Present LEFT POST at J.21.c.67.62.

(c) TOPOGRAPHY.

(i) The principle feature in the Brigade Area is the BASSEVILLEBEEK which flows almost due south from HERENTHAGE CHATEAU and separates the main CANADA STREET - HEDGE STREET - TORR TOP - STIRLING CASTLE Ridge from the TOWER HAMLETS SPUR, and enables the enemy to obtain direct observation on the greater part of the Brigade Area from the South East.

(ii) The BASSEVILLEBEEK Valley is very marshy and consists of a series of shell holes through which the stream flows as best it can. During wet weather, this ground is practically impassable, except by the various duckboard crossings which exist as follows:-

(iii) DUMBARTON TRACK and GLOUCESTER DRIVE at J.20.central.
(Two crossings exist, 20 yards apart)

STOUT TRACK at J.20.d.0.1.

(iv) The ground in the Brigade Area, East of the main ridge has been very badly cut up by shell fire and, except during a hard frost, is practically impassable, except by the existing tracks.

(2)

II. DEFENSIVE ZONES.

(a) Each subsector is organised for defence as follows:-
    (i) Forward Zone.
    (ii) Battle Zone.
    (iii) Rear Zone.

The FORWARD ZONE and BATTLE ZONE are subdivided as follows :-

    (i) Forward Zone - Line of Posts and Supports.
    (ii) Battle Zone - Main Defensive System (Divisional Reserve Line).
                       The Intermediate System.
                       The rear System (Corps Line).

(b) FORWARD ZONE.

This consists of small defensive posts and lengths of fire trench (JULIA TRENCH and WILLICK TRENCH which is being extended Northwards towards PERTH AVENUE).

A wire obstacle exists along the front and is being strengthened.

All isolated posts in this system are being wired for all round defence and the intervals between them wired so as to shepherd hostile patrols and raiding parties into localities swept by Lewis Gun fire.

Splinter-proof cover is to be provided in which the garrison can shelter.

AMBROSE TRENCH is in Support to WILLICK and JULIA Trenches, and PALESTINE TRENCH will serve as a Support Trench to the Western end of JULIA Trench, and the STOUT WOOD Post Line.

(c) BATTLE ZONE.

Main Defensive System. This system consists at present of strong points which are in progress of being linked up to form a continuous trench North of PALESTINE. Wire exists along the whole front, and is being strengthened. These Strong points (numbered from right to left) are sited as follows :-

    S.P.1   J.25.b.95.70.
    S.P.2   J.26.a.80.90.
    S.P.3-   J.20.d.~~40.30.~~ 45.45.
    S.P.4-   J.20.d.~~70.25.~~ 77.37.

and thence Northwards through KANTINTJE CABARET.

Intermediate System. In order to afford greater depth to the defence, An Intermediate System is under construction between the Main and the Rear Defensive Systems.

This system consists of a number of strong points which will eventually be joined up so as to form a continuous trench.

The wiring of this system has been commenced and some of the strong points have been completed. The siting of the strong points is as follows :-

    I.1.   J.25.b.30.30.
    I.2.   J.25.b.30.90.
    I.3.   J.20.c.30.80.

and thence Northwards through INVERNESS COPSE.

The wiring......

The wiring of the INVERNESS COPSE, HERENTHAGE CHATEAU, DUMBARTON LAKES Area, to form an obstacle in depth across the MENIN Road, is now being carried out.

Rear System. This system consists of a number of strong points and machine gun emplacements sited so as mutually to support each other. The forward strong points are located on the Eastern slopes of the main ridge and the system extends back in depth to a line ZWARTELEEN - HOOGE.

The majority of these strong points have been completed with the exception of the erection of concrete shelters. Wire has been erected in connection with them.

It will be occupied by the Supports of Brigades in the line as accommodation becomes available.

Work on this line is undertaken by the Corps, but Infantry Brigades will, as these strong points are completed, be responsible for the maintenance of those occupied by them.

The strong points are as follows :-

J.19.1.	...	J.19.c.54.40.
J.19.2.	...	J.19.c.83.90.
J.19.3.	...	J.19.b.05.20.
I.30.1.	...	I.30.b.15.00.
I.30.2.	...	I.30.b.45.35.
I.30.3.	...	I.30.b.99.99.
I.29.1.	...	I.29.b.99.05.

(d) REAR ZONE.

No work in this Zone will be undertaken until the necessity arises. The front line of this Zone will run approximately from the LILLE GATE through SWAN CHATEAU and CHATEAU SEGARD. This line is to be reconnoitred by Divisional and Brigade Staffs and plans prepared for its defence.

(4)

III. DISTRIBUTION OF TROOPS.

Outpost and Main Defensive Systems.

    1 Battalion
    9 Light Trench Mortars
    1 Newton 6" Trench Mortar
    2 Vickers Machine Guns

Distributed as follows:-

(a) **In Outpost System.** Three companies in the Post and Front Trench Line, with one platoon in each case in close support along the line BEDOUIN - PALESTINE - AMBROSE.
    Three Light Trench Mortars (vide Appendix 'B')

(b) **Main Defensive System.** Battalion H.Q. One Company in Main Divisional Line distributed between S.P.3, STEVENS TRENCH and Northwards towards PERTH AVENUE.
    Six Light Trench Mortars (vide Appendix 'B')
    One 6" Newton Trench Mortar (vide Map).
    Two Vickers Machine guns (vide Appendix 'C').

(c) **Intermediate System.**
    Eight Vickers Machine Guns in J.19 and J.25, (vide Appendix 'C').

(d) **Rear System.**
    One Battalion.
    H.Q. and 1 Company in CANADA TUNNELS.
    1 Company in MOUNT SORREL.
    1 Company in HEDGE STREET.
    1 Company (less 1 platoon and 1 Lewis gun Section) in ILIAD TRENCH.
    1 Platoon in S.P.1.
    1 Lewis Gun Section in S.P.2
Eight Reserve Vickers machine guns and teams in TOR TOP.
One section Trench Mortar Battery at ELZENWALLE.
One Battalion in Reserve at H.35.c., SCOTTISH WOOD CAMP.
Brigade Headquarters at BEDFORD HOUSE.
Advanced Brigade H.Q. at TOR TOP.

IV. PRINCIPLES OF DEFENCE.

(a) The post line will be held at all costs and garrisons of posts will not withdraw, even if outflanked. Should a post or any portion of our line be temporarily lost, supporting platoons will at once counter-attack, assisted by neighbouring posts.

(b) A vigorous policy of patrolling in No Man's Land will be maintained, and any gaps between Companies and Brigades on either flank will be constantly patrolled at night.

(c) The defence of the front line system is organized in depth in that PALESTINE TRENCH is wired on both sides for defence to a flank, with the object of holding the enemy in a pocket.

(d) Main Defensive System. The Reserves of the Battalions in the outpost system will normally be located in this system and, with the exception of definite garrisons detailed for the defence of each strong point, will be available for immediate counter-attack.
Intermediate and Rear Systems.

(e) Definite garrisons will be told off for the Strong Points in these systems and on "Precautionary Action" being ordered, the Support Battalion will be prepared to occupy I.1. and I.2. and the seven posts in the Corps Line between MOUNT SORREL and PERTH AVENUE, map location of which is given in Section II, para. (c), under "Rear System".

(f) Counter Attack. The dispositions of troops in the forward area will be such that the following troops are available for immediate counter-attack:-
   (i) In each Company   -   1 Platoon
   (ii) In each Battalion -   1 Company

These troops are to be detailed for counter attack and will not be used to reinforce or as garrisons of strong points. In the event of the enemy obtaining a footing in any portion of the Defensive System, he will under the orders of the Commander on the spot, be immediately counter attacked by local reserves maintained at suitable positions within the Defensive System.

The quicker such counter attack can be delivered the better. Battalion Commanders are responsible that all subordinate commanders in the line down to and including platoon commanders are prepared to organise a counter-attack on the spot without reference to their superiors.

In the event of an immediate counter attack failing, a deliberate counter attack will be carried out under Divisional instructions.

The Infantry Battalions in Reserve will be used for a deliberate counter attack after artillery preparation and under an artillery barrage, or to prevent the enemy extending his initial success and to maintain the position while a deliberate counter-attack is being prepared by Corps.

V. ACTION IN CASE OF ATTACK.

1. PROBABLE FORMS OF ATTACK.

Various forms of attack open to the enemy are :-
(a) An attack on a large scale with the object of gaining the main MOUNT SORREL - CLAPHAM JUNCTION Ridge.
(b) An attack to gain the high ground of the TOWER HAMLETS Spur, with the object of denying observation to the east and obtaining direct observation of the ground east of the MOUNT SORREL - CLAPHAM JUNCTION Ridge.
(c) A minor operation to capture some tactical point.
(d) A raid.

Any of the above might be attempted with or without a previous bombardment.

Gas Projectors may be used in conjunction with or prior to (a), (b) and (c).

Tanks may also be employed in (a) and (b), and fleets of low flying aeroplanes will probably be employed.

2.
In case of any of the above contingencies :-

(a) The front line Battalion will act in accordance with Section 4 of this Defence Scheme, paras. (a), (c), (d) and (f).

All subordinate commanders in the line will make out a written plan, illustrated by a sketch, showing what their arrangements are for reinforcing the line, or launching counter attacks, not only on their immediate front, but anywhere in the area occupied by the corresponding unit or formation on either flank. The plans should include a scheme for temporarily moving forward or back out of the front line in case of an annihilating barrage being put down on the line, with a view to minimising casualties, and immediately re-occupying the line on the barrage lifting. These plans will be asked for and discussed by visiting officers. Whenever possible, all plans should be rehearsed by troops who are detailed to carry them out. Subordinate leaders especially must reconnoitre the ground.

(b) The Support Battalion will be prepared to act as laid down in Section 4, para. (e).

Troops quartered in the tunnelled dugout systems will act as laid down in Support Battalion Defence Scheme, which will pay particular attention to the following points :-
   (i) Exits from tunnelled systems which should be allotted to each unit down to platoons.
  (ii) Allotments of posts.
 (iii) Routes to the posts.

Troops in occupation of tunnelled dugouts will be practised in getting out of them quickly and quietly with and without gas masks on, at least twice a week, and always after a relief in the tunnel.

Extra S.A.A. up to 170 rounds per man will be issued. 25 will be issued with shovels.

The Battalion will not move until orders to do so are received from Brigade Headquarters.

When the move is ordered, it will be carried out by sections in single file, in accordance with plan, from pre-arranged exits to the strong points to be occupied in

(7)

the Corps Line unless otherwise ordered.

In the event of the enemy breaking through the Division on the right flank, the Support Battalion will at once be prepared to form a defensive flank. If on the right flank, along the line S.P.1 and S.P.2 in Divisional Reserve Line - Post P.1. in Intermediate Line - MOUNT SORREL.

(b) The Reserve Battalion of the Brigade will not move from its camp without reference to Divisional Headquarters.

It would probably assemble between SWAN CHATEAU and KRUISSTRAATHOEK with head of column at SWAN CHATEAU.

In addition to the above, the Reserve Battalion may be called upon to assist the Divisions on the flanks, moving under orders to be issued by Divisional Headquarters. The Battalion would march from SCOTTISH WOOD CAMP to a place of assembly on the KRUISSTRAATHOEK VITUIS CABARET (I.19.d.35.30) Road, in the event of the Division on our right requiring assistance.

In the case of assistance being called for by the Division on the Left, the battalion would assemble at MANAWATU CAMP, I.14.d.

Arrangements have also been made for the Reserve Brigade of Flank Divisions to concentrate for the assistance of this Division as follows :-

Right Division.
(a) Brigade H.Q. at BEDFORD HOUSE, I.26.a.9.4.
(b) Two Battalions on VIERSTRAAT - ELZENWALLE Road with head of column at ELZENWALLE.
(c) Two Battalions on RIDGE WOOD - SCOTTISH WOOD - CHATEAU SEGARD Road, with head of column at cross roads H.30.c.3.8.

Left Division.
(a) Brigade H.Q. at LILLE GATE, YPRES.
(b) One Battalion on the WARRINGTON ROAD with head of column at the junction of WARRINGTON ROAD and the ZILLEBEKE - HELLFIRE CORNER Road, I.16.d.6.5.
(c) One Battalion on the VERBRANDEN Road with head of column at road junction I.28.a.2.9.
(d) One Battalion WESTHOEK RIDGE and RAILWAY WOOD Dugouts.

Officers Commanding Battalions will arrange for officers to reconnoitre roads and forward areas in the Centre Brigade subsector and left Brigade subsector.

(d) Action of Working parties. In case of hostile attack -
(i) Commanders of working parties East of the BASSEVILLE BEEK will report to the nearest Battalion H.Q. for orders. The working parties will take up the best defensive position in the locality of their work.
(ii) Commanders of working parties west of the above line but East of the rear system of the Battle Zone will report to the Battalion Headquarters at CANADA TUNNELS or Adv. Brigade H.Q. at TORR TOP for orders. The working parties will take up the best defensive position in the locality of their work.

(8)

(e) 63rd Machine Gun Company will act as laid down in Appendix 'C'.

(f) 63rd Trench Mortar Battery will act as laid down in Appendix 'B'.

(g) Brigade Headquarters will move to TORR TOP.

VI. PRECAUTIONARY ACTION.

On receipt of the message "Precautionary Action", from Brigade H.Q., the following action will be taken :-

(a) The Front Line Battalions will send out extra patrols and advanced listening posts. *in light or in foggy weather*

(b) The Battalion in Support will equip as laid down in Section V and be prepared to move.

(c) The Battalion in Reserve will be prepared to march at 30 minutes notice, in fighting order.

(d) 63rd M.G.C. Company will act as laid down in Appendix 'C'.

(e) 63rd T.M.Battery will act as laid down in Appendix 'B'.

(f) Brigade Headquarters will move forward to TORR TOP.

(g) Each Battalion will send 4 additional runners to report at Advanced Brigade H.Q. at TORR TOP to maintain communications.

(h) Working parties will act as in case of attack.

(i) Transports will send an orderly to Brigade Transport Officer and will be prepared to march at 30 minutes notice.
S.A.A. and tools will be loaded up.

(j) All infantry will be completed up to 170 rounds S.A.A. per man.

APPENDIX 'A'

COMMUNICATIONS.

I. TELEPHONE.
II. POWER BUZZER & AMPLIFIER.
III. VISUAL.
IV. PIGEONS.
V. ROCKETS.
VI. D.Rs and RUNNERS.

I. TELEPHONE.

1. (a) Companies connected to Battalion by Ground Cable; Laterals between Companies by Ground Cable.
   (b) Battalion to Adv. Brigade by Ground Cable. Direct Lateral to Battalion on Left. Lateral to Battalion on right via Adv. Brigade.
   (c) Adv. Brigade to Brigade H.Q. on Corps Buried system.
   (d) Direct lateral to Flanking Brigades.
   (e) Machine Gun Position at J.19.d.65.57 is connected to Advanced Brigade H.Q., TORR TOP, by ground cable and J.19.d.65.57 is likewise connected by ground cable to the HET PAPPOTJE battery of four guns, and through this battery with two guns at J.26.a.05.45.

2. Maintenance.
   Brigade to Adv. Brigade ... Corps Area Detachment
   Adv. Brigade to Battalion ... Bde. Signal Section
   Battalion to Companies ... Battn. Signallers.

II. POWER BUZZER & AMPLIFIER.

1. (a) Power Buzzer from Right Company H.Q. in line working to Amplifier at Battalion H.Q. in line.
   (b) Power Buzzer and Amplifier at Battn. H.Q. in line working to Divnl. Wireless Centre (J.19.a.50.90).

2. Maintenance.
   These are manned and maintained by Battalion Signals under direct supervision of Divnl. Wireless Officer.

III. VISUAL.

(a) Lamp from Right Company H.Q. in line to Adv. Bde. - EQ 46
(b) Lamp from Battalion H.Q. in line to Adv. Bde. - EQ 46.
(c) Lamp from Adv. Brigade to Brigade H.Q.

IV. PIGEONS.

The Battalion in line receives 6 birds daily :-
2 at Right Company.
2 at Left Company.
2 at Battalion H.Q.

V. ROCKETS.

Rocket emplacements are installed at Battalion H.Q. and Support Company H.Q. and a supply (3) of rockets are available for each position.

VI. RUNNERS.

A motor cyclist is attached to Brigade H.Q. to be used as required.
Cyclist orderly delivers to and collects from Reserve Battalion. Regular Runner service is established between Brigade and Adv. Brigade. Battns. in line collect from and deliver to Adv. Brigade.

APPENDIX 'B'

LIGHT TRENCH MORTARS.
----

1. GENERAL.

The 63rd Trench Mortar Battery is organised on the TOWER HAMLETS for offensive and defensive work.

For offensive work the 3" Stokes Mortars are fired with the sling from shell-holes and rough positions away from the emplacements so as not to give away and draw retaliation on the silent positions from which S.O.S. barrage is fired.

For defensive work, the mortars are so situated that all the mortars in the area can, if required, switch their fire and cover any portion of the front attacked; or again the mortars have picked S.O.S. lines covering the whole front.

The emplacements have been made in depth, so that, in the event of the enemy successfully attacking the forward zone and driving us out of the front and support lines, a heavy barrage can immediately be put down covering the main Divisional Reserve line.

To make this possible, in addition to having 200 rounds at each of the four silent positions in STEVENS and AMBROSE Trenches, there are 300 rounds stacked at each of the four Reserve positions behind the main Divisional Reserve Line.

2. DISTRIBUTION.

Forward Mortars.
1. In AMBROSE TRENCH at J.21.c.25.35 with zero on J.21.d.15.45.
2. In AMBROSE TRENCH at J.21.c.25.30 with zero on J.27.a.30.35.
3. In STEVENS TRENCH at J.20.d.85.25 with zero on J.27.a.50.95.
4. In STEVENS TRENCH at J.20.d.55.20 with zero on J.21.c.50.15.

Reserve Mortars.
5. At J.20.d.45.55 with zero line at 90° (True).
6. At J.20.d.45.55 with zero line at 150° (True).
7. At J.20.d.50.45 with zero line at 150° (True).
8. At J.20.d.50.45 with zero line at 160° (True).

3. PERSONNEL.

There are in normal times, teams of 3 men per mortar on the Ridge, (i.e.) two sections and two officers in charge. Besides these, 1 officer and 1 section is in TORR TOP TUNNELS and 2 officers and 1 section is in Reserve at ELZEN'ALLE.

In the event of "Precautionary Action" the section in TORR TOP and a third officer will move up on to the Ridge and will be replaced by two officers and the Reserve Section in TORR TOP. The Battery in normal times thus relieves itself.

4. ANTI-AIRCRAFT DEFENCE.

The mortars being placed in depth a natural box barrage can automatically be put up for use against low flying hostile aeroplanes, 50 rounds per mortar being kept for this purpose.

APPENDIX 'C'

MACHINE GUNS

1. GENERAL.

    Machine gun defence is based on

    (a) Forward guns which can bring direct fire to bear on enemy who may succeed in penetrating our line, from a short range. Of these, there are two in this sector. One is at J.20.d.5.2, near STEVENS TRENCH and the other at J.21.c.10.65.

    (b) Rear guns which fire on S.O.S., on likely places for enemy reserves and reinforcements, and with the additional power of bringing direct fire on the enemy in case of a break through at medium and short range. Of these there are in the sector, 10, as under :-
        At J.26.a.10.60   ... 2 guns
        At or near J.25.b.25.90 ... 4 guns
        At J.19.d.60.55   ... 4 guns.

    (c)   In addition to the above, arrangements have been made for co-operation of 6 guns of 1st Australian Infantry Brigade, firing from the neighbourhood of KING'S CASTLE on S.O.S. lines on the area HALF FARM - BELLY GATES and thence N.E. to about J.27.a.85.95.

    (d)   In addition to these there are eight guns with reserve teams of 63rd M.G.Company in TOR TOP Tunnels.

2. AMMUNITION SUPPLY, ETC.

    Ammunition dumps have been established as follows :-
        50,000 rounds   HEDGE STREET
        50,000 rounds   TOR TOP.
    In addition, each gun will maintain at least 14 belt boxes and 14,000 rounds S.A.A. at each gun position. Two of the belt boxes will be loaded with A.P. Ammunition and will be clearly marked.

3.   Two days' Reserve Rations, and 6 gallons of water per gun, are maintained at the gun positions.

4. ACTION AGAINST HOSTILE TANKS.

    In the event of hostile tanks attacking, not more than one gun where there are a pair or more guns will fire at the tanks. The other guns will fire on the enemy's Infantry.

5.   H.Q., 63rd M.G.Company are in telephonic communication with Brigades and all the rear guns are connected up.

6.   On "Precautionary Action" being ordered, 63rd M.G.Company will send two guns to positions near CANADA TUNNELS, two guns to HEDGE STREET and two guns to man positions at TORR TOP. The remaining two guns will remain at the disposition of G.O.C. 63rd Inf. Bde. In addition the Company in

Reserve will send up one section to TURK TOP Defences to act under the orders of G.O.C. 63rd Inf. Bde.

7.   Arrangements are being made by which, in the event of enemy operations against the TOWER HAMLETS SPUR, other machine guns of the Division can be bring
    indirect fire to bear by means of a switch to cover the front.

APPENDIX 'D'

ARTILLERY COOPERATION.

1. 63rd Infantry Brigade front is covered by Southern Group Artillery, Headquarters at BEDFORD HOUSE.
The Group consists of two 18-pdr and one 4.5" How. Batteries situated as follows :-
    4   18 pdr guns at ARMAGH HOUSE.
    2   18 pdr guns at HILL 60.
    6   18 pdr guns about I.28.b.central.
    6   4.5" Hows. at VERBRANDEN MOLEN
        18 pdrs S.O.S. lines are distributed along the front.
        4.5" Hows. barrage along 150 yards East of 18 pdrs...

2. Arrangements exist by which support can be obtained from Batteries of the Groups on our right and left if required.

3. An officer of the Group acts as Liaison Officer at Headquarters of the Battalion in the line. His tour of duty is three days.

4. O.Ps at J.26.b.2.1 and I.36.b.5.8 are manned daily from one hour before dawn until dusk.

5. A Group Rocket Station for transmission of S.O.S. Rocket signals is established at HILL 60. S.O.S. Rockets can also be seen from each Battery Lookout Place.

6. Each Battery of the Group has in addition to its normal position one alternative position. There are also constructed positions for 8 reinforcing batteries and O.Ps for same.

MUTUAL SUPPORT BARRAGES

SOUTHERN GROUP.

Code Call	Support given by	Support given to	Action.
HELP SOUTH	Southern Group	Division on Right	1 18 pdr Battery J.27.c.15.00 to J.28.d.55.14. 1 How. on STAGGER FARM. 1 How. on CAPITAL FARM.
HELP GEE LUVELT	Division on Right	Southern Group	1 18 pdr Battery J.27.c.15.00 to J.27.a.65.80 1 How. on STAGGER FARM. 1 How. on CAPITAL FARM.
HELP GEE TEE	Southern Group	Centre Group	Left hand 18 pdr Battery on its S.O.S. lines. 1 How. on STAGGER FARM. 1 How. on J.27.b.45.50.
HELP BELFORT	Centre Group	Southern Group	2 18 pdrs on LEWIS HOUSE 1 How. on GLASS HOUSES, J.28.b. 1 How. on STONE FARM.
SPECIAL HELP	Division on right	Southern Group	1 18 pdr Battery. Area CAPITAL FARM - STAGGER FARM - TROT HOUSE - HARGATE FARM. 1 18 pdr battery. Area J.27.c.9.8 - J.27.a.98.75 - J.21.d.35.65 - J.21.d.50.60. 6 Hows on TROT HOUSE, HARGATE FARM, CAPITAL FARM, STAGGER FARM.

APPENDIX (E).

ADMINISTRATIVE

1. AMMUNITION.

(a) The Brigade Ammunition Dump is at CANADA STREET (I.30.a.3.4.
The establishment of the Dump is as follows :-

S.A.A.	500,000
Hand Grenades (Mills)	1,000
Rifle do. do.	720
Males do. (No.20)	500
S.O.S. day	100
do. night	40
Very Lights 1"	1,500
Ground Flares	1,200
Stokes Ammunition	600
M.S.K. Bombs	100

The Dump is in charge of the Brigade Bombing Officer, upon whom demands for ammunition will be made.

(b) FRONT LINE. Establishments will be maintained as follows:-

S.A.A. at Battalion H.Q.	75,000	
do. each Coy H.Q.	10,000	
do. each Platoon H.Q.	2,000	
Hand Grenades (Mills)	480	at Battn. H.Q.
Rifle do. do.	480	do.
Very Pistol Ammunition	300	rds. do.
S.O.S. day	30	do.
S.O.S. (night) (grenades)	30	at Battn. H.Q.
do. do. do.	12	at Company H.Q.
Ground Flares	300	at Battn. H.Q.

(c) ILIAD TRENCH.

S.A.A.	40,000	) The Battalion in
Rifle Grenades	240	) Support will be
S.O.S.	6	) responsible that
		) these Stores are

(d) TORR TOP.

		) kept in good order,
S.A.A.	20,000	) maintained and
Hand Grenades	144	) handed over.
Rifle Grenades	100	)
S.O.S.	6	)

(e) RESERVE BATTALION (SCOTTISH WOOD CAMP).

Establishment maintained in Magazine :-

S.A.A.	20,000
Hand Grenades	480
Rifle Grenades	240
No.20 Grenades	240
Very Lights	150
Ground Flares	530
Message Rockets	6
'P' Bombs	100

The contents of the Magazine will be handed over to the Reserve Battalion at each relief.

1. AMMUNITION (continued)

   (f) STRONG POINTS. All occupied Strong Points will contain minimum reserves of ammunition as follows :-

   S.A.A.   5000 rounds
   Rifle Grenades   100

   The Battalion occupying these posts will be responsible for the condition and maintenance of such reserves.
   Strong points to be occupied in the event of "Precautionary Action" will as and when they are completed, be equipped with S.A.A. and rifle grenades as above. In the event of the Strong points being occupied before completion, the Battalion occupying them will be responsible that a reserve of ammunition is taken.

   (g) MACHINE GUNS. The 63rd Machine Gun Coy will maintain a reserve of S.A.A. as laid down and will not draw from the Brigade Dump except under circumstances of tactical necessity or on indent counter-signed by the Staff Captain.

   (h) ARMOUR PIERCING AMMUNITION.
   In accordance with Anti-Tank Measures laid down, each Lewis Gun has been provided with not less than 2 Magazines filled with A.P. S.A.A. and each Vickers Gun with not less than 2 belts. These will be clearly marked in order that they may be distinguished from other Magazines and Belts. In addition, a reserve of 3000 rounds is maintained at Brigade Dump.

   (i) STOKES AMMUNITION.
   An establishment of not less than :-
   200 rounds per Mortar with 4 forward Mortars
   300   ,,   ,,   ,,   4 Reserve Mortars
   is maintained at the Gun positions and a Reserve of 800 rounds at forward Battalion Headquarters.

   (j) GROUND FLARES
   These are distributed in depth as follows :-
   At Battalion and Company Headquarters in front Line 300
   Support and Reserve Battalions each have a supply of 530 ready for issue.
   A Reserve of 1200 is kept at the Brigade Dump.

2. RATIONS & WATER.

   (a) RATIONS. 440 Reserve Rations are maintained at Front Line Battalion Headquarters and 660 at Support Battalion Headquarters. 1000 Reserve Rations are maintained at SCOTTISH WOOD CAMP.

   (b) WATER. Reserves of water are maintained as follows :-
   Front Line Battalion Headquarters   100 tins.
   Each Company Headquarters   10 tins
   Each Machine Gun position   5 tins
   Support Battalion Headquarters   50 tins
   Reserve Battalion   500 extra water bottles.

   The Reserve Battalion will ensure that full water bottles are available at 1 hour's notice.

   (c) STRONG POINTS. The Battalion occupying strong points will ensure that a minimum of 5 tins is kept and turned over at each strong post. Strong Points to be occupied in the event of "PRECAUTIONARY ACTION" will be equipped with reserves of water by the Battalion occupying them.

3. BATTLE EQUIPMENT.

(a) SOLIDIFIED ALCOHOL. 100 tins are held in reserve for battle purposes.

(b) SANDBAGS. A reserve of not less than 1000 sandbags is maintained at each of the 3 Battalion Headquarters. In the event of active operations each man will carry 2 sandbags.

(c) TOOLS. A sufficiency of picks and shovels is maintained at CANADA STREET for Support Battalion and the Reserve Battn. is equipped with 60 picks and 240 shovels in the Magazine.

NOTE :- Stores for Battle equipment are issued to Companies of Support Battalion ready for immediate distribution.

4. R.E. MATERIAL. R.E. Dumps are situated as follows :-
   MAIN DUMP CAFE BELGE   H.29.b.5.2.
   Advanced Divisional Dumps. DICKEBUSCH I.20.a.5.8.
                              CANADA STREET   I.30.a.9.4.

   Demands for R.E. Material will normally be made on 154th Field Company R.E. CANADA STREET

5. SUPPLIES & TRANSPORT.
   (a) For front line Battalion, Supplies are convoyed by limber to LANGTON SIDING, thence by Pack Mule to Battalion Headquarters.
   (b) For Support Battn. by wheeled Transport to CANADA STREET.

6. MEDICAL.
   (a) Evacuation of wounded via Regimental Aid Post to Advanced Dressing Station J. STAN at I.28.b.8.6. and WOODCOTE HOUSE.
   (b) Stretchers and blankets. A sufficiency of these stores is at the disposal of O.s C. Field Ambulance in the forward Area.
   (c) Walking Wounded. All Roads from Regimental Aid Posts will be marked by flags along the following route - DUMBARTON LAKES- PERTH AVENUE - PLUMERS DRIVE SOUTH - GADSTAND. - STOUT TRACK - GREEN JACKET DRIVE - MORLAND AVENUE - CANSTAND.
   (d) Stretcher bearers. Additional stretcher bearers will be sent forward to reinforce all bearer relay posts on the receipt of the message "Precautionary action".

7. STRAGGLERS POSTS will be established at :-
   First Line :- (a) Track Junction at I.30.a.6.1.) with collecting
                 (b) do.   do.   J.25.a.05.95.) Station at
                 (c) do.   do.   J.19.c.4.5.) CANADA STREET
       To be detailed as follows from Regimental Police :-
                 (a) 8th Lincolns
                 (b) 8th Somerset L.I.
                 (c) 4th Middlesex.
   Second Line. SHRAPNEL CORNER.   I.20.a.5.5.
                 MANOR HALT   I.28.a.2.0.
                 ZILLEBEKE   I.22.b.8.4.
       with collecting Station WOODCOTE HOUSE I.20.c.3.2.
   Under arrangements to be made by A.P.M. 37th Division.

SECRET   Copy No. 1

35rd Infantry Brigade Order No. 196

Reference Sheet: March 4th 1918
28, 1:40,000

1. (a)   On the night March 5/6th, 4th Middlesex Regt. will
relieve 8th Somerset L.I. in the Line; 8th Somerset L.I.
will, upon relief, withdraw into Support at BLAST TUNNELS.

   (b)   8th Lincolnshire Regt. will remain in Reserve at SCOTTISH
WOOD CAMP, S.55.c.

2.   All details of the above relief will be arranged between
Commanding Officers concerned.

3.   No troops will move forward of the TOR TOP — MOUNT
SORREL Ridge before 6 pm.

4.   No post, trench or strong point will be vacated until
relieved.

5.   All trench stores, maps defence schemes, etc. will
be handed over and receipts taken, copies of which will be
sent to this office.

6.   Completion of relief will be reported to this office
in B.A.B. Code.

                                           (Sgd) B Sheringham
                                                   Captain,
                                                   Brigade Major,
Issued at 1 pm   35rd Infantry Brigade.

Distribution.	Copy No.		Copy No.
War Diary & File	1 - 5	C.R.E.	21
Brigade Staff	6 - 8	B.G.R.A.	22
8th Lincolns	9	111th Inf. Bde.	23
8th Somerset L.I.	10	112th Inf. Bde.	24
4th Middlesex Regt.	11	1st Aust. Inf. Bde.	25
35rd Machine Gun Company	12	Brigade Gas Officer	26
65rd T.M.Battery	13	Brigade Transport Offr.	27
154th Fd. Co., R.E.	14	Brigade Supply Officer	28
No. 2 Coy., Train	15	37th M.G.Battalion/	29
50th Fd. Ambulance	16	Area Commandant,	
Southern Group, Arty	17	KRUISSTRAATHOEK Area	30
Centre Group, Arty.	18	Brigade School	31
37th Division	19 - 20		

63rd Infantry Brigade No. 8952

37th Division

REPORT ON OPERATIONS, MARCH 8/9TH, 1918.

Reference G 6125 dated 11.3.18,

At 9.30 am on 8th inst., word was received from the Battalion in the line (4th Middlesex Regt), that the enemy was heavily shelling our line with 10.5 cm, 7.7 am and some 15 cm, particular attention being paid to PALESTINE and BEDOUIN Trenches, and causing some casualties. At 11.30 am the shelling was reported heavier than ever and Support Battalion was ordered to send up one platoon and one Lewis Gun to man the Reserve Line.

At 12.10 pm, the shelling was reported continuous and, further casualties being reported, the G.O.C. decided to send up two platoons with two Lewis Guns instead of one platoon and one Lewis Gun, front and support Battalions being notified.

At 4.35 pm, Brigade H.Q. moved forward to TORR TOP, arriving at 5.50 pm

At 5.55 pm S.O.S. was reported on our front and Support Battalion was ordered to send one section from each garrison to strong points in the Corps Line.

At 6.20 pm, the Right Brigade (Australians) reported S.O.S. on our right near the junction. Australians were asked if their machine guns were firing on BERRY COTTS.

At 6.30 pm, under orders issued by G.S.O.1, one company of Reserve Battalion was sent up to CANADA TUNNELS, but was not to be used without reference to Division.

O.K. was reported by visual at 6.35 pm from all Companies and Battalions but at 6.40 pm, S.O.S. was reported on our front by Support Battalion ~~and one Company in Reserve was ordered up.~~

At 7.15 pm the Artillery slackened and died down and at 7.24 pm a runner was sent through to the front Battalion asking for a report.

At 7.27 pm, Brigade on Right reported O.K. on their front and at 7.40 pm a report was received from Left Brigade that the enemy had succeeded in entering JOPPA and JERICHO.

At 8.03 pm the following message was received from the Battalion in the Line :-

"Situation as follows aaa No attack has been made on our front "but we have been heavily shelled until 6.30 pm, since when quite "quiet on our front; spasmodic shelling on our left aaa Casualties "about 65 aaa Left and right companies light aaa Centre and Support "companies about 25 casualties each aaa Am arranging for constant "patrolling on my front and am keeping touch with Battalion on left "who report their right and centre companies as comparatively O.K. "but their left company has suffered very heavily aaa They think "enemy have penetrated K.R.R's on their left aaa They are arranging "to form a defensive flank aaa Our communications with you are now "alright aaa We have no officer casualties reported aaa Quiet "prevails on whole front at present moment aaa Our rations have "arrived also 2 platoons S.L.Infy."

At 8.43 pm front line battalion was warned of the importance of occupying STUART'S SAP. Support Battalion was instructed to send up a special carrying party with corrugated iron for repairs to damaged trenches, front line battalion being instructed to carry on with repairs in every way possible.

At 10.30 pm the Brigade Major visited the front line and found all O.K.; PALESTINE, BEDOUIN abd AMBROSE Trenches were considerably damaged.

OVER.

(2)

At 12.10 am on 9th inst., Southern Group Artillery reported that they would shortly be in a better position to assist.

The Support Battalion reported the arrival of the Company from Reserve at 12.35 am.

At 9.40 am, a report was received from Division that the trenches on the left of the Divisional front had been retaken.

The Official casualties for March 8th and 8/9th were:

Killed in Action	2nd Lieut. J.H. Headley.
	16 other ranks.
Wounded	43 other ranks.
	all of 4th Middlesex Regt.

Brigadier General,
Comdg. 63rd Infantry Brigade.

14.3.18

63rd Infantry Brigade No. A/5

8th Lincolnshire Regt.
8th Somerset L.I.
4th Middlesex Regt.
63rd Machine Gun Company
63rd T.M. Battery

The enemy succeeded in occupying a portion of our trenches on the left of the Divisional Front, in the POLDERHOEK System last night. He was counter-attacked this morning and driven out.

The following message has been received from the Corps:- "Corps Commander wishes to congratulate the Division, especially the two Battalions immediately concerned upon the successful defence in last night's attack."

The Brigadier wishes to express his sympathy with 4th Middlesex Regt. upon the losses suffered by them, and thanks them for the gallantry and endurance displayed by all ranks under a heavy bombardment.

Captain,
Brigade Major,
63rd Infantry Brigade.

9.3.18

63rd T.M.Battery

63RD
INFANTRY
BRIGADE.
No. 8924
Date 15/3/18

  The Brigadier wishes to thank the officers N.C.Os and men of the 63rd Trench Mortar Battery for the good work done by them during the enemy bombardment of our trenches on March 8th. He very much appreciates the way in which their mortars were handled on that occasion.

                Captain,
              Brigade Major,
10.3.18   63rd Infantry Brigade.

SECRET

Copy No. 1

63rd Infantry Brigade Order No. 197

Reference Sheet:
28, 1:40,000

March 8th 1918.

1. (a) On the night March 9/10th, 8th Lincolnshire Regt. will relieve 4th Middlesex Regt. in the line; 4th Middlesex Regt., upon relief, will withdraw to Support in and about CANADA TUNNELS.

   (b) As 4th Middlesex arrive into Support, 8th Somerset L.I. will withdraw into Reserve at SCOTTISH WOOD CAMP, H.35.c.

2. Two trains (Light Railway) have been arranged for to convey 8th Lincolns from VIJVERHOEK SIDING at 4.30 pm and 4.45 pm respectively to MANOR HALT. 4th Middlesex Regt. will detail officers to supervise the entraining and detraining.
    The same transport will convey 8th Somerset L.I. from MANOR HALT to VIJVERHOEK in two trains which will leave MANOR HALT under arrangements to be made by O.C. 8th Somerset L.I., who will detail an entraining officer.
    Probable time of departure for first train — 9.45 pm.

3. All details of the above reliefs will be arranged between Commanding Officers concerned.

4. No troops will move forward of the TORR TOP – MOUNT SORREL Ridge before 6 pm. Troops will move in parties not larger than platoons, with a distance of 200 yards between platoons.

5. All trench stores, defence schemes, etc. will be handed over and receipts taken, copies of which will be forwarded to this office.

6. Completion of relief will be reported to this office in B.A.B. Code.

C.J. de B. Sheringham
Captain,
Brigade Major,
63rd Infantry Brigade.

Issued at 1 pm

Distribution	Copy No.		Copy No.
or Diary & File			
Brigade Staff	1 – 3	Centre Group Arty	17
8th Lincolns	4 – 8	37th Division	18 – 19
8th Somersets	9	C.R.E.	21
4th Middlesex Regt.	10	B.G.R.A.	22
63rd M.G.Company	11	111th Inf. Bde.	23
63rd T.M.Battery	12	112th Inf. Bde.	24
154th Fd. Co. R.E.	13	1st Aust. Inf. Bde.	25
No. 2 Coy. Train	14	Bde. Transport Offr.	26
Southern Group, Arty.	15	37th M.G.Battn.	27
	16	Bde. School	28
G.L.R.O. XXII Corps		29	

SECRET.   Copy No. 1
              63rd Infantry Brigade Order No. 198.

Ref; Sheet 28, 1:40,000   March 13th 1918

1. (a) On night March 15/16th, 8th Somerset L.I. will relieve
   8th Lincolnshire Regt. in the line; 8th Lincolns, upon relief,
   will withdraw to Support in and about CANADA TUNNELS.
   (b) As 8th Lincolns arrive in Support, 4th Middlesex Regt.
   will withdraw into Reserve at SCOTTISH WOOD CAMP.

2.   Two trains (Light Railway) have been arranged for to convey 8th Somerset L.I. from VIJVERHOEK SIDING at 6 pm and 6.15
   pm respectively to MANOR HALT. 8th Somerset L.I. will detail
   officers to supervise the entraining and detraining.
      The same transport will convey 4th Middlesex from MANOR
   HALT to VIJVERHOEK in two trains which will leave MANOR HALT
   under arrangements to be made by O.C. 4th Middlesex Regt. who
   will detail an entraining officer.
      Probable time of departure of first train - 11 pm.

3.   All details of the above reliefs will be arranged between
   Commanding Officers concerned.

4.   No troops will move forward of the TOR TOP - MT. SORREL
   Ridge before 7.15 pm. Troops will move in parties not larger
   than platoons, with a distance of 200 yards between platoons.

5.   All trench stores, defence schemes, etc., will be handed
   over and receipts taken, copies of which will be forwarded to
   this office.

6.   O.C. 8th Lincolnshire Regt. will leave two platoons to
   garrison the Reserve Line in place of 1 Company 8th Somerset
   L.I. employed on Special work.

7.   Completion of reliefs will be notified to this office in
   B.A.B.Code.

                                              C.F.B.Sheringham
                                                    Captain,
Issued at 10 pm   Brigade Major,
                                              63rd Infantry Brigade.

Distribution.
War Diary & File   1 - 3   37th Division   18 - 19
Brigade Staff   4 - 6   C.R.E.   20
8th Lincolns   9   B.G.R.A.   21
8th Somersets   10   111th Inf. Bde.   22
4th Middlesex   11   112th Inf. Bde.   23
63rd T.M.Battery   12   1st Aust. Inf. Bde.   24
154th Field Co., R.E.   13   57th M.G.Battalion   25
9th N. Staffs (Pnrs)   14   Bde. Transport Offr.   26
No. 2 Coy. Train   15   Bde. School   27
Southern Group, Arty.   16   C.L.L.O., XXII Corps   28
Centre Group, Arty.   17

8th Lincoln Regt.   63rd Infantry Brigade No. 9106.

      The Brigade Commander wishes to thank all ranks, especially your Right Company, for the manner in which they conducted themselves last night. It is most satisfactory to know that the enemy made a determined attempt to raid us and failed, and great credit is due to those who prevented this attempt from being successful.

                                                        Captain.
                                                 Brigade Major.
15.3.18.   63rd Infantry Brigade.

OUTLINE OF PROJECT FOR A RAID.

The Commanding Officer should, at least 10 days before the raid, forward the project for the raid to Brigade Headquarters. In it he should state -

(i) Proposed date.

(ii) Strength and composition of raiding party, including R.E. etc.

(iii) The objective and objects of the raid.

(iv) The time of the day or night at which the raid will be carried out, and reasons for selecting that time.

(v) An outline of the plan of the raid.

(vi) Targets to be dealt with by the Artillery (C.R.A. will decide whether they will be dealt with by Divisional or Heavy Artillery or trench mortars).

(vii) Targets for Light Trench Mortars, and number of Light Trench Mortars it is proposed to employ.

(viii) Targets for Machine guns and number of machine guns he requires in the front line for dealing with direct targets or strengthening the sides of the box barrage.

N.B. A list giving the co-ordinates of all points from which enemy machine guns are expected or are though likely to open fire should be given.

(ix) Whether feints are required on either or both flanks.

(x) Whether a smoke barrage is required in connection with the raid itself by guns or Stokes Mortars, or in connection with the feints on the flanks.

(xi) Requirements from the R.E., e.g., Bangalore torpedoes or charges for blowing up enemy dugouts.

(xii) Requirements from the R.A.M.C. Position of Aid Post.

(xiii) Duration of the raid; signals for withdrawal, and whether any special signals are required.

(xiv) Signalling arrangements.

(xv) Number of waiting officers and men which will be provided to replace casualties up to Zero (all of whom will have to be practised for the raid).

(xvi) The place at which a copy of the trenches to be raided will be laid out and days and time at which practices will be carried out will be given.

MINOR OPERATION, NIGHT MARCH 18/19TH, 1918.

9030   Original Instructions.
           Battalion Operation Orders.

9030/1   ZERO HOUR and Withdrawal Signal.

9030/2   Lights (Flank Brigades)

9030/3   Trench Mortars

9030/4   Instructions re final details - Dummy figures.

9030/5   Report on Operation.

SECRET.   63rd Infantry Brigade No. 9030
                                    March 13th 1918.
37th Division
8th Somerset L.I.

OPERATION.   1.   8th Bn. Somerset L.I. will carry out a minor operation, taking the form of a raid against the enemy's front line on or about March 18th, 1918, detailed plans for which will be submitted to this office on March 14th. The exact date and ZERO hour will be notified later to all concerned.

OBJECTIVE.   2.   The point in the enemy's system to be raided is a pillbox known by the name of 'The GENERAL'S DUGOUT', situated at J.27.a.40.75, and the trench running southwards from J.21.c.50.00 along the west side of the GENERAL'S DUGOUT to about J.27.a.35.60.

OBJECTS.   3.   To capture or kill the garrison.
To obtain identifications.
To obtain information as to what use is made of the GENERAL'S DUGOUT.
To destroy the tree in the vicinity of the DUGOUT.

STRENGTH AND COMPOSITION OF PARTY.   4.   The Strength of the party will be 2 officers and 51 O.R.

Its composition :-

(a) Assault Party, consisting of
    1 officer, 1 sergt., 2 Corpls and 14 O.R. (including 2 signallers).
(b) Covering party (centre) consisting of
    1 officer, 1 sergt., 1 corpl, 10 O.R., with 1 Lewis Gun.
(c) Right Flank Party, consisting of
    1 Sergt., 1 corpl., 6 O.R., with 1 Lewis Gun.
(d) Left Flank party, consisting of
    1 Sergt., 2 Corpls., 8 O.R., with 1 Lewis Gun.
(e) Demolition Party (Tree), consisting of
    1 R.E. N.C.O. and 2 O.R.

TIME.   5.   It is proposed to carry out the operation at about 2 am, but the exact hour will be decided nearer the date and will to some extent depend on weather conditions.
Bright starlight is preferred.

GENERAL PLAN.   6.   (a) A 5-minutes bombardment of the line LEWIS HOUSE - GENERAL'S DUGOUT - BERRY COTTS - HAMP FARM, (intense on GENERAL'S DUGOUT and the area within 40 yards of it, the last minute of which is to include a bombardment with specially prepared bombs to simulate gas on the area within the objective.
(b) The Barrage will then lift from the above line on to a line about 200 yards east and south east of GENERAL'S DUGOUT, remaining on HAMP FARM and on LEWIS HOUSE. This will enable the raiding party at ZERO plus 5 to move forward and enter the enemy trenches.
(c) The raiding party will have formed up in the southern part of JULIA TRENCH and will have moved forward along tapes laid through gaps in our wire specially prepared early in the evening from our lines.
The Assault party will be followed by the covering party and flank parties who, on reaching the enemy's trenches, will move through the assault party and to the right and left respectively.
The left covering party will move North along and to the east of the enemy trench, will capture or kill the garrison of the enemy machine gun post at J.21.c.50.00 and will cover the left flank of the raiding party from the vicinity of this point.

(2)

ARTILLERY.

7. Targets to be engaged by the artillery will be as follows:-
(a) <u>From ZERO - ZERO plus 5.</u>
    LEWIS HOUSE and its vicinity specially on its southwest side.
    Trenches from J.21.c.50.00, west of and through GENERAL'S DUGOUT, J.27.a.40.75 to a point about J.27.a. 05.10.
    BERRY COTTS.
    HAMP FARM.
(b) <u>From ZERO plus 5 onwards during the operation till ZERO plus 20.</u>
    The following points should receive some attention:- CAPITAL FARM, MARGATE FARM, SWAGGER FARM, TROT HOUSE and tracks thence to front line.
    GHELUVELT Area, including wood.
(c) Demonstrations on the North of the Divisional front and towards the south of the 1st Australian Inf. Bde. front would be of assistance in confusing the enemy as to the real point of the attack.
(d) Enemy wire should be cut from 16th inst. onwards at several points in front of the Divisional front so as not to excite suspicion at any special point.
(e) It is considered that after the enemy S.O.S. has gone up, the heavy artillery might effectively open fire with a view to counter-battery destructive fire on enemy batteries which are known to fire on the TOWER HAMLETS ridge.

TRENCH MORTARS.

8. It is proposed to employ trench mortars as follows :-
<u>Medium 6" NEWTON Mortars</u> under the direction of B.G.R.A., 37th Division, on preparatory wirecutting, and on the targets already mentioned in para. 7.
<u>Light 3" STOKES Mortars</u> as follows :-
    During the bombardment from ZERO to ZERO plus 5 -
4 mortars on enemy trenches from J.21.c.50.00 to J.21.a.35.60.
4 mortars on enemy positions from J.27.a.40.75 to J.27.a.05.50.
1 mortar on SUNKEN ROAD, J.27.d.90.95.
    From ZERO plus 5 to ZERO plus 20 -
These mortars will switch their fire on the following points :-
4 on to BERRY COTTS
2 on to HAMP FARM
2 on to J.27.a.05.10.
1 remaining on SUNKEN ROAD, J.27.d.90.95.

MACHINE GUNS & LEWIS GUNS.

9. The targets set forth below will require to be engaged by direct fire and in addition two Vickers machine guns should be moved up to the front line to engage and silence any machine gun which may open fire from a hitherto silent position from either flank during the progress of the raid. A number of Lewis Guns will also be held in readiness in position for this purpose.
    It would assist the operation if O.C. 37th M.G.Battn. would consider bringing fire to bear on the enemy machine guns located in GHELUVELT WOOD or on any machine guns which are known to bring fire on to the ground near JULIA TRENCH.
    1st Australian Infantry Brigade will also be asked to cooperate with machine guns in neighbourhood of KING'S CASTLE on present S.O.S. lines - BERRY COTTS, switching 200 yards further east at ZERO plus 5.
    Special targets to be engaged are as follows :-
<u>Machine Guns</u> - J.21.c.90.45, J.21.c.95.65, J.21.d.50.74, J.21.d.62.92.
<u>Trench Mortars</u> - J.21.d.05.25.

(3)

FEINTS. 10. DUMMY FIGURES will be set up to simulate an attack and to draw hostile rifle and machine gun fire off actual raiding party as follows:-
    (a) Opposite No. 3 post of Right Company, J.26.b.85.65.
    (b) Opposite Southern portion of KILLECK TRENCH, J.21.c.5) 50.30.)

R.E. 11. O.C. 152nd Field Coy., R.E. will detail 1 N.C.O. and 2 O.R. trained in the use of explosives to report to O.C. 8th Somerset L.I., with a view to participating in the raid and destroying the tree in the neighbourhood of the GENERAL'S DUGOUT.

A special R.E. party should also report to O.C. 8th Somerset L.I., to be trained and held in readiness with BANGALORE torpedoes in case it should be necessary to cut wire which is not anticipated.

R.A.M.C. 12. It is considered that if there are six additional bearers at BODMIN COPSE bearer post, no further special assistance will be required from R.A.M.C. The Regimental Aid Post is at J.20.d.40.72.

DURATION. 13. It is expected that the raid will last about 15 minutes.

SIGNAL FOR WITHDRAWAL. 14. The Signal for withdrawal of the raiding party will be two green very lights fired in quick succession, unless otherwise advised.

SIGNALLING. 15. A Field Telephone, manned by two signallers, will be used and a line run out to the nearest point in enemy trench immediately west of GENERAL'S DUGOUT.

TRAINED RESERVE; TRAINING; PRACTICE TRENCHES. 16. In reserve in case of casualties up to ZERO are 2 officers and 15 O.R., all of whom are being trained in the details of the raid in case of need.

The raid is practised daily on ground where enemy trenches have been laid out, between 11 am and 12.30 pm in the neighbourhood of SCOTTISH WOOD CAMP, H.35.central.

(sd) C.J.de B.SHERINGHAM, Captain,
Brigade Major,
for G.O.C., 63rd Infantry Brigade.

OPERATION ORDERS.

1. **Strength of Raiding Party** 2 officers, 57 O.R.
    divided into Assault, Covering and Demolition Parties as follows:

2. **Composition.**
    A. **Assault Party.** 1 officer, 1 sergt., 2 Corpls., 14 O.R. (including 2 signallers, 2 rifle grenadiers and 1 runner).
    B. **Centre Covering Party.** 1 officer, 1 sergt. 1 corpl., 10 O.R. with 1 Lewis gun (including 2 Lewis gunners 3 rifle grenadiers, 1 runner.)
    C. **Right Covering Party.** 1 Sergt., 1 Corpl., 6 O.R., with 1 Lewis Gun (including 2 Lewis gunners and 2 rifle grenadiers).
    D. **Left Covering Party.** 1 Sergt., 2 Corpls., 10 O.R. with 1 Lewis Gun (including 2 Lewis Gunners and 3 rifle grenadiers).
    E. **Demolition Party.** R.E., 1 N.C.O., 2 O.R.

    4 Stretcher Bearers will move forward with 'B' Party.

3. **Duties of Parties.**
    A. Will attack and overcome any resistance on our side of GENERAL'S DUGOUT and attack and deal with occupants of dugout.

    B. Will pass through A Party and take up position beyond dugout to resist any enemy counter attack and cover retirement of A and E Parties.

    C. Will move on right flank of B, hold ground about 30 - 40 yds South of dugout against counter attack and cover retirement of A and E parties.

    D. Will move on left flank of B to trench immediately North of dugout, move North along and East to East of trench running North, capture or kill garrison of enemy M.G. post at J.21.c.50.00 and cover left flank of A from vicinity of that point.

    E. Will follow B party from our trenches, go to tree immediately South of dugout, place charge and inform O.C. A party when this is done. After signal to withdraw has been given and acted upon by each party, fuze will be lit.

    Stretcher Bearers will move forward in rear of B Party as far as trench immediately W. of dugout where they will remain until required.
    In addition to above, 4 stretcher bearers of A Company, 8th Somerset L.I. will be held in readiness in JULIA TRENCH during the raid to assist in bringing in casualties.

4. **Dispositions for Attack.**
    At ZERO - 40 minutes, the whole party will move from Reserve line N. of STEVENS TRENCH in following order to JULIA TRENCH - A, B, E, C, D. On arrival they will form up in trench opposite their respective gaps in our wire.
    At ZERO plus 4 minutes each party will lead out of trench through gaps in wire and lie down in file along tapes specially laid through gaps earlier in the evening, A party in advance of other parties.

5. **Attack.**
    At ZERO plus 5 minutes the raiding party will advance as quickly as possible towards dugout. All parties will move in file (with one scout about 5 - 10 yds ahead of each column) as far as trench immediately west of dugout extending only in the event of opposition by enemy west of this point.

(2)

'A' Party will clear trench west of dugout and divide into 4 parties as follows :-

1. 1 Cpl. 4 men will clear trench on south of dugout for distance of 15 - 20 yards and take up position in that trench.

2. 1 officer, 1 sergt., 4 men, will pass dugout on each side and capture or kill occupants.

3. 1 Cpl. and 4 men will pass dugout on left side, clear trench running N.E. from rear/for distance of 15 - 20 yards
of dugout
and hold that trench.

4. 2 signallers with Field telephone will remain in trench west of dugout and establish a station at that point (having run out a line from JULIA TRENCH as they moved forward in rear of 'A' party).

After 'B' party have passed through 'A' party, any prisoners captured in the dugout will be despatched at once in charge of two men previously told off for this duty to JULIA TRENCH, care having been taken to separate officers, N.C.Os and men immediately after capture. Any machine guns captured in dugout will be carried back by prisoners who will also be used as stretcher bearers for any of our wounded.

'B' party will follow 'A' party closely across No Man's Land (reinforcing 'A' party in case of determined enemy resistance at the dugout) and pass through them, taking up a position, extended to two paces about 30 - 40 yards east of dugout. On taking up this position, touch will at once be obtained with C and D parties and maintained throughout the operation.

'C' party will move across No Man's Land on right flank of B party to south end of trench immediately west of dugout, clear trench running S.E., and take up position, extended to 2 paces, across this trench, about 30 yards from dugout.

'D' party will move on left flank of B party to North end of trench running immediately west of dugout, where it will divide into 2 sections as follows :-

1. 1 Sergt. and 4 men clearing trench running North towards enemy M.G. post at J.21.c.50.00.

2. 1 Cpl. and 6 men with 1 Lewis gun, moving Northwards to the East of trench leading to J.21.c.50.00.

These parties will converge at the above point, kill or capture garrison, and take up position in vicinity of post to repel counter attack and cover retirement of A party.

Touch with left of B party will be maintained throughout operation.

'E' party will move forward in rear of D party at ZERO plus 5 minutes, place charge in tree, taking notice of any evidence of the tree having been used by the enemy as an observation post, and inform O.C. A party when fuze is ready for lighting.

WITHDRAWAL.   The signal for withdrawal will be   .
This will be fired by O.C. A party after E party have reported that fuze is ready for lighting.

A party will at once withdraw as quickly as possible along tape leading back to JULIA TRENCH (this tape will have been laid by at ZERO plus 5 by man following in rear of D party), covered by B, C and D parties.

C and D parties will then withdraw, covered for a short distance by B party. B party will withdraw, first to trench west of dugout and cover N.E. while fuze to charge laid in tree is ignited; when this is done, B party will at once withdraw to JULIA TRENCH, having thrown 2 R.S.K. bombs into dugout, care being taken that the guiding tape is brough in at the same time.

Stretcher bearers will withdraw with B party.

All parties will be checked on reaching JULIA TRENCH and O.C. Raid will notify O.C. 8th Somerset L.I. of return of whole party by telephone and by runner, using the word 'BOX'.

Every endeavour will be made to bring in any casualties before the parties withdraw.

In the event of none of the enemy being captured alive, identifications will be obtained from enemy killed.

Officers in charge A and B parties and N.C.Os i/c C and D parties, will each have one man detailed as runners from their respective parties.

Captured documents and identifications will be sent back to JULIA TRENCH and handed over to O.C. Raid at once.

REPORT CENTRE.   No. 2 post, JULIA TRENCH, J.27.c.25.95.

A counter sign will be issued.

ADMINISTRATIVE INSTRUCTIONS.

Hands and faces of all ranks will be blackened and bayonets will be blackened by smoke.

All ranks will wear cap comforters.

Raid identity discs will be issued to all ranks and all means of identification will be removed from clothing.

All letters, pay-books, etc., will be placed in sealed envelopes and handed over to the Company Quartermaster Sergeant at SCOTTISH WOOD CAMP before party moves up to the line.

Each man will be in possession of one packet of cough lozenges.

All ranks will be medically examined on the 18th instant and any men who are suffering from colds will not be allowed to participate in the raid.

ARMS & EQUIPMENT

All N.C.Os and men (except No.1 of Lewis Gun teams who will be armed with revolvers) will carry rifle with bayonet fixed and four rounds in the magazine and one in the breech, except rifle grenadiers who will have 5 rounds in the magazine, cut-off closed and one round blank in breech.

All ranks except rifle grenadiers will carry two hand grenades- one in each side pocket of tunic.

Each rifle grenadier will carry 6 rifle grenades in special haversack.

Spare hand grenades to the number of 1 per man will be carried by a man of each party in a bucket.

No.2 of each Lewis Gun team will carry 4 drums.

50% of each party will carry wire cutters.

B party will carry 4 M.S.K.bombs.

All N.C.Os and men will wear 1 bandolier S.A.A.

O.C., A party will carry an electric torch.

The O.C., A party and his two senior N.C.Os will each carry VERY Pistol and 4 lights.

All ranks armed with revolvers will carry 12 spare rounds in pockets.

All ranks will wear box respirators in 'Alert' position.

All ranks will wear steel helmets until Zero - 10 minutes when these will be dumped in JULIA TRENCH.

1 man of A Company will carry a sandbag for bringing back documents etc..

Hot tea and rum will be issued in Reserve Line both before and after the raid.

The reserve of trained Officer N.C.Os and men will move with the party previous to raid as far as JULIA TRENCH where they will remain during the raid or until called upon to reinforce the raiding party.

SECRET.   63rd Infantry Brigade No. 9030/1
                         March 18th 1918.

        Reference this office No. 9030 dated March 13th, 1918,

1.   ZERO HOUR will be 2.30 am on March 19th, 1918.

2.   Watches will be synchronized at BEDFORD HOUSE at noon
and 6 pm and at Advanced Brigade Headquarters, TORR TOP, at
7 pm on March 18th.

3.   The withdrawal signal for the raiding party will be
two Green Very lights fired in quick succession from the
vicinity of GENERAL'S DUGOUT.

        Arrangements have been made for this signal to be repeated
from three other points on the Divisional front and at one
point on the 1st Australian Brigade front.

                                    (sd) C.J.de B.SHERINGHAM,
                                              Captain,
                                           Brigade Major,
                                        63rd Infantry Brigade.

TO:-
        8th Somerset L.I.
        8th Lincolnshire Regt.
        4th Middlesex Regt.
        63rd T.M.Battery
        'A' Coy., 37th M.G.Battn.
        37th Div. Arty.
        37th M.G.Battalion
        Southern Group Artillery.
        111th Infantry Brigade
        112th Infantry Brigade
        1st Aust. Inf. Brigade.
        37th Division
        O.C.Raid
        War Diary
        File.

63rd Infantry Brigade No. 9050/5

39th Division

MINOR
REPORT ON OPERATION CARRIED OUT ON NIGHT MARCH 18/19th 1918.

The following is report on the minor operation carried out by 8th Somerset L.I. on night March 18/19th, 1918.

Reference this office No. 9050 and subsequent correspondence.

The raiding party consisted of 3 officers and 57 other ranks. The party embussed at SCOTTISH WOOD CAMP at 10.30 pm on 18th inst. and arrived at front Battalion H.Q., B J.20.d.4.7, at midnight. After a hot meal at 1 am, 19th inst. they moved off at 1.45 am to JULIA TRENCH where they were in position at 2.20 am.

The artillery barrage came down punctually at 2.30 am and was very even and accurate, so much so that at 2.35 am when it had been arranged for the 6" NEWTON Trench Mortars to lift on to targets further in rear the raiders were able to leave our trenches and get clear of our wire.

By Zero plus 4 our party was clear of the wire while the artillery was still firing on S.O.S. lines.

Upon the artillery lifting at ZERO plus 4 on to targets further east, the raiders crawled still further forward until they were in shell holes within approximately 20 yards of the Stokes Mortar barrage which is reported as being fired very evenly and effectively on the GENERAL'S DUGOUT and the trenches from J.21.c.5.0 southwards.

At about ZERO plus 5 the centre party saw five of the enemy in the trench about 30 yards north of GENERAL'S DUGOUT. This party opened fire with their rifles, but they pressed on to the trench and some of them fired back and threw bombs in the direction of the enemy party. The raiding party as they approached, saw 7 or 8 of the enemy about 25 yards south of the GENERAL'S DUGOUT. These were seen running away and were bombed and were fired on. The raiding party pressed on but by the time they had crossed the trench the enemy were lost to view in the dust and smoke caused by the heavy fire. They were last seen going in the direction of BERRY COTTS.

In the trench to the south of the dugout was a machine gun emplacement in which was a belt of ammunition. The party reported a little shelter similar to our English shelter not badly damaged by our fire, but with the front knocked in. The raiding party proceeded as far south of the dugout as was possible taking into consideration the flanking machine gun barrage fired from No. 4 post, Right Company, but no trace of the enemy could be found.

As the left party entered the trench North of the dugout, about 6 of the enemy were seen running away.

The signal for withdrawal was fired at 2.50 am approximately and the whole party reached our own trenches without casualties at about 2.55 am.

The enemy retaliatory barrage was weak and fell in the neighbourhood of SUNKEN trench at the Support line.

As the left party withdrew in accordance with the withdrawal signal, some of the enemy were seen from the direction of LEWIS HOUSE. The Lewis Gunner fired two magazines at this party and dispersed them before following the withdrawing raiding party.

The tree to the south of the GENERAL'S DUGOUT was destroyed the charge exploding as the last man of the raiding party were approaching our own line.

SECRET   63rd Infantry Brigade No. 9030/3

63rd Trench Mortar Battery
112th Trench Mortar Battery
1st Australian Infantry Brigade
8th Somerset L.I.
O.C.Raid

      Reference this office No. 9030m para. 8, the following is the 3" Stokes Mortar Programme :-

    Nos. 1 and 2, KILLICK TRENCH, J.21.c.4.5, fire from ZERO to ZERO plus 5 on J.27.a.5.9, each mortar to traverse $4\frac{1}{2}°$ each way from central. At Zero plus 5 the mortars will lift and barrage J.27.a.00.45 to J.27.a.00.30.

    Nos. 3 and 4, BEDOUIN TRENCH, J.26.b.8085 fire from ZERO to ZERO plus 5 on J.27.a.45.85 to J.27.a.35.55, each mortar to traverse $4\frac{1}{2}°$ each way.
    At Zero plus 5 the mortars will lift and fire on and engage M.G. at HAMP FARM.

    Nos. 5, 6, 7 and 8 will fire from Zero to Zero plus 5 on J.27.a.35.55 to J.27.a.00.45, all mortars to traverse $4\frac{1}{2}°$ each way.
    At Zero plus 5 the mortars will lift and fire on J.27.a.00.55 to J.26.d.75.95, SUNKEN ROAD.
    No. 9 Mortar will fire from ZERO to ZERO plus 20 on posts in SUNKEN ROAD.

    Map reference of Nos. 5, 6, 7, 8 and 9 - BITTER WOOD, J.26.b.35.55.

    O.C. 112th T.M.Battery will arrange to bombard LEWIS HOUSE and the vicinity with three 3" Stokes Mortars from Zero till Zero plus 25.

    Specially prepared smoke bombs will be fired from 112th T.M.Battery on LEWIS HOUSE and by 63rd T.M.Battery on HAMP FARM and SUNKEN ROAD, J.26.d.75.95 at Zero plus 4.

                          (sd) C.J. de B. SHERINGHAM,
                                       Captain,
                                    Brigade Major,
28.3.18   63rd Infantry Brigade.

(2)

The GENERAL'S DUGOUT was found to be badly knocked about. No actual slits could be seen, but when P.B.X. bombs were thrown into the dugout before leaving, smoke was seen issuing from the dugout.

The ground all round the dugout is very wet and there was no direct evidence of the dugout being used for observation purposes.

Our own barrage gradually slackened and finally ceased when the party was reaching the front Battalion H.Q. at 3.15 am.

The fact that there were no casualties from the time that the party left our trenches until the time of their return is attributed
(1) to the careful neutralisation of all known enemy machine gun
    posts by direct machine gun and T.M. fire,
(2) to the use of dummies which were erected to the Earthworks
North of the objective at a point east of the southern end of KILLEM TRENCH, and opposite No. 3 post of the Right Company.

Both these dummy parties were engaged by the enemy, particularly the Northern party which apparently kept the machine guns in the direction of LEWIS HOUSE very busy.

Casualties: 1 O.R. slightly wounded by enemy granatenwerfer bomb
              in our trenches on the way up to the front line.

                                    (Sd.) E.L.Challenor,
                                          Brigadier General,
March 19th 1918   Comdg. 63rd Infantry Brigade.

63rd Infantry Brigade No. 9030/2

SECRET.

111th Infantry Brigade.
112th Infantry Brigade.
1st Aust. Inf. Brigade.

    Can you arrange to fire two green lights after you see two green lights go up at GENERAL'S DUGOUT tonight from some point in your front line ?

(sd) C.J.de B.SHERRINGHAM, Captain,
Brigade Major,
63rd Infantry Brigade.

18.3.18

SECRET

63rd Infantry Brigade No. 9030/4

8th Somerset L.I.
37th Divnl. Artillery
O.C. Raid
63rd T.M. Battery
Southern Group, Artillery
'A' Coy., 37th M.G. Battn.
112th Infantry Brigade.
1st Aust. Inf. Brigade.

---

1.   O.C. 8th Somerset L.I. will consider the advisability of demonstrating with dummy figures near the Southern end of KILLICK TRENCH and No. 3 Post, Right Company, with the object of drawing any enemy machine gun fire away from the raiding party. He will also arrange for Lewis Guns to cover the ground and engage any hostile machine guns on right or left flanks.

2.   O.C. 'A' Company, 37th M.G. Battalion
   (a) will post two Vickers Machine guns in No. 5 post, JULIA Trench in readiness to cover the left flank of the raiding party, or engage any hostile machine gun in enemy trench which may attempt to fire.
   (b) will post two machine guns in No. 4 Post, right company, to cover right flank of raiding party and fire on enemy posts and trenches between J.26.b.97.39 to about J.27.a.15.55.

3.   O.C. 8th Somerset L.I. will arrange to communicate with this office and O.C. Southern Group, Artillery, as soon as raiding party has returned to our lines. The word 'BOX' will be sent through. This will be the signal to the artillery to cease fire.

(sd) C.J.de B. SHERINGHAM, Captain,
Brigade Major,
63rd Infantry Brigade.

18.3.18

SECRET   Copy No. 1

63rd Infantry Brigade Order No. 199.

Ref. Sheet 28 1:40,000   March 19th 1918.

1. (a) On night March 21/22nd, 4th Middlesex Regt. will relieve 8th Somerset L.I. in the line; 8th Somerset. L.I., upon relief, will withdraw to support in and around CANADA TUNNELS.
(b) As 8th Somerset L.I. arrive in support, 8th Lincolns will withdraw into Reserve at SCOTTISH WOOD CAMP.

2. Two trains (Light Railway) have been arranged for to convoy 8th Middlesex Regt. from VIJVERHOEK SIDING at 6.30 pm and 6.45 pm respectively to LAMBTON SIDING. 4th Middlesex will detail officers to supervise the entraining and detraining.
The same transport will convey 8th Lincolns from LAMBTON SIDING to VIJVERHOEK SIDING in two trains which will leave LAMBTON SIDING under arrangements to be made by O.C. 8th Lincolnshire Regt. who will detail an entraining officer.
Probable time of departure of first train - 11.30 pm.

3. All details of the above reliefs will be arranged between Commanding Officers concerned.

4. No troops will move forward of the TOR TOP - MT. SORREL Ridge before 7.45 pm. Troops will move in parties not larger than platoons, with a distance of 200 yards between platoons.

5. All trench stores, defence schemes, air photos, etc, will be handed over and receipts taken, copies of which will be forwarded to Brigade H.Q.

6. Completion of reliefs will be notified to this office in B.A.B.Code.

            Captain,
       for Brigade Major,
       63rd Infantry Brigade.

Issued at 5 pm

Distribution.	Copy No.		
War Diary & File	1 - 3	37th Division	18 - 19
Brigade Staff	4 - 8	C.R.E.	20
8th Lincolnshire Regt.	9	D.G.R.A.	21
8th Somerset L.I.	10	111th Inf. Bde.	22
4th Middlesex Regt.	11	112th Inf. Bde.	23
63rd T.M.Battery	12	1st Aust. Inf. Bde.	24
154th Field Coy., R.E.	13	37th M.G.Battalion	25
9th N. Staffs (Pnrs)	14	Bde. Transport Off.	26
No. 2 Coy. Train	15	Bde. School	27
Southern Group, Arty.	16	C.L.R.O. XXII Corps	28
Centre Group, Arty.	17		

SECRET.

DEFENCE SCHEME

FRONT LINE BATTALION (RIGHT SUBSECTOR).

I. DESCRIPTION OF BATTALION AREA.

(a) FRONT.   The front held by the battalion extends from the BASSEVILLEBEEK at J.26.d.4.9 on the right to J.21.c. 70.55 on the left. It is the right subsector of the 37th Divisional Front and is about 1200 yards long. The 112th Infantry Brigade is on the left, astride the MENIN Road. The 1st Australian Brigade is on the right of the Battalion, southwards from the BASSEVILLEBEEK.

(b) BOUNDARIES. Battalion Boundary on South; Front line at J.26.d.40.90 along the BASSEVILLEBEEK to J.26.b.30.40. Present right post at J.26.b.60.50.
      Battalion Boundary on North; Front line at J.21.c.70.55 - J.20.d.25.90 - J.20.a.20.30.

(c) TOPOGRAPHY. The principal feature in the right subsector lies west of the forward battalion area. This is the BASSEVILLEBEEK Valley which is very marshy and, except in very dry weather, practically impassable except by existing tracks and duckboard crossings. These are
   DUMBARTON TRACK)   Close together at
   GLOUCESTER DRIVE)   about J.20.central.

   STOUT TRACK at J.20.d.0.1.

   All communication with the rear is across this valley.
   The subsector held by the forward battalion lies on top of the TOWER HAMLETS SPUR on the left, bending westward off the spur in the right centre and running westwards down the western slope of the spur to the BASSEVILLEBEEK VALLEY.

II. DISPOSITIONS.

   The forward battalion occupies the forward zone and main defensive system of the Battle Zone of the Brigade Area, disposed as follows :-

missing and prisoners were nearly all too high. "A considerable percentage under this heading "are due to men having strayed from their units,

(2)

<u>N.B.</u> Companies organized in three platoons.

3 Companies in front line.
1 Company in Support,
disposed as follows :-

<u>RIGHT COMPANY</u>   2 platoons holding posts 1, 2, 3/3a, 4 and 5 in J.26.b. by night; 2 posts only held by day.
1 platoon in BEDOUIN TRENCH.
Coy. H.Q. BEDOUIN TRENCH, J.26.b.75.90.

<u>CENTRE COMPANY</u>   2 platoons in JULIA TRENCH.
1 platoon in AMBROSE TRENCH.
Coy. H.Q. at AMBROSE Fm, J.21.c.20.15.

<u>LEFT COMPANY</u>   2 platoons in MILLICH TRENCH.
1 platoon, Northern end of AMBROSE Tr.
(with L.G. post at J.21.c.15.65).
Coy. H.Q., AMBROSE TRENCH, J.21.c.25.35.

<u>SUPPORT COMPANY</u>   1 platoon in S.P.3, J.20.d.30.25.
2 platoons in PALESTINE and STEVENS Tr.
Coy. H.Q. at PALESTINE TRENCH, J.20.d.)
40.30.)

<u>BATTALION H.Q. & DETAILS.</u>   J.20.d.40.70.

III. <u>PRECAUTIONARY ACTION.</u>

In the event of 'Precautionary Action' being ordered
1. The Battalion will 'Stand to'.
2. Front line Companies will (if by night or foggy) send out patrols.
3. H.Q. details will occupy the main line.

IV.
(a)   In the event of attack -
The post line will be held at all costs and garrisons of posts will not withdraw, even if outflanked. Should a post or any portion of our line be temporarily lost, supporting platoons will at once counter attack, assisted by neighbouring posts.

(b)   A vigourous policy of patrolling in No Man's Land will be maintained, and any gaps between Companies and Brigades on either flank will be constantly patrolled at night.

(c)   The defence of the front line system is organized in depth, in that PALESTINE TRENCH is wired on both sides for defence to a flank, with the object of holding the enemy in a pocket.

(3)

(d) **Main Defensive System.** The Reserve of the Battalion in the Outpost System will normally be located in this system and, with the exception of definite garrisons detailed for the defence of each strong point, will be available for immediate counter attack.

(e) **Counter attack.** The dispositions of troops in the forward area will be such that the following troops are available for immediate counter-attack :-
  (i) In each Company   -   1 platoon
  (ii) In each Battalion   -   1 Company

These troops are to be detailed for counter attack and will not be used to reinforce or as garrisons of strong points. In the event of the enemy obtaining a footing in any portion of the Defensive System, he will, under the orders of the Commander on the spot, be immediately counter-attacked by local reserves maintained at suitable positions within the Defensive System.

The quicker such counter attack can be delivered the better. Battalion Commanders are responsible that all subordinate commanders in the line ~~down to and including platoon commanders~~ are prepared to organize a counter attack on the spot without reference to their superiors.

In the event of an immediate counter attack failing a deliberate counter attack will be carried out under Divisional instructions.

The Infantry Battalion in Reserve will be used for a deliberate counter attack after artillery preparation and under an artillery barrage, or to prevent the enemy extending his initial success and to maintain the position while a deliberate counter attack is being prepared by Corps.

The Support Company (less 1 platoon holding S.P. " 3 and 4) form the Battalion Reserve under the orders of the Battalion Commander.

In the event of
(a) An attack to gain the high ground of the TOWER HAMLETS Spur, with the object of denying observation to the east and obtaining direct observation on the ground east of the MOUNT SORREL - CLAPHAM JUNCTION Ridge.

(4)

(b)　　A minor operation to capture some tactical point.
(c)　　A raid,

the company (less 1 platoon) would be used for immediate counter attack.

　　In the event of
(d) an attack on a large scale with the object of gaining the main MOUNT SORREL - CLAPHAM JUNCTION Ridge,

the company would garrison the Main Line Trench running North from STEVENS TRENCH and would be reinforced by H.Q. details.
　　This line would be held at all costs with a view to preventing the enemy gaining the Eastern edge of the TOWER HAMLETS ridge with observation over the BASSEVILLEBEEK and ground to the westward.

　　In the event of (d) as above :-
(i) If the attack is to the North of PALESTINE TRENCH, the Support Company will advance overland from STEVENS TRENCH via the gaps cut and marked in our wire.
(ii) Should the attack be to the South of PALESTINE TRENCH, the Support Coy. will move up PALESTINE TRENCH and deploy for attack in BEDOUIN TRENCH.

NOTE: All working parties reporting to Battalion H.Q. would be used as the occasion required, normally they would be used to reinforce the garrison of the STEVENS TRENCH - MAIN LINE position.

ATTACKS ON FLANK BATTALIONS

V.

　　In the event of the unit on our Left Flank giving way, the exposed flank will be protected by L.G. fire from the N. end of KILLICK TRENCH and Post at J.21.c.15.65.
　　The Support Platoon of the Left Company will advance and occupy the old trench running between the N. end of KILLICK TRENCH and the L.G. Post referred to above.
　　In the event of the unit on our Right Flank giving way, the exposed flank will be covered by L.G. and rifle fire from S.P.1, S.P.2, S.P.3 and the Southern end of BEDOUIN TRENCH.

VI.　ENEMY BARRAGE.　In the event of a heavy hostile barrage being put down on our front line system, O.C. Companies affected will arrange to move a portion or whole of their commands to a shell hole line in front of the line barraged. This line will be previously reconnoitred and taped out and platoons practised in occupying it quickly. The original line will be reoccupied as soon as the barrage lifts or the shelling ceases.

APPENDIX E - S.O.S. SIGNAL

S.O.S. Stations are established at each Coy. H.Q. and Battn. H.Q. Relay posts are established at J.19.d.60.55 and J.25.b.90.90 Look out Stations are established at TORR TOP and CANADA TUNNELS.

The S.O.S. will be fired -
(i) when the enemy are actually seen to be attacking.
(ii) in the event of a heavy hostile T.M. barrage on our line.

APPENDIX F - COMMUNICATIONS.

1. TELEPHONE.
(a) Coys. are connected to Battn. H.Q. by ground cable; laterals between Companies by ground cable.

(b) Battalion to Adv. Brigade by ground cable; direct lateral to Battn. on left.

2. POWER BUZZER and AMPLIFIER.
(a) Power Buzzer from Right Coy. H.Q. in line working to Battn. H.Q. in line. The message might also be read by Centre Battn. H.Q.

(b) Power Buzzer and Amplifier at Battn. H.Q. in line working to Divnl. Wireless Centre, J.19.a.5.9.

3. VISUAL.
(a) Lamps from Right, Centre and Left Coys in line to Adv. Brigade H.Q., EQ 46.
(b) Lamp from Battn. H.Q. in line to Advanced Bde. H.Q., EQ 46. Messages could also be read from CANADA TUNNELS.
(c) Lamp from Adv. Bde. H.Q. to Bde. H.Q.

4. PIGEON.
The Battalion in Line received 8 birds daily.
    2 at Right Coy. H.Q.
    2 at Centre Coy. H.Q.
    2 at Left Coy. H.Q.
    2 at Battn. H.Q.

5. ROCKETS.
Rocket emplacements are installed at Battn. H.Q. and Support Coy. H.Q. and a supply (3) of rockets are available at each position.

6. RUNNERS.
Battn. in line collect from and deliver to Adv. Bde. In the event of attack or Precautionary Action, 2 runners should be sent to J.19.d.60.55 (BODMIN COPSE Test Box) as a runner relay post and 2 runners to Adv. Bde. H.Q. at TORR TOP.

SECRET. Copy No. 1

63rd Infantry Brigade Order No. 200.

Reference Sheet 2.2, 1:10,000   March 24th 1918.

1. On night 24/25th March, 49th Division is extending its right southwards, taking over from 37th Division as far south as the EUTELBEEK. The Northern Divisional Boundary will then be :-
EUTELBEEK - J.15.central - J.15.a.30.60 - J.8.d.70.20 - thence as at present.

2. On night March 25/26th -
   (a) 37th Division is extending its right southwards, taking over from 1st Australian Division from J.26.d.40.90 to J.32.a.70.35. The Southern Divisional Boundary will then be Post 6, J.32.a.70.35 and FORTH FARM (inclusive) - GROENENBURG FARM exclusive - I.36.b.60.70 - I.30.c.0.0. - Railway at I.28.b.80.40.
   (b) 111th Infantry Brigade will relieve 112th Infantry Brigade in Centre subsector. 112th Infantry Brigade will upon relief withdraw into Divisional Reserve disposed as follows :-

Brigade Headquarters	WASHINGTON AVENUE
One Battalion	MANITATU CAMP
One Battalion	MAIDI CAMP
One Battalion and Trench Mortar Battery	MALPLAQUET CAMP.

   (c) On night March 25/26th 63rd Infantry Brigade will extend its right as above in relief of 1st Australian Inf. Bde. as far south as Post 6, J.32.a.70.35.
   That part of 1st Australian Inf. Bde. front from J.32.a.70.35 to J.32.c.00.55 will be taken over by 3rd Australian Infantry Brigade.

3. On night March 25/26th, 8th Lincolnshire Regt. will relieve 3rd Australian Battalion in the line as above from J.26.d.40.90 to J.32.a.70.35.

4. Trains will leave VIJVERHOEK SIDING at 7.00 pm and 7.15 pm respectively and will convey the Battalion thence to LAMBTON SIDING, I.21.d.75.35.
   All other details of relief will be arranged between Commanding Officers concerned.

5. A consolidated return showing defence schemes, maps, trench stores etc. taken over will be forwarded to this office.

6. Completion of relief will be notified to this office by sending the Code word 'THANKS'.

7. Command of the line as far south as J.32.a.70.35 will pass to G.O.C. 63rd Infantry Brigade on completion of relief.

8. All movement forward of the line MOUNT SORREL - HILL 60 will be after dark.
   From detraining point a distance of 200 yards will be maintained between platoons.

9........

- 2 -

9. The 63rd Infantry Brigade will then be disposed as follows:-

   Right Subsector:

      8th Lincolnshire Regt. with 2 Coys. in front posts.
                                 1 Coy. and 1 platoon
                                     in support about
                                   'THE GLEN'.
                                 1 Coy. less 1 platoon
                                   in Reserve in
                                   PAGE AVENUE.
                                 Battn. H.Q. at
                                 I.36.a.30.99.

   Left Subsector:

      As at present.

      Support Battalion as at present with 1 platoon in
                                   Reserve Line, PAYTIS
                                   TRENCH, J.20.d.
                                   Battn. H.Q. in
                                   CANADA TUNNELS.

                                   (signature)
                                   Captain,
                                   Brigade Major,
Issued at 9 p.m.   63rd Infantry Brigade.

Distribution	Copy No.
War Diary & File	1 - 3
Brigade Staff	4 - 8
8th Lincolnshire Regt.	9
8th Somerset L.I.	10
4th Middlesex Regt.	11
53rd T.M. Battery	12
154th Field Company, R.E.	13
9th N. Staffs Regt. (Pioneers)	14
No. 2 Coy. Train	15
Southern Group, Artillery	16
Centre Group, Artillery	17
50th Field Ambulance	18
37th Division	19 - 20
C.R.E.	21
G.R.A.	22
111th Infantry Brigade	23
112th Infantry Brigade	24
1st Aust. Inf. Brigade	25
3rd Aust. Inf. Brigade	26
37th M.G. Battalion	27
Brigade Transport Officer	28
Brigade Gas Officer	30
Brigade School	31
C.L.O., XXII Corps	32

SECRET. Copy No. 1.

63rd Infantry Brigade Order No. 201.

Ref. Sheet, 28, 1:40,000   March 25th 1918.

1. On night March 27/28th, 8th Somerset L.I. will relieve 4th Middlesex Regt. in the line. 4th Middlesex Regt. upon relief will withdraw into support in and around CANADA TUNNELS.

2. All details of the above relief will be arranged between Commanding Officers concerned.

3. No troops will move forward of the TOR TOP - MOUNT SORREL Ridge before 7.45 pm. Troops will move in parties not larger than platoons, with a distance of 200 yards between platoons.

4. All trench Stores, defence schemes, air photos, etc. will be handed over and receipts taken, copies of which will be forwarded to Brigade H.Q.

5. Completion of relief will be notified to this office by use of the code word 'PORT'.

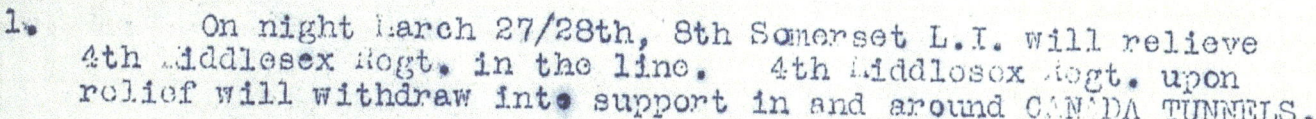
Captain,
Brigade Major,
Issued at 1.30 pm   63rd Infantry Brigade.

Distribution	Copy No.
War Diary & File	1 - 3
Brigade Staff	4 - 8
8th Lincolnshire Regt.	9
8th Somerset L.I.	10
4th Middlesex Regt.	11
63rd T.M.Battery	12
154th Field Coy., R.E.	13
9th N. Staffs (Pnrs)	14
No. 2 Coy. Train	15
Southern Group, Arty.	16
Centre Group, Arty.	17
37th Division	18 - 19
C.R.E.	20
C.R.A.	21
111th Inf. Bde.	22
112th Inf. Bde.	23
37th M.G.Battalion	24
Brigade Transport Offr.	25
Brigade School	26

SECRET   Copy No. 1

63rd Infantry Brigade Order No. 203

March 28th 1918

1. (a) 37th Division (less artillery and No. 1 Coy. Train) with H.Q. and 3 sections 37th Div. M.T. Coy. and S.A.A.Section of D.A.C. will be transferred from XXII Corps to Third Army.

   (b) 37th Division (less artillery and No. 1 Coy. Train) will move by rail on March 28/29th to MONDICOURT - PAS - BOUQUEMAISONS Area.

   (c) 63rd Inf. Bde. Group and 4th Middlesex Regt. will move in accordance with table attached.

2. 63rd Infantry Brigade Group for the purpose of entrainment will be as follows :-
   63rd Infantry Brigade (less 4th Middlesex Regt.)
   153rd Field Company, R.E.
   'C' Coy., 37th M.G.Battalion
   No. 2 Coy. Train
   ½ S.A.A.Section, 37th D.A.C.

3. (a) Entraining Stations will be as follows :-
   For 63rd Inf. Bde. Group   CAESTRE
   For 4th Middlesex Regt.   HOPOUTRE

   (b) Detraining Stations will be as follows :-
   For 63rd Inf. Bde. Group   MONDICOURT - PAS
   For 4th Middlesex Regt.   BOUQUEMAISONS

4. 63rd Inf. Bde. Entraining Officer :-
   Captain H.A.MAYNARD, M.C., 4th Middlesex Regt.

   63rd Inf. Bde. Detraining Officer :-
   Staff Captain.

   Each unit will detail its own entraining officer who should report to the Brigade Entraining Officer with a marching out state in <u>triplicate</u>.

   Billeting Officer in the new area :-
   Captain C.S.WILLIS, 8th Lincolnshire Regt.

   153rd Field Company, R.E. will detail 1 officer and 100 other ranks to act as a loading party at the entraining station. This party will report to Captain H.A.MAYNARD, M.C. at 6.25 am on 29th inst.

   The Company of 8th Lincolnshire Regt. proceeding on the 1st train leaving CAESTRE at 9.25 am will furnish an unloading party of 1 officer and 100 other ranks at MONDICOURT - PAS. This party will report to the Staff Captain immediately on detrainment and will remain on duty until the troops from the last train have marched off.

   Each Unit of 63rd Inf. Bde. Group will send on billeting parties under a billeting officer to report to Capt. WILLIS at CAESTRE at 8.10 am. Two days' rations in addition to the unconsumed portion of the current day's ration, and iron ration will be carried. Billeting parties should consist of not more than 1 officer and 6 O.R. and should if possible have cycles.

5. All transport will arrive at entraining stations 3 hours prior to departure of trains and all personnel 1½ hours prior to departure.

6. Complete marching out states showing number of men, animals, 4-wheeled vehicles, 2 wheeled vehicles and bicycles will be handed to the R.T.O. by the Brigade Entraining Officer with a copy for the officer in charge of each train.

8. HEAD COLLARS and head ropes for securing horses in trucks will be provided by units.

9. LASHINGS for vehicles will be provided by Railway authorities.

10. VEHICLES: Supply and Baggage wagons of the Divnl. Train will accompany the units which they serve. The O.C. Divnl. Train will arrange for these wagons to be handed over to units.

11. WATER CARTS and COOKERS: Water carts will be entrained full and cookers with 24 hours fuel.

12. WATERING HORSES: All horses will, as far as possible, be watered just prior to entraining.

13. One motor ambulance will be on duty at each entraining and detraining station.

14. PICQUETS: The senior officer on each train will ensure that picquets are posted at each end of the train at all stops to prevent troops leaving.

15. SUPPLIES: All troops will entrain with unexpired portion of rations 28th and complete rations for 29th and 30th. Rations for consumption 30th will be drawn in Brigade Group Billeting areas at 4 pm, 27th and will remain on supply wagons which accompany units by train. Rations for consumption 29th inst. will consist of Preserved rations and will be issued to all troops entraining as follows :-
CAESTRE 7.30 am   CAESTRE - CASSEL Main Road, ½ mile west of CAESTRE.
HOPOUTRE 7.30 am   HOPOUTRE Station.
Preserved rations and forage for consumption 29th will be carried on the man and animal.

16. STRAGGLERS: All stragglers arriving at entraining stations after the Divn. has left will be directed to Div. Wing, Corps Reinforcement Camp, BERTHEN.

17. Acknowledge.

Captain,
Brigade Major,
63rd Infantry Brigade.

Issued at 4 pm

Distribution	Copy No.		
War Diary & File	1 - 3	49th Field Ambulance	17
Brigade Staff	4 - 8	37th Division	18 - 19
8th Lincolnshire Regt.	9	111th Inf. Bde.	20
8th Somerset L.I.	10	112th Inf. Bde.	21
4th Middlesex Regt.	11	Area Cmdt.	
63rd T.M.Battery	12	GODEWAERSVELDE	22
163rd Field Company, R.E.	13	R.T.O. CAESTRE	23
No. 2 Coy. Train	14	Bde. Entraining Officer	24
'C' Coy, 37th M.G.Bn.	15	Bde. Supply Officer	25
S.A.A. Sect. D.A.C.	16	Bde. Billeting Officer	26

SECRET   (15)   Copy No. 24

63rd Infantry Brigade Order No. 202.

March 27th 1918

1.   On night March 27/28th, 63rd Infantry Brigade will be relieved in the line by XXII Corps Mounted Troops (South of the BASSEVILLEBEEK) and by 4th York & Lancaster Regt. (North of the BASSEVILLEBEEK).

2.   Upon relief, moves will be made as per march table attached.

3.   For the purpose of the move, the following units will be grouped with the 63rd Inf. Bde. as 63rd Inf. Bde. Group :-

        153rd Field Company, R.E.
        49th Field Ambulance
        No. 2 Coy. Train
        9th N. Staffs (Pnrs) (less 1 company with
                                       cooker and team)
        'C' Coy. 37th M.G. Battalion
        Mobile Vet. Section.

4.   Units will be prepared to entrain on 28th inst. for an unknown destination.

5.   All trench stores, defence schemes, maps, aeroplane photographs, details of proposed work, etc., will be handed over on relief and receipts obtained.

6.   Completion of all reliefs and moves will be reported to Brigade Headquarters.

7.   Two lorries per Battalion are being supplied to assist moving of surplus kit.

                                       Captain,
Issued at 5.30 pm   Brigade Major,
TO :-   63rd Infantry Brigade.

8th Lincolnshire Regt.	1	C.R.E.	11
8th Somerset L.I.	2	C.R.A.	12
4th Middlesex Regt.	3	37th Division	13 - 14
63rd T.M. Battery	4	111th Inf. Bde.	16
153rd Field Coy., R.E.	5	112th Inf. Bde.	17
49th Field Ambulance	6	3rd Aust. Inf. Bde.	18
No. 2 Coy. Train	7	148th Inf. Bde.	19
9th N. Staffs (Pnrs)	8	XXII Corps M't'd Troops	20
'C' Coy., 37th M.G.Bn.	9	Bde. Transport Offr.	21
Mobile Vet. Sect.	10	37th M.G. Battn.	22

MARCH TABLE to accompany Bde. Ops. Order No. ... of ...

Ser. No.	Date	Unit	From	To	Remarks
1	27/28	4th Middlesex	Line	FLETRE	By bus from SHRAPNEL CORNER at about midnight. To march on relief to this pt. via THE HALT. TRANSPORT FAR.
2	"	8th Lincolns	Line	"	By bus from KRUISSTRAATHOEK X Roads, H.30.d.3.2 at about midnight. To march to this point via SPOIL BANK, ST. ELOI – VOORMEZEELE.
3	"	86th Somersets	Support	BERTHEN	By train from LAMBTON SDG at about 9.30pm to REMY SIDING, POPERINGHE, marching thence to BERTHEN.
4	"	63rd T.M.Bty	Line and Details	BERTHEN	By bus from SHRAPNEL CORNER at midnight
5	"	4th Middlesex	Details	FLETRE	By train from LARKHOF SDG. at 8.30 pm
		8th Lincolns		"	"
		8th Somersets		BERTHEN	"
6	"	153rd Fd. Co. RE	Present Camp	GODEWAERS- VELDE	By train from LARKHOF SDG. at 8.30 pm
7	"	49th Fd. Amb.		"	"
8	"	No. 2 Co. Train		"	As ordered by O.C. Divnl. Train
9	"	Mob.Vet.Sect.		"	As ordered by O.C. Mob. Vet. Sect.
10	"	63rd Inf. Bde.HQ	BEDFORD HOUSE	GODEWAERS- VELDE	

2 Limbers will report at NORTH DUMP at 10.30 pm to convey extra baggage of 8th Lincolns to KRUISSTRAATHOEK X Roads. 2 Limbers will report at CANADA DUMP at 10.30 pm to convey extra baggage of 4th Middlesex to SHRAPNEL CORNER. 1 Limber will report to CANADA DUMP & TORR TOP to convey mortars and moss kit of 63rd T.M.Battery to SHRAPNEL CORNER.
Transport will meet 8th Somerset L.I. at REMY SIDING to take moss kit etc.
On arrival at REMY SDG. units will move off in the following order :- 153rd Fd. Co. RE, Details 4th Middlesex, Details 8th Lincolns, 49th Fd. Amb., Details 8th Somersets.
Transport of units has moved to the above destinations.
Units will arrange to send 2 cyclist orderlies to Bde. H.Q. at GODEWAERSVELDE by 10 am on 28th.

C Col MG Bn will move under orders of CC 37th h.q 13.11.n

SECRET.   Copy No. 1   (17)

63rd Infantry Brigade Order No. 204

March 30th 1918

was
1. (a)   37th Division ~~was~~ transferred to IV Corps at midnight
         29/30th March.

   (b)   37th Division will move to IV Corps Area on March 30th.

2.   37th Division will relieve 62nd Division (A.A. SOUASTRE)
         in the line on night March 31st/1st April, under orders which
         will be issued later.

3.   63rd Infantry Brigade will be prepared to take over the
         left subsector of the line on that night.

4.   Units will hold reconnoitring parties in readiness to
         move on the afternoon of March 30th to the line. Parties
         will spend the night March 30/31st in the line.
         Transport arrangements will be notified later.

5.   Machine gun reliefs will take place on night April 1/2nd.

6.   Brigade H.Q. will close at PAS at 12 noon, 30th inst.
         and reopen at HENU at the same hour.

7.   Refilling point for 63rd Inf. Bde. - Brickfields, on the
         PAS - MONDICOURT Road, at 2 pm. on 30th inst.

8.   ACKNOWLEDGE.

                                            C.J. B. Sheringham
                                                  Captain,
                                              Brigade Major,
Issued at 10 am.   63rd Infantry Brigade.

Distribution.   Copy No.

War Diary & File   1 - 3
Brigade Staff   4 - 8
8th Lincolnshire Regt.   9
8th Somerset L.I.   10
4th Middlesex Regt.   11
63rd T.M. Battery   12
153rd Field Coy., R.E.   13
'C' Coy., 37th M.G.Bn.   14
37th M.C. Bn.   15
No. 2 Coy. Train   16
S.A.A. Section, 37th D.A.C.   17
49th Field Ambulance.   18
254th Employment Coy.   19
37th Division   20 - 21
111th Inf. Bde.   22
112th Inf. Bde.   23
62nd Division   24
'A' Bde. 62nd Divn.   25
Brigade Transport Offr.   26
Brigade Supply Officer   27
R.T.O. MONDICOURT   28
Area Comdt. MONDICOURT   29

63rd Infantry Brigade No. 9509

SECRET.

8th Lincolnshire Regt.
8th Somerset L.I.
4th Middlesex Regt.
63rd T.M.Battery
153rd Field Company, R.E.
37th M.G.Battalion
No. 2 Coy. Train
S.A.A. Section, D.A.C.
49th Field Ambulance
37th Division
111th Inf. Bde.
112th Inf. Bde.
4th Aust. Inf. Bde.
187th Inf. Bde.
Brigade Transport Officer
Brigade Supply Officer

Paras. 2 to 5 (inclusive) of 63rd Infantry Brigade Order No. 204 dated 30.3.18 are cancelled.

(signed)
Captain,
Brigade Major,
63rd Infantry Brigade.

31.3.18

TABLE TO ACCOMPANY 63rd Inf. Bde. Order No. 203 dated 28.3.18

Ser. No.	Date	Unit	To arrive LESTRE STATION	Serial No. of Train	Remarks.
		'A' TABLE FOR UNITS of 63rd Infantry Brigade Group.			
1.	Mar.29th	1 Coy., 8th Lincolns with Cooker and team	8.10 am hrs	13	
2.	"	'C' Coy., 37th M.G.Battn.	8.15 am	13	O.C. No. 13 Train -
3.	"	63rd Inf. Bde. H.Q. and Signal Section	8.20 am	13	Brigade Major,
4.	"	63rd T.M.Battery	8.25 am	13	
5.	"	8th Lincolnshire Regt. (less 1 Coy. with Cooker and team)	11.20 am	15	O.C.Train, O.C. 8th Lincolns
6.	"	8th Somerset L.I. (less 1 Coy. with Cooker and team).	14.20 pm	17	O.C. Train, O.C. 8th Somersets
7.	"	153rd Field Coy. R.E.	17.15 pm	19	
8.	"	1 Coy. 8th Somersets with Cooker and team.	17.20 pm	19	O.C. Train -
9.	"	No. 2 Coy. Divnl. Train	17.25 pm	19	O.C. 153rd Field Coy. R.
10.	"	Half S.A.A. Section, 37th B.A.C.	18.20 pm	21	O.C. Train, O.C.S.A.A.Section, I.A.C.
		'B' TABLE FOR UNITS MOVING with 111th Inf. Bde. Group.			
1.	"	49th Field Ambulance	8.50 am at Harbours Sh	14	
2.	"	4th Middlesex Regt. (less 1 Coy. with cooker and team).	11.50 pm	16	O.C. 4th Middlesex Regt. O.C. Train. Lorries will convoy Battn. from FLETRE under orders issued separately.

- 2 -

Ser. No.	Date	Unit	To arrive at HOPOUTRE Station	Serial no. of train	Remarks.
3	March 29th	1 Coy. 4th Middlesex Regt.	14.50 pm	18	

Units will march from Detraining Stations in the same order after obtaining permission of the Brigade Entraining Officer to move off.

Units transport will be at entraining Station 2 hours before the times stated in Column 5, i.e. three hours before the respective trains start, and will move to the entraining stations and from the Detraining Stations in the same order with permission of Brigade representative.

Wounded	1,335	27,507
Missing	370	17,588
	2,298	51,807

NOMINAL ROLL OF OFFICERS.

63rd Infantry Brigade Headquarters

Brigadier General E.L.CHALLENOR, C.M.G., D.S.O.   Commanding.
  (Leicestershire Regiment)

Captain C.J.de B.SHERINGHAM   Brigade Major
  (Queen's Own Cameron Highlanders)

Captain P.W.SKELLEY   Staff Captain
  (New Zealand Staff Corps)

2nd Lieut. R.A.FORREST   Brigade Intelligence
  (8th Somerset Light Infantry)   Officer

NOMINAL ROLL OF OFFICERS

8th Battalion, The Lincolnshire Regiment.

Rank and Name		Present Employment	How Trained	Arrived in France
Lt.-Col.	Webb Bowen W.I., DSO	Commanding		18.9.16
Major	Phelips R.M.	2nd i/Command		25.7.17
Captain	Latham F.W.	Coy. Comdr.		7.4.17
"	Heffer H.E., MC	Adjutant		5.10.14
Lieut.	Christie E.J.A.	Asst. Adjutant		2.8.17
"	Wiggins A.B.	Transport Offr.	Bombing	19.6.17
Captain	Hansell F.J½	Coy. Comdr.	Lewis Gun	30.1.17
"	Moss W.	Coy. Comdr.		19.4.17
"	Robinson A.R.	Coy. Comdr.		27.9.16
"	Hine S.T.	Signal Offr.	Signalling	25.6.16
Lieut.	Gooseman F.L.	Platoon Comdr.		17.12.17
2nd Lt.	Hamilton C.G.H.	Plaroon Offr.	Signlling	6.10.17
"	Askey C.H.L.	Platoon Comdr.		21.5.17
"	McDonald J.R.	XXII Corps School		2.6.17
"	Draper P.	Platoon Comdr.		1.8.17
"	Peadon P.H.	Platoon Comadr.		12.10.17
"	Woollatt F.L.	Platoon Comdr.		12.10.17
"	Owen E.J.	Bombing Officer	Bombing	12.10.17
"	Beales F.C.	152nd Fd.Co.RE		21.5.17
"	Sutcliffe J.G.	Platoon Comdr.		8.5.17
"	Mitchell A.T.	Sick	Lewis Gun	21.8.17
"	Moody H.F.	Platoon Comdr.		20.8.17
"	Lowe C.	Platoon Cpmdr.		17.10.17
"	Bousfield W.R.	Bn. Gas Offr.		17.10.17
"	Naylor T.	Platoon Comdr.		17.10.17
"	Garvey H.H.	Platoon Comdr.		17.5.17
"	Mills F.	Platoon Cpmdr.		17.10.17
Captain	Taylor F., MC	Quartermaster		11.9.15

NOMINAL ROLL OF OFFICERS

8th Battalion, The Somerset Light Infantry

Rank and Name		Present Employment	How Trained	Arrived
Lt.Col.	Richardson H.S.C.	Commanding		3.5.17
Major	Hardyman J.H.M. MC	37th Div.	Staff duties	24.2.17
Major	Jenkyns S.S.	A/2nd i/c		
Major	Ostle H.K.E.	Sick		
Captain	Baker H.G., MC.	Coy. Comdr.	Signalling	8.9.16 17.12.1
"	Peard C.J.	Coy. Comdr.		17.12.17
"	Madden C.H.	Coy. Comdr½	L.G., M.G., Gas	31.7.17
"	Pople H.K., MC	Coy. Comdr.	L.G., Musketry	14.7.17
Lieut.	Pring H.O.	Adjutant		15.2.17
"	Pike H.	Transport Offr.	Transport duties	10.9.15
"	Willatt V.G.	63rd Bde. Sig.Sch.	Signalling	20.7.16
"	Plant V.L.	Musketry Offr.	Musketry	26.7.17
"	Cox D.H.	Bombing Offr.	Bombing	26.6.17
"	Bennett P.H.R.	Asst. Adjt.	General Courses	26.7.17
"	Austin H.K.	Bn. Gas Offr.	Bombing, Gas	11.8.17
"	Cresswell J.J.	Platoon Comdr.	Transport duties	11.2.18
"	Bustard T.S.	Platoon Comdr.		11.2.18
2nd Lt.	Bodey L.C.	Platoon Comdr.	General Courses	2.5.17
"	Pickard F.J.	Platoon Comdr.	Musketry	14.7.17
"	Radford J.A.	Platoon Comdr.	Gas Course	26.7.17
"	Stone H.G.½	Signal Officer	Signalling	11.8.17
"	Hearder G.H.	Platoon Comdr.	General Course	11.8.17
"	Pfaff E.	37th Divn.	Transport duties	11.8.17
"	Deeming W.	Platoon Comdr.	Intelligence	
"	Hewitt J.P.	Platoon Comdr.	Gas, General	15.12.17
"	Button R.H.	Platoon Comdr.	General Course	15.12.17
"	Drakeford H.A.	Platoon Comdr.	General Course	29.12.17
"	Hayes W.E.	Platoon Comdr.	Gas Course	29.12.17
"	Dyte S.T.	Platoon Comdr.	General Course	28.12.17
"	Jones P.J.	Platoon Comdr.		29.12.17
"	Lock J.	Platoon Comdr.	Musketry	21.12.17
"	Forrest R.A.	63rd Bde. HQ	Intelligence	
"	Woodmansey K.G.	Bde. School		
"	Goad A.E.	Bde. Gas Offr.		
"	Walne H.A.	Bde. Transport Offr.		
"	Gaunt B.W.	63rd T.M.B.		
"	Stears S.G.	63rd T.M.B		
"	Owen A.C.	Sick		11.2.18
Lieut. & Q.M.	D.G.Campbell	Quartermaster		-.3.16
Lieut.	Scott W., M.O.R.C.	M.O.		

NOMINAL ROLL OF OFFICERS.

4th Battalion, The Middlesex Regiment.

Rank and Name		Present Employment	How Trained	Arrived in France
Lt.-Col.	H.A.O.Hanley, DSO, MC	Commanding		5.11.14
Major	C.R.Hay	37th Div. Wing		28.6.17
Major	P.Grove White	2nd in command	Staff Gas	11.8.14
Captain	H.A.Maynard, MC	Attd. 63rd Bde. HQ	Staff duties	
"	P.W. Smith MC	Coy. Comdr.	Army School	19.7.16
"	E.Procter	,,		
"	S.Mirams	Attd. 63rd Bde. HQ	Staff Duties	5.6.16
"	F.W.Scholefield	Coy. Comdr.	Lewis Gun	15.7.16
"	J.P.Jamieson	Coy. Comdr.	Lewis Gun	7.5.17
"	G.N.Viner	A/Adjutant		1.1.17
Lieut.	E.A.H.Fenn	Sick	Army School	13.7.16
"	A.G.Mitchell	Bn. Gas Officer	Gas	19.7.16
"	F.F.Moorat	2nd i/c Coy.	Gas	3.12.17
"	Bowser H.F.	37th Div. Wing	Sniping	1.2.15
"	E.C.Moryoseph	Platoon Offr.	Lewis Gun	17.9.17
"	H.R.Odling	37th Div. Wing	Signalling	19.4.17
"	R.E.Taylor	37th Div. Q	Q duties	29.5.16
"	O.N.Martin	37th Div. Salvage	Lewis Gun	13.7.16
"	R.G.Williams	Platoon Offr.	Bombing	15.7.16
"	J.H.Hodgson MM	Transport Offr.	Bombing	28.8.16
"	J.C.Lyal, MC, DCM	37th Div.Wing	Lewis Gun	12.12.16
"	T. De Val	Asst. Adjt.	Corps School	10.5.17
"	G.Chipperfield	Intelligence Off.	Intelligence duties	
2nd Lt.	H.F.Backhouse	Platoon Offr.	Trench Mortars	21.4.16
"	A.J.Klaiber	Platoon Offr.	Corps School	11.8.17
"	H.S.Yates	37th Div. Wing.	Bombing	11.8.17
"	A.G.Andrews	Lewis Gun Offr.	Lewis Gun.	11.8.17
"	H.M.Chaundy	Lewis	Lewis Gun	11.8.17
"	E.Elmore	Platoon Offr.	Gas	17.9.17
"	R.A.K.Stuart, MC	Platoon Offr.	Army School	23.9.17
"	W.A.Bloy	Sick	Corps School	9.11.17
"	F.F.Marshall	Platoon Offr.	Musketry	9.11.17
"	G.A.Pierce	Platoon Offr.	Musketry	19.11.17
"	J.L.Selfe	Attd. 152 Fd½Co.RE		2.12.17
"	F.W.Elliott	Platoon Offr.		2.12.17
"	H.W.Herman	Sick	Corps School	30.12.17
"	J.E.Harrington	Platoon Offr.	Corps School	30.12.17
"	C.V.Caine	Town Major	Corps School	1.1.18
"	S.R.Wilkins, MC	Signal Offr.	Signalling	
"	L.E.Moore	Platoon Offr.	General Course	16.7.17
"	K.T.Swan	Platoon Offr.	Traffic duties	19.11.17
"	J.K.Ross	Platoon Offr.	Trench Mortars	19.11.17
"	A.H.Payne	Bde. Dump Offr.		19.11.17
"	C.G.Spalding	Platoon Offr.	Intelligence	
"	C.H.Woolvin	Platoon Offr.	Corps School	1.1.18
"	W.T.Powell	Platoon Offr.	Bombing	
"	J.H.Baird	Platoon Offr.	Musketry	19.11.17
Captain	AMOR, E.H.	Quartermaster		18.10.15
Captain	W.A.Milner, R.A.M.C. (T)	Medical Officer		
Captain Rev.	P.S.Douglas, C.F.	Chaplain.		

NOMINAL ROLL OF OFFICERS.

63rd Trench Mortar Battery.

Rank and Name		Employed	Embarked
Captain	Akerman, J.P., MC	Commanding	8.9.15
Lieut.	Harris M.W.S.		28.5.16
Lieut.	Gaunt B.W.		13.12.16
2nd Lt.	Brown F., MC		7.10.17
2nd Lt.	Stears, S.G.		11.10.17

CASUALTIES DURING MARCH, 1918.

Unit	IN TRENCHES							OUT OF TRENCHES							Total Casualties in and out of Trenches	SICK			GRAND TOTAL	Remarks
	Officers			Other Rks			Total	Officers			Other Rks			Total		Officers	Other Ranks	Total		
	Killed	Wounded	Missing	Killed	Wounded	Missing		Killed	Wounded	Missing	Killed	Wounded	Missing							
8th Lincolnshire Regt.	-	1a	-	10	33	-	44	-	1b	-	-	8	-	9	53	1c	26	27	80	a Lt. A.White b 2/Lt. J.H.Gray c 2/Lt. AT.Mitchell
8th Somerset L.I.	-	-	-	8	48	-	56	-	-	-	1	-	-	1	57	2d	69	71	128	d Major H.K.E.Ostle 2/Lt. A.C.Owen
4th Middlesex Regt.	2e	-	-	21	52	-	75	-	1f	-	-	1	-	2	77	4g	122	126	203	e 2/Lt. Hedley J.H 2/Lt. Millican f 2/Lt. Benda P MM g 2/Lt. Bloy W.A. 2/Lt. Herman H.W
63rd Trench Mortar Battery	-	-	-	-	4	-	4	-	-	-	-	-	-	-	4	-	11	11	15	Lieut.Moryoseph Lieut.Fenn E.A.H.
Total	2	1	-	39	137	-	179	-	2	-	-	9	-	12	191	7	228	235	426	

63rd Infantry Brigade.

REINFORCEMENTS RECEIVED DURING MARCH, 1918.

Unit.	Officers	Other Ranks	Date of arrival.
8th Lincolnshire Regt.	-	78	3.3.18
	-	23	6.3.18
	1 a	-	11.3.18
	-	22	19.3.18
	-	23	19.3.18
	-	6	26.3.18
	-	6	28.3.18
	1	**158**	
8th Somerset L.I.	-	72	3.3.18
	1 b	32	6.3.18
	6 c	-	8.3.18
	1 d	-	10.3.18
	-	10	19.3.18
	-	4	23.3.18
	-	3	26.3.18
	-	7	27.3.18
	8	**128**	
4th Middlesex Regt.	1 e	1	1.3.18
	-	5	3.3.18
	-	33	6.3.18
	1 f	-	13.3.18
	-	21	19.3.18
	-	46	23.3.18
	-	61	26.3.18
	-	8	28.3.18
	2	**175**	
63rd Trench Mortar Battery	-	10	4.3.18

Total reinforcements during March, 1918: 1 officers, 471 O.R.

```
a  2nd Lieut.  F. Mills                  8th Lincolnshire Regt.

b  2nd Lieut.  R.A. Forrest              8th Somerset L.I.
c  Major       H.K.E. Ostle, MC              ,,
   2nd Lieut.  K.G. Woodmansey               ,,
   2nd Lieut.  A.E. Goad                     ,,
   2nd Lieut.  H.A. Walne, MC                ,,
   2nd Lieut.  B.W. Gaunt                    ,,
   2nd Lieut.  S.G. Stears                   ,,
d  Major       S.S. Jenkyns                  ,,

e  2nd Lieut.  J.H. Hedley               4th Middlesex Regt.
f  2nd Lieut.  L.E. Moore                    ,,
```

63rd Infantry Brigade

STRENGTH OF UNITS, MARCH 31st, 1918.

UNIT	STRENGTH		DETAILS INCLUDED	
	Officers	Other Rks	Officers	Other Rks.
8th Lincolnshire Regt.	29	937	3	132
8th Somerset L.I.	39	892	14	221
4th Middlesex Regt.	48	922	16	198
63rd Trench Mortar Battery	5	70	-	2
TOTAL	121	2821	33	553

37th Division.

B. H. Q.

63rd INFANTRY BRIGADE.

APRIL 1918.

Appendices attached :- List follows War Diary.

Operation Orders.
Report on Operations 5th April 1918.
Nominal Roll of Officers.
Defensive Arrangements.
Casualties.
Reinforcements.
Strengths.

ORIGINAL COPY

WAR DIARY

63rd Infantry Brigade

APRIL, 1918.

Army Form C. 2118.

WAR DIARY
or
INTELLIGENCE SUMMARY
(Erase heading not required.)

Instructions regarding War Diaries and Intelligence Summaries are contained in F. S. Regs., Part II. and the Staff Manual respectively. Title pages will be prepared in manuscript.

Place	Date	Hour	Summary of Events and Information	Remarks references to Appendices
	April			
Trenches	1		On night 1/2nd April, 63rd Infantry Brigade relieved 187th Infantry Brigade (62nd Division) and one battalion 125th Infantry Brigade (42nd Division) in the ROSSIGNOL WOOD Sector of the line in front of GOMMECOURT (O.O. No. 205). The weather at the time was very cold and wet and the ground was in very bad condition. O.O. 205	1
"	2		On night 2/3rd the Brigade extended its right and took over about 1000 yards of front from 4th Australian Infantry Brigade, O.O. No. 206	2
"	3		Orders issued for an operation to be carried out with a view to straightening the line and improving our position, tanks to cooperate ...... O.O. 207	3
"	4		This operation took place at 5.30 am under extremely bad weather conditions. Close upon 200 prisoners were taken and 3 machine guns captured (see detailed report)	4
"	5		The Brigade was relieved by 111th Infantry Brigade and went into support in the PURPLE LINE, in front of GOMMECOURT (O.O. No. 206), and provided working parties for digging, wiring and improving the PURPLE LINE System.	5
GOMME-COURT	6/7			
GOMMECOURT	8			
Trenches	9/10		The Brigade relieved 112th Infantry Brigade in the line, O.O. No. 209	6
"	12/13		The Brigade extended its left, taking over about 500 yards of front from 111th Infantry Brigade, O.O. No. 210.	7
	14		63rd Infantry Brigade Defensive Arrangements issued, No. 229/1 G.	7a
	14/15		4th Middlesex Regt. relieved 8th Lincolnshire Regt. in the left subsector of the line, O.O. 211.	8

A7092. W: W.128.9/M:293. 750.600. 4/17. D. D. & L., Ltd. Forms/C2118/14

Army Form C. 2118.

WAR DIARY
or
INTELLIGENCE SUMMARY

(Erase heading not required.)

Instructions regarding War Diaries and Intelligence Summaries are contained in F. S. Regs., Part II. and the Staff Manual respectively. Title pages will be prepared in manuscript.

Place	Date	Hour	Summary of Events and Information	Remarks references Appendi.
HENU	15/16		The Brigade was relieved by 126th Infantry Brigade (42nd Division) and withdrew into Corps Reserve at HENU, O.O. No. 212	9
AUTHIE	16 to 23		The Brigade moved to AUTHIE WOOD (Camp) (O.O. No. 213). While in Corps Reserve, the Brigade was placed under the orders of G.O.C. New Zealand Division for Defence and Counter attack. The weather while at AUTHIE continued to be cold, with rain at times. (O.O. 214)	10 11
	23/24		Work was done on the RED LINE and a certain amount of Lewis Gun and Bombing Training was carried out. The duties of the Brigade while in Corps Reserve are set out in O.O. 214.	
Trenches	23/24		The Brigade moved up and relieved 187th Infantry Brigade (62nd Division) in the BUCQUOY - BIEZ WOOD sector of the line, with two battalions in the line and one in support, O.O. 215 Our patrols were very active during this tour in the line.	12
"	27/28		The Support Battalion, 8th Lincolnshire Regt., relieved the right front Battalion, 4th Middlesex Regt., O.O. 216 The weather now was much warmer and generally fine.	13
"	28		63rd Infantry Brigade Defensive arrangements issued Two Military Medals and one Croix de Guerre were awarded to the Brigade during the month	14

May
15th 1918

[signature]
Brigadier General,
Comdg. 63rd Infantry Brigade.

63rd Infantry Brigade

WAR DIARY

April, 1918.

List of Appendices.	No. of Appendix.
63rd Infantry Brigade O. No. 205	1
63rd Infantry Brigade O. No. 206	2
63rd Infantry Brigade O. No. 207	3
Report on Operations, April 5th, 1918	4
63rd Infantry Brigade O. No. 208	5
63rd Infantry Brigade O. No. 209	6
63rd Infantry Brigade O. No. 210	7
63rd Infantry Brigade Defensive Arrangements, 229/1G	7a
63rd Infantry Brigade O. No. 211	8
63rd Infantry Brigade O. No. 212	9
63rd Infantry Brigade O. No. 213	10
63rd Infantry Brigade O. No. 214	11
63rd Infantry Brigade O. No. 215	12
63rd Infantry Brigade O. No. 216	13
63rd Infantry Brigade Defensive Arrangements	14
Nominal rolls of officers	15
Casualties during April, 1918	16
Reinforcements received during April, 1918	17
Strength of units, April 30th, 1918.	18

SECRET.   Copy No.

63rd Infantry Brigade Order No. 205.

Reference Sheet: March 31st 1918
57 D N.E., Edn. local,
1:20,000

1. (a) 37th Division (less artillery) will relieve 62nd Division (less artillery) in the line on nights March 31st/1st April and April 1st/2nd.
   (b) Command of the line will pass to G.O.C. 37th Division on completion of reliefs on night April 1/2nd.
   (c) Upon completion of reliefs, the artillery covering the front, 4th Australian Infantry Brigade and two machine gun squadrons come under the command of G.O.C. 37th Division.

2. (a) 112th Infantry Brigade will relieve 186th Infantry Brigade in the left sector on night March 31st/April 1st.
   (b) 63rd Infantry Brigade will relieve 187th Infantry Brigade and one Battalion 185th Infantry Brigade in the right sector on night April 1/2nd.
   (c) 111th Infantry Brigade will relieve 185th Infantry Brigade (less one Battalion) and part of 125th Infantry Brigade in Support on night April 1/2nd.
   (d) Units of 63rd Infantry Brigade will move in accordance with March table to be issued separately.
   (e) Command of the right sector will pass to G.O.C. 63rd Infantry Brigade on completion of relief.

3. 4th Australian Infantry Brigade is holding the line on the right of 63rd Infantry Brigade.

4. 187th Infantry Brigade is patrolling the front before and during relief. On completion of relief, Os.C. 8th Somerset L.I. and 8th Lincolnshire Regt. will push out advanced listening posts to cover the front.

5. The password for night April 1st/2nd will be 'TURNIPS'.

6. Guides will be at a point on the SOUASTRE - FONQUEVILLERS Road 300 yards west of Road junction at E.26.b.90.15 from 7 pm onwards.

7. Administrative arrangements will be issued separately.

8. A consolidated return of all trench stores, maps, etc. will be forwarded to Brigade Headquarters together with a map showing all posts and trenches taken over and dispositions, by 12 noon on April 2nd.

9. Brigade Headquarters will close at HENU at 8 pm, reopening on arrival at RETTIMOY FARM, E.30.d.95.65.

10. Completion of relief will be reported to Brigade H.Q. by sending the code word 'THANKS.'

Issued at 9 pm
                                                           Captain,
                                                           Brigade Major,
TO:-   63rd Infantry Brigade.
War Diary & File   1 - 3   S.A.A. Sect., D.A.C.   16
Brigade Staff   4 - 8   50th Field Ambulance   17
8th Lincolnshire Regt.   9   37th Division   18 - 19
8th Somerset L.I.   10   111th Inf. Bde.   20
4th Middlesex Regt.   11   112th Inf. Bde.   21
63rd T.M.Battery   12   4th Aust. Inf. Bde.   22
153rd Field Coy., R.E.   13   187th Inf. Bde.   23
37th M.G.Battalion   14   Brigade Transport Offr. 24
No. 2 Coy. Train   15   Brigade Supply Officer 25
                                   A.D.M.S. 37 Div.   26
                                   C.R.E. 37 Div.   27
                                   B.G.R.A.   28

MARCH TABLE TO ACCOMPANY 63RD INF. BDE. ORD.R NO. 205 dated 31.3.18.

Ser. No.	Date	Unit	In relief of	From	To	To pass starting pt. Road junction D.19.b.80.45 at	Remarks
1	Apr. 1st	4th Mid.Dlesex Regt.	2/7th West Yorks (185th Inf. Bde.)	HEBU	K.6.a. - K.6.central - K.6.d. to L.1.c.central with Battn. H.Q. and 1 Coy. at HAMM and about E.30.d.50.85.	6 pm	Not to pass Road junction SOUASTRE FORK,E.25.b.90.15 before 8 pm
2	"	8th Somerset L.I.	2/4th York & Lancs. 2/4th K.O.Y.L.I.	"	K.12.c.3.8 - L.1.c.6.4 - L.1.c.1.1 - L.1.c.5.2 - K.12.b.5.6 - K.12.b.60.99 Trenches running south to ROSSIGNOL WOOD at K.12.a. C.7 and K.12.c.99.30 and K.12.b.15.95, with Battn. HQ. at K.6.d.7.3.	5.30 pm	Not to pass E.25.b.90.15 before 8 pm.
3	"	8th Lincolnshire Regt.	2/5th K.O.Y.L.I. 187th Pioneer Coy.	"	K.11.b.05.30 to K.6.c.20.35. thence to K.6.c.65.05 - K.5.c.20.35 - K.5.d.45.90 with Bn. H.Q. and 1 Coy. at and around K.5.c.2.7.	7 pm	Not to pass E.25.1 90.15 before 9 pm.
4	"	63rd T.M.Battery	187th T.M.Battery		Line, with K.C. at K.4.b. 3.5.	7.20 pm	
5	"	63rd Inf. Bde. HQ	187th Inf. Bde. HQ		RETTEMOY FARM	-	-

A distance of 500 yards should be maintained between battalions. No movement east of FORK ROADS D.23.c.50.40 in larger bodies than platoons, and a distance of 10 yards should be maintained between platoons east of SOUASTRE.

ACKNOWLEDGE. (Units of Brigade).

S E C R E T.

Amendment to 63rd Infantry Brigade Order No.206.

2nd April 1918.

Paragraphs 3 and 4 are cancelled and the following substituted.

"3. O.C. 8th Lincolns will detail his Right Company Commander to report to Brigade Headquarters at 1:30 p.m. to-day, to go with the Brigade Major to K.4.b.3.5. to meet representatives of 4th Australian Brigade and 14th Australian Battalion.

4. As the extension of the present Right of the 8th Lincolns may necessitate the readjustment of the boundary between 8th Lincolns and 8th Somerset L.I. xxxxxxxxxxxxxxxxxxxxxxxxxxxxxxxxxxxxxx O.C. 8th Lincolns xxxxxxxx and O.C. 8th Somerset L.I. will report to Brigade Headquarters to-day at 5 p.m. O.C. 4th Middlesex Regt. will also be present.

Sgd. G. de B. SHERINGHAM, Captain.
Brigade Major.
63rd Infantry Brigade.

Distribution.
As for Brigade Order No.206.

SECRET   Copy No. 1

63rd INFANTRY BRIGADE ORDER No.206.

Reference Map.
1/20,000 Sheet 57d. N.E.   2nd April 1918.

---

1. On night 2nd - 3rd April, 63rd Infantry Brigade, will extend its right and take over from 4th Australian Infantry Brigade the frontage from the present Right of the 63rd Infantry Brigade in COD Trench up to and including the old German Front Line Trench about K.11.c.65.50.

2. O.C. 8th Lincolns will arrange with O.C. 14th Australian Infantry Battalion to extend his Right as above to K.11.c.65.50.

3. As this extension of the present Right of the 8th Lincolns may necessitate the re-adjustment of the boundary between 8th Lincolns and 8th Somerset L.I., O.C. 8th Somerset L.I. will arrange to be present at Headquarters O.C. 8th Lincolns at K.6.c.2.7. at 2:30 p.m. to-day 2nd instant.

4. A re-presentative of 63rd Infantry Brigade H.Q., 4th Australian Infantry Brigade H.Q. and 14th Australian Infantry Battalion will also be present.

5. O.C. 8th Lincolns will arrange with O.C. 14th Australian Infantry Battalion for this part of the front to be covered by advanced listening posts or Patrols, before, during and after this re-adjustment of the Front.

6. 4th Australian Infantry Brigade is arranging to maintain the existing posts in the old No Man's Land and will join them up so as to form a continuous line between the old British Front Line about K.11.c.15.20 and the old German Front Line at K.11.c.65.50.

7. Completion of re-adjustment will be notified to this Office by wiring Code word "Not required".

8. ACKNOWLEDGE.

                                                            Captain.
                                            Brigade Major.
                                      63rd Infantry Brigade.

DISTRIBUTION.	Copy No.
War Diary	1 - 3.
Staff & File	4 - 8.
8th Lincolns Regt.	9
8th Somerset L.I.	10
4th Middlesex Rgt	11
63rd T.M.Battery	12
4th Aust. Inf. Bde	13
111th Inf. Bde	14
112th Inf. Bde	15
37th Division	16
152 Field Coy. R.E.	17
9th N. Staffs	18
O.C. Group R.A.	19

SECRET.   Copy No. 1.

63rd INFANTRY BRIGADE ORDER No.207.

Reference Map.
Sheet 57D. N.E.
1:20,000.
                                                                    3rd April, 1918.

1. After extending its right to K.11.c.65.50 on night 2nd/3rd April, 63rd Infantry Brigade will hold a front extending along general line from K.11.c.65.50 on the RIGHT, through K.11.b.05.60 - K.6.c. 50.15 - L.1.c.50.20 with various saps and advance posts in front of this general line.

2. On "Z" day, at ZERO hour, 63rd Infantry Brigade will advance its front to general line K.17.b.10.75, along SUNKEN ROAD, running Eastwards to K.12.d.65.30, thence along trench running E.N.E. to L.7.c.10.50, thence N.E. to L.7.c.50.90, joining up with 112th Infantry Brigade at this point.
   4th Australian Infantry Brigade will push forward their line so as to connect up with 63rd Infantry Brigade RIGHT at K.17.b.10.75.

3. "Z" day and ZERO hour will be notified later.

4. 8th Lincolnshire Regt. will attack on the RIGHT.
   8th SOMERSET L.I. will attack on the left.
   They will form up on the line of COD TRENCH running from K.11.c. 65.50, N.E. to K.6.c.25.25. The dividing line between 8th Lincolns and 8th Somersets will be SUNKEN ROAD running S.E. from K.11.b.10. 60 through CRUCIFIX K.11.b.90.20 to K.12.d.20.80, thence South to K.12.d.35.25. The SUNKEN ROAD inclusive to 8th Somersets.
   The Infantry will follow the Tanks, and will attack in waves, each wave to be allotted a definite objective, special parties being detailed to mop up.
   4th Middlesex Regt. after ZERO will move forward two Companies into COD TRENCH in reserve.

5. TANKS.
   12 Tanks will cooperate with 63rd Infantry Brigade in this operation. These tanks will form up sometime before ZERO hour N.E. of trench running from K.11.a.15.60 to K.5.d.45.85.
   6 Tanks have been allotted to 8th Somersets to cooperate in taking their objective, and 6 Tanks to 8th Lincolns in taking their objective.
   Further details as to the routes to be followed by the Tanks in their advance on their objective will be issued as soon as possible.

6. Each Battalion will attack with two Companies in depth, each company on a one platoon front. One Company will be in close support and one Company in Reserve.

7. 63rd Trench Mortar Battery will cooperate in the attack, and will detail two Mortars to move forward with each Battalion. These Mortars will be used against any strong point which holds up the advance, and as a reserve of fire to consolidate the position against counter attack.

8. Artillery and Machine Gun arrangements will be notified separately.

- 2 -

9. Material and fighting Equipment will be issued in accordance with arrangements to be notified later.

10. MEDICAL ARRANGEMENTS. Advanced Dressing Station will be established at N.5.d.45.85 - thence along trench on to Road running N. into GOMMECOURT.

11. PRISONERS. Any prisoners taken will be sent back to COD TRENCH and will be handed over to a party to be detailed by O.C. 4th Middlesex Regt.

12. Watches will be synchronized at 63rd Infantry Brigade H.Q. at 12 noon and 9 p.m.

13. Os.C. 8th Somersets and 8th Lincolns will detail one platoon of their reserve companies to carry forward reserves of S.A.A., Grenades etc. to the front companies.

14. One mile additional cable is being issued to each Battalion to enable forward communication to be maintained.
    Visual communication will be established in every case.

15. After objective has been reached and during consolidation units will be prepared to light flares in response to signals of contact aeroplane which will call for these before protective barrage has died down.

    After objective has been reached and as part of consolidation any trenches leading towards enemy from newly established line will be blocked at a point at least 50 yards East of the line.

    ACKNOWLEDGE.

    Issued at 7 a.m. 3rd April 1918.

                                                    Captain.
                                                    Brigade Major.
                                                    63rd Infantry Brigade.

DISTRIBUTION :-
                        Copy No.
    War Diary   1 - 4
    Staff & File   5 - 8
    8th Lincolns   9
    8th Somerset L.I.   10
    4th Middlesex   11
    63rd T.M. Battery   12
    111th Inf.Brigade   13
    112th Inf.Brigade   14
    4th Australian Bde.   15
    37th Division   16-17
    C.R.E.   18
    C.R.A. 63nd Divn.   19
    D.M.G.C.   20
    O.C. Group, R.A.   21
    Senior Liaison Officer
              Group R.A.   22
    9th North Staffs.   23
    A.D.M.S. 37 Divn.   24

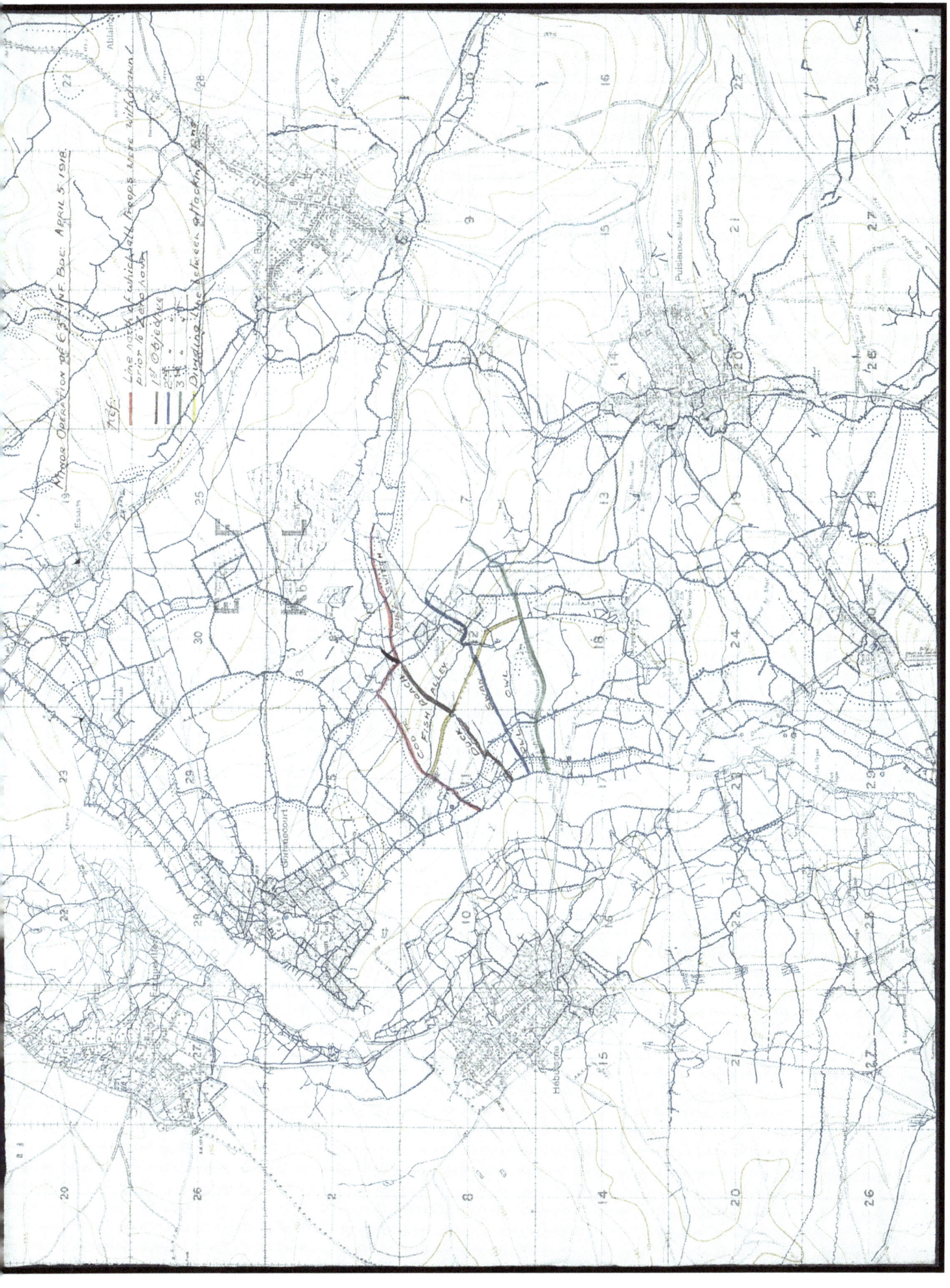

SECRET.   Copy No. 1

COMMUNICATIONS.

Reference 63rd Infantry Brigade Order No.207.

1.   A Forward Report Centre (F.R.C.) will be established at Trench Junction at K.12.a.1.5.

2.   O's C. 8th Lincolns and 8th Somerset L.I. will detail their Intelligence Officers to be at this point with one runner from each Company.

COMMUNICATIONS from this Report Centre

(a)   Brigade Signal Section will establish Visual Centre for Contact Aeroplane.

(b)   8th Somerset L.I. will establish Power Buzzer at this point working to Amplifier (F.I.D.) at K.6.c.3.6.

(c)   O.C. 4th Middlesex will detail 4 signallers to report to Signalling Officer 8th Somerset L.I. to lay wire from 8th Lincolns Signal Office to this report Centre.

(d)   When this means of communication (c) has been established 2 of these Signallers will act as operators, the remaining 2 signallers will assist Lance Corporal EVANS, of Brigade Signal Section with the visual at this point.
       The Visual Station will establish communication with Battalion Headquarters K.6.c.3.6.
       They can also get into touch with 8th Lincolns Visual Centre K.11.b.2.8.

                                                Captain,
                                             Brigade Major.
                                           63rd Infantry Brigade.

DISTRIBUTION.

	Copy No.		Copy No.
War Diary	1 - 4	C.R.E.	18
Staff & File	5 - 8	C.R.A. 63nd Divn	19
8th Lincolns	9	D.A.G.C.	20
8th Somersets	10	O.C. Group R.A.	21
4th Middlesex	11	Senior Liaison	
63rd T.M.Battery	12	Officer Group R.A.	22
111th Inf. Bde	13	9th North Staffs	23
112th Inf. Bde	14	152 Field Coy R.E.	24
4th Aus. Inf. Bde	15	153 Field Coy R.E.	25
37th Divn.	16 - 17	A.D.M.S. 37th Divn.	26
		O.C. Tanks	27

SECRET.

63rd Infantry Brigade No. 119 G.

8th Lincolnshire Regt.
8th Somerset L.I.
4th Middlesex Regt.

Herewith tracings as promised. These tracings have been somewhat delayed as it has been necessary to bring them up to date, only a certain number of the trenches being marked.

Each Officer and as many Platoon Sergeants and Section Commanders as possible, should have a copy of this tracing, and it is suggested that the objective of the particular Section or platoon be marked on this tracing, so that the Officer or N.C.O. concerned can get thoroughly familiar with his own particular task and commit to memory so far as possible his own objective and the intervening section of trenches or ground to be passed over.

A copy of the orders issued by you should be submitted to this Office at the earliest possible moment, so that they may be co-ordinated.

O.C. 4th Middlesex Regt. will also submit orders to reserve Companies and will hold in readiness a carrying party of 1 officer and 2 N.C.O's and 20 men to carry forward the material with a view to assisting in consolidating of captured trenches.

Please submit, at once, your suggestion as to Zero hour, giving reasons and report on observation made. It is important to consider at what hour a Tank would be visible at 200 yards distance.

As many maps as possible herewith. Others to follow.

Captain.
Brigade Major.
63rd Infantry Brigade.

3.4.18.

SECRET.
Copy No. 3

63rd INFANTRY BRIGADE INSTRUCTION No.1.

Reference 63rd Infantry Brigade Order No.207.

1. A Barrage of Machine Guns has been arranged consisting of 50 Machine Guns firing from E.30, K.4, 5, 6, 9 and 10, and L.2. These guns will concentrate on targets as follows:- From K.17 central through K.18.b.00.50, K.18.b.60.65, L.7.c.40.10, L.8.c10.00

2. Forward Machine Guns will operate as under:-
(a) One gun from K.11.b.52.70. and one gun from K.8.d.85.05. will move under an officer of "D" Coy. 37th M.G.Battalion, to positions in vicinity of the CRUCIFIX in K.11.b. where they can best cover the consolidation of the final objective and inflict loss on the enemy.
(b) Four guns from L.1.c. will advance under an officer of "C" Coy. 37th M.G. Battalion, and act as a battery of opportunity and cover the consolidation of the final objective.
(c) Two guns from K.10.c. will move under an officer of no.10 Squadron M.G.C. to positions in K.11.c. from which they can best cover the consolidation of the final objective by direct fire.
"Forward" machine guns will not advance with the assaulting troops but at the discretion of the officer commanding them.

3. ACKNOWLEDGE.

(signed)
Captain,
Brigade Major.
63rd Infantry Brigade.

4.4.18.

DISTRIBUTION:-

	Copy No.		Copy No.
War Diary	1 - 4	C.R.E.	18
Staff & File	5 - 8	C.R.A. XI 62nd Div.	19
8th Lincolns	9	D.M.G.C.	20
8th Somersets	10	O.C.Group, R.A.	21
4th Middlesex	11	Senior Liaison	
63rd T.M.Battery	12	Officer Group R.A.	22
111th Inf.Bde.	13	9th North Staffs	23
112th Inf.Bde.	14	152 Field Co.R.E.	24
4th Aus.Inf.Bde.	15	153 Field Co.R.E.	25
37th Division.	16 - 17	A.D.M.S.37 Divn.	26

SECRET.   Copy No. 1

63rd INFANTRY BRIGADE INSTRUCTION No.2

Reference 63rd Infantry Brigade Order No.207.

1. 12 TANKS under the command of O.C. "A" Coy. 10th Battalion Tanks will cooperate with 63rd Infantry Brigade in the operation.

2. These Tanks will move as follows:-
   (a) One Tank will move along line N.E. of ROSSIGNOL WOOD.
   (b) Five Tanks will advance along S.W. side of ROSSIGNOL WOOD between ROSSIGNOL WOOD and the SUNKEN ROAD running S.E. from CRUCIFIX.
   (c) Two Tanks will advance from a point in the old NO MAN'S LAND at about K.11.c.50.80. S.E. to final objective, moving along S.W. side of old GERMAN FRONT LINE.
   (d) Two Tanks will advance from K.11.a.90.40 in a S.E. direction to the final objective just north of the old German front line system through K.11.d.50.80 and K.11.d.90.20.
   (e) Two more Tanks will advance along a line in a S.E. direction to the final objective so as to deal with the ground between SUNKEN ROAD running S.E. from CRUCIFIX and old German front system.

   On arrival at line of final objective Tanks will remain for 3 minutes, at the end of which time they will sail Eastwards across the front of the line of the final objective, wheeling North round the N. and N.E. side of ROSSIGNOL WOOD, thence Northwards through K.6.

3. All Ranks will be warned that the tanks will withdraw as laid down in para.2 so that this movement gives rise to no misapprehension or surprise.

4. Arrangements have been made for intermittent Artillery and M.G. fire between ZERO and ZERO minus 30 so as to deaden the sound of the Tanks advancing from PIKE TRENCH to COD TRENCH (co-ordinances of PIKE TRENCH K.11.a.10.60 to K.5.d.40.87).

5. Intermittent shelling will also be carried out between 12 midnight and 2 a.m. so as to enable the Tanks to get into position without being discovered N.W. of PIKE TRENCH.

6. ACKNOWLEDGE.

                                                    C.J. de P. Sheringham
                                                    Captain.
                                                    Brigade Major.
4.4.18.   63rd Infantry Brigade.

DISTRIBUTION:-

	Copy No.		Copy No.
War Diary	1 - 4	C.R.E.	18
Staff & File	5 - 8	C.R.A. 62nd Divn.	19
8th Lincolns	9	D.A.G.C.	20
8th Somersets	10	O.C.Group, R.A.	21
4th Middlesex	11	Senior Liaison Officer	
63rd T.M.Battery	12	Group R.A.	22
111th Inf.Bde.	13	9th North Staffs.	23
112th Inf.Bde.	14	152 Field Co.R.E.	24
4th Aus.Inf.Bde.	15	153 Field Co.R.E.	25
37th Divn.	16 - 17	A.D.M.S.37 Divn.	26

63rd Infantry Brigade No.G.140.

SECRET.   Copy No. 1

ADDITIONAL GENERAL INSTRUCTIONS.

Reference 63rd Infantry Brigade Order No.207.

1. "Z" day will be 5th April, 1918.
   ZERO HOUR will be notified later.

2. 4th Australian Infantry Brigade is advancing its line on the RIGHT of 63rd Infantry Brigade so that the front of 16th Australian Battalion will conform with the front of 8th Lincolns from K.17.b. 10.75. through the 16 POPLARS at K.17.a.40.70.

3. G.O.C. 112th Infantry Brigade has arranged to withdraw 6th Battn. Bedford Regt. from the trenches now held by them on the LEFT of 8th Somerset L.I. by ZERO minus one hour on the 5th inst. The withdrawal will be carried out slowly throughout the night and the front thus vacated will be covered by Lewis Guns placed in selected positions behind the present front line. These guns will not be withdrawn until the new line of the 63rd Infantry Brigade has been established.
   1st Essex Regt. will extend their RIGHT from L.7. central to join up with new LEFT of 8th Somerset L.I. on final objective at L.7.a.45.00.
   A demonstration will be carried out by 1st Essex Regt. and 13th Royal Fusiliers against enemy trenches in L.8.a and b., to take the form of Rifle and Lewis Gun fire, so as to simulate an attack, and if wind is favourable smoke candles will be used with a view to screening the attack from the high ground about SERRE.
   Upon completion of the operations 112th Infantry Brigade will be disposed as follows:-
   1st Essex Regiment will be on RIGHT.
   13th Royal Fusiliers will be on LEFT, and
   6th Bedfords in SUPPORT in and about E.30.

4. The Infantry will move forward in formation shewn in attached sketch behind the advancing Tanks at 100 yards distance, but should any Tanks breakdown it must be impressed on all ranks that they should continue their advance, following the barrage as closely as possible. The Artillery and M.G. barrage has been so arranged as to make the advance of the Infantry possible whether Tanks cooperate or not.
   On the left however as Tanks are not moving through but are moving forward on both sides of ROSSIGNOL WOOD, 8th Somerset L.I. will follow Tanks as close as possible so as to advance through wood in close cooperation with advance of Tanks on either side.

5. MEDICAL ARRANGEMENTS. O.C. 8th Somerset L.I. will be responsible for establishing advanced Dressing Station at K.5.d.45.85.

6. PRISONERS. O.C. 4th Middlesex Regt. will arrange for any prisoners sent back to COD TRENCH to be marched thence to Brigade Headquarters, where he will mount a guard on them. Orders will be issued for their further disposal.

7. Watches will be synchronized at 9 P.M. at Brigade Headquarters.

- 2 -

8. O.C. Right Group R.A. and O.C. 37th M.G. Battn. will arrange for intermittent shooting to cover movement of Tanks as provided for in Instruction No.2 (TANKS) para.4.

9. Os.C. 8th Somerset L.I. and 8th Lincolns will each arrange an S.O.S. Relay Station, notifying map locations to this office.

10. O.C. 153 Field Co.R.E. will move forward a supply of wire and pickets as near to our present front line as possible with a view to assisting in the consolidation of the captured trenches as early as possible.

11. A separate Barrage Map shewing Field Artillery arrangements has been issued down to Company Commanders.
    During the protective barrage the ground gained will be consolidated in depth and posts will be established in front of it so as to deny to the enemy the Sunken Road in K.17.b. and K.18.a. and b and to obtain observation of the LA LOUVIERE F.R. Valley.

12. A Contact Aeroplane will call for flares at about ZERO plus 60, i.e. before protective barrage dies down.
    Flares in groups of not less than three in a group will be lit by the most forward troops.

13. O.C. 4th Middlesex Regt. will arrange to be at Brigade Headquarters with 2 runners per Company from ZERO minus 30 minutes and onwards. He will also detail an Officer to get into touch with O.C. Right Company, 6th Bedfords, so as to maintain close touch throughout the operation.

C.J.C.P. Sheringham
Captain.
Brigade Major.
63rd Infantry Brigade.

4.4.18.

DISTRIBUTION:-

	Copy No.		Copy No.
War Diary	1 - 4	C.R.E.	18
Staff & File	5 - 8	C.R.A. 62nd Divn.	19
8th Lincolns	9	D.A.G.C.	20
8th Somersets	10	O.C.Group R.A.	21
4th Middlesex	11	Senior Liaison	
63rd T.M.Battery	12	Officer Group R.A.	22
111th Inf.Bde.	13	9th North Staffs.	23
112th Inf.Bde.	14	152 Field Co.R.E.	24
4th Aus.Inf.Bde.	15	153 Field Co.R.E.	25
37th Divn.	16 - 17	A.D.M.S.37 Divn.	26

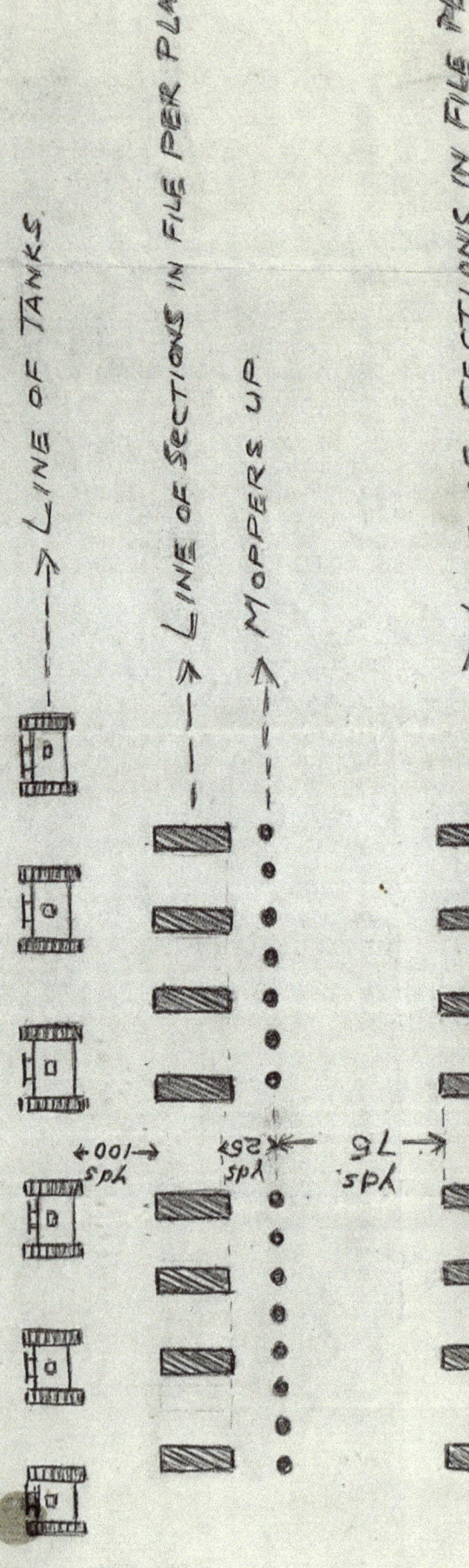

6th Lincolnshire Regt.　　　　　63rd Infantry Brigade No. 449
8th Somerset L.I.
4th Middlesex Regt.
63rd T.M. Battery.

The following extract from 37th Divisional instructions are repeated to you for your information and necessary action:-

INFORMATION.

2.　　The necessity of passing back constant and accurate information regarding the situation during and after the operation must be impressed on all ranks.　　Hourly reports commencing at ZERO plus 60 will be forwarded to Divisional Headquarters by telegram during 'Z' day by the Infantry Brigade in the line.

　　　　x　　x　　x　　x　　x　　x

ACTION OF INFANTRY.

3.　　　x　　x　　x　　x　　x　　x

Careful arrangements must be made to ensure that all the assaulting Infantry do not get deflected towards the old German trench system on the right or ROSSIGNOL WOOD on the left, so that the valley between these objectives is neglected.

　　　　x　　x　　x　　x　　x　　x

5.　　Maps showing the trenches normally occupied by our troops may be carried by personnel taking part in the attack, provided that the trenches occupied and Headquarters are not specially marked.

Reference para. 2.　　From Zero onwards to Zero plus 60 information will be sent through as frequently as possible. From Zero plus 60 xxxxxxxxxxxxxxxxxxxxxxxx onwards situation reports will be sent through every half-hour to 8 a.m. and after that, hourly. Any information of special importance will of course be wired through at once.

Reference para. 5 re Maps.　　All ranks should remember that no maps showing our dispositions or documents of a Secret nature, such as would be of value to the enemy should be taken into action.

ACKNOWLEDGE.

G. A. Sheringham

Captain.
Brigade Major.
63rd Infantry Brigade.

4.4.18.
N.

8th Lincolnshire Regt.　　　　　　　　63rd Infantry Brigade No. 145 G.
8th Somerset L.I.
4th Middlesex Regt.
63rd Trench Mortar Bty.

1. Reference 8th Bn. Lincolnshire Regt. Order para.7. and 4th Middlesex Order para.17.

   In the event of difficulty being met with at the final objective, Os. C. 8th Lincolns and 8th Somerset L.I. will apply to Brigade H.Q.
   O.C. 4th Middlesex will be at Brigade H.Q. where he will receive instructions.

2. Identification tracing showing Artillery Barrage arrangements was sent to you this morning. This will have shown you that on the front of 8th Lincolns the original arrangements for barrage have been modified owing to the nature of the ground.
   The barrage will lift from 1st objective to 2nd objective. Tanks will precede the advance of the Infantry and it is thought that the lifts shown in the diagram will enable to Tanks and Infantry to operate more successfully.. This should be thoroughly explained to all Company Commanders who should make certain that all ranks understand the arrangements.
   On the Front of the 8th Somerset L.I., on the other hand, the barrage has been arranged in accordance with the original plan - 100 yards every 3 minutes, with 5 minutes between Zero and Zero plus 5 and Zero plus 22 and Zero plus 27.

3. Reference 8th Lincolns Order para.17. O.C. Tanks considers from his previous experience that no Signals are required.

4. Should there be any points not clear to Commanding Officers, requiring elucidation, an Officer should be sent to Brigade Headquarters with a view to having the matter cleared up.

　　　　　　　　　　　　　　　　　　　　　　Captain.
　　　　　　　　　　　　　　　　　　　　Brigade Major.
　　　　　　　　　　　　　　　　　　　63rd Infantry Brigade.

4.4.18.
N.

8th Lincolnshire Regt.
8th Somerset L.I.
4th Middlesex Regt.
63rd T.M. Battery.
57th Division.
4th Australian Brigade.
111th Inf. Brigade.
112th Inf. Brigade.
37th M.G. Battalion.
153rd Field Co.R.E.
13th K.R.R.C.

63rd Infantry Brigade No.158 G.

Reference Map Sheet 57 D. S.2.
1:20,000.

1. On the night April 5th/6th the 63rd Infantry Brigade will be disposed as follows:-
  (a) 8th Lincolns on the Right from K.11.c.85.30, N.E. along GOD TRENCH to SUNKEN ROAD in K.11.b.05.60 with supports (including One Platoon 4th Middlesex) about NAMELESS FARM.
  Touch has been established with 4th Australian Brigade on RIGHT.

  (b) On the LEFT of the Lincolns 8th Somerset L.I. together with two companies 4th Middlesex Regt. will hold trench from SUNKEN ROAD at K.11.b.05.60 along FISH ALLEY to its junction with ROACH at K.12.a.10.45, thence North to K.6.c.60.10 with supports in GOD TRENCH between SUNKEN ROAD and K.6.c.20.20.

  (c) On their LEFT one company 4th Middlesex from this last point to about K.6.d.70.20 keeping touch with

  (d) 1 Company 8th Somerset L.I. in hook shaped trench North of ROSSIGNOL WOOD running North to about K.12.b.80.50. This Company is reported in touch with 6th Bedfords on their LEFT.

  (e) In support of the above mentioned troops 1 Company 4th Middlesex less 1 Platoon about K.6. central.

  (f) Headquarters 8th Lincolns   K.6.c.30.65.
      do   8th Somersets   K.6.c.40.75.
      do   4th Middlesex   K.6.c.40.75.
      Line

2. The Map covered by the above map co-ordinates will be held at all costs.

3. 13th Battn. K.R.R.C. having been placed at the disposal of the G.O.C. 63rd Infantry Brigade to be used as a Reserve is disposed as follows:-

    1 Company in trench running from K.6.d.50.50 to L.1.c.90.60.
    2 Companies from K.5.d.85.75 Northwards to E.30.c.40.50, and
    1 Company from K.5.a.55.10 to K.5.a.70.80, with Battn. H.Qrs. at E.25.d.80.75.

4. Every effort will be made to prepare fire steps and to consolidate with a view to possible enemy counter attacks. Any trenches running from our present Front Line will be blocked and held. Officers Commanding will endeavour to sort out the men under their Command as far as possible.

5. Arrangements have been made to carry forward rations and water to K.6.a.50.75 from which point they will be carried forward by carrying parties to be arranged by 13th K.R.R.C. to 8th Somersets and 8th Lincolns.
  O.C. 4th Middlesex will arrange to collect his Battalion's rations and water from this point and will distribute. Guides will be sent to the above point to await arrival of transport. O.C. 13th K.R.R.C. will arrange to have an officer at this point who will detail carrying parties from 13th K.R.R.C. on arrival of rations.

6. Acknowledge by Wire and by Bearer.

5.4.18.

Captain.
Brigade Major.
63rd Infantry Brigade.

8th Lincolnshire Regt.
8th Somerset L.I.
4th Middlesex Regt.
63rd Trench Mortar Bty.

63rd Infantry Brigade No.1636.

1. It is suggested in view of the fact that the Units are somewhat mixed up on the Brigade Front,
that Commanding Officers confer together at Headquarters 8th Somerset L.I. and detail an Officer to be responsible for an area, i.e. this Officer to decide when the troops of any of the 3 Battalions occupying such-and-such area are relieved. Otherwise it is feared that the relief may be difficult to carry out or else considerable delay will take place.
The Officer responsible for this Area will also be responsible for the advance Listening Posts to cover the front before and during the relief. Arrangements will be made with relieving Units to cover the Front after relief.

2. It is further suggested that O.C. 8th Somerset L.I. and O.C. 4th Middlesex Regt. hand over their respective Sectors to the other two Commanding Officers together in the same H.Q., owing to the mixed up state of their Units.

3. It may be possible to relieve certain areas in day-light.

4. It is absolutely imperative that Units should bring out sufficient Petrol Tins to make up their mobile reserve. There are a very large number of Petrol Tins lying about and there are none available at Division or Corps. If therefore the Division were ordered to move or a situation arose necessitating the Brigade returning to the Line at short notice we should be without means of providing water.
The seriousness of this must be impressed on all Officers.

5. Every effort is being made to arrange Baths to-morrow and onwards.

6. The Brigadier wishes special attention to be paid to feet.

Captain.
Brigade Major.
63rd Infantry Brigade.

6.4.18.
N.

63rd Infantry Brigade No. 9601

REPORT ON OPERATION CARRIED OUT on 5.4.1918.

Zero hour for the attack was fixed for 5.30 am. The assembly for the operation was rendered most difficult owing to the extremely dark night, the heavy rain and the consequent muddy state of trenches, which greatly added to the difficulty of getting into their positions for the troops undertaking the attack.

For the purpose of describing the operation, the attack will be dealt with by summarising the experiences of the right Battalion firstly, and secondly, those of the left Battalion.

On the right - the advance of 8th Lincolnshire Regt. commenced to time. No tanks being able to advance on our front, our right section suffered severely within 50 yards of jumping off, also our left platoon within 150 yards of jumping off, from machine gun fire. Considerable resistance was experienced from the first objective where approximately 100 prisoners were taken, and 60 to 90 killed or wounded on entering the trench. In this conflict all tree lines were engaged and the position captured by 5.45 am.

Resistance in the second objective was not heavy, but considerable machine gun fire from both flanks. Having taken this objective, bombing became general on the right. The line was cleared with the exception of two strong points roughly in the final objective on our right, and at 7.45 am this position was being consolidated. The carrying platoon and blocking party had now been absorbed into the line.

At 9 am lorries containing enemy were seen travelling towards ROSSIGNOL WOOD.

This position was maintained some hours. About midday the enemy was reinforced. We were not in touch with 8th Somersets on our left or Australians on our right., and our small garrison in SWAN Trench was gradually driven southwards into the trench system. At about 1 pm, in the trench system on our right the enemy advanced from his two strong points and succeeded in cutting our troops in half. From this time we were outnumbered, and owing to lack of bombs, we had to withdraw, and a rearguard action began which lasted for three hours, till we withdrew in good order into our original front line. Very heavy casualties were inflicted on the enemy in this action. Whilst retiring a party destroyed all machine guns in DUCK Trench.

During this action the conduct of the men was beyond all praise and their musketry powers exceeded all expectations.

The original front line was occupied about 5.30 pm.

Two of our machine guns consolidated in CRUCIFIX and did good work throughout the day on ROSSIGNOL WOOD.

We accounted for fourteen enemy machine guns. Our T.Ms were cut up badly before reaching the first objective, 2/Lt. BROWN being killed.

Contact aeroplane was given flares at 2.30 pm but the position could not have been definite as we were withdrawing at the time.

A Foremost visual station under 2/Lt. HAMILTON was established at K.11.c.6.5 and was kept in working order until personnel were bombed out of position.

At about 3 pm, at least 200 enemy were seen debouching from south side of ROSSIGNOL WOOD and these were severely handled by machine guns Lewis guns and rifle fire.

On the left - There was some hesitation at ZERO Hour among 8th Som. L.I. owing to the non appearance of six expected tanks. This caused the leading wave to somewhat lose the barrage which, however, failed to touch the first objective of the front allotted to this Battalion, all the shells bursting beyond it. The first objective was reached and captured with little resistance from the enemy in a heavy mist. Many enemy were found here and about 50 prisoners were taken.

OVER.

The second wave then advanced towards the second objective but on the western edge of ROSSIGNOL WOOD the advance was held up and little further progress was made on the right, owing to the heavy rifle and machine gun fire from ROSSIGNOL WOOD.

On the left, the wood was entered by our troops who fought their way forward, capturing some prisoners and machine guns and eventually established their left close to the second objective. Owing to the thickness of the wood touch with the company on the right was lost and the left company was heavily counter attacked by enemy bombing parties and machine guns, which, however, failed to dislodge them. They were then shelled and owing to heavy casualties, lack of bombs, diminished strength and the extent of the line, were forced to withdraw to the north side of the wood.

Before withdrawing to HOOK Trench, covering parties were arranged for. Whilst in HOOK trench some bombs were collected, the company reorganised and a further attempt made to gain the position, but owing to further casualties and to the fact that touch had not been obtained with the right, it was not possible to hold the 2nd objective at this point.

The company on the right made repeated attempts to get forward suffering many casualties in doing so, and were heavily counter-attacked. The enemy suffered heavily from rifle and Lewis gun fire brought to bear from our first objective. He however succeeded in surrounding and capturing about 1 officer and 20 men on the left of the left company close to the wood. The rifles of this party were badly clogged with mud and they had run out of bombs.

A report centre was established by 2nd Lt. H.K.AUSTIN at K.11.b.95.25 from which point much valuable information was received during the day. A forward signal station was also established, cable being run out as the advance proceeded. Many messages were received from this source.

From the Support Battalion, 4th Middlesex Regt., one company was moved up to COD TRENCH, taking the place of one company of 8th Lincolns, between K.11.b.1.6 and K.5.d.8.1. at 6 am. This Company was subsequently moved further to the right, its place being taken by 'C' Company.

At about 8.45 am a message was received from 8th Lincolns that progress was held up by machine gun fire and that rifle grenades were wanted. These were sent forward.

At 10.30 am, 1½ platoons with one Lewis gun were sent forward to hold ROACH Trench. At the same time one officer and 20 men reinforced 8th Somerset L.I. in ROSSIGNOL WOOD. Meanwhile, enemy supports were kept under observation from COD Trench. The enemy was seen to come up in small sections in file to mass in the trench system south of ROSSIGNOL WOOD.

The reserve company supplied parties for carrying bombs, T.M. ammunition, etc. and at 12.30 pm those of this company not so engaged were moved up into COD Trench to cover the retirement of 8th Somerset L.I. and 8th Lincolnshire Regt. Touch was kept with the Australians throughout the operation.

The enemy brought his troops from PUISIEUX, reinforcing by sending small sections at a time over the ridge.

One platoon was ordered to support 8th Somerset L.I. in ROACH Trench and on arrival found the enemy were bombing north up this trench. An immediate counter attack was organised and the enemy driven back.

At 8.30 am I decided, in view of the size of the front and the failure on the part of the tanks to cooperate, that it was inadvisable to push in my reserves (4th Middlesex Regt.) further than COD Trench.

At 11 am I requested that a Battalion of the Reserve Brigade might be put at my disposal so that I might utilize two companies 4th Middlesex Regt. in an organised attack on ROSSIGNOL WOOD from the north, but until able to make good the line ROACH – DUCK, with a the fourth battalion I did not consider it advisable to commit the remaining two companies of my reserve in a further attack. I requested that the fourth battalion be sent up so that I might

Over

prepare a deliberate attack with the cooperation of an artillery barrage, having, in the meantime, established the co-ordinates of the front line.

At 11.06 am a message was received that information had been obtained from a German prisoner than an attack with five German Divisions had been planned on generally the Corps front for the morning of the 5th inst. and had only been postponed on account of the weather.

At 12.20 pm a report was received that BUCQUOY had been heavily attacked and that part or whole of the village taken by the enemy. I at once warned O.C. 4th Middlesex Regt. that my original intention to attack ROSSIGNOL WOOD must be abandoned and my reserve kept in hand ready to deal with any situation which might develop on my own front or on the front of the Brigade on my left.

I made this decision owing to the information received about BUCQUOY, and because I felt that if the information from the prisoner of the intended attack were true, the forces opposite my front must be very much stronger than was expected. I accordingly issued instructions with a view to making good the ROACH - DUCK line and it was only owing to lack of bombs and to the clogged condition of rifles occasioned by the mud that 8th Lincolns were forced to withdraw as stated above.

Two Trench Mortars were detailed to cooperate in the advance of each Battalion. On the right, so the officer in charge and some of the party were killed. 30 rounds were however fired on CRUCIFIX with good results. The remaining ammunition, owing to the wet and mud was rendered unserviceable.

Some 50 rounds were fired by the left mortar on the enemy in ROSSIGNOL WOOD, with excellent results, contributing somewhat to the successful advance of the left company.

The following points appear to be worthy of special attention:-

1. Those responsible for the tanks were unduly optimistic. It would appear to be better to give up all idea of using tanks in weather such as we experienced on the 5th inst. It would have been better to have known definitely that the tanks would be unable to cooperate.

2. The artillery and machine gun barrages were most saitsfactory and the cooperation of the artillery group was excellent.

3. Communications forward of Brigade Headquarters were extraordinarily good, only once being interrupted owing to the progress of tanks. I enclose a separate report.

The value of Visual, and Power Buzzer and Amplifier as means of communication was never greater.

4. Considerably greater resistance was encountered than was ever expected, owing perhaps to the intended attack by the enemy.

5. As far as I am able to estimate, the enemy casualties must have been heavy, amounting to some 800, including prisoners, so far as can be gathered from the accounts of the officers in charge of the attacking troops. This is independent of casualties inflicted by artillery fire further to the rear.

6. Enemy strong points that have been specially reported are located at K.11.d.3.2, K.11.d.8.3 and K.12.d.5.8. At the last mentioned place there are two T.Ms.

OVER

-2-

In conclusion, I consider that the behaviour of these Battalions, which were composed largely of very young soldiers, was beyond all praise. The operation called for the greatest endurance owing to the heavy condition of the ground and trenches and very heavily taxed the endurance of all ranks. Leadership was in all cases good and the men used their rifles to a greater extent than could have been hoped for.

The withdrawal became necessary owing to the difficulty of getting up bombs and to the very large enemy reinforcements who were equipped with bombs. It was carried out excellently and in good order and reflects the greatest credit on all ranks.

Casualties incurred by the Brigade in the operation are as follows :-

8th Lincolnshire Regt.

Died of Wounds	2nd Lt. C.H.L.ASKEY
Wounded	2nd Lt. C. LOWE
	2nd Lt. P.H.PEADON
Wounded and Missing	2nd Lt. H.F.MOODY

Total Officers 4

Killed	26 other ranks
Wounded	91 other ranks
Wound Missing	81 other ranks @

Total O.R. 198

@ Undoubtedly some of these have been evacuated.

4th Middlesex Regt.

Killed	2nd Lt. L.E.MOORE
Gassed	2nd Lt. J.E.HARRINGTON
	2nd Lt. T. ELLIOT

Total Officers 3

Killed	2 other ranks
Died of Wounds	2 other ranks
Wounded	10 other ranks
Gassed	2 other ranks
Missing	12 other ranks

Total O.R. 28

63rd T.M.Battery

Killed	2nd Lt. F. BROWN, MC
Killed	1 O.R.
Wounded	5 O.R.

Total 1 officer
6 O.R.

8th Somerset L.I.

Killed	2/Lt. H.G.STONE	Killed	7 other ranks
	2/Lt. J.F.HEWITT	Wounded	74 O.R.
	2/Lt. H.A.DRAKEFORD	Wounded &	
Wounded	Capt. H.G.BAKER	Missing	3 O.R.
	2/Lt. F.J.PICKARD	Missing, believed killed	41 O.R.
	2/Lt. G.H.HEARDER	Missing, believed P.O.W.	26 O.R.
Wd. & Msg.	2/Lt. V.L.PLANT		
Missing	2/Lt. S.T.DYTE		
bld. P.O.W.	2/Lt. F.J.JONES		
	2/Lt. W.E.HAYES		

April 9th 1918.

Challenor
Brigadier General,
Comdg. 63rd Infantry Brigade.

J 57/13.

REPORT ON COMMUNICATIONS OF 63RD INFANTRY BRIGADE
DURING OPERATION AT ROSSIGNOL WOOD, APRIL 5TH, 1918.

I. Communications forward of Brigade Headquarters.
II. Communications rear of Brigade Headquarters.

I. FORWARD COMMUNICATIONS.

A Forward Report Centre was established at Trench junction in first objective and did good work; although a special report has been sent in on this centre, it is referred to in this report.

(a) Telephone.
(b) Visual
(c) Power Buzzer and Amplifier
(d) Runners

(a) Battalions' (3) H.Q. were in touch by phone throughout the whole battle and practically every minute of the battle was reported to Brigade by this means. One Battalion Signalling Officer established a Battalion Forward Station in touch with Battalion H.Q. by phone and transmitted some very valuable information by this means. This centre kept in touch by phone for some hours until unfortunately the position became untenable and the officer himself was killed.

Telephonic communication was arranged to work from Forward Report Centre but did not reach that point although I have reason to believe that this line was used to transmit information.

An old Bosche bury was picked up by Brigade Signal Section between Brigade and Battalion and only necessitated 400 yards of ground line to one Battalion. As both Battalion H.Q. were near each other with a 100 yards lateral between, both were practically on the bury and there is no doubt that this greatly assisted communication.

(b) Visual - This means was largely used forward of Battalion H.Q. and good work was done.

At report centre a Visual Central Station was established and some very important messages and reports were received at the station.

Visual Transmitting Stations were established at Battalion H.Q. These Stations received messages but as Battalions were always on the phone to Brigade, the Brigade H.Q. Visual Station was not used although established and in touch all the time.

(c) Power Buzzer - This means of communication was established between 1 Battalion H.Q. and Brigade H.Q. two-way working, but as telephonic communication held throughout, this was not taken advantage of.

At Forward Report Centre a Power Buzzer was established working to the Amplifier at Battalion H.Q. and exceptionally good work was sent back in very good time by this means.

As far as is traceable, 12 messages were transmitted, 10 of these being very important and I think a special report on this Power Buzzer work (one-way) is called for.

(d) Runners - These were used to a fair extent in front of Battalion H.Q. but again owing to telephonic communication from Battalions to Brigade, no runners were used behind Battalions.

II. REAR COMMUNICATIONS............

II. REAR COMMUNICATIONS. (Brigade to Division)

(a) Telephone
(b) Visual
(c) Wireless

(a) Telephone - This was the least satisfactory part of communications, owing to the heavy shelling.
　　As there were many disconnections, the progress of the battle could not be sent back as regularly as desired.
　　Here again an old Bosche bury was utilized as far as possible and was a big advantage.

(b) Visual - Rain and fog prevented this means being used over the distance.

(c) Wireless - At one time during break in wires to Division, wireless was used, two messages being sent through in clear.

NOTE: When tanks are to be used in attack, tank route should be known, if ground line is used.

　　　　　　　　　　(sd) J. STEWART, 2/Lt., R.E.,
　　　　　　　　　　　　　　O.C. Signals,
　　　　　　　　　　　　63rd Infantry Brigade.

9.4.18

37th Division No. G. 1516.

5th April 1918.

63rd Inf. Bde.   (18)   Cmdt. AA S
111th Inf. Bde.   (18)   T.M.B.
112th Inf. Bde.   (18)   S.C.
C.R.E.   (4)   Opns
C.R.A.   (1)
Sth N. Staffs.   (5)
A.D.M.S.   (4)
4th Aust. Inf. Bde.   (18)
A.P.M.
D.A.D.O.S.
D.A.D.V.S.
Div. Train   (5)
Div. M.G. Bn.   (5)
37th Signal Coy. R.E.
Camp Comdt.
'Q'.

G.O.C. Second Army has wired many congratulations from whole of Second Army on today's operations.
The Divisional Commander hopes that as many all ranks as possibly will be informed.

(Signed)
Lieut-Colonel,
General Staff, 37th Division.

37th Division No. G.5303

5th April 1918.

63rd Inf. Bde. (18)
111th " " (19)
112th " " (18)
C.R.E. (4)
C.R.A. (1)
9th F.Staffs (5)
A.D.M.S. (4)
4th Aus.Inf.Bde. (13)
A.P.M.
D.A.D.O.S.
D.A.D.V.S.
Div. Train
Div. G. Batt'n (5)
37th Signal Co. (5)
Camp Comdt
'Q'

G.O.C. XXII Corps has wired his congratulations from whole of XXII Corps on today's operations.

The Divisional Commander hopes that as many all ranks as possible will be informed.

Matthew Hendy
Lieut-Colonel
General Staff, 37th Division.

IV Corps No. 76/1/2.G.

37th Division No. G.6657.

8th April 1918.

37th Division

The Corps Commander wishes to thank the troops of the 63rd Brigade for the manner in which they carried out the attack on the morning of the 5th April. The weather and the state of the ground rendered movement very difficult. The resistance encountered was stronger than was expected and it is extremely likely that the attack by the 63rd Brigade forestalled and broke up a strong German attack. The results of the attack by the 63rd Brigade were the capture of close on 200 prisoners and 3 machine guns and severe losses were inflicted on the enemy.

           sd/ R. G. Parker,
           Brigadier-General
7th April 1918.   General Staff, IV Corps.

63rd Inf. Bde.

  For your information

         [signed] T. S. Cowan
          Lieut-Colonel
         General Staff, 37th Division.

SECRET. 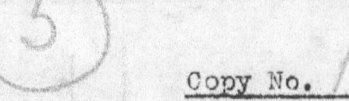 Copy No. 1

63rd INFANTRY BRIGADE ORDER No. 203.

Reference Map, Sheet 57 D. N.E.
Scale – 1:20,000.   6th April, 1918.

1. (a) On the night 6/7th April 111th Infantry Brigade will relieve 63rd Infantry Brigade in the Line in the RIGHT Sector in accordance with Table attached.

   (b) Upon relief the RIGHT Sector front will be taken over by the 111th Infantry Brigade in three Sub-sectors with a Battalion to each Sub-sector. The boundaries between Battalions will be as follows:-
   RIGHT Battalion from K.11.c.55.60 to a line drawn from CRUCIFIX to K.5. Central.
   CENTRE Battalion from the above boundary to a line drawn from K.6.c.70.05 to K.6.a.50.99, with trench junction inclusive to Centre Battalion.
   LEFT Battalion from this boundary to the left at K.12.b. 30.50.

2. All details of Relief will be arranged between Commanding Officers concerned.

3. No Post or Trench will be vacated until relieved and patrolling will be constant before, during and after relief.

4. Defence schemes, details of work in progress and proposed and any maps showing dispositions will be handed over and receipts taken. Receipts will be taken for any Trench stores handed over.

5. Completion of relief will be wired to this office by the code word "CONGRATS".

6. Upon relief 63rd Brigade H.Qs. will be transferred to FONQUEVILLERS CHURCH.

7. ACKNOWLEDGE. (Units of 63rd Infantry Brigade by WIRE).

                                                          Captain.
                                                       Brigade Major.
                                                   63rd Infantry Brigade.

6th April, 1918.

DISTRIBUTION:-

	Copy No.		Copy No.
War Diary	1 – 4	C.R.E.	18
Staff & File	5 – 8	No.2 Coy. Train	19
9th Lincolns	9	A.D.M.S. 37 Divn.	20
8th Somerset L.I.	10	37th M.G. Battn.	21
4th Middlesex	11	153 Field Co.R.E.	22
63rd T.M.Battery	12	Right Group, R.A.	23
111th Brigade	13	Senior Liaison	
112th Brigade	14	Officer, Group R.A	24
4th Aus. Inf. Bde.	15	Brigade T.O.	25
37th Division	16-17	Bde. Supply Officer	26
		9th North Staffs.	27

TABLE to accompany 63rd Infantry Brigade Order No.208.

Serial No.	UNIT	Relieved by	Will move on relief to	Remarks.
1.	8th Lincolns Regt.	13th Rifle Brigade	Trenches and Dug-outs about K.4.c. and d. and L.5.a. and c.	At present in occupation of 13th Rifle Brigade.
2.	4th Middlesex Regt.	10th Royal Fusiliers.	Trenches and Dug-outs about E.28.d.	(Lately in occupation of 13th K.R.R.C.
3.	8th Somerset L.I.	13th K.R.R.C.	Trenches and Dug-outs about E.29.a	At present in occupation of 10th Royal Fusiliers.
4.	63rd Trench Mortar Bty.	111th Trench Mortar Bty	FONCUEVILLERS	
5.	63rd Inf. Bde H.Q.	111th Inf. Bde H.Q.	FONCUEVILLERS	

N.B. Units' Reconnoitring parties under an Officer will be sent back at once with not more than one guide per platoon to meet outcoming troops.

SECRET. Copy No. 1

63rd Infantry Brigade Order No. 209.

Reference Map:
57D N.E., 1:20,000 April 8 1918.

1.   On night April 9/10th 63rd Infantry Brigade will relieve 112th Infantry Brigade in the line from K.12.b.7.4 to L.2.d.3.3. Relief will be carried out as follows :-

   8th Lincolnshire Regt. will relieve 6th Bedfords in the RIGHT subsector, with Battn. H.Q. at L.1.c.90.10.
   4th Middlesex Regt. will relieve 1st Essex Regt. in the LEFT subsector, with Battalion H.Q. at L.1.c.50.40.
   8th Somerset L.I. will relieve 13th R. Fusiliers in Support with Battalion H.Q. at E.30.b.5.5.
   63rd T.M.Battery will relieve 112th T.M.Battery, with H.Q. at RETTIMOY FARM.

2.   All details of relief will be arranged between Commanding Officers concerned.

3.   Completion of relief will be reported to this office by use of the code word 'CONGRATS'.

4.   The password to be used in the front line will be 'NEW YORK'. This password is being used by 112th Infantry Brigade on night 9/10th April and will be taken over by units of this Brigade.

5.   All trench stores, defence schemes, details of work in progress and proposed, and any maps showing dispositions will be taken over and receipts given.

6.   Guides for 4th Middlesex Regt. and 8th Lincolns will be at K.6.a.50.80 at 8.30 pm (on the tram line near the railway junction).

7.   Brigade H.Q. will close at FONQUEVILLERS Church at 10 pm and reopen at the same time at RETTIMOY FARM.

8.   ACKNOWLEDGE (Units of Bde. only)

                                          C.A.B. Sheringham
                                          Captain,
                                          Brigade Major,
Issued at 11 pm   63rd Infantry Brigade.

Distribution.	Copy No.		
War Diary & File	1 - 3	4th Aust. Inf. Bde.	19
Brigade Staff	4 - 8	37th Division	20 - 21
8th Lincolnshire Regt.	9	C.R.E.	22
,, ,, Rear HQ	10	No. 2 Coy. Train	23
8th Somerset L.I.	11	A.D.M.S. 37th Divn.	24
,, ,, Rear HQ	12	37th M.G.Battn.	25
4th Middlesex Regt.	13	153rd Field Coy., R.E.	26
,, ,, Rear HQ	14	Right Group, R.A.	27
63rd T.M.Battery	15	Senior Liaison Offr.	28
,, ,, Rear HQ	16	Brigade Transport Offr.	29
111th Inf. Bde.	17	Brigade Supply Offr.	30
112th Inf. Bde.	18	9th N. Staffs (Pnrs).	31

SECRET.   Copy No...... 2

63rd INFANTRY BRIGADE ORDER No.210.

Ref. Map 1/20,000   11th April 1918.
Sheet 57 D N.E.

1. 37th Division will extend its RIGHT and take over the front of the N.Z. Division to a point on the line running East and West through K.21.d.0.0.
    The 62nd Division is extending its RIGHT and taking over the Front of the 37th Division to L.7.b.85.15.

2. On completion of this adjustment the Southern boundary of the Division will run :-
    K.21.d.0.0. - K.14.d.0.0. - thence due West along the grid line South of SAILLY-AU-BOIS.
    Northern Boundary will run:-
    L.7.b.85.15 - L.1.d.2.5. - South-west face of RIEZ WOOD to K.6.b.57. - thence to the old boundary at E.30.a.0.3.

3. The Divisional Front will be organised in four Brigade Sectors in depth as follows :-

    RIGHT BRIGADE SECTOR.   4th Australian Inf Bde. from K.21.d.0.0. to K.16.c.2.3.   Headquarters J.16.a.6.6.

    RIGHT CENTRE BRIGADE SECTOR.   111th Inf. Bde from K.16.c.2.3. to K.11.c.75.50.   Headquarters E.27.b.2.7.

    LEFT CENTRE BRIGADE SECTOR.   112th Inf. Bde. from K.11.c.75.50 to K.12.b.0.8.   Headquarters E.28.d.8.8.

    LEFT BRIGADE SECTOR.   63rd Inf. Bde. from K.12.b.0.8. to L.7.b.85.15.   Headquarters E.28.d.7.5.

4. On the night of the 12th/13th April -
    (a) The 62nd Division take over the Front of the 63rd Inf. Bde. to L.7.b.85.15.
    (b) The 63rd Inf. Bde will take over the 111th Inf. Bde Front from K.12.b.7.7. to K.12.b.0.8.
    (c) The 112th Inf. Bde will take over the Front of the 111th Inf. Bde from K.12.b.0.8. to K.11.c.7.4.
        The relieved troops of the 111th Inf. Bde will be withdrawn into Divisional Reserve in the purple Line.   The troops of the 111th Inf. Bde holding the line from K.11.c.7.4. to K.16.b.4.5. will temporarily come under the orders of the 112th Inf. Bde.

5. On the night of the 13/14th April -
    (a) The 111th Inf. Bde. will take over the front of the 4th Aust. Inf. Bde. from K.16.b.4.5. to K.16.c.2.3.
    (b) The 4th Aust. Inf. Bde. will extend their right and take over the front of the N.Z. Division as far South as K.21.d.0.0.

6. On the night April 12th/13th -
    (a) 8th Lincolns will extend their LEFT so as to take over from 4th 4th Middlesex Regt. up to L.7.b.85.15.
    (b) 8th Somerset L.I. will take over from 13th Bn. K.R.R.C. from K.12.a.08. to K.12.b.7.7., and from 8th Lincolns all posts East of the grid line running N. & S. between Squares K.12. and L.7.
        All other details of relief will be arranged between Battalion Commanders concerned.

7. 4th Middlesex Regt. will be relieved from L.7.b.85.15. to their present LEFT by "A" Bn. 187th Infantry Brigade, and will with-draw to Trenches and Dug-outs in E.29.a.
    O.C. 4th Middlesex Regt. will detail an advance party to reconnoitre this accommodation early on the 12th inst.

8. Arrangements will be made to cover the Front by Patrols or advanced d listening posts before, during and after relief.

9. Battalions will be distributed in their Sectors as far as possible in depth and all Units will forward to this Office a Map showing their dispositions within 24 hours of completion of relief.

10. A duplicate copy of all receipts taken for all Trench Stores Maps, &c will be forwarded to this Office.

11. ~~Completion~~ Completion of relief will be reported to this Office by use of the Code-word "SANDBAGS".

12. ACKNOWLEDGE (Units of this Brigade by wire).

                                                      Captain.
                                            Brigade Major.
                                        63rd Infantry Brigade.

DISTRIBUTION.	Copy No.
War Diary & File	1 - 3
Brigade Staff	4 - 8
8th Lincolnshire Rgt.	9
do. (Rear H.Q.)	10
8th Somerset L.I.	11
do. (Rear H.Q.)	12
4th Middlesex Regt	13
do. (Rear H.Q.)	14
63rd T.M.Battery	15
do. (Rear H.Q.)	16
111th Inf. Brigade	17
112th Inf. Brigade	18
4th Aust. Inf. Bde	19
37th Division	20 - 21
C.R.E.	22
No.2 Coy Train	23
A.D.M.S. 37th Divn.	24
37th M.G. Bn.	25
154 Field Coy R.E.	26
Right Group R.A.	27
Senior Liaison Officer	28
Brigade Transport Offr	29
Brigade Supply Officer	30
9th North Staffs. (Pnrs)	31

ADDENDUM to 63rd INFANTRY BRIGADE DEFENCE ARRANGEMENTS.

In case of attack 154th Field Coy R.E. will take up positions in the PURPLE SYSTEM as follows :-

Two Sections in the 2nd PURPLE LINE in E.28.d.50.10 to E.28.d.90.80.

Two Sections in 3rd PURPLE LINE in E.28.c.55.30 to E.28.b.55.35.

O.C. 154th Field Coy R.E. in case of receiving "PRECAUTIONARY MEASURES" will at once send 2 Orderlies to Brigade Headquarters.

                                Captain.
                         Brigade Major.
14.4.18.   63rd Infantry Brigade.

DISTRIBUTION :-

All recipients of 63rd Infantry Brigade Provisional Defensive arrangements.

SECRET.   Copy No.

                              63rd Infantry Brigade No. 229/1 G.

           AMENDMENTS TO 63rd INFANTRY BRIGADE

           PROVISIONAL DEFENSIVE ARRANGEMENTS.

Reference Map.
Sheet 57D. N.E.
   1:20,000.   14th April, 1918.

PARA. 5, Sub-para. (c) is cancelled, and the following substituted:-

       "   The Reserve Battalion is responsible for the defence of
       the PURPLE LINE, and will be disposed as follows:- One
       Company from E.30.a.10.15 to E.29.d.30.85. One Company
       from E.29.d.30.85 to E.29.c.50.50. One Company from E.29.
       c.50.50 to K.5.a.60.50., and one Company in the second
       PURPLE LINE about E.29.a.50.20 and E.29.a.50.50 with
       Battalion Headquarters at E.29.a.45.60.
            This Battalion will be reserved for the defence of this
       line and will not be used for counter attack to retake any
       portions of the front system without direct orders from
       Brigade Headquarters."

PARA. 10, Sub-para. (b) is cancelled, and the following substituted:-

       "   The Reserve Battalion will occupy first and second
       PURPLE LINES as laid down in para. 5."

                                          G. B. Sheringham
                                                      Captain.
                                                  Brigade Major.
14.4.18.   63rd Infantry Brigade.

DISTRIBUTION:-

       All recipients of 63rd Infantry Brigade Provisional
       Defensive Arrangements.

SECRET.

Copy No. 1

63rd Infantry Brigade No. 229 G.

63rd INFANTRY BRIGADE
PROVISIONAL DEFENSIVE ARRANGEMENTS.

Reference Map
Sheet 57D. N.E.
1:20,000.

12th April, 1918.

1. The 37th Divisional front (with 4th Australian Infantry Brigade attached) is extending its RIGHT on nights 12/13th and 13/14th April so as to hold the line from K.21.d.0.0. to L.7.b.85.15.

2. 63rd Infantry Brigade holds the LEFT Brigade Sector from K.12.b.0.8. to L.7.b.85.15. with 187th Infantry Brigade on the LEFT (i.e. to the North) and 112th Infantry Brigade on the RIGHT (i.e. to the South).

3. The Northern and Southern boundaries and the successive main lines of resistance are shewn on attached map.

4. The sphere of responsibility for defence of the sector is as shewn on this map.

5. (a) The LEFT front Battalion should be disposed in depth so far as possible with its reserves in or about L.1.c. with one platoon to garrison northern end of CHUB TRENCH.
   (b) The RIGHT front Battalion will hold the line with two companies in the line, one company in Support about K.6.d. and K.6.central with one platoon in CHUB TRENCH, and one company in Reserve in SALMON TRENCH.
   (c) The Reserve Battalion is responsible for the defence of the PURPLE LINE and will be disposed in the First PURPLE LINE (i.e. from E.30.a.2.2. to K.5.a.6.5) in the first instance.
   This Battalion will be reserved for the defence of this line and will not be used for counter attack to retake any portions of the front system without direct orders from Brigade Hdqrs.

6. POLICY OF DEFENCE.
   (a) The defence of the successive lines must necessarily consist of a number of more or less independent posts, which must be sited so far as possible so as to command all avenues of approach. Os.C. Battalions will site these posts most carefully and will arrange at once to distribute at least one box of S.A.A. to each post, and will arrange for a supply of grenades in these successive lines at all posts where trenches run into these main lines from an Easterly direction.
   Indents should be sent in to the Staff Captain at once and every effort will be made to get these supplies forward by the Light Railway to a point on the Railway as required by Os.C. forward Battalions.
   (b) The Troops holding the front system must offer the greatest possible resistance to the enemy.
   (c) The garrison of each line if driven out by overwhelming attack must retire fighting, and will reorganise behind the next line, occupying defensive localities to cover the withdrawal of those in front of them. If troops on the flank are forced back there must be no general withdrawal. A defensive flank must be formed by those troops which are still holding out; this should be quite practicable if troops are kept in good depth.
   (d) The PURPLE Line must be held against all attacks.
   (e) Should the front line troops be obliged to fall back, they will take up positions in the support and reserve trenches of the PURPLE LINE shewn on attached map.

- 2 -

7. **FLANKS.**
   (a) The front, support and reserve line systems of the flank Brigades are shewn on attached map "A".
   (b) Units will send an N.C.O. and two runners to the Headquarters of Units on their flanks. The closest possible liaison is of the utmost importance.

8. **ACTION OF 63rd INFANTRY BRIGADE IN CASE OF WITHDRAWAL BEING ORDERED.**
   It is essential that all Officers and N.C.Os. should know the successive main lines of resistance as shewn on attached map. It is not possible to issue copies of this map below Battalion Commanders as it is not considered advisable for Officers to be carrying maps so marked in front of Battalion H.Q., but in view of the fact that the rear lines of defence do not run parallel with the present front line it must be impressed on all Officers and N.C.Os. that in the event of a withdrawal being ordered troops must fight a rear-guard action moving back in a Westerly direction and not diagonally from the present front in a North-westerly direction.

9. The greatest possible effort will at once be made by all ranks to improve the posts they are occupying. These posts should be at least fire-stepped and everything possible done to improve the field of fire. This work must be carried out by night as well as by day in shifts even if it involves a strain on the garrison.

   SHOULD PRECAUTIONARY MEASURES BE ORDERED:-
10. (a) All ranks will be issued with extra bandolier of ammunition.
    (b) The Reserve Battalion will be prepared to move to the first PURPLE Line and take up a defensive position therein at 30 minutes notice.
    (c) The greatest vigilance must be observed by all ranks against Gas.
    (d) Front Line Battalions will push out protective patrols. Support Companies will double sentries and be prepared to man their positions at a moments notice.

11. ACKNOWLEDGE.

                                                    Captain.
                                                    Brigade Major.
                                                    63rd Infantry Brigade.
12.4.18.

DISTRIBUTION:-

	Copy No.		Copy No.
War Diary	1 - 3	187th Infantry Bde.	15
Staff & File	4 - 8	4th Aus. Inf. Bde.	16
8th Lincolnshire Regt.	9	37th Division	17-18
8th Somerset L.I.	10	C.R.E.	19
4th Middlesex Regt.	11	154 Field Co. R.E.	20
63rd T.M. Battery	12	37th M.G. Battalion	21
111th Infantry Bde.	13	O.C. 'D' Group,	
112th Infantry Bde.	14	37th M.G. Battn.	22
		O.C.R.A. Group	23
		B.G.R.A.	24

SECRET　　　　　　　　　　　　　　　　　　　　　　　Copy No. 1.

63rd INFANTRY BRIGADE ORDER No.211.

Ref. Map.
Sheet 57D.N.E.　　　　　　　　　　　　　　　　　14th April, 1918.
1:20,000.

1. 4th Battn. Middlesex Regt. will relieve 8th Battn Lincolnshire Regt. in the LEFT sub-sector on the night 14/15th April. 8th Battn. Lincolnshire Regt. upon relief will withdraw into Trenches and Dugouts in and about E.29.a. with Battalion Headquarters at E.29.a.4.7.

2. All details of relief will be arranged between Commanding Officers concerned.
   There will be no movement before 7.45 p.m. except for the usual advance parties.

3. Defence orders for the respective areas will be handed over by the Commanding Officers along with any maps shewing dispositions, trench stores &c. and receipts taken. A copy of each receipt will be forwarded to this office.

4. A plan shewing existing dispositions, number of posts with map locations will be forwarded to this office within 24 hours of relief.

5. Arrangements will be made for patrolling the front before, during and after relief.

6. Completion of relief will be notified to this office by use of the code word 'CERTAINLY'.

7. ACKNOWLEDGE BY WIRE (Units of Brigade only).

ISSUED AT 7 A.M.

　　　　　　　　　　　　　　　　　　　　　　　　Captain.
　　　　　　　　　　　　　　　　　　　　　　Brigade Major.
14.4.18　　　　　　　　　　　　　　　　　63rd Infantry Brigade.

DISTRIBUTION:-

	Copy No.		Copy No.
War Diary	1 - 3	187th Inf. Bde.	17
Staff & File	4 - 8	112th Inf. Bde.	18
8th Lincolnshire Regt.	9	37th Division	19 - 20
-do-　　Rear	10	37th M.G.Battn.	21
8th Somerset L.I.	11	O.C.'D' Group,	
-do-　　Rear	12	37th M.G.Bn.	22
4th Middlesex Regt.	13	Left Group, R.A.	23
-do-　　Rear	14	Senior Liaison Officer	24
63rd T.M.Battery	15	154 Field Co. R.E.	25
Rear	16	No.2 Coy. Train	26
		Brigade Transport Offr.	27
		Brigade Supply Officer	28

SECRET.   Copy No. 1

63rd INFANTRY BRIGADE ORDER No.212.

Reference Map.
  Sheet 57D.N.E.   16th April 1918.
  1:20,000.

1.   The 37th Division less Artillery will be relieved in the
Line by the 42nd Division less Artillery on the nights 15/16th
and 16/17th April. 37th Division upon relief will withdraw into
Corps Reserve.

2.   On the night 15/16th 63rd Infantry Brigade will be relieved
in the LEFT sector by the 126th Infantry Brigade, and will withdraw
upon relief to the area HENU - D.13.b. in accordance with table to
be issued later.
        On the night 16/17th 111th and 112th Infantry Brigades will
be relieved in the Line by the 125th and 127th Infantry Brigades
respectively, and will withdraw - 111th Inf.Bde. to ST.LEGER -
BOIS DU WARNIMONT area - 112th Inf.Bde. to LOUVENCOURT area.

3.   Reconnoitring parties from the incoming units will come
forward to-day - 14/15th - and advance parties for attachment for
24 hours will also arrive at a time to be notified later. Guides
to meet these parties will be sent to Brigade Headquarters.

4.   Arrangements will be made by the rear details of each unit
to reconnoitre the new area as soon as further particulars are
available.

5.   All details of relief will be arranged between Commanding
Officers concerned.

6.   Programmes of work in hand or proposed, disposition maps,
defence schemes, aeroplane photos and any documents relating to
the sector will be handed over and receipts taken. Copies of these
receipts, along with copies of all receipts taken for trench stores,
will be forwarded to this office within 24 hours of relief.

7.   Completion of relief will be notified to this office by use
of the code word 'APPROVED'.

8.   ACKNOWLEDGE BY WIRE (Units of Brigade only).

ISSUED AT 3.30 P.M.

                                                    Captain.
                                                 Brigade Major.
14.4.18.   63rd Infantry Brigade.

DISTRIBUTION:-

	Copy No.		Copy No.
War Diary	1 - 3	126th Inf.Bde.	20
Staff & File	4 - 8	37th Division	21 - 22
8th Lincolnshire Regt.	9	37th M.G.Battn.	23
-do- Rear	10	O.C.'D' Group,37 M.G.Bn	24
8th Somerset L.I.	11	Left Group, R.A.	25
-do- Rear	12	B.G.R.A.	26
4th Middlesex Regt.	13	Senior Liaison Officer	27
-do- Rear	14	C.R.E.	28
63rd T.M.Battery	15	154 Field Co. R.E.	29
-do- Rear	16	A.D.M.S. 37th Divn.	30
127th Infantry Bde.	17	No.2 Coy. Train	31
111th Infantry Bde.	18	Brigade Supply Officer	32
112th Infantry Bde.	19	Brigade Transport Offr.	33

66

TABLE TO ACCOMPANY
63rd INFANTRY BRIGADE ORDER NO. 212.

Serial No.	Date.	Unit	From	To	Relieved by	Guides to be at E.28.c.60.5 at	Remarks.
	Night						
1	15/16th	4th Middlesex Regt.	Left sub-sector	HENU area	5th East Lancs.Regt.	7.15 p.m.	Units will be responsible that movement East of the CHATEAU DE LA HAIE - BIENVILLERS ROAD is carried out in parties not exceeding one platoon in strength at 200 yards intervals.
2	do	8th Somerset L.I.	Right sub-sector.	do	10th Manchester Regt.	7.30 p.m.	
3	do	8th Lincoln-shire Regt.	Reserve	do	8th Manchester Regt.	8.0 p.m.	
4	do	63rd T.M. Battery.	Line	do	126th T.M. Battery.	7.15 p.m.	

Guides to meet outcoming troops are being arranged by the Rear Headquarters of each unit and will be on the SOUASTRE - HENU ROAD on the eastern outskirts of HENU.

C.A.B. Pluntham
Captain.
Brigade Major.
63rd Infantry Brigade.

15.4.18.

SECRET.   Copy No. _____

63rd Infantry Brigade Order No. 213.

                                              April 16th 1918.

1.   On 16th inst. 63rd Inf. Bde. will move to AUTHIE WOOD
area and will take over camps vacated by 171st Inf. Bde.

2.   March Table is issued herewith.

3.   Transport will move independently; all stores must be
clear of HENU by 1 pm.
        One lorry per Battalion and half a lorry for T.M.Battery
will be available and units will detail guides to be at cross
roads, D.19.a.3.2, at 12 noon.

4.   Billeting parties of 1 officer and 6 N.C.Os (T.M.Battery
1 N.C.O.) will report to Captain C.H.S.WILLIS, 8th Lincoln
Regt. at Town Major's Office, AUTHIE, at 10 am.

5.   Arrival in billets will be notified to Brigade H.Q. by
runner.

6.   ACKNOWLEDGE (Units of Brigade Only).

                                        _____ Captain,
                                              for Brigade Major,
Issued at 2 am   63rd Infantry Brigade.

Distribution.   Copy No.
War Diary & File   1 - 3
Brigade Staff   4 - 8
8th Lincolnshire Regt.   9
8th Somerset L.I.   10
4th Middlesex Regt.   11
63rd T.M.Battery   12
No. 2 Coy. Train   13
Brigade Supply Officer   14
Brigade Transport Offr.   15
152nd Field Coy., R.E.   16
37th Division   17 - 18
111th Inf. Bde.   19
112th Inf. Bde.   20
A.D.M.S.   21
57th Divnl. Composite Bn.   22

MARCH TABLE to accompany 63rd Inf. Bde. Order No. 213 dated 16.4.18.

Serial No.	Unit	From	To	Starting Point	Time to pass starting pt.	Route
1	8th Lincolnshire Regt.	HEBU	AUTHIE WOOD (L.16.b and d)	Cross Roads D.19.c.55.65	11.30 am	D.19.c. - D.30. central - I.10. - AUTHIE
2	8th Somerset L.I.	"	"	"	11.45 am	-do-
3	4th Middlesex Regt.	"	"	"	12.00 noon	-do-
4	63rd Inf. Bde. H.	"	"	"	12.15 pm	-do-
5	63rd T.M.Battery	"	"	"	12.20 pm	-do-

N.B. The following distances will be maintained :-
100 yards between Companies
500 yards between Battalions.

SECRET.   Copy No. 1

63rd Infantry Brigade Order No. 214

Reference Sheet: April 17th 1918.
57 D, 1:40,000

1. 63rd Infantry Brigade and 'A' Company, 37th M.G.Battn. will come under orders of G.O.C. New Zealand Division in case of attack.

2. In this case 49th Field Ambulance will supply bearer sub-divisions to accompany 63rd Inf. Bde.

3. In case of enemy bombardment or threatened attack, 63rd Inf. Bde., 'A' Coy., 37th M.G. Bn., and bearer subdivisions of 49th Field Ambulance will move to positions of readiness about J.19.central, where they will be disposed as follows :-
   (a) 63rd Inf. Bde. H.Q.   J.19.d.0.8.
   (b) 4th Middlesex Regt.   S. of AUTHIE - BUS-LES-
                                          ARTOIS Road about J.19.d.2.4.
   (c) 8th Somerset L.I.   N. of AUTHIE - BUS-LES-
                                          ARTOIS Road about J.19.d.5.6.
   (d) 8th Lincolnshire Regt.   N. of AUTHIE - BUS-LES-
                                          ARTOIS Road about J.19.central.
   (e) 'A' Coy., 37th M.G.Bn.
        Personnel   -   N. of AUTHIE - BUS-LES-
                                          ARTOIS Road about J.19.c.3.9.
        Transport   -   S. of AUTHIE - BUS-LES-
                                          ARTOIS Road about J.19.c.10.75.
   (f) Bearer Sub-divisions   J.19.c.30.75.
       49th Field Ambulance
   (g) Forward echelon of first line transport will be disposed S. of AUTHIE - BUS-LES-ARTOIS Road in J.24.d., as far as possible under cover of the wood.

   (h) O.C. 63rd T.M.Battery will detail two mortars and teams to accompany each Infantry Battalion. The remaining mortars and teams will remain with Rear Details.

4. On receipt of the order 'MOVE', units will move to their positions of assembly as above in J.19., passing the starting point, I.18.b.85.55, as follows :-
   63rd Inf. Bde. H.Q.   Zero plus 25 minutes
   8th Somerset L.I.   Zero plus 30 minutes
   4th Middlesex Regt.   Zero plus 40 minutes
   8th Lincolnshire Regt.   Zero plus 50 minutes
   ~~63rd T.M.Battery~~   ~~Zero plus 60 minutes~~
   'A' Coy., 37th M.G.Bn.   Zero plus 65 minutes
   Bearer Sub-divisions, 49th F.A. Zero plus 75 minutes

   ZERO Hour will be notified to all concerned.

   First line transport of 'A' M.G.Company will move with the Company. All other first line transport will move under orders of Brigade Transport Officer, following in rear of the infantry.

5. 63rd Inf. Bde. will be prepared to carry out the following:-

   (a) To relieve two Battalions and one M.G.Company of New Zealand Division in occupation of the PURPLE LINE from P.10.cent. to K.14.cent., in which case 4th Middlesex Regt. would take over the right subsector from P.10.cent. as far north as a line drawn E. & W. through cross roads J.36.a. and J.35.b. 8th Somerset L.I. would

(2)

take over the left subsector from cross roads, J.36.a. to K.14. central.

(b) To manoeuvre in the area BEAUSSART - FORCEVILLE - ENGLEBELMER - MAILLY - MAILLET to protect the right flank of the Division, in which case 4th Middlesex Regt. will be prepared to cover this manoeuvre.

(c) To manoeuvre in the vicinity of SAILLY-au-BOIS to protect the left flank of the Division, in which case 8th Somerset L.I. will be prepared to cover the manoeuvre.

(d) To counter-attack to recapture BEAUSSART, COLINCAMPS or COURCELLES.

6. Units of the Reserve Brigade of New Zealand Division (H.Q. BUS-LES-ARTOIS), will supply units of 63rd Inf. Bde. will all information regarding the PURPLE LINE.
H.Q. of Battalions are located at the following points :-
J.34.b.2.6   J.22.d.central
J.18.d.55.25   P.9.a.2.8
N.Z. M.G. Battalion - J.26.a.25.45 (BUS).

7. In the event of heavy enemy barrage, the following routes to the forward area should be used :-
(a) J.25.central - P.2.central - P.16.central.
(b) J.20.central - J.22.central - thence either J.35.central or J.23.central.

8. In the event of attack, 37th Division has been ordered to move two Infantry Brigades into positions of assembly behind the RED Line between the Corps Right Boundary and J.14.central and to establish its Battle H.Q. at BUS-les-ARTOIS.

9. Brigade Signal Officer will reconnoitre the ground with a view to establishing communication forward from BUS-les-ARTOIS in case of 63rd Inf. Bde. being ordered to carry out any of those operations.

10. On 63rd Inf. Bde. being ordered to assembly positions in J.19.,
(a) Captain C.H.S. WILLIS, 8th Lincolnshire Regt., will report to H.Q. New Zealand Division, BUS-les-ARTOIS, with a mounted orderly, to act as liaison officer throughout the operations.

(b) Os.C. 4th Middlesex Regt. and 8th Lincolnshire Regt. will each detail one officer mounted, each accompanied by a mounted orderly, to report to General Staff Office, 37th Division H.Q., AUTHIE.

(c) Each Battalion will detail one officer mounted, accompanied by a mounted orderly, to report to Brigade H.Q., J.19.d.0.8, to act as liaison officer between their respective Battalions and Brigade H.Q. during the operations.

11. Administrative Instructions will be issued separately.

12. ACKNOWLEDGE.

Issued at 12.60 midnight.

A. B. Sheringham,
Captain,
Brigade Major,
63rd Infantry Brigade.

Distribution.

War Diary & File	1 - 3	Brigade Transport Officer	15
Brigade Staff	4 - 8	37th Division	16 - 17
8th Lincolnshire Regt.	9	111th Inf. Bde.	18
8th Somerset L.I.	10	112th Inf. Bde.	19
4th Middlesex Regt.	11	N.Z. Division	20
63rd T.M. Battery	12	1st N.Z. Inf. Bde.	21
'A' Coy., 37th M.G. Bn.	13	2nd N.Z. Inf. Bde.	22
49th Fd. Ambulance	14	3rd N.Z. (Rifle) Bde.	23
		37th M.G. Battn.	24

COMMUNICATIONS.

Reference Sheet:
57 D, 1:40,000

Reference: 63rd Inf. Bde. Order No. 214 dated 17.4.18.

1. On receipt of the order "MOVE" Battalions will make up the number of runners attached to Brigade Headquarters to 8 (4 pairs). 152nd Field Company, R.E. will detail 4 runners and "A" Coy.,
   37th Machine Gun Battalion will detail 2 runners to report to Brigade H.Q.
   These runners will join Brigade H.Q. at the Assembly Point, J.19.d.0.8.

2. If positions taken up by units are not already in telephonic communication, this means of communication will be established as soon as possible.

3. In the event of the Brigade holding the PURPLE System, a Brigade Central Visual Station will be established on HILL 153 J.28.a.60.90.

4. In the event of the Brigade forming a Left flank defence, Brigade Central Visual Station will be the same as for holding the PURPLE System, i.e., HILL 153, J.28.a.60.90.

5. In the event of the Brigade forming a Right Flank Defence, Brigade Central Visual Station will be established at the WINDMILL, J.34.b.20.65.

6. Power Buzzers will be sent to Battalions in the line as soon as possible after positions have been taken up.
   Amplifier Station will be established at Brigade Central Visual Station.

J. Stewart 2nd Lieut.,
for Brigade Major,
63rd Infantry Brigade.

20.4.18.

Copy to:- 37th Division
8th Lincolnshire Regt.
8th Somerset L.I.
4th Middlesex Regt.
63rd T.M.Battery
"A" Coy., 37th M.G?Battn.
152nd Field Coy., R.E.

SECRET.   VERY URGENT

63rd INFANTRY BRIGADE
ADMINISTRATIVE INSTRUCTIONS.

Reference 63rd Infantry Brigade Order No.214.
(Defence Orders while in IV Corps Reserve)

ACTION IN CASE OF ATTACK.

63rd Infantry Brigade No.9682 is cancelled and the following substituted. On the issue of the order "MOVE" the following action will be taken:-

1. **TRANSPORT.**

    (a) Each Battalion will form a Mobile Reserve of Ammunition and Tools consisting of:-
    - 4 Lewis Gun Limbers
    - 1 S.A.A. Limber
    - Tool Limbers
    - Medical Cart
    - Ammunition Mules.

    Battalion Mobile Reserves will move to the position of assembly under orders issued by the Brigade Transport Officer.

    (b) A Brigade Mobile Reserve under the Command of 2nd Lieut. G.H.PIERCE, 4th Middlesex Regt. will be formed as under:-
    - 2 Brigade H.Q. Tool Wagons.
    - 2 S.A.A. Limbers per Battalion.
    - 1 Grenade Limber   do
    - 1 G.S. Wagon to carry Stokes Shells.

    On receipt of the order "MOVE" these wagons will be loaded and the teams will be harnessed and will stand by ready to move on receipt of orders from G.O.C. Brigade.

    (c) 3 Cookers and 1 Water cart per Battalion will follow the Brigade to the place of assembly. These will probably return to the Transport Lines when Battalions move forward from the assembly position.

    (d) All surplus pack-saddlery will be placed on the Limbers sent to join the Brigade Ammunition Reserve.

2. **TENTAGE.**

    All tents will be left standing in their present positions.

3. **SURPLUS STORES & BAGGAGE.**

    All stores, blankets, baggage etc., surplus to what can be carried on train transport, and men's packs, will be collected by Details left behind and stacked in Battalion Dumps near to the main road where they can be readily loaded on to lorries.

4. **TRENCH MORTARS.**

    One Light Trench Mortar Team and 20 rounds Ammunition will move with each Battalion. Mortar and Ammunition to be carried in hand carts.
    A reserve of 3 L.T.Ms. and 60 shells will be carried in a G.S. wagon with the Brigade Mobile Reserve.

5. **WATER.**

    Water can be obtained from wells fitted with pumps at COURCELLES - BEAUSSART. There are also wells at COLINCAMPS and BERTRANCOURT.
    Water carts must always be filled at dusk and kept full in readiness to move at any time during the night.
    Water bottles must always be kept full.

- 2 -

6. **AMMUNITION.**
   1. **DUMPS.**   The following S.A.A. Dumps exist:-
      (a) In PURPLE LINE -
         (i) J.3.d.2.3.   (FORCEVILLE - BERTRANCOURT Road)
         (ii) J.28.d.2.7.   (COURCELLES - BUS Road)
         (iii) J.28.c.3.3. (SAILLY - BERTRANCOURT Road)
         ∅ (iiii) J.30.d.3.7. (BERTRANCOURT - COURCELLES Road)
            ∅ is a N.Z.Bde Dump of mixed ammunition.

      (b) In RED LINE system.-
         (i) I.34.a.3.3.   (VAUCHELLES - LOUVENCOURT Road)   )
         (ii) I.28.d.3.3.   (LOUVENCOURT - THEIVRES track)   ) X
         (iii) 0.4.b.central (X track S. of LOUVENCOURT)   )
                X - Mixed dumps.
         (iv) O.11.d.4.1.   (LEALVILLERS - LOUVENCOURT Road))
         (v) 0.5.c.3.3.   (do   -   do   )   )
         (vi) I.34.a.3.4.   (VAUCHELLES - LOUVENCOURT Road)   ) ∅
         (vii) I.24.a.3.4. (BUS - AUTHIE Road)   )
             ∅ - M.G.Ammn. 45,000 each.

      (c) N.Z.Div. A.R.Bs.-
         (i) O.12.b.3.3.   (AGNEUX - LOUVENCOURT Road)
         (ii) 0.6.c.3.2.   (do   -   do   )
         (iii) I.35.b.3.3. (LOUVENCOURT)

      (d) Corps Reserve at I.14.d. (AUTHIE-MARIEUX Road).

      (e) ST.LEGER Railhead I.12.b.2.2. (in emergency).

      (f) ACHE Railhead P.13.d. (in emergency).

   2. **FIGHTING EQUIPMENT.**
        The following will be issued to each Battalion as fighting equipment, to be issued to the men before marching off:-

            S.A.A. and Grenades (including a proportion of No.36
               in accordance with S.S.135.   Grenades)
        This will be issued unopened to units and kept under guard in Camp Magazine, and not distributed until required.

   3. **SYSTEM OF SUPPLY.**
        Arrangements will be made to ensure the supply of ammunition independently of the above dumps, although these will be used whenever possible, the Mobile Reserve being kept intact.
             A chain will be formed as under:-
      (i)   D.A.C. to Brigade Ammunition Reserve - by D.A.C. S.A.A. carts.
      (ii) Brigade Ammunition Reserve to Battalion Ammunition Reserve -
               (full limbers will be sent forward in exchange for empty ones).
      (iii) Battalion Ammunition Reserve to Firing Line - Pack animals.
             Should the situation be such as to necessitate a more extensive use of pack animals, Battalion Commanders will notify the Officer i/c Brigade Reserve who will then send forward a proportion of his animals equipped with pack-saddlery. The Officer i/c Brigade Ammunition Reserve will keep O.C. S.A.A. Section D.A.C. informed as to the situation by means of D.A.A. orderlies attached to him. He will at once notify D.A.C. of any change in the location of the Brigade Ammunition Reserve.
             The animals with Battalion Ammunition Reserve will not be used as pack animals; these Reserves must be kept mobile.

7. **SUPPLIES.**
      (i)   Units 1st Line Transport will be prepared to receive Iron Rations on the following scale:-
                500 per Battalion.
                240 for Bde. H.Q. (includes T.M.B. and M.G.
                                     Coy. attached).
      (ii) Trench Rations will be indented for for 50% fighting strength of units.

- 3 -

 (iii) Chewing Gum will be issued and held in reserve as fighting equipment.

8. **MEDICAL.** The 49th Fld.Amb., less 2 tent Sub-divisions, has been attached to the Brigade and will move as follows:-
 Bearer sub-division will march to place of assembly.
 Remainder will stand by to wait orders.

9. **REAR HEADQUARTERS.**
 Rear Brigade Headquarters will be established in AUTHIE WOOD.

10. **SURPLUS PERSONNEL AND DETAILS NOT TAKEN INTO BATTLE.**
 All personnel less Transport and Q.M.Details, including drums, not to be taken into battle, will, as soon as the Camp has been cleared be assembled at Brigade Headquarters. The senior officer of each Battalion will report to Major P.GROVE WHITE, 4th Middlesex Regt., who will organise this Detail into the Brigade Company. He will apply to the Town Major AUTHIE for accommodation which will be allotted in the Camp at present occupied by Brigade. The details will form one Company of 37th Divisional Composite Battalion under the Command of Lt.Col. F.W.MOFFITT, D.S.O., 1st Bn. Essex Regt., whose address will be given by the Town Major AUTHIE.

11. **TRANSPORT & Q.M.STORES.**
 These will remain in present position pending receipt of further orders.

12. **ACKNOWLEDGE.**

          (Sd) H.A.MAYNARD, Captain.
             Staff Captain.
            63rd Infantry Brigade.

Distribution.

8th Lincolnshire Regt.	1
8th Somerset L.I.	2
4th Middlesex Regt.	3
63rd Trench Mortar Battery	4
63rd Brigade Transport Offr.	5
37th M.G.Battalion	6
"A" Coy. 37th M.G.Battn.	7
49th Field Ambulance	8
S.A.A.Section, D.A.C.	9
No.2 Coy. Train.	10
Supply Officer 63rd Inf.Bde.	11

SECRET.   Copy No. 1.

63rd Infantry Brigade Order No. 215

Reference Sheet:
57 D, 1:40,000   April 21st 1918.   less Arty

1. On nights 23/24th and 24/25th April, 37th Division is relieving 62nd Division in the line in the BUCQUOY - ABLAINZEVELLE Sector from L.2.c.9.1 to the south, to F.22.b.8.8 to the north.

2. (a) On night 23/24th April, 63rd Infantry Brigade will relieve 187th Infantry Brigade in the right subsector in accordance with March Table which will be issued later.

   (b) 111th Infantry Brigade will relieve 185th Infantry Brigade in the left subsector.

   (c) The inter-brigade boundary is at L.3.b.3.4.

3. Lorries have been asked for to be at AUTHIE CHURCH at 4 pm, 22nd inst, to take forward advance parties.
   These parties will be met at a point on the GOMMECOURT - PIGEON WOOD Road, E.29.a.70.00 at 8.30 pm and will spend 24 hours in the line attached to the unit holding the area to be taken over by their respective Battalions.

4. Guides from units of 187th Infantry Brigade will meet incoming units at E.29.a.70.00. at 8.30 pm on 23rd inst.

5. All Defence Schemes, maps showing dispositions, trench stores, etc., will be taken over, and a map showing dispositions together with a list showing all trench stores taken over will be sent to this office within 24 hours of relief.

6. Completion of relief will be notified to this office by use of the word 'RECEIVED'.

7. Administrative Arrangements will be issued separately.

8. ACKNOWLEDGE.

                                            C.J.de B. Sheringham
Issued at 2 pm.   Captain,
                                               Brigade Major,
Distribution   63rd Infantry Brigade.

War Diary & File   1 - 3   C.R.A. 37th Division   24
Brigade Staff   4 - 8   I.M.G.C.   25
8th Lincolnshire Regt.   9   'A' Coy., 37th M.G.Bn.   26
8th Somerset L.I.   10   New Zealand Divn.   27
4th Middlesex Regt.   11   62nd Division   28
63rd T.M. Battery   12   A.P.M., 37th Divn.   29
Brigade Transport Officer   13
152nd Field Company R.E.   14
No. 2 Coy. Train   15
C.R.E.   16
A.D.M.S.   17
37th Division   18 - 19
112th Inf. Bde.   20
111th Inf. Bde.   21
187th Inf. Bde.   22
Brigade Supply Officer   23

AMENDMENT TO 63RD INF. BDE ORDER NO. 215 DATED 21.4.18.

Para. 4, line 2,

for "2.30 pm" read "8.30 pm".

C.J.de B.SHERINGHAM, Captain,
Brigade Major,
21.4.18   63rd Infantry Brigade.

To all recipients of 63rd Inf. Bde. Order No. 215 dated 21.4.18.

MARCH TABLE TO ACCOMPANY 63RD INF. BDE. ORDER NO. 215 DATED 21.4.18.

Ser. No.	Date	Unit	From	To	To pass starting point at I.16.b.90.65 at	Route	Remarks
1	23.4.18	8th Somerset L.I.	AUTHIE WOOD	Line (Left)	2.30 pm	ST.LEGER-les-AUTHIE – COUIN – J.1.b.05.20 – SOUASTRE – FONQUEVILLERS – GOMMECOURT	Units moving into the line will stage in the neighbourhood of SOUASTRE in old rest camp about D.22.c.3.5.
2	23.4.18	4th Middlesex Regt.	AUTHIE WOOD	Line (Right)	2.45 pm		
3	23.4.18	8th Lincolnshire Regt.	AUTHIE WOOD	Support	3.00 pm		
4	23.4.18	63rd T.M.Battery	AUTHIE WOOD	Line	3.15 pm		
5	23.4.18	63rd Inf. Bde. HQ	AUTHIE	La BRAYELLE Fm, E.23.d.8.1.	–		

All movements of formed parties of troops East and N.E. of SOUASTRE will be by parties not larger than platoons moving at 200 yards interval.

SECRET  Copy No. 1.

63rd Infantry Brigade Order No. 216

April 26th 1918.

1. On the night April 27/28th April, 8th Lincolnshire Regt. will relieve 4th Middlesex Regt. in the right subsector. Upon relief, 4th Middlesex Regt. will withdraw into trenches now occupied by 8th Lincolnshire Regt. in E.30.b., F.25 and F.26.

2. All details of relief will be arranged between Commanding Officers concerned.

3. Completion of relief will be notified to this office by use of the code word 'THANKS'.

4. All Trench Stores, Defence Schemes, Maps showing dispositions, work in progress and proposed, will be handed over and consolidated returns showing material handed over will be sent to this office within 24 hrs. of completion of relief.

5. ACKNOWLEDGE (Units of Brigade only).

Captain,
Brigade Major,
Issued at 5 pm.   63rd Infantry Brigade.

Distribution.   Copy No.

War Diary & File   1 - 3
Brigade Staff   4 - 8
8th Lincolnshire Regt. 9
  -do-   Rear HQ   10
8th Somerset L.I.   11
  -do-   Rear HQ   12
4th Middlesex Regt.   13
  -do-   Rear HQ   14
63rd T.M.Battery   15
  -do-   Rear HQ   16
'C' Coy., 37th M.G.Bn. 17
152nd Field Company RE 18
Brigade Transport Officer 19
37th Division   20 - 21
111th Infantry Brigade 22
112th Infantry Brigade 23
126th Infantry Brigade 24
C.R.A.   25
C.R.E.   26
Right Group, R.F.A.   27
37th M.G.Battalion   28
49th Field Amb.   29
Bde Supply Officer   30

SECRET.   Copy No. 18

63rd Infantry Brigade.

DEFENSIVE ARRANGEMENTS.   April 28th 1918

Reference Sheet:
57D N.E., 1:20,000

I. BOUNDARIES.

1. 37th Division holds the front line from L.2.c.9.1 on the right to F.22.b.8.8 on the left, on a two-brigade front with one brigade in reserve.

   The Northern and Southern boundaries of the Division and the Inter-brigade boundary are as shown on the attached map.

2. 63rd Infantry Brigade holds the Right Brigade Sector on a two-battalion front with one Battalion in Reserve. Inter-battalion boundary and the dispositions of all units of the Brigade are as shown on the map.

II. MAP.

The First Defensive Line is that shown coloured RED.
The second Defensive Line (MAIN) is coloured BLUE.
The support line and system of trenches immediately in rear the BLUE Line are coloured GREEN.
The Reserve Line is coloured BROWN.
The PURPLE Line is held by the Reserve Brigade.

III. TOPOGRAPHY.

The main features of the Divisional Area are :-

1. The main ESSARTS - GOMMECOURT Ridge.
2. HENLEY HILL, with its two spurs running
   (a) Due east to ABLAINZEVELLE and
   (b) S.E. to BUCQUOY.
3. The valley running N.W. towards BIEZ WOOD from L.22.b. through L.15 and L.8 and 9.
4. The valley running S.W. to F.19.d from AYETTE through F.15 and 20.

The forward slopes of HENLEY HILL are under direct observation from the direction of ABLAINZEVELLE and the high ground S.W. of that village, but the enemy can see little of the valley in F.27.

The southern slopes of the spur running S.E. towards BUCQUOY are under observation from the direction of FORK WOOD.

The enemy at present has no close observation of the area and cannot obtain such observation without securing the western exit from BUCQUOY in F.27.c and 26.d. and the spur to the south of this exit - L.2.b.

It is of the utmost importance therefore that these points be denied to him. Once they are gained it would be difficult to hold HENLEY HILL, the slopes of which could be swept by M.G.fire.

IV. DISPOSITIONS.

(a) All units are disposed in depth and a portion of each unit, whether a company or a battalion, will be held in reserve.

Should O.C. Right or Left Battalion propose to employ their reserve company for counter attack or to reinforce, Brigade H.Q. will be advised.

(b) The Support Battalion is at the disposal of the Brigade Commander and will be prepared for any of the following orders from Brigade H.Q. -

1. To reinforce any threatened portion of the Brigade front.
2. To counterattack should the enemy gain a footing in the forward zone of the Brigade front.

-2-

3. To hold the BROWN LINE.
In the event of attack, O.C. Support Battalion will at once arrange for an officer to keep in touch with each of the front line battalions, whose duty it will be to keep O.C. Support Battalion advised of any development of the situation.

V. POLICY OF DEFENCE.
(a) The defence of the successive lines must necessarily consist of a number of more or less independent posts, which must be sited so far as possible to command all avenues of approach. Os.C. Battalions will site these posts most carefully and will see that each post is provided with a reserve supply of S.A.A. and will arrange for a supply of grenades in these successive lines, particularly at all posts where trenches run into these main lines from an easterly direction.

(b) Troops holding the front system must offer the greatest possible resistance to the enemy. Every inch of ground must be obstinately defended. There should be no withdrawal from any line of resistance and the fact that a post is gained by the enemy is to be no justification for the posts on the flanks withdrawing. A post that holds out is often the means of breaking up an enemy attack and allows time for a counter attack to restore the situation. A defensive flank must be formed by those troops which are still holding out. This should be quite practicable if troops are disposed in good depth.

With the above in view, all unit commanders down to section commanders are responsible for the improvement of their positions. Posts should be sited with a view to their field of fire. They should be wired and firestopped and all trenches leading into our system from the enemy's should be blocked and filled in for 50 yards.

VI. FLANKS.
Units will send a N.C.O. and 2 runners to the Headquarters of units on their flanks. The closest possible liaison is of the utmost importance. A Liaison officer will be sent by Brigade H.Q. to flank Brigades.

VII. ACTION OF WORKING PARTIES IN CASE OF ATTACK.
Any working parties forward of the PURPLE Line will man the nearest trench and will send a representative to the nearest Battalion H.Q.

VIII. STOKES MORTARS.
Stokes Mortars are in position as follows :-
(a) Covering the Post line and, particularly, likely approaches of the enemy, with S.O.S. lines laid on such points, four)
L.2.d.35.85   L.3.a.00.60.   mortars)
L.2.b.70.15   L.3.a.05.75.

(b) Covering the Second (MAIN) Defensive line, 4 mortars :-
L.2.a.35.60   F.26.d.30.35.
L.3.a.47.70   F.26.d.40.40.

(c) Reserve positions have been prepared and are being stocked, to cover the BROWN LINE, as follows :-
Two guns   F.25.c.65.95, with S.O.S. lines on L.1.a.45.95
                                                and F.25.c.65.10.
One gun   F.25.c.95.95,   "   "   on F.25.d.25.25.
One gun   F.25.d.25.95,   "   "   on F.25.d.95.65.
Two guns   F.25.d.50.95,   "   "   on F.25.d.90.85
                                                and F.25.d.85.85.
Two guns   F.25.b.85.35, to protect strong point.

IX. MACHINE GUNS.
One Company of the Divisional Machine Gun Battalion is in action on the Brigade front disposed in depth, dispositions and S.O.S. lines of which are shown on attached map.

X. ARTILLERY.

The Brigade is covered by two Brigades of 37th Divnl. Artillery (123rd and 124th Brigades R.F.A.) Their S.O.S. lines are shown on the attached map.

S.O.S. relay stations have been established at the following points:-

Double Company H.Q.	The Château, BUCQUOY)	Left
Battalion H.Q.	F.26.a.7.1)	Battalion
Battalion H.Q.	)	
Left & Right Coy. H.Q.	(	Right
Support Coy. H.Q.	(	Battalion
F.25.c.45.40	)	
Battalion H.Q. and all Company H.Q.		Support Battalion.
L.2.d.4.9	)	
F.25.d.5.1	)	Company
F.26.a.9.3	)	M.G.
F.26.b.8.9	)	Battalion.
E.23.d.46.00	)	

The S.O.S. signal is a rifle grenade signal, RED over GREEN over RED, which should be fired in the event of the enemy being seen advancing against our positions, or in the event of a very heavy T.M. or artillery bombardment on our front line.

XI. COMMUNICATIONS.

(1) Telephone
(2) Visual
(3) Power Buzzer
(4) Pigeons
(5) Runners.

1.(a) With the exception of 500 yards of ground cable Adv. Brigade and 2 line Battalions are connected by buried cable to Brigade H.Q.

(b) The Support Battalion is conneceted by ground cable to Adv. Brigade.

(c) Artillery Group and Machine Gun Company are connected by ground cable to Brigade H.Q. Exchange.

(d) All companies are connected to Battalions by ground cable.

2.(a) This means of communication is established from all Battalions to Brigade Visual Centre. This Centre is 300 yds. from Brigade H.Q. and is connected to same by phone.

(b) Visual is also established from Brigade H.Q. to Adv. Division.

3.(a) This means is established from both line Battalions to Brigade H.Q. -
1-way working to Left Battalion,
2-way working to right Battalion.

(b) 2-way working is established between Brigade H.Q. and Adv. Division.

4. 2 Pigeons are available daily, making one bird to each Battalion in line.

XII. ANTI-GAS MEASURES

A supply of bleaching powder will be kept, in sealed tins, if possible, in each post.

Sentries will be fully instructed in the action to be taken by them in the event of
(a) Gas Cloud
(b) Gas shelling
(c) Use of projectors by the enemy.

Small Box Respirators will be inspected daily, Dugouts which it is possible to render gas proof will be made so as soon as possible.

-4-

XIII. ANTI-TANK ARRANGEMENTS.

Two guns are being placed in forward positions to deal with any possible employment of tanks by the enemy. In addition, each machine gun and Lewis Gun should be supplied with specially marked belts and magazines filled with Armour Piercing Ammunition.

XIV. ANTI-AIRCRAFT DEFENCE MEASURES.

A.A. Lewis guns and machine guns are in position at the following points :-

Lewis Guns.
    L.2.b.85.28   L.3.a.32.83.
    F.26.d.75.45.   F.26.c.60.95.
    F.25.b.40.80   F.25.c.50.50.
    F.25.c.50.95   E.30.b.50.10.
    E.30.d.50.95   E.30.b.40.45.

Machine guns   F.26.b.60.85   F.26.a.85.10.

XV. OBSERVATION POSTS.

Brigade Observation Posts are established at
1. L.1.d.20.10.
2. F.25.d.15.85.
3. F.26.c.35.95.

Nos. 1 and 2 are connected by telephone with Brigade Headquarters.
No. 3 communicates important information through Left Battalion H.Q.

XVI. ADMINISTRATIVE ARRANGEMENTS.

These will be issued separately as Appendix 'A'.

XVII. PRECAUTIONARY ACTION.

(a) Should 'Precautionary Measures' be ordered, all ranks will be issued with an extra bandolier of ammunition.
(b) Support Battalion will double sentries and will be prepared to stand to at short notice.
(c) Greatest vigilance must be observed by all ranks against gas.
(d) Front line Battalions will push/protective patrols. Support Companies will double sentries and be prepared to man their positions at a moment's notice.

RIGHT BRIGADE COMMUNICATIONS

(Less Corps Cons.) 29.4.18.

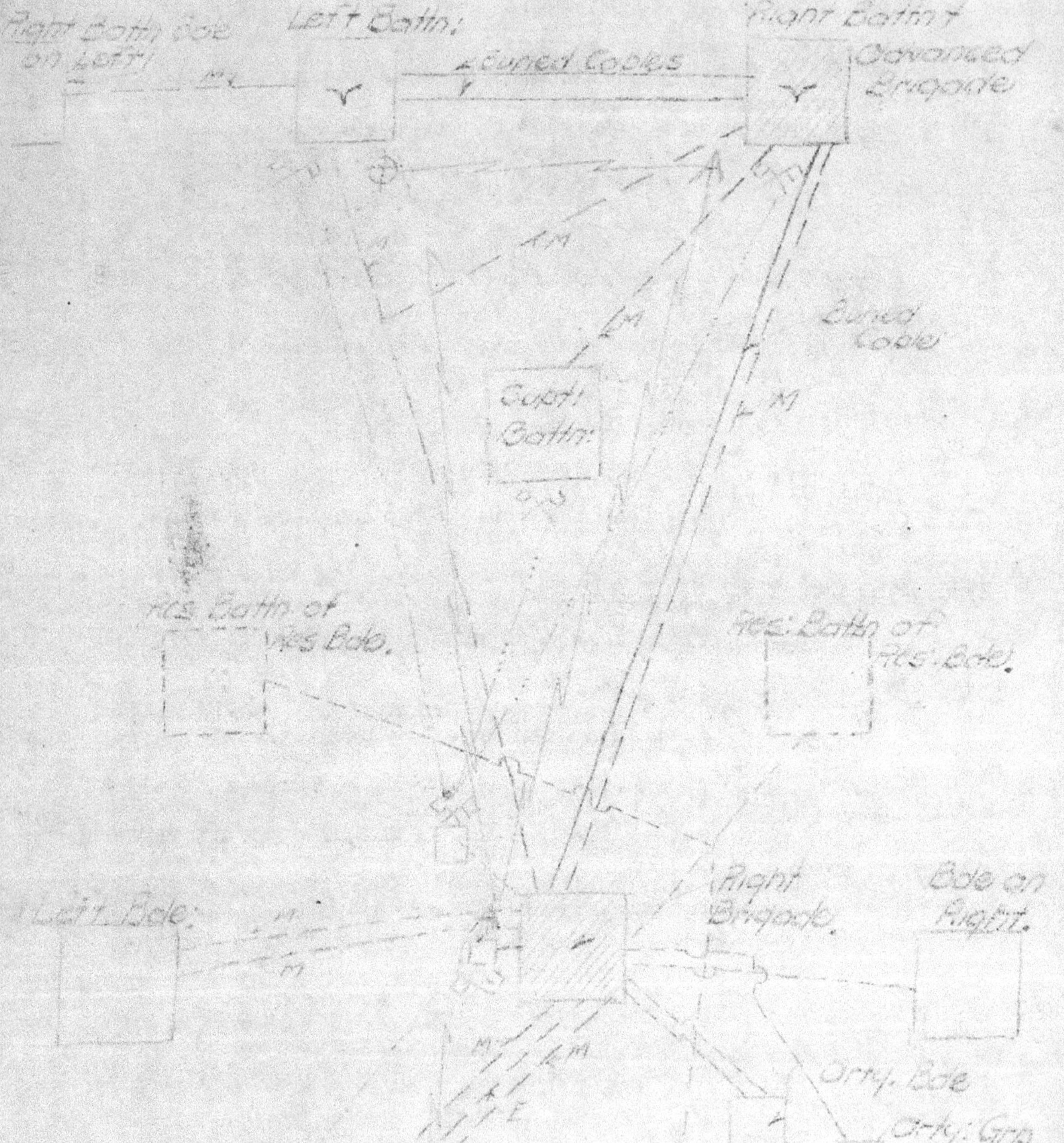
Right Battn Bde on Left.
Left Battn.
Buried Cables
Right Battn + Advanced Brigade
Buried Cable
Suppt: Battn.
Res. Battn of Res. Bde.
Res: Battn of Res. Bde.
Left Bde.
Right Brigade.
Bde on Right.
Arty. Bde
Arty: Grp.
Reserve Bde.
Divnl. Division.

J Stewart 2/Lt RE
OC Sigs 63rd Inf Bde.

63rd INFANTRY BRIGADE DEFENSIVE ARRANGEMENTS
APPENDIX "A"
ADMINISTRATIVE ARRANGEMENTS.

1. **LOCATION OF UNITS.** (Rear Echelons).

   The Rear Echelons of Units are located as follows :-

	Billet No.60	SOUASTRE.	Transport :-	
Brigade H.Q.				
8th Lincolns.	"	70	"	D.21.d.50.60
8th Som. L.I.	"	57	"	D.21.d.15.50
4th Midx.	"	72	"	D.21.c.1.90
63rd T.M.Bty	"	48	"	

2. **AMMUNITION.** Divisional Grenade Dump is located at D.19.c. central.

   Brigade Dumps :- Brigade Headquarters (Mixed Dump).
   F.26.c.20.65 (S.A.A. 180,000)
   There is a Reserve of S.A.A. and Grenades at each Front Line Battalion and Company H.Q.

   Units indent on the Staff Captain for their requirements, which are sent up by Limber with the Rations.

3. **RATIONS & WATER.**
   (a) Rations for all Units are carried forward by horse Transport.
   The following routes are used :-
   RIGHT BATTALION. SOUASTRE - FONQUEVILLERS - GOMMECOURT - Green Roads in F.19.c. - Track running S.W. through F.25.a. - HETTIMOY FARM.
   LEFT BATTALION. SOUASTRE - FONQUEVILLERS - GOMMECOURT - Trench Roads in F.19.c. - ESSARTS - BUCQUOY.

   SUPPORT BATTALION. SOUASTRE - FONQUEVILLERS - GOMMECOURT - PIGEON WOOD Road.

   BRIGADE HEADQUARTERS. SOUASTRE - FONQUEVILLERS - LA BRAYELLE ROAD - LA BRAYELLE FARM.

   (b) **WATER.** Water for all Units is carried forward in Petrol Tins.

   (c) **COOKING. FRONT LINE BATTALIONS :-** Hot Food for the men of Front Line Battalions is sent up nightly from Quartermasters' Stores. No Cooking is possible except by means of Tommy's Cookers.
   SUPPORT BATTALION.- Company Cookhouses have been established.

4. **R.E. MATERIAL.** Indents are submitted to O.C. 152nd Field Company R.E. Material is delivered to Dump at F.25.b.80.40. by the R.E.

5. **MEDICAL.** The evacuation from the Line is under the administration of O.C. 40th Field Ambulance.

   (a). **Regimental Aid Posts.** Right Bn. F.26.c.9.7.
   Left " F.26.a.5.1.
   Support E.30.d.4.9.
   (b). **Bearer and Relay Posts.** E.24.d.6.7.
   E.23.d.4.8.
   E.22.d.2.5.
   (c). **Car Loading Post.** E.21.D.1.1. FONQUEVILLERS.
   (d). **Advanced Dressing Station.** E.2.d. central. BIENVILLERS.
   (e). **Main Dressing Station.** T.27.a.1.2. SOUASTRE.

6. **PREVENTION OF TRENCH FEET.**
   (a) A Depot has been established at HETTIMOY FARM for treatment of men showing a tendency to Trench Foot. Men may be sent here from the Line to have their feet washed, massaged and treated with soap and camphor powder. After treatment they return to the Line.
   (b) Wet socks are sent by Units to their Quarter-master's Stores on returning Ration Limbers and dry socks in exchange are sent up nightly with the rations.

7. **ANTI-GAS STORES.**

   (a) **BLEACHING POWDER.** A supply of Bleaching Powder in bulk is maintained at each Battalion H.Q. In addition, each Unit carries with it into the Line from 100 to 150 small tins, a number of which are kept at each H.Q. down to Platoon H.Q., and in every dug-out, post and occupied fire-bay.

   (b) **CLOTHING.** A reserve of clothing is available for issue to Units in the event of clothing worn by the men becoming contaminated with Mustard gas.

   This is distributed in the Line as follows :-

Brigade H.Q.	Suits B.D.	25	Sets under-clothing	10
Right Bn. H.Q.	"	50	"	25
Left do.	"	50	"	25
Support do.	"	50	"	25

   In addition to the above, a reserve is kept at Advanced Dressing Station, Main Dressing Station and at Billet 62 BOUASTRE (Divisional Gas Officer).

   Any clothing which is contaminated will be returned to the Divisional Gas Officer, BOUASTRE. A letter stating whether the clothing has been splashed with liquid or merely been exposed to vapour will invariably accompany clothing returned.

   (c) ~~GONG & RATTLES.~~ ~~This is issued on the scale of 1 per Coy.~~ 50 Gongs ~~Bombers.~~ ~~Rifles are not available.~~ + 5/ Rattles are distributed among units. These are en charge as Trench Stores

8. **SALVAGE.** Returning Ration Limbers will be utilised to convey Salvage back to the Main Divisional Dump at BOUASTRE.

9. **ADV. DRES. STN OF BDE CAGE.** BOUASTRE.

10. **BURIALS.** There is a Military Cemetery at BERNEVILLES B.7.b.4.1.

NOMINAL ROLL OF OFFICERS.

53rd Infantry Brigade Headquarters

Brigadier General E.L.CHALLENOR, C.M.G.,D.S.O.   Commanding.
    (Leicestershire Regiment)

Captain C.J.de B.SHERINGHAM   Brigade Major.
    (Queen's Own Cameron Highlanders)

Captain H.A.MAYNARD, M.C.   Staff Captain.
    (Middlesex Regiment)

2/Lieut. R.A.FORREST.   Brigade Intelligence Officer.
    (8th Somerset Light Infantry)

8th BATTALION LINCOLNSHIRE REGIMENT

NOMINAL ROLL OF OFFICERS

Rank & Name	How Employed	Trained In	Arrived in France
Major. R.M.PHELIPS.	Commanding Officer		21. 7.17.
Major. A.T.HITCH.	2nd in Command		1. 4.18.
Capt. H.E.HEFFER,M.C.	Adjutant		9. 7.17.
Capt. S.T.HINE	Coy. Commndr	Signalling	25. 6.16.
Capt. F.W.LATHAM.	Coy. Commndr		7. 4.17.
Capt. W.MOSS.	Coy. Commndr		19. 4.17.
Capt. A.R.ROBINSON.	Coy. Commndr	Lewis Gun	10. 7.16.
Capt. F.TAYLOR,M.C.	Quartermstr.		11. 9.15.
Lieut. E.J.A.CHRISTIE.	Asst/Adjt.		2. 8.17.
Lieut. A.B.WIGGINS.	Transport Off		19. 6.17.
Lieut. F.J.HANSELL.	Hospital	Lewis Gun	30. 1.17.
Lieut. F.L.GOOSEMAN			17.12.17.
Lieut. F.W.ALLBONES		Signalling	24. 4.18.
2/Lieut. G.P.JONES.	Intell.Offr.	Sniping	17.10.17.
2/Lieut. E.J.OWEN.	Bombing Off.	Bombing	12.10.17.
2/Lieut. C.G.H.HAMILTON.	Signal Offr.	Signalling	6.10.17.
2/Lieut. J.R.MACDONNELL	XXII Corps School		2. 6.17.
2/Lieut. P.DRAPER.			1. 8.17.
2/Lieut. F.C.BEALES.	152 Field Co. R.E.		21. 5.17.
2/Lieut. J.G.SUTCLIFFE.			8. 5.17.
2/Lieut. T.NAYLOR.			17.10.17.
2/Lieut. H.H.GARVEY.			17. 5.17.
2/Lieut. F.D.J.FORGE.			5. 4.18.
2/Lieut. H.BROOKES.			5. 4.18.
2/Lieut. J.R.HALL.			3. 4.18.
2/Lieut. A.B.CRAIG.			22. 4.18.
2/Lieut. H.G.CROOK.			22. 4.18.
2/Lieut. C.H.BRADLEY.			22. 4.18.
2/Lieut. D.W.FLINT.			22. 4.18.
2/Lieut. F.M.FILMORE.			22. 4.18.
2/Lieut. S.KNEEBONE.			22. 4.18.
2/Lieut. H.F.MEHEW.			22. 4.18.
2/Lieut. A.S.MATHEWMAN.			22. 4.18.
2/Lieut. H.SMALLEY.			22. 4.18.
2/Lieut. J.SCORGIE.			22. 4.18.
2/Lieut. J.WANNAN.			22. 4.18.
2/Lieut. J.MCBEAN.			20. 4.18.
2/Lieut. A.N.SELBIE.			24. 4.18.
Capt. C.H.S.WILLIS.	63 Inf.Bde.		

8th BATTALIONS SOMERSET LIGHT INFANTRY

NOMINAL ROLL OF OFFICERS

Rank & Name	How Employed	Trained In	Arrived in France
Lt.Col. S.S. JENKYNS.	Commanding Officer	:	
Lieut. H.O. PRING.	Adjutant	:	15. 2.17.
Major. J.H.M. HARDYMAN.	2nd in Commd	Staff Duties	24. 2.17.
Capt. C.J. PEARD.	Coy Commander	:	17.12.17.
Capt. F. AYRES.	Coy Commander	L.G., M.G. Bombing	18.11.15.
A/Capt. C.H. MADDEN.	Coy Commander	L.G., M.G. Gas	31. 7.17.
A/Capt. H.K. POPLE.	Coy Commander	L.G. Musketry	14. 7.17.
Capt. B. HOLT.	Transport	:	20. 4.18.
Lieut. H. PIKE.	Transport Off	Transport Duties	10. 9.16.
Lieut. V.G. WILLATT.	Bde. Sig. Sch.	Signalling	20. 7.16.
Lieut. D.H. COX.	Bombing Offr.	Bombing	16. 6.17.
Lieut. P.H.R. BENNETT.	Asst/Adjt.	General Courses	26. 7.17.
Lieut. H.K. AUSTIN.	Gas Officer	Bombing. Gas	11. 8.17.
Lieut. J.J. CRESSWELL.	Divl. Tspt.	Transport Duties	11. 2.18.
Lieut. T.S. BUSTARD.	Platoon Cmdr.	:	11. 2.18.
Lieut. H.A. WALNE.	B.T.O.	Transport Duties	12. 3.18. ∅
Lieut. O. BRIGGS.	Platoon Cmdr.	T.M. Course.	16.12.17.
Lieut. D.J.L. ROUTH.	Platoon Cmdr.	Gas Course	3. 4.18.
2/Lieut. L.C. BODEY.	Platoon Cmdr.	General Courses	2. 5.17.
2/Lieut. J.A. RADFORD.	Platoon Cmdr.	Gas Course	26.7.17.
2/Lieut. E. PFAFF.	37 Divn.	Transport Duties	11. 8.17.
2/Lieut. R.H. BUTTON.	Platoon Cmdr.	General Courses	15.12.17.
2/Lieut. R.A. FORREST.	63 Inf. Bde.	Intelligence	6. 3.18.
2/Lieut. K.G. WOODMANSEY	Bde. School	Lewis Gun	9.12.16.
2/Lieut. A.E. GOAD.	63 Inf. Bde.	Gas	4.12.17.
2/Lieut. A.C. OWEN.	Platoon Cmdr.	P.T., B.F., Bombing	11. 2.18.
2/Lieut. F.T.M. COOK.	Platoon Cmdr.	M.G., Gas.	3. 4.18.
2/Lieut. C.Y. FAUX.	Platoon Cmdr.	Lewis Gun.	6. 4.18.
2/Lieut. S. FRANKCOM.	Platoon Cmdr.	Musketry.	6. 4.18.
2/Lieut. W.D. WILLATT.	Platoon Cmdr.	Gas Courses	3. 4.18.
2/Lieut. C. RIGBY.	Platoon Cmdr.	Musketry	20. 1.18.
2/Lieut. E.M. EYRES.	Platoon Comdr.	General Course	5. 1.18.
2/Lieut. R. ERSKINE.	Platoon Cmdr.	:	20. 4.18.
2/Lieut. W.A.G. SNELGROVE.	Platoon Cmdr.	:	20. 4.18.
2/Lieut. A.P. MASON.	Platoon Cmdr.	:	20. 4.18.
2/Lieut. G. JACKLIN.	Platoon Cmdr.	:	20. 4.18.
2/Lieut. W.E. BYWATER.	Platoon Cmdr.	:	20. 4.18.
2/Lieut. A.G. SCHURIG.	Platoon Cmdr.	:	20. 4.18.
2/Lieut. W. DEEMING.	Platoon Cmdr.	Intelligence	25.10.17.
Lieut. D.G. CAMPBELL.	Quartermaster	:	
Lieut. S.R. MAXEINER.	Medical Officer (M.O.R.C.) attached.		

∅ Date of posting.

4th BATTALION MIDDLESEX REGT.

NOMINAL ROLL OF OFFICERS

Rank & Name	How Employed	Trained In	Date of Embarkation
Lt.Col. H.A.O.HANLEY, D.S.O. M.C.	Commanding Officer		5.11.14.
Major. C.R.HAY.	37 Div. Wing.		28. 6.17.
Major. P.GROVE WHITE.	2nd in Commnd	Gas	11. 8.14.
Capt. E.PROCTER.	Coy. Commandr.		28. 5.16.
Capt. P.W.SMITH, M.C.	do.	Army School	19. 7.16.
Capt. S.MIRAMS.	37th Divn.	Staff Duties	5. 6.16.
Capt. F.W.SCHOLEFIELD.	Coy. Commandr.	Lewis Gun	15. 7.16.
Capt. J.P.JAMIESON.	do.	Lewis Gun	7. 5.17.
Capt. G.N.VINER.	A/Adjutant		1. 1.17.
Lieut. E.A.H.FENN.	Hospital	Army School	13. 7.16.
Lieut. A.G.MITCHELL.	Bn. Gas Offr.	Gas	19. 7.16.
Lieut. F.F.MOORAT.	2nd i/c.Coy.	Gas	3.12.17.
Lieut. H.F.BOWSER.	37 Div. Wing.	Sniping	1. 2.15.
Lieut. R.G.WILLIAMS.	Platoon Offr.	Bombing	15. 7.16.
Lieut. J.H.HODSON, M.M.	Trans.Offr.	Bombing	28. 4.16.
Lieut. J.C.LYAL, M.C., D.C.M.	37 Div. Wing.	Lewis Gun	12.12.16.
Lieut. T.DE VAL.	Asst/Adjt.	Corps School	10. 5.17.
Lieut. G.CHIPPERFIELD.	Intell. Offr.	Intelligence	
2/Lieut. H.F.BACKHOUSE	Platoon Offr.	T.M.	21. 4.16.
2/Lieut. A.J.KLAIBER.	Platoon Offr.	Corps School	11. 8.17.
2/Lieut. H.S.YATES.	37 Div. Wing.	Bombing	11. 8.17.
2/Lieut. A.G.ANDREWS.	L.G.Officer.	Lewis Gun	11. 8.17.
2/Lieut. H.M.CHAUNDY.	Platoon Offr.	Lewis Gun	11. 8.17.
2/Lieut. E.ELMORE.	Platoon Offr.	Gas	17. 9.17.
2/Lieut. R.A.K.STUART, M.C.	Hospital	Army School	23. 9.17.
2/Lieut. W.A.BLOY.	Hospital	Corps School	9.11.17.
2/Lieut. F.F.MARSHALL.	Platoon Offr.	Musketry	9.11.17.
2/Lieut. G.A.PIERCE.	Platoon Offr.	Musketry	19.11.17.
2/Lieut. J.L.SELFE.	152 Field Co.		2.12.17.
2/Lieut. C.V.CAINE.	Platoon Offr.	Corps School	1. 1.18.
2/Lieut. S.R.WILKINS, M.C.	Sig. Officer.	Signalling	23. 2.17.
2/Lieut. J.K.ROSS.	Platoon Offr.	T.M.	19.11.17.
2/Lieut. A.H.PAYNE.	Bde.Dump Off.		19.11.17.
2/Lieut. C.H.WOOLVIN.	Platoon Offr.	Corps School	1. 1.16.
2/Lieut. J.H.BAIRD.	Platoon Offr.	Musketry	19.11.17.
2/Lieut. J.E.HARRINGTON.	Platoon Offr.	Corps School	30.12.17.
2/Lieut. J.C.LINDSAY.	Platoon Offr.		17. 4.18.
2/Lieut. P.PATER.	Platoon Offr.		17. 4.18.
2/Lieut. J.ROSS.	Platoon Offr.		17. 4.18.
2/Lieut. A.M.P.WILSON.	Platoon Offr.		17. 4.18.
2/Lieut. H.P.SUTCLIFFE.	Platoon Offr.		17.4 .18.
Capt. E.H.AMOR.	Quartermstr.		10.10.15.

63rd TRENCH MORTAR BATTERY

) NOMINAL ROLL OF OFFICERS

Rank & Name	How Employed	Trained In	Arrived in France
Capt. J.P.AKERMAN	O.C. 63rd T.M.Bty.		8. 9.15.
Lieut. M.W.S.HARRIS.	63rd T.M.Battery		28. 5.16.
Lieut. B.W.GAUNT.	do.		13.12.16.
2/Lieut. S.G.STEARS.	do.		11.10.17.

CASUALTIES DURING APRIL, 1918.

UNIT	IN TRENCHES						OUT OF TRENCHES						Total casualties in and out of trenches.	SICK			GRAND TOTAL	Remarks.
	Officers			Other Rks.			Officers			Other Rks								
	Killed	Wounded	Missing	Killed	Wounded	Missing	Total	Killed	Wounded	Missing	Killed	Wounded	Missing	Total		Officers	Other Ranks	Total		
8th Lincolnshire Regt.	-	5	1	30	130	64	230	-	-	-	-	-	-	-	230	1	79	80	310	See Attached slip for particulars of officer casualties.
8th Somerset L.I.	3	5	3	13	85	84	193	-	-	-	-	-	-	-	193	-	102	102	295	
4th Middlesex Regt.	2	5	-	7	63	-	77	-	-	-	-	-	-	-	77	2	139	141	218	
63rd Trench Mortar Battery	1	1	-	2	3	-	7	-	-	-	-	-	-	-	7	-	9	9	16	
TOTAL	6	16	4	52	281	148	507	-	-	-	-	-	-	-	507	3	329	332	839	

PARTICULARS OF OFFICER CASUALTIES

8th Lincolnshire Regt.   WOUNDED - 2/Lt. C.LOWE.
                                   2/Lt. P.H.PEADON, d. of w. 7.4.18.
                                   2/Lt. C.H.L.ASKEY,   do. 6.4.18.
                                   2/Lt. H.F.MOODY, wounded & missing.
                                   2/Lt. F.L.WOOLLATT.
                                   2/Lt. W.R.BOUSFIELD.
                         SICK -   Lt. F.J.HANSELL.

8th Somerset L.I.   KILLED -

                         WOUNDED -

                         MISSING -

4th Middlesex Regt.   KILLED - 2/Lt. L.E.MOORE.
                                   2/Lt. T.W.POWELL.

                         WOUNDED - Lt. H.R.ODLING.
                                   Lt. E.C.MORYOSEPH.
                                   2/Lt. F.W.ELLIOTT.
                                   2/Lt. J.E.HARRINGTON.
                                   2/Lt. K.T.SWAN.

                         SICK -   2/Lt. R.A.K.STUART.
                                   2/Lt. C.G.SPALDING.

63rd T.M. Battery.   KILLED -
                         WOUNDED -

63rd Infantry Brigade

REINFORCEMENTS
RECEIVED
DURING
APRIL, 1918.

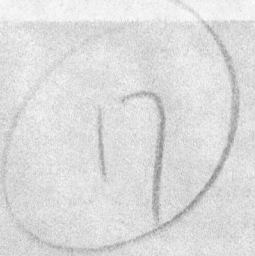

	Officers	Other Ranks	Date
8th Lincolnshire Regt.	1 a	-	5.4.18
	-	25	7.4.18
	-	52	10.4.18
	-	6	11.4.18
	1 b	20	14.4.18
	-	90	16.4.18
	2 c	-	18.4.18
	-	3	19.4.18
	-	9	23.4.18
	11 d	-	22.4.18
	3 e	5	27.4.18
	18	210	
8th Somerset L.I.	-	7	1.4.18
	2 f	-	7.4.18
	-	215	10.4.18
	-	65	11.4.18
	5 g	-	16.4.18
	3 h	-	18.4.18
	-	6	20.4.18
	7 i	24	25.4.18
	-	5	29.4.18
	17	322	
4th Middlesex Regt.	-	17	8.4.18
	-	6	11.4.18
	-	42	13.4.18
	-	6	16.4.18
	-	8	17.4.18
	-	2	19.4.18
	5 j	-	20.4.18
	-	8	23.4.18
	-	9	27.4.18
	-	4	28.4.18
	2	3	29.4.18
	1 k	4	30.4.18
	6	109	

Total reinforcements received during April, 1918,

41 officers, 641 other ranks.

For explanation see over.

a	Major	A.T. HITCH	8th Lincolnshire Regt.
b	2nd Lieut.	F.D.J. FORGE	"
c	" "	H. BROOKS	"
	" "	J.R. HALL	"
d	" "	A.B. CRAIG	"
	" "	CROOK H.G.	"
	" "	C.H. BRADLEY	"
	" "	D.W. FLINT	"
	" "	F.M. FILMORE	"
	" "	S. KNEEBONE	"
	" "	H.F. MEHEW	"
	" "	A.S. MATHEWMAN	"
	" "	H. SMALLEY	"
	" "	J. SCORGIE	"
	" "	J. WANNAN	"
e	Lieut.	F.W. ALLBONES	"
	2nd Lieut.	J. McBEAN	"
	" "	A.N. SELBIE	"
f	Captain	F. AYRES	8th Somerset Light Infantry
	Lieut.	O. BRIGGS	"
g	Lieut.	D.J.L. ROUTH	"
	2nd Lieut.	F.T.M. COOK	"
	" "	C.Y. FAUX	"
	" "	S. FRANCKOM	"
	" "	W.D. WILLATT	"
h	" "	C. RIGBY	"
	" "	H.M. EYRES	"
	" "	E.L. YARKER	"
i	Captain	B. HOLT	"
	2nd Lieut.	W.A.G. SNELGROVE	"
	" "	G. JACKLIN	"
	" "	A.G. SCHURIG	"
	" "	R. ERSKINE	"
	" "	A.P. MASON	"
	" "	W.E. BYWATER	"
j	2nd Lieut.	J.C. LINDSAY	4th Middlesex Regt.
	" "	P. PATER	"
	" "	J. ROSS	"
	" "	A.M.P. WILSON	"
	" "	H.P. SUTCLIFFE	"
k	" "	J.E. HARRINGTON	"

63rd Infantry Brigade

STRENGTH OF UNITS, APRIL 30th, 1918.

UNIT.	STRENGTH		DETAILS INCLUDED	
	Officers	Other Rks	Officers	Other Rks.
8th Lincolnshire Regt.	40	820	7	108
8th Somerset L.I.	38	829	3	106
4th Middlesex Regt.	42	831	18	205
63rd Trench Mortar Battery.	4	62	-	2
TOTAL.	124	2542	28	421

ORIGINAL COPY.

WAR DIARY

63rd Infantry Brigade.

MAY, 1918.

Army Form C. 2118.

WAR DIARY
or
~~INTELLIGENCE SUMMARY~~

(Erase heading not required.)

Instructions regarding War Diaries and Intelligence Summaries are contained in F. S. Regs., Part II. and the Staff Manual respectively. Title pages will be prepared in manuscript.

Place	Date	Hour	Summary of Events and Information	Remarks and references to Appendices
BUCQUOY	May 1		On the night 1/2nd 63rd Inf. Bde. was relieved in the line by 112th Inf. Bde. and withdrew into Divisional Reserve. 63rd Inf. Bde. O. No. 217	1
SOUASTRE	2 – 8th		Bathing at SOUASTRE and FONQUEVILLERS. Working parties daily in the forward area under R.E. during the period in Reserve for the Battalions at ESSARTS and FONQUEVILLERS.	
"	4		Working parties found.	
"	5		On night 5/6th 8th Somerset L.I. relieved 8th Lincolnshire Regt. in the ESSARTS Area 63rd Inf. Bde. O. No. 218	2
"	6		Working parties found.	
"	7		Working parties found.	
"	8		Defensive arrangements for Reserve Brigade issued, 63rd Inf. Bde. No. 536 G	3
LA BRAYELLE FARM	9		63rd Inf. Bde. relieved 111th Inf. Bde. in the left sector of 37th Divisional front, (ABLAINZEVELLE – BUCQUOY Sector) – 63rd Inf. Bde. O. No. 219	4
"	10		Quiet day. Misty but fine.	
"	11		Enemy artillery more active. Short barrage on dead ground front line and QUESNOY FARM.	
"	12		Enemy artillery again active. Clearer day – movement of enemy seen and engaged.	
"	13		Enemy aircraft very active over forward areas. Quiet day. On night 13/14th 4th Middlesex Regt. relieved 8th Somerset L.I. in the left subsector of 63rd Inf. Bde. front.–63rd Inf. Bde. O. No. 220.	5
"	14		Enemy aircraft again active. Intermittent hostile shelling.	
"	15		Quiet day. Enemy relief observed and dealt with by our artillery.	

Army Form C. 2118.

WAR DIARY
or
INTELLIGENCE SUMMARY.
(Erase heading not required.)

Instructions regarding War Diaries and Intelligence Summaries are contained in F. S. Regs., Part II. and the Staff Manual respectively. Title pages will be prepared in manuscript.

Place	Date	Hour	Summary of Events and Information	Remarks and references to Appendices
	May			
ST. LEGER	16		Defensive arrangements, Left Brigade, Left Division, 63rd Inf. Bde. No. 669 G issued. On night 16/17th, 186th Inf. Bde. (62nd Division) relieved 63rd Inf. Bde. in the left sector of 37th Divisional front, 63rd Inf. Bde. withdrawing to billets and camps at ST.LEGER. 63rd Inf. Bde. Order No. 221	5a
"	17		Relief complete at 1.30 am 17th. 51 patrols were out on the Brigade front during the tour.	6
"	18		On relief being complete, 63rd Inf. Bde. came under orders of New Zealand Division for counter attack purposes. Resting and Bathing.	
"	19		Bathing and cleaning up.	
"	20		Church parades. At noon 63rd Inf. Bde. ceased to be at disposal of New Zealand Division and came into Corps Reserve, 63rd Inf. Bde. No. 702 G	7
"	21		Training and shooting on ranges.	
"	22		One Battalion (8th Somerset L.I.) working party under R.E. supervision at SAILLY-AU-BOIS. Remainder training and on ranges.	
"	23		8th Lincolnshire Regt. on R.E. working party. Practice manning of the RED LINE carried out.	
"	23		4th Middlesex Regt. on R.E. working party. Training and ranges. Lecture by Corps Commdr. warning order received of relief of 2nd New Zealand Brigade in the PURPLE LINE by 63rd Inf. Bde.	
BUS-LES-ARTOIS	24		63rd Inf. Bde. relieved 2nd New Zealand Brigade in the PURPLE LINE, 63rd Inf. Bde. Order 223. Very wet during tour.	8
"	25		working parties/(8th Lincolnshire Regt., 250, 8th Somerset L.I. and 4th Middlesex Regt., 160 each). Baths at BERTRANCOURT. daily during relief. 320 500	
"	26		working parties as above.	

Army Form C. 2118.

WAR DIARY
or
INTELLIGENCE SUMMARY.

(Erase heading not required.)

Place	Date	Hour	Summary of Events and Information	Remarks and references to Appendices
	May			
BUS-LES-ARTOIS	27		Working parties on PURPLE LINE. Slight gas shelling on our forward battalions.	
"	28		Working parties on PURPLE LINE. Quiet day.	
"	29		Working parties on PURPLE LINE. Quiet day. Role of Reserve Brigade holding PURPLE LINE, 63rd Inf. Bde. No. 702/3 issued	8a
AUTHIE	30		On night 30/31st 111th Inf. Bde. relieved 63rd Inf. Bde. in the PURPLE LINE, relief being complete at 12.41 am, 31st, 63rd Inf. Bde. Order No. 224 During the tour in the PURPLE LINE the weather was very fine and warm.	9
"	31		Cleaning up and on ranges.	

June 2nd 1918

Brigadier General,
Comdg. 63rd Infantry Brigade.

ORIGINAL COPY

WAR DIARY

63rd Infantry Brigade

JUNE, 1918.

Army Form C. 2118.

WAR DIARY
or
INTELLIGENCE SUMMARY

(Erase heading not required.)

Instructions regarding War Diaries and Intelligence Summaries are contained in F.S. Regs., Part II. and the Staff Manual respectively. Title pages will be prepared in manuscript.

Place	Date JUNE	Hour	Summary of Events and Information	Remarks and references to Appendices
AUTHIE	1st		Training and shooting on range. 37th Division in G.H.Q. Reserve.	
"	2nd		Church parades and recreation. 63rd Inf. Bde. No. 895 G issued	1
"	3rd		Training and firing on range	
"	4th		Order issued for relief of 125th Inf. Bde. (42nd Division) in COUIN Area, and cancelled later. Warning order issued for move South. Transport moved at night by march route to CANAPLES Area.	2
PICQUIGNY sur-SOMME	5th		63rd Inf. Bde. moved by bus to PICQUIGNY-sur-SOMME; transport by march route from CANAPLES to PICQUIGNY-sur-SOMME. Movement by night. 37th Division transferred to XXII Corps, Fourth Army. 63rd Inf. Bde. Order No. 226	
"	6th		63rd Inf. Bde. debussed at PICQUIGNY at 8 am. 37th Division in readiness to move at a moment's notice.	3
"	7th		Resting. Demonstration to troops of new armoured car.	
"	8th		Officers reconnoitred country in area occupied by XXXI French Corps, H.Q. DURY, South of AMIENS. BOVES - COTTENCHY Area. Men training.	
"	9th		Church parades. Division warned to move at once - standing to.	
LOEUILLY	10th		63rd Infantry Brigade moved by bus (French) to LOEUILLY Area, 4th Middlesex Regt. and 8th Lincolnshire Regt. in LOEUILLY, 8th Somerset L.I. in PROUZEL. 63rd Inf. Bde. No. 963/1 - 5 G	4
"	11th		French second line reconnoitred by officers - GUYENCOURT - AILLY-SUR-SOMME.	5
"	12th		4th Middlesex Regt. moved by march route to ORESMAUX, 63rd Inf. Bde. Order No. 227	6
"	13th		8th Somerset L.I. moved by march route to ST. SAUFLIEU, 63rd Inf. Bde. Order No. 228	
"	14th		Staff ride preparatory to Brigade Scheme.	
"	15th		Brigade Scheme (open warfare) carried out in neighbourhood of ORESMAUX. Area BOVES - ST. NICOLAS - TRONVILLE WOOD reconnoitred by officers. 4th Middlesex Regt. moved to LOEUILLY and 8th Lincolnshire Regt. to ORESMAUX, 63rd Inf. Bde. Order No. 229 In the evening, 63rd Inf. Bde. (less 8th Somerset L.I.) moved by march route to RUMIGNY.	7
RUMIGNY	16th		63rd Inf. Bde. Order No. 230 Church parades. Commanding officers reconnoitred assembly positions in vicinity of BOIS DE BOVES, and crossings of the River AVRE.	8
"	17th		Visit of XXII Corps Commander. Tactical open warfare training by battalions. Reconnoitring parties from the R. AVRE from BOVES to COTTENCHY. 63rd Inf. Bde. instructions No. 1	
"	18th		Training. 63rd Inf. Bde. Instructions No. 2	9
"	19th		Wet Day. Training in morning. 63rd Infantry Brigade relieved by 5eme R.I., 5eme (French) Division, and proceeded by march route to PROUZEL and PLACHY-BUYON, 4th Middlesex Regt. to PLACHY-BUYON, 8th Somerset L.I. to PROUZEL; 8th Lincolnshire Regt. and 63rd T.M.B. remained at	10

Army Form C. 2118.

WAR DIARY .1.

~~INTELLIGENCE~~ SUMMARY.

(Erase heading not required.)

Instructions regarding War Diaries and Intelligence Summaries are contained in F.S. Regs., Part II. and the Staff Manual respectively. Title pages will be prepared in manuscript.

Place	Date	Hour	Summary of Events and Information	Remarks and references to Appendices
			-2-	
PROUZEL	19th (contd)		RUMIGNY. Transport Billeting parties sent forward. 63rd Inf. Bde. Order No. 231	11
			Notes on Handing Over to 5eme R.I., 5eme French Division	12
"	20th		Billeting parties sent forward. Transport moved by road to FLESSELLES, 63rd Inf. Bde. Order No. 232.	13
COUIN	21st		63rd Inf. Bde. moved by train from PROUZEL and SALEUX to MONDICOURT, thence by march route to COUIN. Transport moved by road from FLESSELLES to COUIN. Move complete in the evening 63rd Infantry Brigade Order No. 232	
			37th Division transferred to IV Corps, Third Army, to G.H.Q. and IV Corps Reserve 63rd Infantry Brigade No. 1078 G	14
"	22nd		Wet during evening.	
"	23rd		Training and on range.	
"	24th		Church parades. Forward parties sent to reconnoitre line (BUCQUOY - ABLAINZEVELLE Sector). training.	
LA BRAYELLE FARM	25th		63rd Infantry Brigade relieved 187th Inf. Bde., 62nd Division, in the line (BUCQUOY - ABLAINZEVELLE Sector) left sector of 37th Divisional front), 63rd Inf. Bde. Order No. 233	15
"	26th		Relief complete at 4.40 am. Quiet day in trenches. 63rd Inf. Bde. No. 1155 G issued	16
"	27th		Quiet during day. Left support line heavily shelled with 10.5 cm during evening. Enemy aircraft very active.	
"	28th		Left Sector staffed intermittently during night 27/28th and in early morning - small calibre. Valley West of ESSARTS lightly shelled with gas. 63rd Inf. Bde. Order No. 234 issued	17
"	29th		Quiet day.	
"	30th		Slightly increased enemy artillery activity, especially North of QUESNOY FARM. Two enemy aircraft brought down in his lines. Good deal of enemy movement observed in the evening behind enemy's lines. Possible relief.	
			The month was fine and dry, practically without a break.	

July 2nd 1918

Y Challenor
Brigadier General,
Comdg. 63rd Infantry Brigade.

SECRET

APPENDIX 'A' to
63rd Inf. Bde.
Order No. 242 of
22.6.1918.

ARTILLERY COOPERATION.

1. Barrages will be put down as under :-

(a) <u>37th D.A. 18-pdrs.</u> - 'Z' 10 'L' 4.

<u>Zero to Zero plus 4.</u>   ...   L.2.d.57.25 - L.2.d.20.19.

<u>Zero plus 4 to Zero plus 6</u>   Lift to line L.2.d.61.11 -
L.2.d.30.00
<u>Zero plus 6 onwards</u>   ...   Standing Barrage.

'Z'	4	L.3.c.20.36 - L.3.c.50.05
	2	L.8.b.90.70 - L.8.b.71.61
'L'	2	L.8.b.71.61 - L.8.b.60.60
	2	L.8.b.60.60 - L.8.b.49.52
'Z'	2	L.8.b.49.52 - L.8.b.37.51
	2	L.8.b.37.51 - L.8.b.27.50

(b) <u>37th D.A. 4.5 Hows.</u> - 'Z' 6 'L' 10.

<u>Zero to Zero plus 5.</u>

'Z'	6	L.2.d.75.27 - L.3.c.14.10.	
'L'	6	On points L.2.d.20.05	On points L.8.b.10.89
		L.2.d.10.00	L.8.b.00.80
		L.8.b.17.91	L.8.b.20.85
	4	On points L.2.d.71.20	On points L.3.c.40.18
		L.2.d.65.18	L.3.c.51.28

<u>Zero plus 5 onwards.</u>

'Z'   6)
         (L.3.c.50.05 - L.8.b.80.55.
'L'   6)
      4   L.3.c.40.18 and L.3.c.51.28.

(c) The N.Z.D.A. is cooperating as under :-

<u>Zero onwards.</u>   Trench L.8.a.91.70 - L.8.c.90.52.

2. <u>Rates of Fire and Ammunition.</u>

<u>18 pdrs.</u> Zero to Zero plus 6   4 rds per gun per minute.
25% A to 75% AX

Zero plus 6 to Zero plus 16   3 rds per gun per minute.
Zero plus 16 to Zero plus 20 2 "   "   "   "   "
Zero plus 20 to Zero plus 25 1 "   "   "   "   "
Zero plus 25 onwards   ½ "   "   "   "   "
     50% A to 50% AX.   No. 106 Fuze

4.5 Hows.

Zero to Zero plus 5.　　　3 rds per how per minute
　　　　　　　　　　　　　　(No. 101 fuze)
Zero plus 5 to Zero plus 16.　2 rds per how per minute
Zero plus 16 to Zero plus 20　1½ "　"　"　"　"
Zero plus 20 to Zero plus 25　½ "　"　"　"　"
Zero plus 25 onwards　　　　¼ "　"　"　"　"

50% 106 fuze, except where otherwise stated.

3.　Arrangements have been made with the heavy artillery to bombard objectives as under :-

Hows.
Zero to Zero plus　Sunk Road L.3.d.96.25 - L.8.b.90.80.
Zero to Zero plus 5　Sunk Road L.3.c.50.05 - L.8.b.80.55.
Zero plus 5 onwards　Trench　L.9.b.20.65 - L.9.b.00.01.
Zero onwards ...　　　...　L.8.b.80.55 - L.8.b.70.00
　　　　　　　　　　　　　FORK WOOD
　　　　　　　　　　　　　Area L.3.c. & d.
　　　　　　　　　　　　　L.9.c.30.95
　　　　　　　　　　　　　BUCQUOY, S. of E. & W. line through
　　　　　　　　　　　　　L.3.c.90.70.
　　　　T.M. L.9.c.30.80　T.M. L.9.a.50.95.
　　　　T.M. L.9.c.35.90　T.M. L.9.b.45.75

60 pdrs.　Enfilade trench system L.9.b.20 - L.10.a.70.00.

4.　37th Divnl. Trench Mortars will cooperate as under :-

(a) Zero to Zero plus 4 -
　　3 T.M.　L.2.d.30.10 - L.2.d.70.20
　　(6 rounds per mortar per minute)

　　Zero plus 4 onwards -
　　2 T.M.　Lift to L.3.c.50.30 - L.3.c.65.50
　　1 T.M.　Lift to M.G. Area about L.3.c.60.15.
　　(3 rounds per mortar per minute)

(b) Zero onwards -
　　1 T.M.　M.G. L.9.a.90.90.
　　1 T.M.　L.3.c.50.30 - L.3.c.65.50.
　　(3 rounds per mortar per minute).

5.　Arrangements will be made with C.B.S.O. to carry out C.B. work with available batteries, from Zero onwards.

ORIGINAL COPY

WAR DIARY

63rd Infantry Brigade

JULY, 1918

Army Form C. 2118.

WAR DIARY
or
INTELLIGENCE SUMMARY.
(Erase heading not required.)

Instructions regarding War Diaries and Intelligence Summaries are contained in F. S. Regs., Part II. and the Staff Manual respectively. Title pages will be prepared in manuscript.

Place	Date	Hour	Summary of Events and Information	Remarks and references to Appendices
	JULY			
LA BRAYELLE FARM	1		On the night 1/2nd 8th Lincolnshire Regt. relieved 4th Middlesex Regt. in the left subsector of 63rd Inf.Bde. front; relief complete 12.40 am - 63rd Inf. Bde. Order No. 235	1
	2		Enemy artillery active on area held by support battn. Trench Mortars rather active. 63rd Infantry Brigade No. 1296 G issued	2
	3		Quiet day in trenches. Much movement behind enemy's lines observed and dealt with by our artillery.	
	4		At 12.50 am a gas projector attack was successfully carried out on ABLAINZEVELLE, 850 drums being projected. artillery, machine guns and trench mortars cooperated in harassing the village and approaches. Smoke and thermite shells were also used. Retaliation was slight. During the day a good deal of movement was again seen in the enemy lines. 400 rounds of gas on the support battalion area.	
	5		Quiet day in trenches.	
	6		Quiet day.	
SOUASTRE	7		Quiet day. On night 7/8th 63rd Inf. Bde. was relieved by 111th Inf. Bde. in the left subsector of 37th Divnl. front and withdrew into Reserve area; relief complete 1.30 am. Order 236. 63rd Infantry Brigade No. 1340 G (Defence Scheme Reserve Brigade) issued	3 4
	8		Baths and cleaning.(Throughout the tour the weather was very dry. 65 patrols out during the tour)	
	9		Range and working parties. Slight rain.	
	10		Range and working parties. 8th Lincolnshire Regt. relieved 8th Middlesex Regt. 8th Somerset L.I. relieved 8th Lincolnshire Regt. on night 10/11th, 63rd Inf. Bde. Order No. 237 ..	5
	11		Working parties and range. Wet day.	
	12		Working parties and range.	
THE 'Z'	13		On night 13/14th 63rd Inf. Bde. relieved 112th Inf. Bde. in the right subsector of 37th Divnl. front; relief complete 2.45 am. 63rd Inf. Bde. Order No. 238	6
	14		Quiet day in trenches. Wet.	
	15		Enemy artillery more active.	
	16		Quiet day. Very fine - visibility good. Much movement of enemy in full marching order in vicinity of PUISIEUX. Relief. Artillery active on roads.	
	17		On night 16/17th 8th Somerset L.I. relieved 8th Lincolnshire Regt. in the left subsector of the Brigade front, relief complete 2.15 am 18th. 63rd Inf. Bde. Order No. 239	7
	18		A party of Boches attempted to raid one of our posts but they were driven off. The body of a German officer of the 164th I.R. (111th Divn.) was found in front of this post on the 18th. Quiet day. 'A' Coy., 4th Middlesex Regt. was relieved by a coy. of 8th Lincolnshire Regt. and withdrawn to SOUASTRE for training. 63rd Inf. Bde. Order No. 240	8

WAR DIARY / INTELLIGENCE SUMMARY

Army Form C. 2118.

Place	Date	Hour	Summary of Events and Information	Remarks and references to Appendices
THE 'Z'	19		Enemy artillery more active. 63rd Inf. Bde. No. 1537 G issued	9
	20		Enemy artillery very active in early morning on BIEZ WOOD and area immediately east, small calibre. Information received at 1 pm that the enemy had retired on our right flank and had evacuated ROSSIGNOL WOOD. In view of this patrols were pushed out by our right battalion but met with strong M.G. and T.M. fire and had to return. Boche posts had not been withdrawn on our front. At 17.30 the enemy put down a light barrage on HEDGE, CLIFF and WASP TRENCHES. No withdrawal opposite our front.	
	21		Enemy artillery very quiet. 8th Lincolnshire Regt. relieved 4th Middlesex Regt. in the right subsector of the brigade front. 63rd Inf. Bde. Order. 241	10
	22		Quiet day in trenches.	
	23		Wet day. Prisoner of M.G. 76th I.R. (111th Divn.) (normal) captured S.W. of BUCQUOY by 8th Somerset L.I.	
	24		At 1.45 am a raid on the enemy trenches S.W. of BUCQUOY was carried out by 4th Middlesex Regt. (1 Coy). Artillery, trench mortars and machine guns cooperated - 63rd Inf. Bde. Order No. 242. 6 prisoners of 76th I.R. (111th Div) and 1 Lewis gun were captured and casualties inflicted on the enemy. Two dugouts were destroyed and a T.M. dump blown up. None of our men were missing and our casualties were very slight. Weak artillery and T.M. retaliation on our forward area.	11
	25		Enemy artillery active on our right forward area owing to minor operation of N.Z. Brigade on our right at 5 pm. Quieter morning. At 5.30 pm the enemy put down a barrage of all calibres on our right subsector and the sector of the brigade on our right. Brigade on right sent up S.O.S. at 7.15 pm Enemy attacked ROSSIGNOL WOOD; our front was not attacked. Our posts dealt with movement of parties of enemy advancing on sector on our right and inflicted casualties. Our artillery cooperated in the S.O.S.	
SOUASTRE	26		On night 26/27th 111th Inf. Bde. relieved 63rd Inf. Bde. in the right subsector of the 37th Divnl. front. Relief complete 2.10 am. Very wet. 63rd Inf. Bde. Order 243	12
	27		During this tour in the line the weather had been very unsettled. 60 patrols out.	
	28		Cleaning and baths at SOUASTRE. Working parties under R.E.	
	29		Large working parties under R.E.	
	30		On night 29/30th 8th Lincolnshire Regt. relieved 8th Somerset L.I. in the forward area 63rd Infantry Brigade Order No. 244. Demonstration of Bangalore torpedoes to Battalions.	13
	31		20 rounds 15 cm fired into SOUASTRE by hostile H.V. gun. Small Box respirators of all units were tested in lachrymatory gas whilst at SOUASTRE.	

Signed, Brigadier General, Comdg. 63rd Infantry Brigade.

REPORT ON RAID CARRIED OUT BY 4TH MIDDLESEX REGT. ON NIGHT
24TH/25TH JULY, 1918.

Copy of 63rd Infantry Brigade Order No. 242 and Appendices is attached.

1. The raiding party consisted of four officers and 114 other ranks, including 2 Royal Engineers, and Stretcher Bearers.

2. The party was conveyed to HANNESCAMPS by busses from SOUASTRE where they had been training for a period of four days. They arrived in dugouts in LA BRAYELLE AVENUE about 10 pm. After a hot meal the four platoons were moved independently to their assembly positions as detailed in 63rd Infantry Brigade Order No. 242. As the trenches were very muddy and waterlogged and the light was good they moved by an overland route. All parties were in position by 1.30 am, July 24th. The Bangalore Torpedoes had been carried up earlier in the day.

3. The artillery, trench mortars and machine guns opened fire punctually at Zero hour, 1.45. am. Their fire was reported by the parties to be accurate and effective.
   At Zero the raiding party advanced in four columns as arranged, No. 1 platoon on the left flank, No. 2 Platoon, left centre, No. 3 platoon right centre and No. 4 platoon on the right flank.

4. The progress of the raid is best shown by giving in detail the reports of the Platoon Commanders.

5. No.1 Platoon (Platoon Commander, No. 13047 Sergt. C.H.REANEY).

"At about Zero plus 2, we left 'K' post and came across three "belts of concertina wire which did not prove much of an obstacle. "At the third belt the enemy threw some hand grenades which fell "amongst the men and somewhat disorganised the sections. The "section commanders quickly got their sections together again and "we rushed the post but met with no resistance. The garrison "surrendered and five prisoners were sent back. With one man, I went "round the trench and saw one of the enemy running away with a "machine gun. This was captured together with the gunner and it "proved to be a British Lewis Gun with magazine attached. I then "sent my bombing post down the trench to guard our flank and pro-"ceeded with four men down a C.T. Here we found several dugouts, "three of which were fired with No. 27 grenades. No enemy were "encountered here.
"When the signal for return went up we came back through the "trench and found that the Bangalore Torpedoes had not been used. "We fired them, one in a shelter and one in a grenade dump.
"There was no enemy machine gun fire.
"The state of the enemy trenches was bad with the exception of "the post. No enemy dead were seen. The German equipment in "the post was packed up with bayonets in scabbards."

6. No. 2 Platoon (Platoon Commander, 2/Lt. H.F.BACKHOUSE).

"At Zero plus 2 the column left 'H' Post, the Bangalore "Torpedo Section leading. There was no hostile fire of any "description and direction was easily kept. The ground was "overgrown with grass and the going was good. We crossed the "old trench North of the Sunken Road. This trench is very shallow "and overgrown and did not appear to have been used recently. "We then crossed the Sunken Road which was also overgrown and "hardly recognisable at this point. The rear section was dropped "here. The Section Commanders reported no sign of any enemy works "in the road except a large crater about L.2.d.45.30 which showed "signs of having been occupied. About 70 yards South of the road
"

"a belt of knee-high wire was encountered; this proved to be no
"obstacle. 30 yards further on we crossed the second trench, also
"overgrown, about 6 feet deep and showing signs of occasional use.
"One section was dropped here. Three dugout shafts were found, two
"of them evidently belonging to one dugout. There were no signs of
"recent occupation. 'P' bombs were thrown down one shaft, igniting
"woodwork, and Mills' grenades down the other two. Three Mills'
"grenade boxes were found here, 2 empty and one full; these grenades
"were used to throw down the dugouts. Some old British waterproof
"sheets were also found. The remaining two sections of the column
"then moved forward and ran into a thick belt of plain and barbed
"concertina wire in bad repair, which was crossed without difficulty.
"15 yards beyond this wire was the final objective. This trench was
"5 feet deep and very narrow and showed signs of frequent use. One
"section went to the right and one to the left, both parties gaining
"touch with the platoons on the flanks. One shaft was found in
"this trench and was fired with 'P' bombs. No enemy were encountered.
"At Zero plus 20 the return signal was observed and the platoon
"returned to their starting point by a tape which had been run out
"during the advance."

7. **No. 3 Platoon (Platoon Commander, 2nd Lieut. P.F.MARSHALL).**

"The platoon moved forward at Zero plus 3. The ground was good
"and there was no wire North of the road. One section remained at
"the sunken road. A belt of plain concertina wire, which was easily
"trampled down, was found about 15 yards in front of the trench which
"was entered at L.2.d.40.10. There is a fork in the trench here;
"one section went along to the right and one section to the left as
"far as the track running S.E. at L.2.d.25.05. A dugout was found
"at L.2.d.37.10; this was fired with 'P' bombs. Several shelters
"were destroyed. No bombs or S.A.A. were found but there was a
"granatenwerfer dump at L.2.d.37.10 which was blown up. The trench
"was narrow and very wet and muddy. There was no enemy rifle or
"machine gun fire. On the return signal being fired the party
"returned to the starting point along a tape which was picked
"up by the last man."

8. **No.4 Platoon (Platoon Commander, 2/Lt. A.S.YATES).**

"Just before the platoon left their starting point a trench
"mortar fell into the trench inflicting several casualties. The
"men, however, at once closed up and moved forward out of the
"trench. Three belts of wire were encountered North of the Sunken
"Road; the first two were thin and easily cut with wirecutters;
"the third consisted of knife rests, and a gap was blown with a
"Bangalore Torpedo. On reaching the Sunken Road we found several
"belts of wire, but as these ran across the road they did not
"hinder the progress of the party. About half way between the road
"and the enemy trench at L.2.d.26.10 was another belt of barbed
"concertina wire, on which we used our second Bangalore Torpedo.
"We were getting through the gap when the signal to return was
"sent up, and came back through the trench running from Sunken Road
"towards our line, L.2.d.32.20 to L.2.d.32.30. This trench appears
"to be used but was unoccupied. There was an empty shaft at L.2.d.31.
"27. No enemy were seen and there was no rifle or machine gun fire.
"The signal for the Raiding party to withdraw (one red followed
"by one Green Very Light) was sent up at Zero plus 20 from the
"report centre, O.C. Raid having become a casualty.
"At Zero plus 38 signal for the Artillery to cease fire (three
"Green Very Lights) was fired from the same point."

9. **Enemy Retaliation.**

Enemy put down a light barrage on our Right flank at about
Zero plus 10 minutes.
Two Medium T.Ms opened fire on CLIFF TRENCH from the direction
of BUCQUOY at Zero plus 5 minutes.

10.

(3)

10. The 8th LINCOLNSHIRE Regt. cooperated on the Right flank against the enemy posts previously located at L.2.c.75.10 in WASP Trench, and at L.8.a.45.98 in OAK Trench. Their action, however, was hampered by the artillery protecting the Right flank of the Raid, which remained in these posts throughout the raid, and rendering it impossible to approach them

The enemy had carried out a relief between 11 p.m. and 12.30 a.m. and it is thought that the other Posts which had been previously located had not yet been occupied by the relieving battalion. This points to bad discipline. It is possible that the posts ran away, as the prisoners stated that several of them had been killed by the bombardment.

11. Remarks.

Everything went according to plan and there was no hitch anywhere. The artillery barrage was excellent and much appreciated by the Raiding party. The wire encountered was not formidable and proves that the enemy's wiring of his outpost line is really no obstacle.

That the enemy had a considerable number of Machine Guns covering the area raided was evident in the afternoon before the raid when an attempt was made to push out patrols in cooperation with the Division on our Right. These were all, however, neutralized by artillery during the raid, and the Raiding party were not troubled in any way by Machine Gun fire.

12. Total Prisoners captured.

6 O.Rs.

13. Material captured.

1 Lewis Gun.

14. Casualties incurred during raid.

Killed ... 5 other ranks (Trench Mortar)
Wounded ... Captain S.MIRAMS (Shell)
8 other ranks (shell and trench mortar)

Brigadier General,
Comdg. 73rd Infantry Brigade.

July 25th 1918

SECRET

REPORT ON RAID CARRIED OUT BY 4TH MIDDLESEX REGT ON NIGHT 24/25TH JULY 1918.

Copy of 63rd Infantry Brigade Order No.242 and Appendices is attached.

---

1. The raiding party consisted of four officers and 114 other ranks, including 2 Royal Engineers, and Stretcher Bearers.

2. The party was conveyed to HANNESCAMPS by busses from SOUASTRE where they had been training for a period of four days. They arrived in dugouts in LA BRAYELLE AVENUE about 10.0pm. After a hot meal the four platoons were moved independently to their assembly positions as detailed in 63rd Infantry Brigade Order No. 242. As the trenches were very muddy and waterlogged and the light was good they moved by an overland route. All parties were in position by 1.30am, July 24th. The Bangalore torpedoes had been carried up earlier in the day.

3. The artillery, trench mortars and machine guns opened fire punctually at Zero hour, 1.45am. Their fire was reported by the parties to be accurate and effective.
   At Zero the raiding party advanced in four columns as arranged, No.1 Platoon on the left flank, No.2 Platoon, left centre, No.3 Platoon right centre, and No.4 Platoon on the right flank.

4. The progress of the raid is best shown by giving in detail the reports of the Platoon Commanders.

5. No.1 Platoon (Platoon Commander, No.13047 Sergt.C.H.Reaney)

   "At about Zero plus 2, we left 'K' post and came across three belts of concertina wire which did not prove much of an obstacle. At the third belt the enemy threw some hand grenades which fell amongst the men and somewhat disorganised the sections. The section commanders quickly got their sections together again and we rushed the post but met with no resistance. The garrison surrendered and five prisoners were sent back. With one man I went round the trench and saw one of the enemy running away with a machine gun. This was captured together with the gunner and it proved to be a British Lewis Gun with magazine attached. I then sent my bombing post down the trench to guard my flank and proceeded with four men down a C.T. Here we found several dugouts, three of which were fired with No. 27 grenades. No enemy were encountered here.
   When the signal for return went up we came back through the trench and found that the Bangalore torpedoes had not been used. We fired them, one in a shelter and one in a grenade dump.
   There was no enemy machine gun fire.
   The state of the enemy trenches was bad, with the exception of the post. No enemy dead were seen. The German equipment in the post was packed up with bayonets in scabbards."

6. No.2 Platoon (Platoon Commander 2/Lt. H.F.Backhouse)

   "At Zero plus 2 the column left 'H' post, the Bangalore Torpedo Section leading. There was no hostile fire of any description and direction was easily kept. The ground was overgrown with grass and the going was good. We crossed the old trench North of the sunken road. This trench is very shallow and overgrown and did not appear to have been used recently. We then crossed the sunken road, which was also overgrown and hardly recognisable at this point. The rear section was dropped here. The Section Commanders reported no sign of any enemy works in the road except a large crater about L.2.d.45.30. which showed signs of having been occupied. About 70 yards South of the road,
   a belt/

a belt of knee high wire was encountered; this proved to be no obstacle. 30 yards further on we crossed the second trench, also overgrown, about 6 feet deep and showing signs of occasional use. One section was dropped here. Three dugout shafts were found, two of them evidently belonging to one dugout. There were no signs of recent occupation. 'P' bombs were thrown down one shaft, igniting woodwork, and Mills Grenades down the other two. Three Mills Grenade boxes were found here, 2 empty and one full; these grenades were used to thrown down the dugouts. Some old British waterproof sheets were also found. The remaining two sections of the column then moved forward and ran into a thick belt of plain and barbed concertina wire in bad repair, which was crossed without difficulty. 15 yards beyond this wire was the final objective. This trench was 5 feet deep and very narrow and showed signs of frequent use. One section went to the right and one to the left, both parties gaining touch with the platoons on the flanks. One shaft was found in this trench and was fired with 'P' bombs. No enemy were encountered. At Zero plus 20 the return signal was observed and the platoon returned to their starting point by a tape which had been run out during the advance."

7. No. 3 Platoon (Platoon Commander, 2/Lieut. F.F.Marshall)

"The platoon moved forward at Zero plus 3. The ground was good and there was no wire North of the road. One section remained at the sunken road. A belt of plain concertina wire, which was easily trampled down, was found about 15 yards in front of the trench, which was entered at L.2.d.40.10. There is a fork in the trench here; one section went along to the right and one section to the left as far as the track running S.E. at L.2.d.25.05. A dugout was found at L.2.d.37.10.; this was fired with 'P' bombs. Several shelters were destroyed. No bombs or S.A.A. were found but there was a granatenwerfer dump at L.2.d.37.10. which was blown up. The trench was narrow and very wet and muddy. There was no enemy rifle or machine gun fire. On the return signal being fired the party returned to the starting point along a tape which was picked up by the last man."

8. No.4 Platoon (Platoon Commander 2/Lieut. A.S.Yates.)

"Just before the platoon left their starting point a trench mortar shell fell into the trench inflicting several casualties. The men, however, at once closed up and moved forward out of the trench. Three belts of wire were encountered North of the sunken road; the first two were thin and easily cut with wirecutters; the third consisted of knife rests, and a gap was blown with a Bangalore torpedo. On reaching the sunken road we found several belts of wire, but as these ran across the road they did not hinder the progress of the party. About half way across the road and the enemy trench at L.2.d.26.10. was another belt of barbed concertina wire, on which we used our second Bangalore torpedo. We were getting through the gap when the signal to return was sent up, and came back through the trench running from sunken road towards our line,L.2.d.32.20. to L.2.d.32.30. This trench appears to be used, but was unoccupied. There was an empty shaft at L.2.d.31.27. No enemy were seen, and there was no rifle or machine gun fire.

The signal for the raiding party to withdraw (one red followed by one Green Very light) was sent up at Zero plus 20 from the report centre, O.C.Raid having become a casualty.

At Zero plus 38 signal for the Artillery to cease fire (three Green Very lights) was fired from the same point."

9. Enemy Retaliation.

Enemy put down a light barrage on our Right flank at about Zero plus 10 minutes.

Two Medium T.Ms opened fire on CLIFF TRENCH from the direction of BUCQUOY at Zero plus 5 minutes.

10. The 8th Bn. Lincolnshire Regt co-operated on the Right flank against the enemy posts previously located at L.2.c.75.10. in WASP TRENCH, and at L.8.a.45.98. in OAK TRENCH. Their action, however, was hampered by the artillery protecting the Right flank of the Raid, which remained in these posts throughout the raid, and rendering it impossible to approach them.

The enemy/

The enemy had carried out a relief between 11.0pm and 12.30 am and it is thought that the other posts which had been previously located had not yet been occupied by the relieving battalion. This points to bad discipline. It is possible that the posts ran away, as the prisoners stated that several men had been killed by the bombardment.

11. Remarks.

Everything went according to plan and there was no hitch anywhere. The artillery barrage was excellent and much appreciated by the Raiding party. The wire encountered was not formidable and proves that the enemy's wiring of his outpost line is really no obstacle.

That the enemy had a considerable number of machine guns covering the area raided was evident in the afternoon before the raid when an attempt was made to push out patrols in co-operation with the Division on our Right. These were all, however, neutralised by artillery during the raid, and the Raiding party were not troubled in any way by Machine Gun fire.

12. Total prisoners captured.

6 O.Rs.

13. Material captured.

1 Lewis Gun.

14. Casualties incurred during raid.

Killed . . . . 5 other ranks (Trench Mortar)
Wounded . . . Captain S.Mirams (shell)
8 other ranks (shell and trench mortar)

sd/ E. L. Challenor,

Brigadier-General
Comdg 63rd Infantry Brigade.

July 25th 1918.

SECRET.   Copy No. _____.

                     63rd Infantry Brigade Order No. 242
                     ─────────────────────────────────────

Reference Map: July 22nd 1918.
57D N.E., 1:20,000

1.   4th Middlesex Regt. will carry out a minor operation on
        night 23/24th July with the object of raiding the enemy's posts
        and trenches in L.2.d.

2. STRENGTH.
        The raiding party will consist of 4 officers and 100 other
        ranks, including R.E. and Stretcher Bearers.

3. OBJECTIVES.
        Enemy posts in L.2.d., SUNKEN ROAD running from L.2.d.10.05
        to L.2.d.60.45, and trench running from L.2.d.25.00 to L.2.d.
        75.30.
        Map attached shows area to be raided and enemy posts and
        machine guns which have been definitely located.

4. OBJECTS OF RAID.
        To inflict casualties on the enemy and obtain identification.

5. PLAN.
        The raiding party will advance in four columns under an
        artillery, trench mortar and machine gun barrage. The follow-
        ing will be the assembly positions and starting points of the
        four platoons :-
            Left   ...   ...   L.2.d.8.65 (X Post)
            Left Centre ...   ...   L.2.a.25.85 (SUNKEN TRENCH)
            Right Centre ...   L.2.c.25.15 (CRIPP TRENCH)
            Right   ...   ...   L.2.c.25.40 (WASP SUPPORT TRENCH)
        Each column will leave one section at SUNKEN ROAD, L.2.d.
        10.05 - L.2.d.60.45 to mop up any enemy found there, to protect
        the flanks of the raiding party and to cover their withdrawal.

6. ACTION OF TROOPS ON FLANKS.
        (a) 8th Somerset L.I. will be prepared to cooperate on left)
                                                                flank)
        by engaging with rifle grenades or Lewis gun fire any active
        hostile machine guns, especially the machine gun at L.3.c.30.35.

        (b) 8th Lincolnshire Regt. will cooperate to protect the right
        flank of the raiding party by engaging the attention of the
        enemy post at L.2.c.75.15, by bombing down the eastern end of
        WASP TRENCH. A party of 1 officer and 12 O.R. will be detailed
        for this task.
        2 3" Stokes Mortars will bombard this post from Zero to
        Zero plus 2 minutes.

7. WIRECUTTING.
        Each of the four parties will be equipped with two Bangalore
        Torpedoes for the purpose of cutting the enemy's wire. 50%
        of the raiding party will be equipped with wirecutters.

8. DURATION OF RAID.
        20 - 25 minutes. Artillery and Trench Mortars will cease
        fire at Zero plus 30 minutes.

9. SIGNAL TO WITHDRAW.
        One red followed by one green light fired from a 1" Very
        pistol by O.C. Raiding party.

                                                            F.T.C.

-2-

10. For details of Artillery, Machine Gun and Trench Mortar cooperation see Appendices A, B and C respectively.

11. **DIVERSIONS.**
Divisions on flanks are creating diversions by artillery in order to mislead the enemy as to the exact area to be raided.

12. **SMOKE SCREENS.**
No. 3 Special Company, R.E. will, at Zero hour, put down smoke screens in L.3.central and on enemy trenches in T.3.d. and L.9.b.

13. **MEDICAL.**
Arrangements have been made with O.C. 50th Field Ambulance for two additional sections of bearers to be located at BOUTEMOY FARM and an ambulance to be on LA BRAXELLE Road near the 'Z' from 5 am, 24th July.

14. **SYNCHRONIZATION OF WATCHES.**
Watches will be synchronised at 63rd Infantry Brigade Headquarters, E.33.c.75.35, at 7 pm on 23rd inst.

15. **ZERO HOUR.**
Zero Hour will be 1.45 am on July 24th, 1918.

16. **MAPS.**
Maps are attached to copies of units marked @ below.

17. **ACKNOWLEDGE.**

Issued at 7 am.

Captain,
A/Brigade Major,
63rd Infantry Brigade.

Distribution.
8th Lincolnshire Regt.	1 @
8th Somerset L.I.	2
4th Middlesex Regt.	3 @
63rd T.M.Battery	4 @
Right Group Machine Guns	5
Left Group, Machine Guns	6
37th Machine Gun Battalion	7
37th Division	8 @
112th Infantry Brigade	9
2nd N.Z. Infantry Brigade	10 - 11
C.R.A.	12
'Z' Group, R.F.A.	13 @
No. 3 Special Company, R.E.	14
A.D.M.S.	15
50th Field Ambulance	16

Note: Appendix 'B' will follow

SECRET

APPENDIX 'B' to
63rd Inf. Bde.
Order No. 242 of
22.7.18.

MACHINE GUNS

'A' and 'C' Companies, 37th M.G. Battalion.

Fire Orders for 'A', 'B' and 'C' Batteries.

1. LOCATION OF BATTERIES :-

   'A' Battery - L.2.a.80.85.
   'B'   "   - L.7.a.90.75.
   'C'   "   - F.27.a.50.15.

2. 'A' Battery. 4 Guns.

   (a) ZERO to ZERO plus 15, rapid fire area L.8.d.30.60 to L.8.d.00.70.

   (b) ZERO plus 15 to ZERO plus 30, bursts of fire.

3. 'B' Battery. 2 Guns.

   (a) ZERO to ZERO plus 15, rapid fire. Barrage on line L.8.b.47.76 to L.8.b.00.70. L.9.a.04.70

   (b) ZERO plus 15 to ZERO plus 30, bursts of fire.

4. 'C' Battery. 6 Guns.

   (a) ZERO to ZERO plus 15, rapid fire on trenches in L.9.b.

   (b) ZERO plus 15 to ZERO plus 30, bursts of fire.

---oOo---

To all recipients of 63rd Inf.Bde. Order No.242, dated 22.7.18.

SECRET.

APPENDIX 'O' to
63rd Inf. Bde.
Order No. 342 of
22.7.1918.

3 - INCH STOKES MORTARS.

63rd Light Trench Mortar Battery will cooperate as under:-

(a) Zero to Zero plus 4 minutes.
```
      1 mortar  ... L.3.c.10.45.
      1   "     ... L.2.d.95.90.
      1   "     ... L.2.d.60.80.
      1   "     ... L.2.d.70.82.
      1   "     ... L.2.d.80.15.
      1   "     ... L.2.d.30.10.
```

(b) Zero plus 4 minutes to Zero plus 30 minutes.
```
      2 mortars .. L.3.c.50.27 - L.3.c.10.45.
      1 mortar  ... L.3.b.20.85 - L.3.b.10.70.
      3 mortars .. L.3.a.90.75 - L.3.a.95.65.
```

(c) 2 Mortars will cooperate as follows :-

Zero to Zero plus 2 minutes.
L.2.c.90.05 - L.2.c.70.10. (German post
in MAIN TRENCH).
Zero plus 2 minutes to Zero plus 30 minutes.
```
      1 mortar  ... L.3.a.55.55
      1 mortar  ... L.3.a.25.40.
```

(d) <u>Rates of Fire.</u>

Zero to Zero plus 4 minutes	...	10 rounds per minute
Zero plus 4 minutes to Zero plus 20 minutes	...	5 rounds per minute
Zero plus 20 minutes to Zero plus 30 minutes	...	3 rounds per minute.

---oOo---

SECRET.

8th Lincolnshire Regt.
4th Middlesex Regt. (for Information).

63rd Infantry Brigade No. 1599.G.

Reference 63rd Infantry Brigade Order No.242.
Para. 6 "Action of Troops on Flank".

O.C. 8th Lincolnshire Regt. will also detail party of bombers and rifle grenadiers to deal with enemy post in OAK Trench (about L.8.a.45.98) located by 2/Lt. ELBIE on 22nd inst. At ZERO plus 2 minutes they will engage the attention of the enemy, and if possible capture the post.
This party should be equipped with wire-cutters.

Captain.
A/Brigade Major.
63rd Infantry Brigade.

22nd July, 1918.

SECRET.   63rd Infantry Brigade No. 1554/5 G

AMENDMENT and ADDENDA to 63rd Infantry Brigade Order No. 242
    dated 22.7.1918.

Para. 8 will be amended to read :-

"Para. 8. DURATION OF RAID.

    "20 - 25 minutes. The barrage will cease at Zero plus
"30 minutes. From Zero plus 30 minutes onwards artillery
"will fire bursts of fire at intervals on the same lines
"until the order to "Cease Fire" is given by O.C. 4th Middlesex
"Regt. This will be sent by telephone or POWER BUZZER to Brigade
"Headquarters.
"   Should the above means of communication break down, a light
"signal will be used: 3 green Very lights will be fired in
"rapid succession from 4th Middlesex Adv. Report Centre at
"L.2.d.25.50. O.C. 4th Middlesex Regt. will establish a relay
"post about F.25.central to repeat this signal to the rear."

    Add the following :-

"Para. 18. All posts withdrawn owing to the bombardment will be
"reoccupied immediately on completion of the operation."

"Para. 19. PRISONERS OF WAR: will be sent to Brigade Headquarters
"E.23.c.75.35.

"Para. 20. REPORTS.

            "The following code words will be used :-
    "RAIDING PARTY ALL IN ...   ...   RUM
    "ARTILLERY CEASE FIRE ...   ...   WORK FINISHED.
    "(No.) PRISONERS   ...   ...   (No.) COILS
    "OUR CASUALTIES APPROX (No.)...   (No.) PICKETS."
    "all posts reoccupied   ...   ...   new work begun.

"Para. 21. Should it be necessary to postpone the raid, the
"code word 'ARTICHOKE' will be sent.

                                        Captain,
                                     A/Brigade Major,
July 23rd 1918.   63rd Infantry Brigade.

ISSUED TO ALL RECIPIENTS OF 63RD INFANTRY BRIGADE ORDER NO. 242
                                            DATED 22.7.18.

AMENDMENT to APPENDIX 'A', 63rd Infantry Brigade Order No. 242
dated 22.7.18.

Para. 3, line 11, Amend to read - "BUCQUY, B. of an E. and N. line
through L.3.c.90.40."

July 22nd 1918

To all recipients of 63rd Infantry Brigade Order No. 242 dated 22.7.18

Captain,
M/Brigade Major,
63rd Infantry Brigade.

ORIGINAL COPY

WAR DIARY

63rd Infantry Brigade

AUGUST, 1918

Army Form C. 2118.

WAR DIARY
or
INTELLIGENCE SUMMARY.
(Erase heading not required.)

Instructions regarding War Diaries and Intelligence Summaries are contained in F.S. Regs., Part II. and the Staff Manual respectively. Title pages will be prepared in manuscript.

Place	Date	Hour	Summary of Events and Information	Remarks and references to Appendices
LA BRAYELLE FARM	August 1		On the night Aug. 1/2nd, 63rd Inf. Bde. relieved 112th Inf. Bde. in the left sector of the 37th Divnl. front. Relief complete 2 am 2nd Aug.	1
	2		Quiet day in trenches. Very wet and misty.	
	3		Enemy very quiet. Artillery activity very slight. Enemy patrol driven off.	
	4		Again quiet. Enemy patrol dispersed.	
	5		Quiet day - wet. On the night 5/6th Aug. 8th Somerset L.I. relieved 4th Middlesex Regt. in the right subsector of 63rd Inf. Bde. front. Relief complete 12.50 am. 63rd Inf. Bde. Order No. 246	2
	6		Quiet day in trenches.	
	7		2 prisoners of 2nd Guard Reserve Division, 15th R.I.R., (relieved 111th Div. and 5th Bav. Res. Div.) captured South of ABLAINZEVELLE by 8th Somerset L.I. Enemy artillery more active on battery positions.	
	8		Again slight increase in enemy artillery activity but on the whole quiet.	
	9		Quiet day. On night 9/10th 4th Middlesex Regt. relieved 8th Lincolnshire Regt. in the left sub-sector of the Brigade front. Relief complete 12.30 am. 63rd Inf. Bde. Order No. 247	3
	10		Enemy artillery active on back areas during morning. G.O.C. proceeded on course to GRANTHAM. Command of the Brigade taken over by Lieut.-Col. "C.B.MOLONY, 4th Middlesex Regt. At 3.55 am under cover of a heavy T.M. barrage on our post line and heavy calibre on our forward system, the enemy, 100 strong, attempted to raid our posts on 250 yards front in F.28. The enemy penetrated out post line but was repulsed and casualties inflicted. The raid had been anticipated and an artillery barrage has been prepared accordingly to fire on given signal. Our M.Gs and T.Ms cooperated. Three of our men were wounded. Report 1886.G.	4
	11		Enemy artillery more active on back areas, otherwise quiet.	
	12		Quiet day. Occasional crashes on area. Cooperated in projector gas attack on right, 1331 G. At 3.15 am 8th Somerset L.I. attempted to drive the enemy out of post in F.28.h. but were unable to gain a footing in trench.	5
	13		On night 13/14th 8th Lincolnshire Regt. relieved 8th Somerset L.I. in the right subsector of the Brigade front. 63rd Inf. Bde. Order No. 248	6
	14		Information received that the enemy had withdrawn from SERRE and that patrols of the Division on our right were pushing forward. Patrols were sent out during the afternoon but enemy was found to be still holding his outpost line. At 4 am 15th 4th Middlesex, and at 5.15 am, 8th Lincolnshire Regt., with artillery preparation attempted to gain a footing in the enemy's main line of resistance but were unsuccessful; the enemy was holding his main line in strength. ABLAINZEVELLE and its Eastern exits were also engaged by Heavy Artillery. 63rd Inf. Bde. Order No. 249	7

P.T.O.

2353 Wt. W2544/1454 700,000 5/15 D.D.&L. A.D.S.S./Forms/C 2118.

Army Form C. 2118.

WAR DIARY
or
INTELLIGENCE SUMMARY.
(Erase heading not required.)

Instructions regarding War Diaries and Intelligence
Summaries are contained in F. S. Regs. Part II.
and the Staff Manual respectively. Title pages
will be prepared in manuscript.

Place	Date	Hour	Summary of Events and Information	Remarks and references to Appendices
LA BRAYELLE FARM	Aug. 15		Enemy artillery quiet. ABLAINZEVELLE and approaches were searched by 6" howitzers during the evening and patrols were pushed out by 4th Middlesex Regt. During the night 8th Lincolnshire Regt. attempted to push patrols into the Cemetery but met with strong resistance and were forced to withdraw. Preliminary bombardments carried out at 8 am, 8.30 am and 9 am by field guns and a barrage at 9.25 – 9.35 am. Covering fire was also opened on ABLAINZEVELLE at 9.25 am. It was quite evident that the enemy was holding his line opposite our front in strength.	
	16.		Quiet day. Occasional crashes over area.	
	17		On night 17/18th Aug. 63rd Inf. Bde. relieved in line by 111th Inf. Bde. Relief complete 12.50 am G.O.C., recalled, returned from England. 63rd Inf. Bde. Order No. 250	8
	18		Resting. Order received from 37th Division to capture high ground east of BUCQUOY.	9
	19		63rd Inf. Bde. Order No. 251	
	20		Relief complete 1.45 am. 63rd Inf. Bde. Order No. 252	10
BUCQUOY L.26.a.8.0	21	4.55 am	On the night 19/20th 63rd Inf. Bde. relieved 112th Inf. Bde. in the right sector of 37th Divnl. front. Reconnoitring line at BUCQUOY and making final arrangements. Zero hour for attack. 63rd Inf. Bde. attacked on the right of the Divnl. sector, 111th Inf. Bde. to the north. Divisions on flanks cooperated. Tanks and cavalry also cooperated. All objectives were taken and 5th Division passed through 63rd Bde. by 6.15 am. 63rd (R.N.) Division passed through 111th Inf. Bde. ACHIET LE PETIT and LOGEAST WOOD were captured. There was a thick fog during the morning.	
	22		Our troops consolidated on the BLUE LINE east of BUCQUOY and in the evening moved to positions of assembly to the west and North of LOGEAST WOOD, ready to support 111th and 112th Inf. Bdes. in attack on ACHIET LE GRAND.	
L.5.a.5.2	23		The Brigade was in reserve to 111th and 112th Inf. Bdes. and passed through them after ACHIET LE GRAND RAILWAY had been captured, pressing on to the Eastern outskirts of BIHUCOURT. M.Gs on the N.W. of the village prevented further progress.	
G.3.a.0.5	24	4.30 am	On the morning of 24th, 8th Somerset L.I. pushed on in conjunction with the New Zealand Division on their right, and captured BIEFVILLERS. At midday 8th Lincolnshire Regt. and 4th Middlesex Regt. were ordered forward to connect up the line and protect the left flank of 8th Somerset L.I. a congratulatory message was received from the Corps Commander and one from the Divisional Commander to 8th Somerset L.I. on the capture of BIEFVILLERS	
Brickworks, ACHIET LE GRAND	25	5 am,	63rd Inf. Bde. attacked the enemy positions on the SAPIGNIES – BAPAUME Road. Our troops reached all their objectives and a position on the SAPIGNIES – BAPAUME Road was taken up. Thick fog made direction difficult. At 6.30 pm the 111th Inf. Bde. passed through 63rd Inf.	11, 12.

P.T.O.

Army Form C. 2118.

WAR DIARY
or
INTELLIGENCE SUMMARY.
(Erase heading not required.)

Place	Date	Hour	Summary of Events and Information	Remarks and references to Appendices
Brickworks ACHIET LE GRAND	25 contd.		Bde. and captured FAVREUIL in conjunction with the New Zealand Division. During the evening 63rd Inf. Bde. withdrew from the line and were replaced by a Brigade of the 5th Division. During rest the Brigade was in the ACHIET LE PETIT area. Our casualties were very light during these operations. The weather was very hot and dry. Report on operations	13
-do-	26		Resting.	
	27		Resting and salving.	
	28		Salving.	
	29		Reorganising and salving.	
	30		Reorganising and salving.	
	31		Training and on range.	

August 31st, 1918

E. Wheeler Capt BdeMajor
for Brigadier General,
Comdg. 63rd Infantry Brigade.

REPORT ON OPERATIONS AUGUST 21ST TO 26TH (INCLUSIVE).

PHASE I.

63rd Inf. Bde. Order No. 251 issued at 7 pm 18.8.18.
Owing to the fact that the operations were to be conducted on a very much larger scale, and 5th and 63rd Divisions and 3rd Division were to pass through 37th and 2nd Divisions respectively, 13th Royal Fusiliers of 112th Infantry Brigade, who had been allotted to the Brigade as a carrying battalion were placed entirely at the disposal of the Brigade. Consequently B.M. 203 was issued ordering 13th Royal Fusiliers to support 4th Middlesex Regt. on the right and 8th Lincolnshire Regt. to support 8th Somerset L.I. on the left, and a new order No. 251 in substitution of the original Order No. 251 was issued at 7 am 20.8.18.

21st   The enemy carried out slight harassing fire on the position with gas shell but did not seriously interfere with the assembly. The Brigade was formed up in position by 3.55 am in accordance with map attached.

The barrage started on the front of 2nd Division rather before Zero hour, 4.55 am.

Our artillery barrage was reported by all ranks to be remarkably good and accurate.

There was a very heavy ground mist when our attack started and very little retaliation by the enemy.

Of the eight tanks allotted to the Brigade, four cooperated with 8th Somerset L.I., doing excellent work. The remaining four lost their way in the fog.

5.50 am   4th Middlesex Regt. reported their right company on objective, which was the high ground to the east of BUCQUOY. Prisoners reported coming in.

6.9 am   ABLAINZEVELLE reported clear.

6.35 am   Left Company 4th Middlesex Regt. reported on objective.

6.38 am   Left Company 8th Somerset L.I. reported on objective.

6.48 am   All three companies 8th Somerset L.I. reported on their objective, and in touch with left company 4th Middlesex Regt also on objective. This completed capture of objective of 63rd Inf. Bde. 5th Division reported going through at 6.15 am. The following are extracts from reports of Battalions :-

4th Middlesex Regt.

"Companies went over in two waves, the first to capture and con-
"solidate the objective and the second to pass through and form an
"outpost line........

"B Company on the right advanced on a compass bearing, a M.G. on
"their right opened fire but was silenced by Cpl. HASWELL who gallantly
"rushed in and killed the men at the gun.

"C Company worked round South of BUCQUOY and gradually forced their
"way up trenches which were held by M.Gs. Cpl. ONYETT and Cpl. JARVIS
"rushed these posts. 2/Lieut. HODGKINSON went through the centre of
"BUCQUOY and pushed up to the enemy advanced post where he took several
"prisoners.

"D Company on the left had a stiff time in BUCQUOY as the tanks
"were not able to function as arranged. A strong point put up a
"great fight with T.Ms and M.Gs but was rushed by Capt. JAMIESON and
"Sergt. PERRY and 3 or 4 men. They got to the final objective about
"5.45 am capturing in all about 50 prisoners and killing a large num-
"ber.

"Shortly after the objective was captured the enemy barraged it
"heavily.

"An advanced Report Centre was established at a derelict tank
"in 'C' Company's objective to which a telephone line was laid shortly
"after the Companies had taken the objective.

"The total captures of the Battalion were 115 prisoners, 7 M.Gs
"and 8 T.Ms."

8th Somerset L.I. were organised with 2 companies in front line and and 2 companies in support :-

"The Battalion advanced straight to its objective with very few
"casualties and quickly got into touch with the units on each flank.

"About 60 prisoners and 6 machine guns were captured.

"Our Battle Headquarters was established at the S.E. tip of the

P.T.O.

"Cemetery immediately the barrage had cleared from it.
"Tanks cooperated very successfully.
"As soon as the objective was gained the Battalion was organised "in depth, two companies in the front line and two companies in support."

Prisoners captured were from 2nd Guard Reserve Division and 4th Bavarian Division. The prisoners captured during this phase of the operations were estimated at 115 by the right Battalion and 68 by the left battalion.

Two Stokes Mortars cooperated with each attacking Battalion and the covering fire of the mortars on the left is reported by the Infantry to have been most effective.

Four Mortars were moved forward to the line of the objective and consolidated so as to cover this line.

153rd Field Coy. RE detailed one section to make a mule track running South of BUCQUOY from WASP TRENCH L.1.d. to the BUCQUOY - ACHIET-LE-PETIT Road L.4.d.9.6. One section was employed on making good for wheeled traffic the road from L.1.d.25.50 - L.3.a.50.05. 2 officers and one section assisted with the siting and digging of strong points from F.28.c. through L.4.a. and c to L.9.b.

'A' Company, 37th M.G.Battn. moved forward 8 guns to cover the objective line to the east of BUCQUOY, siting the guns in pairs as shown on map referred to above.

Communications during the above phase were rendered much more difficult by the fog. A Forward Report Centre was however established at the CRUCIFIX, L.4.a.45.60. Telephonic communication was maintained with interruptions owing to shellfire. Visual was impossible until the fog lifted. Power Buzzer, owing to the trees and the village, and the distance to Brigade H.Q. being over 2,000 yards, was only of limited value. R5 signals only were passed at first, but increased to R7 during the day.

At 7.54 am, word being received from O.C. 8th Somerset L.I. that the ACHIET-LE-PETIT Road badly required clearing in the neighbourhood of the Shrine, O.C. 8th Lincolnshire Regt. was instructed to detail half a company to do this work.

Cavalry patrols reported to have passed through.

At 9.12 am orders were received from Division that 112th Inf. Bde. was to be withdrawn to a position of readiness West of HENLEY HILL. Accordingly at 9.22 am corresponding verbal orders were issued to 8th Lincolnshire Regt. and 13th Royal Fusiliers, confirmed later by B.M.212.

At 10.40 a, G.383 was received from Division giving the order in which Brigades should be prepared to to move - 63rd Inf. Bde. to be ready to hold the BLUE LINE whole.

At 1.30 pm units were ordered to push out patrols to keep in touch with the forward situation.

At 2.4 pm G.386 received from Division confirming enemy counter attack from ACHIET LE GRAND and ordering BLUE LINE to be organised for defence. 63rd Division reported to have lost direction Southwards in fog in the morning.

At 7.25 pm message received that Division would remain responsible for the defence of the BLUE LINE. All ranks rested and fed so as to be available for operations on 22nd if required.

At 12.15 am, 22nd, warning received from Division that troops should be prepared to move at short notice should the enemy counter attack heavily, otherwise no move anticipated before noon 22nd.

Reconnaissance East of BLUE LINE ordered.

PHASE II.

At 3.15 pm warning received from Division re move to positions North of ABLAINZEVELLE in support to 111th Inf. Bde. with a view to attack on ACHIET-LE-GRAND and BIHUCOURT.

Warning order B.M.216 issued and officers sent to reconnoitre ground North of LOGEAST WOOD. Conference at Brigade H.Q. 7 pm called by BM 217

At 7.40

At 7.40 pm G.408 received from Division re move to assembly positions
B.M.218 and B.M.219 re assembly issued at 8 pm and 10 pm respectively
At 7 am 23rd, artillery barrage maps received from Division for the advance on ACHIET LE GRAND.
At 7.45 am Brigade HQ reached L.5.a.5.2. Met Brigade Major, 111th Inf. Bde., Tank Company Commander, O.C. C Coy., 37th M.G.Bn., and O.C. 63rd T.M.Battery. Gave them B.M.220, final instructions for the attack Reached H.Q. 8th Somerset L.I. and met Commanding Officers and handed to them copy of B.M.220. Emphasised importance of maintaining greatest depth possible, at the same time keeping in close touch with 10th Royal Fusiliers.
About 10.20 am wire received from Division stating that G.O.C. 111th Infantry Brigade would have direct call on one Battalion 63rd Infantry Brigade.
Attack commenced at 11 am.
At 11.15 am, conversation with G.S.O.1. explaining our orders and dispositions and that instead of placing one Battalion at the disposal of G.O.C. 111th Infantry Brigade, the G.O.C. had, in the absence of specific orders from Division, disposed the Brigade 4th Middlesex Regt. on right, 8th Lincolnshire Regt. on left, each in depth and keeping in close touch with 111th Infantry Brigade, G.Os.C. 63rd and 111th Infantry Brigades agreeing that the only method of ensuring the necessary support at the right moment was to leave it to the discretion of Battalion Commanders.
At 11.30 am unnumbered message sent to 4th Middlesex Regt. and 8th Lincolnshire Regt. confirming previous instructions re keeping in the greatest depth possible - not to commit more than 2 companies each per Battalion unless the situation absolutely required it.
At 1.20 pm message received from 13th Rifle Brigade at G.4.c. stating that 63rd Inf. Bde. had gone through and that S.A.A. was required could carrying parties be furnished if possible. This message was passed on to 111th Inf. Bde. and Division was asked for a supply tank.
At 3.40 pm B.M.221 issued to Battalions re exploiting success by pushing out to the ground East of BIHUCOURT to general line G.23.central G.18.central, H.7.central.
At 4.15 pm verbal message received from division ordering advance on BIEFVILLERS by 8th Somerset L.I. from support at 5.30 pm in conjunction with troops on right and left. This was confirmed later by wire.
At 4.16 pm 8th Somerset L.I. ordered to go forward.
At 4.38 pm orders re advance communicated to 4th Middlesex Regt. and 8th Lincolnshire Regt. by Intelligence Officer 8th Lincolnshire Regt.
Lieut.-Col. W.B.MOLONY, Commanding 4th Middlesex Regt. put in charge of first operation, i.e., exploiting success by pushing out to general line G.23.central, G.18.central, H.7.central.
This exploitation was attempted but owing to heavy machine gun fire no further advance was possible and 4th Middlesex Regt. and 8th Lincolnshire Regt. withdrew to their original positions (see map).
On arrival at BIHUCOURT at about 5.30 pm, 8th Somerset L.I. found that the enemy had a strong M.G. pocket just south of BIHUCOURT. Later, during night 23/24th a company attacked this pocket, capturing part of it without opposition and driving the enemy some distance East along the trenches in G.16.d.
At 6.45 pm reported to Division that supply tank had not arrived. By arrangements earlier in the day these tanks were to supply dump to be formed at Brickworks.
Situation in G.16.d. - Enemy reported in G.16. Divisional Commander ordered message to be given to 8th Somerset L.I. G.O.C. 111th Infantry Brigade to clear up this pocket.
6.56 pm - message sent through 111th Inf. Bde. to 4th Middlesex Regt. to form defensive flank S.E. of BIHUCOURT.
At 8.30 pm message received timed 7 pm from Lt.-Col. Hardyman reporting failure of attempt to advance from Red Dotted Line at 5.30 pm. No British appear to be East of the Red Line, i.e., BIHUCOURT. 1st Herts failed to get Red Line South of BIHUCOURT cause of difficulty. Enemy machine guns sufficient to hold up any further advance unless regular barrage arranged. Enemy withdrawing guns from high ground East of BIHUCOURT; enemy reported not in strength.
7.10 pm - message received enemy attacking huts East of BIHUCOURT

STOKES MORTARS.

At 11 am 23rd, one mortar was attached to each of 4th Middlesex Regt. and 8th Lincolnshire Regt. The mortar on the right, on arrival at the railway cutting, G.10.c.2.4, gave covering fire to 10th Royal Fusiliers in their advance on ACHIET LE GRAND and later advanced with 4th Middlesex Regt. and dug in, covering the position taken up by them.

The other mortar went forward with the left Battalion (8th Lincolnshire Regt.) to the railway cutting, where the officer in charge, 2nd Lieut. J.WANNAN, was wounded.

R.E.

On night 23/24th, 153rd Field Coy., R.E. assisted the infantry in consolidating their position in the trench running N.E. and S.W. through G.16.a and b.

MACHINE GUNS.

One section was ordered to cooperate with each leading battalion, 4th Middlesex Regt. and 8th Lincolnshire Regt., and one section was given the task of covering the left flank of the attack. The fourth section was retained in reserve with 8th Somerset L.I.. Limbers cooperated in the advance as far as the road running N.E. from LOGEAST WOOD to COURCELLES in A.26.a and b. Here they came under heavy fire and kit was taken off the limbers which returned to the assembly area. No. 2 section detailed to guard the left flank took up position in A.27.c.7.0, 2 guns and G.3.b.2.9, 2 guns, covering the valley towards GOMIECOURT.

Nos. 3 and 4 sections supporting 8th Lincolnshire Regt. and 4th Middlesex Regt. took up positions on high ground in G.3. and G.9.

At 2.30 pm two guns moved forward to G.11.a.0.7 to cover the ground between ACHIET LE GRAND and BIHUCOURT, two guns into position east of the railway at G.10.b.2.8 and two guns at G.4.d.2.1 to cover the left flank, two guns being left at G.9.central and 4 guns at G.3.b. & d.

At 5 pm, No. 4 section was ordered up from reserve to take up positions east of the railway in G.16.a.2.8 to cover the right flank. Company H.Q. moved to A.27.c.5.5.

COMMUNICATIONS.

On the 23rd inst. communications were somewhat difficult at first owing to the role of 63rd Inf. Bde. as Support Brigade, with two battalions moving to the north of LOGEAST WOOD to support 111th Inf. Bde., whilst Brigade H.Q. remained South of the wood in L.5.a. In the afternoon however communication was established with the Infantry, and in the evening the line was connected up from L.5.a. to G.3.c.2.9 which became Brigade H.Q., in close touch with the Group Commander whose H.Q. was about 200 yards away.

TANKS.

At 11.30 am 4 platoons of 8th Somerset L.I. were detailed to work as mopping up parties with 6 tanks allotted to the Division for the attack on ACHIET LE GRAND. These parties met the tanks at G.2.d.9.4 and the advance of the tanks to ACHIET LE GRAND resulted in the surrender of some 200 prisoners and the capture of 15 machine guns.

It is worth mentioning that this number of the enemy were still in position after the barrage had passed over and the success of the advance at this point may be undoubtedly attributed largely to the cooperation between the tanks and the infantry.

PHASE III.

At 10 pm Brigade H.Q. moved to G.3.c.2.9

At 12.15 am 24th, verbal instructions on telephone were received from Division re attack on BIEFVILLERS at 4.30 am 24th.

At 12.30 am conference with Group commander to arrange barrage for 4.30 am.

1.15 am Brigade Major proceeded to line to warn Battalion Commanders of the attack; delivered orders to 8th Lincolnshire Regt. at 1.45 am, to 4th Middlesex Regt. at about 2.15 am, to 8th Somerset L.I. at about 2.50 am, later informing 10th Royal Fusiliers, 13th Royal Fusiliers and 13th K.R.R.C. of the attack. Visited Companies of 8th Somerset L.I. with O.C. 8th Somerset L.I., the last company receiving its orders for the 4.30 am attack ay 3.15 am.

Owing to having received word from Major Anderson that 8th Somerset L.I. were engaged in clearing up the situation in G.16, the Brigadier informed Division that 8th Somerset L.I. would not be able to attack at Zero hour; consequently, at 2.30 am G.O.C. Division authorised the use of a battalion of 111th Infantry Brigade, 13th Rifle Brigade, vice 8th Somerset L.I. In the meantime the Brigade Major had notified all Battalions, and they were getting into position for the attack.

At 3 am word was received by G.O.C. from G.S.O.1 that the Division on the left would do something to cooperate at 7.30 am.

At 3.6 am the officer in charge of tanks reported to G.O.C. and discussed routes etc.

At 3.35 am, G.S.O.2 telephoned Division from Brigade H.Q. that Battalions had not received their orders in time, that 8th Somerset L.I. were engaged, and asked for the attack to be cancelled.

Orders had however been communicated as above and the attack was launched at 4.30 am.

At 5 am the Brigade Major reported to G.O.C. that all Battalions had received their orders and that the attack would commence at Zero as ordered.

The barrage, owing to the shortness of the notice was extremely ragged, as it was bound to be, owing to the fact that many of the guns were in course of being moved when the Division orders were received.

One company of 8th Somerset L.I., and 8th Lincolnshire Regt. moved off, but 8th Lincolnshire Regt. were held up by machine gun fire.

At 5.30 am the New Zealanders advanced on the right, the remaining companies of 8th Somerset L.I. cooperating and overtaking the leading company of 8th Somerset L.I. The advance continued under heavy machine gun fire by section rushes to BIEFVILLERS, which with the assistance of two tanks and the cooperation of the New Zealanders, was taken at 6 am.

In the meantime, touch had been obtained by the Brigadier with 13th Rifle Brigade who were ordered not to advance owing to the fact that orders had been received by all battalions of 63rd Infantry Brigade, making it unnecessary for a battalion of 111th Infantry Brigade to be utilised.

The situation not becoming clear at 8 am, the Brigadier went forward to see what was happening. On learning that 8th Somerset L.I. were in BIEFVILLERS he at once ordered 4th Middlesex Regt. and 8th Somerset L.I. forward to support them and protect their left, one company 4th Middlesex Regt. to be in close support to 8th Somerset L.I., one company to occupy the trenches just west of BIEFVILLERS and the remaining 2 companies to form a defensive flank facing N.E., 8th Lincolnshire Regt. following to positions in G.17., 18., 23. and 24. In spite of heavy shelling, companies reached their positions with very few casualties.

In the meantime 8th Somerset L.I. had been obliged, owing to the left flank being in the air and the extremely heavy bombardment of the village to evacuate the village, and took up a position immediately to the west holding the spur in G.24.b and d.

At about 7.30 am, Lt.-Col. J.H.M.Hardyman, M.C., commanding 8th Somerset L.I., who had previously moved up with his Battalion H.Q. to this point in a tank, was killed by a shell.

During the advance 8th Somerset L.I. captured 3 5.9" howitzers, 30 prisoners and 3 machine guns.

Meanwhile a further section of C Coy., 37th M.G.Bn. was ordered forward to cover the left flank of 8th Somerset L.I.

MACHINE GUNS.

One section took up position on the high ground G.18.a.; No. 2 section South of the railway in G.23.b., the object of these dispositions being to cover the BIHUCOURT - BIEFVILLERS Road and the left flank of the position generally.

COMMUNICATIONS.

At 11 pm 23rd inst., the Brigade Signal Officer ran forward a line to G.4.c.5.4 and the following morning pushed on to G.11.a.4.0. By 7 am the line was carried forward to G.10.d.5.3 and by 7.45 am the line was carried forward to G.17.d.5.1. Upon 3 miles more of cable being sent forward this line was carried forward to G.24.central.

TANKS.

Two tanks cooperated in the advance on BIEFVILLERS, one of which got into difficulties in the sunken road running N. and S. through H.13.c. The other moved south of the village and went round BIEFVILLERS, rejoining the second tank which it pulled out of the road whence both returned to
ACHIET LE GRAND.

PHASE IV.

About 4 pm 24th, G.452 was timed 3 pm was received from Division ordering an advance to the high ground North of BAPAUME. Accordingly O.50 was issued after consultation with the Group Commander, at 5.10 pm. At 5.30 pm O.52 with Zero hour for 2.15 am was issued.

Brigade Headquarters moved forward to the Brick Works, G.9.b.5.0 at 5.40 pm.

About 9.30 pm a message was received from Division stating that the attack on the high ground North of BAPAUME was to be carried out in conjunction with 111th Inf. Bde., orders being issued by Division. This cancelled our orders for a similar attack by the Brigade at 2.15 am.

A telephone message was sent through to 4th Middlesex Regt. advising them that our operation as set forth in O.50 and O.52 was cancelled, but that a similar attack was to take place at a somewhat later hour under orders of Division, particulars of which would be notified. 4th Middlesex Regt. undertook to advise 8th Somerset L.I., 8th Lincolnshire Regt. and C Coy., 37th M.G.Bn.

Order 235 together with artillery arrangements was not received until 11.45 pm. The Group Commander was advised and he telephoned to Divisional Artillery to find out what were the detailed artillery arrangements so far as his Group was concerned.

At 12.53 am 25th, O.53 with orders for the attack was issued - Zero hour 5 am.

At 5 am a heavy fog prevailed which made it very difficult for the troops to keep direction.

At 7.15 am a message was received from 2/Lt. STEWART, RE, who was at Advanced Report Centre in sunken road H.19.a.50.95 that the enemy had put down a smoke screen and a H.E. and gas barrage.

At 7.10 am 4th Middlesex Regt. reported that they had advanced 700 yards and everything going well. Message timed 6.10 am. The objective was captured about 6.30 am.

At 7.34 am prisoners were reported coming down.

The enemy retaliated along the valley G.23.b.8.2 - G.18.d.0.0.

At 8.3 am 4th Middlesex Regt. reported that Battalion had been cut up during advance by machine gun fire from H.8.d; reported 4th Middlesex in touch with 13th K.R.R.C. on main SAPIGNIES - BAPAUME Road and dug in.

Capt. Hine, 8th Lincolnshire Regt., was ordered to take his company forward to establish touch with the New Zealanders on right of 4th Middlesex Regt. Two

Very few Lincolns report on objective. /Armoured cars reported through SAPIGNIES.

At 8.30 a further message was received from 2/Lt. Stewart that Battalions had attacked and reached objective but had found same untenable owing to H.E., gas and smoke barrage - casualties heavy. Battalion H.Q. G.23.b.45.50; estimated casualties JOGE, 250.

At 8.50 am, O.C. 8th Lincolnshire Regt. was ordered to send forward the whole battalion to the support of 4th Middlesex Regt., dribbled up by sections if necessary. O.C. 8th Lincolnshire Regt. informed of position of N.Z.Bn right and ordered to fill gap and report where the New Zealanders' left rested. The gunners were informed of the situation

At 9.12 am the enemy were reported to be heavily shelling BAPAUME; enemy aircraft flying low, dropping 12 bombs and firing their machine guns on our lines. Brigade observers instructed to find out if we had obtained touch on the right with the New Zealanders, and if so at which point.

At 9.10 am 4th Middlesex Regt. reported that original attack was unsuccessful through loss of direction in the fog; battalion reorganizing and now going forward with tanks and armoured cars.

At 9.20 am 4th Middlesex Regt. informed of situation. 4th Middlesex Regt. reported Battalion dug in on final objective along the whole front and touch reported with New Zealanders.

At 9.50 am 2nd Lieut. Stewart reported that machine guns which had been giving trouble at H.15.central had been mopped up by a Whippet tank.

At 10.10 am spoke to O.C. 4th Middlesex Regt. with reference to some Lincolns reported as being alongside him and told him that should no officer of 8th Lincolnshire Regt. be present to take whatever Lincolns were in the vicinity under his immediate command and employ them as he thought best.

Order No. 236 received from Division about 12.10 pm re attack by New Zealanders and 111th Infantry Brigade on FAVREUIL: 63rd Infantry Brigade to follow in support.

O.57 issued at 2 pm.

The Brigade carried on with consolidation.

Order received from 111th Inf. Bde. showing that they had in error issued their order to 8th Somerset L.I. instead of to 8th Lincolnshire Regt. through use of the wrong code word - 'LOCE' instead of 'JOCE'. Consequently at 5.15 pm when O.C. 8th Lincolnshire Regt. was asked for dispositions of his Battalion in support to 111th Infantry Brigade he had received no orders from 111th Inf. Bde. Map location of 111th Inf. Bde. Report Centre at H.8.c.50.40 (Shrine) was given to him and he was ordered to push his H.Q. forward..

At 6.49 pm upon communication again being open to Advanced Report Centre, word was sent direct to Companies of 8th Lincolnshire Regt. to be ready to move at a moment's notice but to remain in their present positions on the SAPIGNIES - BAPAUME Road, and to push forward patrols to keep in touch with the situation, informing them that the attack commenced at 6.30 pm. and that Report Centre of 111th Infantry Brigade was at H.8.c.50.40 (Shrine), to which point they should send orderlies at once.

A message was also sent though this means to 8th Somerset L.I. telling them that the order addressed to them by 111th Infantry Brigade was intended for 8th Lincolnshire Regt.

Messages received between 6.15 pm and 7.25 pm on attack by New Zealanders and 111th Infantry Brigade reported favourable progress.

At 10.59 pm a message was received from G.S.O.1 that 63rd Infantry Brigade was to be relieved that night.

O.59 sent out to units at 2.15 am; also 8th Somerset L.I. instructed to send guides to meet two Battalions of 5th Division coming up to relieve 111th Inf. Bde. to bring them into the trenches in H.13 and 14. These messages were transmitted throuhg out Forward Report Centre in H.19

O.61 sent out through Advanced Report Centre at 2.45 am authorising withdrawal of 8th Somerset L.I. and 4th Middlesex Regt. and 'C' Coy., 37th M.G.Bn. less 1 section attached to 8th Lincolnshire Regt.

8th Lincolnshire Regt. subsequently received direct orders from G.O.C. 111th Infantry Brigade to withdraw.

Staff Captain proceeded to ACHIET LE PETIT to reconnoitre for accommodation and met outgoing units at road junction G.14.b:25.70, just N.E. of ACHIET LE PETIT.

Upon relief units were disposed as follows :-

8th Lincolnshire Regt.	...	Hutted Camp, G.14.b.
8th Somerset L.I.	...	,, G.14.a.
4th Middlesex Regt.	...	,,, G.7 and L.12.
63rd T.M.Battery &) 153rd Field Coy., R.E.)	...	,, G.16.a.

R.E.

In accordance with orders received from Brigade, one section was detailed to cooperate with each Battalion in the advance in the SAPIGNIES BAPAUME Road. These sections reported to their respective Battalions but it was not though necessary by battalion commanders for them to consolidate along the existing line owing to the further advance and the weak resistance offered by the enemy. O.C. 153rd Field Coy., RE went forward and advised the Infantry Company Commanders as to the best line to consolidate.

MACHINE GUNS.

No. 2 and 4 sections 'C' Coy., 37th M.G.Bn. were moved forward to positions in the outpost line East of the village of BIEFVILLERS. Covering parties were provided by 'A' Coy., 4th Middlesex Regt. One section of 'A' Coy., 37th M.G.Bn. was also in this position on the left.

The enemy kept up a heavy bombardment of BIEFVILLERS and the surrounding area and during the night constant machine gun fire was directed from H.20. at a distance of 300 yards.

Coy. H.Q. meantime had been advanced to G.24.c.7.5. Nos. 1 and 3 sections were brought up from their positions in rear, Nos. 2 and 4 sections being able to carry out overhead fire. Owing to the prevailing fog and smoke and gas, fire was indirect, this contingency having been foreseen and the necessary calculations made. In the advance of the infantry each section had 2 guns forward and 2 guns following in rear. These guns advanced in bounds, the teams in rear passing through the forward teams, by whom they were covered. The forward teams of both sections took up positions east of the sunken road in H.20.b. and H.20.d while the teams in rear remained west of the road. As soon as circumstances permitted two teams of the right section were placed at H.14.d.6.2. and two teams in our outpost line at H.15.c.5.7 covered the right and approaches to FAVREUIL. Similarly the left section had two guns forward and two guns west of road. Fleeting targets were engaged N.E. of FAVREUIL on several occasions. At 6 pm during the attack of 111th Inf. Bde. on FAVREUIL, the guns at H.15.c.5.7. were able to give good supporting fire and obtained good targets. 4 guns in H.15.c. and d. fired directly at the retreating enemy about 6.30 pm, killing a considerable number. During the night the positions were consolidated and on the morning of the 26th the company was relieved by 'A' Coy., 5th M.G.Bn.

COMMUNICATIONS.

As already stated communication had been carried forward on 24th inst to report centre G.24.central.

Zero hour being at 5 am, Brigade Signal Officer left Brigade HQ at 4 am and reached the forward Report Centre at 5.30 am with extra cable. He at once carried forward the line to a point in the sunken road at about H.19.a.50.80, from which point he was able to collect messages and watch operations throughout the morning of the 25th. At 2 pm communications were carried still further forward to trench system H.14.c.50.15 and later on 4th Middlesex Regt. carried their line forward to the Quarry in H.14.d.

TANKS.

Tanks did not cooperate on the right in this advance. A Whippet tank mopped up an enemy post at H.15.c.5.7.

In conclusion I wish to express my appreciation of the splendid cooperation and assistance given to the Brigade by the Artillery. During the fighting on 23rd, 24th and 25th August most valuable assistance was given by Lt.-Col. CROFTON, Group Commander of 63rd Divnl. Artillery.

I also wish to place on record the valuable assistance rendered and good judgment shown by Major Beechman, Commanding C Coy.; 37th M.G. Battn.

63rd T.M.Battery pushed forward their mortars with the Infantry and on one occasion during the attack on ACHIET LE GRAND came into action with good results, covering the advance of 10th Royal Fusiliers. Otherwise the long distances and open nature of the fighting made it difficult for them to play a very active part.

I cannot speak too highly of the excellent work of the Brigade Signal Officer, 2nd Lieut. J.STEWART, R.E. who succeeded in keeping forward communication open during the whole advance under very difficult conditions.

The assistance rendered by the tanks was undoubtedly the reason of the small casualties suffered by us. I do not think that the many enemy machine gun nests cleaned up could possibly have been dealt with by infantry and artillery alone without very severe casualties to the former. I wish also to place on record the readiness with which the tank personnel undertook the tasks allotted to them and the great value of their cooperation.

The New Zealanders cooperating on our right were always ready to render any assistance in their power.

I deeply regret the death of Lt.-Col. J.H.M.HARDYMAN, M.C. commanding 8th Somerset L.I. who has throughout the operations proved himself to be a most gallant officer and one whose judgment and appreciation of the situation I always found especially sound.

Brigadier General,
Comdg. 63rd Infantry Brigade.

29.8.18

63rd Infantry Brigade

The following casualties were incurred during the course of the operations from 21st August to 26th August 1918 :-

	KILLED		WOUNDED		MISSING		GASSED		TOTAL	
	Offs.	O.R.	Offs.	O.R.	Offs.	O.R.	Offs.	O.R.	Offs.	O.R.
8th Lincolns	-	22	5	131	-	8	-	21	5	182
8th Somerset L.I.	1	21	5	119	-	11	-	14	6	165
4th Middlesex	2	25	10	202	-	18	-	20	12	265
63rd T.M.Battery	-	-	1	3	-	-	-	-	1	3
Total for Brigade	3	68	21	455	-	37	-	55	24	615

PARTICULARS OF OFFICER CASUALTIES.

8th Lincolnshire Regt.	Wounded:	2/Lt. A.B.Craig	22.8.18
		2/Lt. H.G.Crook	24.8.18
		2/Lt. H.R.Greenwood	24.8.18
		2/Lt. J.E.Rogers	25.8.18
		2/Lt. J.S.Scorgie	25.8.18
8th Somerset L.I.	Killed:	Lt.Col. J.H.Maitland Hardyman, M.C.	24.8.18
	Wounded:	Lt./a/Capt.) G.H.Sims, M.C.	23.8.18
		2/Lt. R.Ersking	23.8.18
		2/Lt. W.A.G.Snelgrove	24.8.18
		2/Lt. C.G.R.Palmer	24.8.18
		2/Lt. H.M.Eyres	25.8.18
		(13th T.R.R.C. attd. 8th Somerset L.I.)	
4th Middlesex Regt.	Killed:	Lt.(a/Capt) F.F.Moorat	24.8.18
		2/Lt. H.F.Backhouse	25.8.18
	Wounded:	2/Lt. (a/Capt.) J.P.Jamieson	25.8.18
		2/Lt. J.H.Baird	23.8.18
		2/Lt. F.M.Meacham	23.8.18
		2/Lt. A.J.Hurding	24.8.18
		2/Lt. BEE.Goodwin	24.8.18
		2/Lt. H.E.Hodgkinson	24.8.18
		2/Lt. W.A.Bloy	25.8.18
		2/Lt. R.W.Seaby	22.8.18
		Lt. E.A.H.Fenn	22.8.18
		2/Lt. J.C.Lindsay	24.8.18
63rd T.M.Battery	Wounded:	2/Lt. J.Wannan (Lincolnshire Regt.)	23.8.18

MATERIAL CAPTURED BY 63RD INF. BDE. DURING
OPERATIONS AUGUST 21ST - AUGUST 26th, 1918

	Prisoners	Guns	M.Gs	Trench Mortars		
				Light	Medium	Heavy
8th Lincolnshire Regt.	50	-	2	-	-	-
8th Somerset L.I.	500	3 (5.9" Hows)	20	1	-	1
4th Middlesex Regt.	200	-	20	8	3	-
TOTAL	750	3	42	9	3	1

NOMINAL ROLL OF OFFICERS

63rd Trench Mortar Battery

Captain AKERMAN J.P., M.C.	Commanding	8.9.15
Lieut. HARRIS, M.W.S., M.C.		28.5.16
Lieut. GAUNT B.W.		13.12.16

NOMINAL ROLL OF OFFICERS.

4th Battalion, Middlesex Regiment.

Rank and Name	Present Employment	How Trained	Arrived
Lt.-Col. Molony W.B.	Commanding		
Major HAY C.R.	37th Div. Rec. Camp		28.6.17
Major GROVE WHITE P.	2nd in command	Gas	11.8.14
Captain PROCTER E.	Coy. Comdr.		28.5.18
Captain MIRAMS S., M.C.	Wounded	Staff duties	5.6.16
Captain JAMIESON J.P.	Wounded	Lewis Gun	7.5.17
Captain VINER G.N.	A/Adjutant		1.1.17
Captain KLAIBER A.J.	Coy. Comdr.	Army School	11.8.17
Lieut. FENN E.A.H.	Wounded	Army School	13.7.16
Lieut. DE VAL	Coy. Comdr.	Corps School	10.5.17
Lieut. CHIPPERFIELD G.	Intelligence Off.	Intelligence	1.9.16
Lieut. HODGES A.J.	Transport Off.		3.5.17
Lieut. BURCH A.A.	Hospital		28.6.18
Lieut. WILKINS S.R., M.C.	Signal Officer	Signalling	23.2.17
Lieut. BUCKNILL J.B.	Platoon Offr.		22.8.18
Lieut. DASHFIELD E.S.	Platoon Offr.		22.8.18
Lieut. MARSHALL L.T.	Platoon Offr.		22.8.18
Lieut. KING C.	Hospital		31.7.18
2nd Lieut. YATES A.S.	Platoon Offr.	Bombing	11.8.17
2nd Lieut. ANDREWS A.G.	Lewis Gun Offr.	Lewis Gun	11.8.17
2nd Lieut. CHAUNDY H.M.	Platoon Offr.	Lewis Gun	11.8.17
2nd Lieut. ELMORE E.	A/Transport Offr.	Gas	17.9.17
2nd Lieut. BLOY W.A.	Wounded	Corps School	9.11.17
2nd Lieut. MARSHALL F.F.	On Course	Musketry	9.11.17
2nd Lieut. PIERCE G.A.	Asst. Adjutant	Musketry	19.11.17
2nd Lieut. SELFE J.L.	Platoon Offr.	R.E. Duties	2.12.17
2nd Lieut. PAYNE A.H.	37th Div. Sig. School	Asst. Instr. Sig.	19.11.17
2nd Lieut. BAIRD J.H.	Wounded	Musketry	19.11.17
2nd Lieut. HARRINGTON J.E.	Platoon Offr.	Bombing	30.12.17
2nd Lieut. PATER P.	Hospital		17.4.18
2nd Lieut. Lindsay J.C.	Wounded	Musketry	17.4.18
2nd Lieut. GOODWIN B.E.	Wounded		10.7.18
2nd Lieut. HODGKINSON H.E.	Wounded		10.7.18
2nd Lieut. HURDING A.J.	Wounded		10.7.18
2nd Lieut. SEABY R.W.	Wounded		29.6.18
2nd Lieut. TURNER W.J.	Platoon Offr.		28.6.18
2nd Lieut. SMITH F.R.	Platoon Offr.		28.6.18
2nd Lieut. GROVE R.	Platoon Offr.		22.8.18
2nd Lieut. McFADDEN R.E.	Platoon Offr.		22.8.18
2nd Lieut. MEACHAM F.H.	Wounded		31.7.18
2nd Lieut. NUTTON W.	Hospital		28.6.18
2nd Lieut. PRITCHARD G.	Hospital		10.7.18
Captain AMOR E.A.	Quartermaster		10.10.15

Lieut. STONE O., U.S.A., R.C. Medical Officer

Captain Rev. DOUGLAS P.S., CF Chaplain

NOMINAL ROLL OF OFFICERS.

8th Battalion, The Lincolnshire Regiment.

Rank and Name	Present Employment	How Trained	Embarked
Lt.-Col. HITCH A.T.	Commanding		1.4.18
Major BOSS J.G.	2nd in command		
Captain HEFFER H.E., M.C.	Adjutant		9.7.17
Captain ALLBONES F.W.	A/Adjutant		24.4.18
Captain HINE S.T.	Town Major	Signalling	25.6.16
Captain LATHAM F.W.	Coy. Comdr.		7.4.17
Captain MOSS W., DSO	Coy. Comdr.		17.4.17
Captain GARVEY H.H.	Coy. Comdr.		17.5.17
Lieut. BAUMBER B.			27.6.18
Lieut. ROWLAND G.M.			24.4.18
Lieut. GODFREY R.J.			4.7.18
Lieut. CHRISTIE E.J.A.	Div. Traffic Control		8.8.17
Lieut. PROCTER J.	Asst. Adjutant		4.7.18
Lieut. WIGGINS A.B.	Transport Officer		19.6.17
Lieut. COOK E.C.	Sick		12.5.18
Lieut. GOOSEMAN F.L.	Coy. Comdr.		17.12.17
Lieut. McDONNELL J.	On leave		2.6.17
2nd Lieut. JONES G.P.	Intelligence Offr.	Sniping	12.10.17
2nd Lieut. OWEN E.J. MC	Coy. Comdr.	Bombing	12.10.17
2nd Lieut. HAMILTON C.G.H., MC	On Course	Signalling	6.10.17
2nd Lieut. BEALES F.C.			21.5.17
2nd Lieut. FORGE F.D.J.			5.4.18
2nd Lieut. BROOKS H.			5.4.18
2nd Lieut. HALL J.R.			5.4.18
2nd Lieut. BRADLEY C.H.			22.4.18
2nd Lieut. KNEEBONE S			22.4.18
2nd Lieut. MATTHEWMAN A.S.			22.4.18
2nd Lieut. SMALLEY H.			22.4.18
2nd Lieut. McBEAN J.			22.4.18
2nd Lieut. SELBIE A.N. MC			22.4.18
2nd Lieut. MANSELL C.J.			16.6.18
2nd Lieut. TYRRELL A.			4.7.18
2nd Lieut. WELBY E.H.			4.7.18
2nd Lieut. BLAKEY J.S.			4.7.18
2nd Lieut. JONES G.			4.7.18
Captain WILLIS C.H.S.	Attd. 37th Div. H.Q.		
Captain THOMAS J.G., MC	Medical Officer		
Captain HARDY T.B. V.C., D.S.O., M.C.	Chaplain		
Lieut. GIBBONS H.	Quartermaster		

NOMINAL ROLL OF OFFICERS

8th Battalion, Somerset Light Infantry

Rank and Name	Present Employment	How Trained	Arrived
Lt.-Col. SHERINGHAM C.J. de B., M.C.	Commanding		
Major PEARD C.J., DSO	2nd in command		15.12.17
Captain PRING H.O.	Adjutant		15.2.17
Captain HOLT B.		LG, MG, Bombing	20.4.18
Captain CARTWRIGHT E.C.	Coy. Comdr.	Bombing	10.7.18
Captain MADDEN C.H.	Coy. Comdr.	Musketry, LG, MG Gas	31.7.17
Captain BENNET W.J.	Coy. Comdr.	Musketry, Bombing Gas, General	31.5.18
Lieut. WILLATT V.G.	Sick	Signalling	20.7.16
Lieut. BENNETT P.H.R.		General	26.7.17
Lieut. AUSTIN H.K.	Intelligence Off.	Bombing, Gas	11.8.17
Lieut. WALNE H.A., MC	Transport Officer		12.3.18
Lieut. BRIGGS O.		T.M.	16.12.17
Lieut. ROUTH D.J.L.	Corps School	Gas	3.4.18
Lieut. WOODMANSEY K.G.	Platoon Comdr.	Lewis Gun	9.12.16
2nd Lieut. PFAFF E.	37th Divn.	Transport	11.8.17
2nd Lieut. BODEY L.C.		Signalling, Gen'l	2.5.17
2nd Lieut. WOOD W.	Sick		31.5.18
2nd Lieut. WARD H.G.	Bde. Gas Officer	Gas	2.6.18
2nd Lieut. COOK F.J.M.	Bn. Gas Officer	Gas, M.G.	3.4.18
2nd Lieut. DEEMING W.	Platoon Comdr.	Intelligence	25.10.17
2nd Lieut. FORD L.N.	Sick	Bombing Gas	31.5.18
2nd Lieut. BYWATER W.E.	Platoon Comdr.		20.4.18
2nd Lieut. SCOTT W.J.	Platoon Comdr.		31.5.18
2nd Lieut. STONE H.	Platoon Comdr.	Lewis Gun	31.5.18
2nd Lieut. TRENT R.T.J.	Sick		11.10.17
2nd Lieut. MILES C.G.	Sick	M.G.	16.7.18
2nd Lieut. McLEOD C.	Platoon Comdr.	Lewis Gun	27.5.18
2nd Lieut. HENDERSON R.	Platoon Comdr.	Gas	13.8.18
2nd Lieut. LUGG J.H.	Platoon Comdr.	Lewis Gun	16.8.18
2nd Lieut. DOMAN L.P.B.	Platoon Comdr.	Lewis Gun	16.8.18
2nd Lieut. MACKAY D.A.	Platoon Comdr.		16.8.18
Lieut. CAMPBELL D.G.	Quartermaster		
Captain BROOKFIELD P., CF	Chaplain		
Lieut. SUMMERS J.W., M.O.R.C.	Medical Officer		

CASUALTIES DURING AUGUST, 1918.

UNIT	IN TRENCHES – Officers Killed	Wounded	Missing	Other Rks Killed	Wounded	Missing	Total	OUT OF TRENCHES – Officers Killed	Wounded	Missing	Other Rks Killed	Missing	Wounded	Total	TOTAL CASUALTIES IN AND OUT OF TRENCHES	SICK Officers	Other Rks	Total	GRAND TOTAL	REMARKS
8th Lincolnshire Regt.		5		24	169	8	206								208	1	51	52	260	a see appendix to report on operations 21st – 26th Aug. 1918.
8th Somerset L.I.	2	6		15	117	12	152								152	4	78	82	234	b Lieut. E.C.Cook. c Lieut. A.C.Owen, M.C. Lt.Col.J.H.M.Hardyman, M.C. d 2/Lt. J.J.Cresswell For remainder see report on operations 21st – 26th Aug. 1918.
~~Middlesex Regt.~~																				
4th Middlesex Regt.	2	10		35	253	13	311								311	6	56	62	373	e 2/Lt. V.G.Willatt 2/Lt. W.Wood 2/Lt. E.C.Miles 2/Lt. R.T.Trent. f,g,see report on operations 21st – 26th Aug. 1918. h Lieut. A.A.Burch Lieut. C.King 2/Lt. W.Nutton 2/Lt. P.Pater 2/Lt. G.Pritchard 2/Lt. F.R.Smith
63rd T.M. Battery		1	1										2	2	2		4	4	6	i 2/Lt. J.Wanman
T O T A L	4	22		72	540	35	671						2	2	673	11	189	200	873	

ORIGINAL COPY.

WAR DIARY

63rd Infantry Brigade

September, 1918.

Army Form C. 2118.

WAR DIARY
or
INTELLIGENCE SUMMARY.
(Erase heading not required.)

Instructions regarding War Diaries and Intelligence Summaries are contained in F. S. Regs., Part II. and the Staff Manual respectively. Title pages will be prepared in manuscript.

Place	Date	Hour	Summary of Events and Information	Remarks and references to Appendices
Brickworks ACHIET LE GRAND.	Septr. 1		Church Parades. Area E. of BAPAUME reconnoitred by officers.	
LEBUCQUIERE	2		Training. Warning order received re relief of 5th Division...63rd Inf.Bde. in the evening 63rd Inf. Bde. relieved 15th Inf. Bde. (5th Divn) in Support. W. of (O. 253.... LEBUCQUIERE.	1
	3		63rd Inf. Bde. Order A.B.1 issued	2
J.32.b.80.80	4		63rd Inf. Bde. took up positions in area E. of LEBUCQUIERE in support of 112th Inf. Bde. who pushed forward E. of HERMIES.	
	4		On the night 5/6th 63rd Inf. Bde. relieved one battalion of the 112th Inf. Bde. in the line and one battalion of the 2nd N.Z. Bde. in the line. 4th Middlesex Regt. in Support. Sector S. of CANAL DU NORD (Right subsector of 37th Divl. front) .....63rd Inf. Bde. Order A.B.5.....	3
	5		The Brigade was then on a two battalion front.	4
GAIKA COPSE	6		Little enemy artillery activity. In the afternoon our patrols pushed forward in the Western outskirts of HAVRINCOURT WOOD.	
	7		Our line was pushed forward into HAVRINCOURT WOOD to CLAYTON CROSS along HUBERT AVENUE to CHEETHAM SWITCH, touch being maintained with our flanks. Enemy Machine Guns very active against our patrols but only slight artillery activity. 63rd Inf. Bde. Order A.B.9.....	5
P.11.b.0.3.	8		Battalions reorganised and established a line in HUBERT AVENUE along N. side of HAVRINCOURT WOOD and down QUADRANGLE with Patrols pushed forward. The wood was harassed all day with small calibre shells. 63rd Inf. Bde. Order A.B.10....	6
	9		Enemy artillery active, harassing HAVRINCOURT WOOD. Patrols were pushed forward during the day to outskirts of Wood. 63rd Inf. Bde. Order 254......	7
	10		Line of trenches N.E. of wood established - TUFNEL AVENUE - QUEER STREET - KNIFE TRENCH and YORKSHIRE HEAP. Patrols pushed forward N. and S. of TRESCAULT. Strong opposition encountered South of Village. Patrols also pushed forward towards Wood south of HAVRINCOURT village. On the night 10/11 a Gas Projector attack was carried out on Eastern edge of HAVRINCOURT village. 63rd Inf. Bde. Order 255.......	8
	11		On the night 11/12th the 63rd Inf. Bde. was relieved in the line. The 4th Middlesex Regt. were relieved by the 111th Inf. Bde. The 8th Somerset L.I. by the 186th Inf. Bde. and the 8th Lincolnshire Regt. by the 187th Inf. Bde. (62nd Divn). 63rd Inf. Bde. withdrawn to Divisional Reserve in the LEBUCQUIERE area.	
LEBUCQUIERE	12		Resting.	9
	13		Cleaning up and bathing.	
	14		Reorganising and on range.	

P.T.O.

Army Form C. 2118.

WAR DIARY
or
INTELLIGENCE SUMMARY.
(Erase heading not required.)

Instructions regarding War Diaries and Intelligence Summaries are contained in F.S. Regs., Part II. and the Staff Manual respectively. Title pages will be prepared in manuscript.

Place	Date	Hour	Summary of Events and Information	Remarks and references to Appendices
LEBUCQUIERE	15		Church Parades. Warning Order received from Divn. to relieve the 111th Inf. Bde. in Support. Enemy aircraft active at night bombing in Reserve area.	
P.11.b.0.3.	16		On the night 15/17th 63rd Inf. Bde. relieved the 111th Inf. Bde. in Support area. Relief was complete before midnight. 4th Middlesex Regt. were in close support to 112th Inf. Bde. in trenches in N.E. corner of HAVRINCOURT WOOD and were under the tactical command of G.O.C. 112th Inf. Bde.	10
			63rd Inf. Bde. Order No.257.	
	17		Quiet day in trenches. 2 battalions in rear support carried on with training.	
	18		In view of probable enemy attack on HAVRINCOURT 8th Somerset L.I. moved to area West of HAVRINCOURT WOOD by 6 a.m. No attack in morning.	
		3.15 p.m.	Heavy enemy bombardment, especially W. edge of HAVRINCOURT WOOD.	
		4.00 p.m.	Enemy attacked TRESCAULT and North of there. Attack held up by 6.30 p.m. and line regained by 1/1st Herts Regt. on one company front which had been broken (40 prisoners taken)	
		8.00 p.m.	8th Somerset L.I. told to relieve 13th Royal Fusiliers (112th Inf. Bde) on right of Front Line.	
			63rd Inf. Bde. Order No.258.	
			63rd Inf. Bde. Instructions for Defence issued (No.2234.G.).	11
PLACE MORTMARTE.	19		Quiet day in trenches. Brigade H.Q. relieved 112th Inf. Bde. at PLACE MORTMARTE. 4th Middlesex Regt. relieved 1/1st Herts Regt. who moved to close support, and 8th Lincolnshire Regt. relieved Centre Battalion, Front Line.	12
			Warning Order received from Divn. that 37th Divn. were being relieved by 42nd Divn.	
	20		63rd Inf. Bde. Warning Order No.2346.G. issued.	13
			Quiet in Front Line, usual shelling. Report of captured German Sergt.Major and increased air activity indicated attack on HAVRINCOURT. Heavy shelling of HAVRINCOURT WOOD from 8 p.m. till midnight.	
			63rd Inf. Bde. Order No.259.	14
	21		Quiet during morning, normal shelling. Attack by 8th Lincolnshire Regt. and 8th Somerset L.I. on junction DERBY TRENCH and BILHEM-CHAPEL WOOD SWITCH and BASS LANE. Attack unsuccessful owing to wire and blocks in our own trenches from short shooting of our heavies.	
			63rd Inf. Bde. Order No.260.	15
	22		63rd Inf. Bde. relieved by 126th Inf. Bde. (42nd Division). Units and Brigade H.Q. moved to LEBUCQUIERE.	
THILLOY	23		63rd Inf. Bde. marched by Battalions to the LA BARQUE - THILLOY area. Resting, bathing and cleaning up.	
			63rd Inf. Bde. Instructions for Defence issued (No.2290.G.).	16

P.T.O.

Army Form C. 2118.

WAR DIARY
or
INTELLIGENCE SUMMARY.
(Erase heading not required.)

Instructions regarding War Diaries and Intelligence Summaries are contained in F. S. Regs., Part II. and the Staff Manual respectively. Title pages will be prepared in manuscript.

Place	Date	Hour	Summary of Events and Information	Remarks and references to Appendices
THILLOY	24		Resting and bathing.	
	25		Platoon and specialist training.	
	26		63rd Inf. Bde. taken over by Brig. Genl. R. OAKLEY, D.S.O. vice Brig. Genl. E.L.CHALLENOR, C.M.G., D.S.O. to command Home Brigade.	
	27		Platoon and specialist training continued.	
	28		Training continued.	
	29		Training continued. Church Parades. Warning order received from Division for move and probable relief of 5th Division. 63rd Inf. Bde. Order No.261........	17
RUYAULCOURT	30		Brigade H.Q. moved to W. of RUYAULCOURT, 4th Middlesex Regt. to NEUVILLE, 8th Lincolnshire Regt. to RUYAULCOURT, 8th Somerset L.I. to BERTHINCOURT. 63rd Inf. Bde. Order No.262........	18
			Reports on operations 3rd to 11th September.........................	19
			Congratulatory message from G.O.C. 63rd Inf. Bde. to Battalions on operations 3/11 Sept...	20
			Reports on operations carried out on 21st September	21

30th September, 1918.

[signature]
Brigadier General.
Commdg. 63rd Inf. Brigade.

REPORT ON OPERATIONS CARRIED OUT 3rd to 11th SEPTEMBER, 1918

by

63rd INFANTRY BRIGADE

─────────────────oOo─────────────────

Reference Sheets:-
57C. NE, SE, NW, SW.
Scale 1:20,000.

On the evening of the 31st August a letter was received from Division in which it was stated that 37th Division would probably relieve one of the Divisions of IV Corps in the Line at an early date, and ordering Brigade and Battalion Commanders to reconnoitre the ground in front and South of BAPAUME. G.O.C. 63rd Infantry Brigade decided to hold a Battalion Commander's Conference, which was held at H.Q. 8th Lincolnshire Regt. at 11.30 a.m. 2nd September. The G.O.C. explained the probable future moves of the Brigade and ordered reconnaissances to be carried out in accordance with the Divisional letter.

2nd Septr.
At 9.30 pm 2nd September a warning order was received from Division that the Division would probably be required to relieve the 5th Division in the Left Sector of the IV Corps area. Late on Septr. 2nd Division Order No.237 was received to the effect that 37th Division would relieve 5th Division in the Line on the night 3/4th September, 112th Infantry Brigade to be leading, 63rd Infantry Brigade to relieve 95th Infantry Brigade in Support, and 111th Infantry Brigade to be in Reserve. All arrangements for relief were to be made by G.Os.C. concerned.

3rd Septr.
Accordingly, on the morning of the 3rd Septr. G.O.C. 63rd Infantry Brigade and the Brigade Major rode over to H.Q. 95th Infantry Brigade, 5th Division, where they were informed that 95th Infantry Brigade were no longer in Support but were now in Reserve, 13th Infantry Brigade having moved forward to gain touch with the enemy who were reported to be retiring on the whole of the 5th Division front. 37th Division were at once informed by telephone of the change in the situation, and orders were issued by G.S.O.1 for the Brigade to stand by pending further instructions.

At about midday 3rd Septr. orders placing the Brigade at half an hour's notice to move were issued (2034/4.G).

At 12.30 pm 112th Infantry Brigade were ordered to move forthwith to FAVREUIL in relief of Right Brigade, 5th Division. When the former Brigade moved forward from FAVREUIL, 63rd Infantry Brigade were to replace them. Accordingly 63rd Infantry Brigade Order No.253 was issued at 1.15 pm to the Brigade Group, consisting of 63rd Infantry Brigade, 'C' Company, 37th M.G.Battalion, and 153 Field Co. R.E.

At 2.25 pm a telephone message was received from Division that the Brigade were to move off at once in relief of 13th Infantry Brigade somewhere East of BEUGNY and West of LEBUCQUIERE. 63rd Infantry Brigade wire No. B.M.8 ordering the time of start to be 3.15 pm was issued. The head of the column passed the Starting Point, Fork Road G.9.d.8.8, at 3.20 pm. On reaching FAVREUIL it was found that 112th Infantry Brigade were not yet clear of that area, and the Brigadier decided to halt and close up the column and have teas just West of FAVREUIL, in the meantime riding forward to Advanced Divisional H.Q. at that place at about 5.30 pm.

At 6 pm the Brigade Intelligence Officer who had been sent forward to get the dispositions of 13th Infantry Brigade reported to the Brigade Major, and on the return of the G.O.C. a Conference of Commanding Officers was called, and instructions as to relief were given in B.M.10 issued at 7 pm.

Troops .....

- 2 -

Troops of 112th Infantry Brigade were to have been clear of FAVREUIL by 6.30 pm but owing to the traffic were not clear until 7.20 pm. 63rd Infantry Brigade followed immediately in rear in the same order of march as previously. The column was held up by traffic on the main road to FREMICOURT and considerably delayed.

Guides from 13th Infantry Brigade were met at the Cross Roads at BEUGNY. Brigade Headquarters opened in the old hutted camp, I.29.b.7.3., at about 10.30 pm. 13th Infantry Brigade were too tired to move that night so it was decided to let both Brigades remain in the area.

4th Septr.

63rd Infantry Brigade Group was reported safely in by 3.30 am, disposed as follows:-

Brigade Headquarters	I.29.b.7.3.
8th Lincolnshire Regt.	I.22.c.
8th Somerset L.I.	I.29.b.
4th Middlesex Regt.	I.29.a.
63rd T.M.Battery	I.30.a.3.5.
153rd Field Co. R.E.	FREMICOURT.
'C' Coy. 37th M.G.Bn.	BEUGNY.

At 1.45 am 37th Division Orders Nos. G.410/2 and 410/3 were received. Accordingly 63rd Infantry Brigade Order A.B.1 was issued at 3.15 am. The advance on the IV Corps front was to recommence at 7 am. As and when 112th Infantry Brigade advanced, 63rd Infantry Brigade were to follow in Support, with 8th SOMERSET L.I. on the Right, 4th MIDDLESEX REGT. on the LEFT, both disposed in depth and each with One Section of 'C' Coy., 37th M.G.Bn., attached; 8th LINCOLNSHIRE REGT. to be in reserve and to move to the area West of LEBUCQUIERE with 63rd T.M.BATTERY. 8th SOMERSET L.I. and 4th MIDDLESEX REGT. were to send forward Officers' patrols to keep in touch with and report on progress of 112th Infantry Brigade. Battalions were to be ready to move at 7 am. Commanding Officers were ordered to attend a Conference at Brigade Headquarters at 6.30 am at which the G.O.C. explained the manner in which he wished Battalions to move forward.

Brigade Headquarters closed at I.29.b.7.3. at 9 am and opened at Advanced Divisional Report Centre at I.30.b.6.1. at that hour.

At 9.20 am B.M.15 was issued ordering 153rd Field Co. R.E. to move to I.30.d. and B.M.17 to 8th LINCOLNSHIRE REGT. ordering them to move to the same area.

At this time the Brigade was approximately disposed on the line of the railway from J.26.c. & d. with 4th MIDDLESEX REGT. on the Left, and 8th SOMERSET L.I. on the Right, each with One Section 'C' Coy. 37th M.G.Bn. attached. The remainder of the Brigade Group was concentrated in I.29. and I.30.

At 11.15 am 8th SOMERSET L.I. and 4th MIDDLESEX REGT. were ordered to push their leading companies slowly forward, the companies of 8th SOMERSET L.I. to be directed on the trenches in P.3.a. and J.33.c., and the companies of 4th MIDDLESEX REGT. directed on J.33.a. and J.27.b. The Support and Reserve companies were to move forward and replace the leading companies as they moved forward (B.M.19).

At 1 pm the situation was as follows:-

8th SOMERSET L.I., with 2 companies in depth, on the approximate line J.33.central, one company J.32.central, Reserve Company in J.31.d.

4th Middlesex Regt. with one company in depth in trench line J.27.d., one company in J.26.a., one company J.19.d., one company J.19.c., and

Remainder of Brigade Group in I.29. and I.30 in Reserve.

There was no substantial change in the situation during the afternoon. At 6.30 pm Brigade Headquarters closed at I.30.b.6.1 and moved to J.32.b.8.8.

At 8 pm a telephone message was received from Division stating that the Brigade would have to take over on a one Battalion front from the New Zealand Division as far South as P.11.a.0.6. on the night

5/6th.....

- 3 -

5/6th September.

5th Septr.

At 2 am 37th Division G.410/4 was received, on which 63rd Infantry Brigade A.B.5 was issued at 6 am, in which it was stated that G.O.C.112th Infantry Brigade would be able to call on 8th Somerset L.I. or 4th Middlesex Regt in case of necessity. Troops were to be rested as much as possible on the 5th instant. 63rd Infantry Brigade would probably be required to take over a two battalion front on the night 5th/6th September, relieving troops of N.Z.Division North of MATHESON Road and troops of the 112th Infantry Brigade South of the Interbrigade boundary which was to be notified later.

A Commanding Officers conference took place at 11-0am: At this conference the probable reliefs and changes of boundary were explained to Commanding Officers.

At 2-0pm: 63rd Infantry Brigade A.B.7 was issued. 37th Division was to extend its Southern Divisional Forward Boundary to MATHESON ROAD, the Northern Divisional Boundary remaining as before. 63rd Infantry Brigade were to be on the right and 112th Infantry Brigade on the left, the inter-brigade boundary to be the line J.32.b.0.0. - K.32 central - thence due East. The Brigade front was to be held by two Battalions in the line, 8th Somerset L.I. on the right and 8th Lincolnshire Regiment on the left, disposed in depth, with inter-battalion boundary on East and West grid line through P.5 and P.6. central. 4th Middlesex Regt would be in reserve disposed approximately 2 Companies in trenches P.2.d. and P.2.b. and 2 Companies in trenches P.3.a and b. O.C.'C' Company, 37th Battalion, M.G.C. was to arrange for machine gun defence in depth West of the Main Line of Resistance which would be on the line of trenches P.2.d.7.9. - J.33.c.7.0. - J.33.a.8.5. The Brigade was to be covered by the 124th and 317th Brigade R.F.A. under the Command of Lt-Col CROFTON, D.S.O. Reliefs were to be completed by 4-0am:

Headquarters and 2 sections of 153rd Field Company R.E. were moved to the SPOIL HEAP, J.33.d.

During the whole of this day the troops were rested as much as possible and the positions remained unaltered.

6th Septr.

The above mentioned reliefs were completed by 3.22am: 6th inst.

At 11.15am: 6th instant, a telephone message was received from G.S.O.1. that the New Zealanders reported having found no enemy in P.24.a.,b and c and 17th Division on their right reported no enemy in P.36. and V.6. 8th Lincolnshire Regiment and 8th Somerset L.I. were told by phone to push out patrols at once to gain touch with the enemy along the whole Brigade front (confirmed by B.M.43)

At 12 noon Brigade Headquarters moved to Copse in I.36.d.9.0.

As a result of these patrols touch with the enemy was reported along the whole Brigade front. Slight hostile movement was observed in HAVRINCOURT WOOD.

In a telephone conversation with 2nd N.Z.Infantry Brigade, O.C. their Left Battalion stated that 8th Somerset L.I. could reach the edge of the wood without artillery preparation. Accordingly B.M.50 was issued at 3.20pm: ordering 8th Somerset L.I. to push forward strong patrols to occupy the Western edge of the wood. 8th Lincolnshire Regiment were to push forward to try to gain the line QUADRANGLE RESERVE - Q.1.a.6.0. - Q.1.a.7.6. - K.31.d.7.0.- CHEETHAM RESERVE - HUBERT AVENUE - K.32. central.

At 4.35pm 8th Somerset L.I. reported small parties of the enemy in full marching order moving about in HAVRINCOURT WOOD and that patrols were fired on by rifles and machine guns whilst in P.6.a.

In the meantime the New Zealanders had been pushing on and had gained the S.W. corner of the Wood, whilst 112th Infantry Brigade on the left had established posts K.32 central and on the SLAG HEAP K.32.a.9.8., and were at that time trying pushing forward to try and establish a post in WIGAN COPSE. In order to conform with this the G.O.C. spoke to 8th Lincolnshire Regiment and told them to swing their line from CHEETHAM RESERVE to HENLEY LANE.

At 7.15 pm a telephone message was received from Division that aeroplane reports stated that HAVRINCOURT WOOD was unoccupied and that the New Zealanders were probably holding METZ.

During this period the forward companies of 4th MIDDLESEX REGT. had been placed, one at the disposal of 8th SOMERSET L.I. and one at the disposal of 8th LINCOLNSHIRE REGT., the company with 8th SOMERSET L.I. to remain in P.10.b. and the company with 8th LINCOLNSHIRE REGT. to move at 6.30 am 7th inst. to the Sunken Road running N.E. from J.35.d.0.0; the remaining two companies of 4th MIDDLESEX REGT. to move to accommodation in the Sunken Road in P.3.central.

At 7.30 pm a message was received from 8th SOMERSET L.I. stating that their two front companies were now going through the wood and the Support company had moved to the old front line and the Reserve company to the Support. No opposition had been met and no enemy seen. The enemy was reported to have shelled the wood at 4.50 pm.

At 11.50 pm a telephone message was received from 8th LINCOLNSHIRE REGT. saying that the advance was going to be continued in three stages, first to QUADRANGLE RESERVE, second to ride running N.E. from Q.1.c. to CHEETHAM RESERVE, third and last to ride running N.E. from Q.1.d.0.2., the left of 8th LINCOLNSHIRE REGT. conforming with 13th ROYAL FUSILIERS (112th Infantry Brigade) - touch at present maintained with the latter at the junction of HENLEY LANE and CHEETHAM SWITCH. On this message 4th MIDDLESEX REGT. were notified that the second company at the disposal of O.C. 8th SOMERSET L.I. would move to the Sunken Road J.35.d. by 6 am 7th inst. and come under orders of O.C. 8th LINCOLNSHIRE REGT.

The line at this time ran approximately - just East of RUYAULCOURT - P.12.b.0.9. - Q.1.d.0.0. - Q.1.central - K.32.central - West end of YORKSHIRE BANK - SQUARE COPSE.

7th Septr.

At 1.25 am wire received from Division placing one battalion of the 112th Infantry Brigade at the disposal of the G.O.C. 63rd Infantry Brigade for the purpose of manning the main line of resistance.

4th MIDDLESEX REGT. were disposed at 9 am - One company J.36.c.0.5, One company PAUPER TRENCH (P.10.b.), One company P.5.a. and One company P.9.b.

Reports received during the morning all tended to show that the enemy was merely fighting a rearguard action, and good progress was made by 8th SOMERSET L.I. and 8th LINCOLNSHIRE REGT. through the wood.

At 1.55 pm Line reported to be Q.2.a.5.0 - Q.2.a.55.75 - K.32.c.45.70 - K.32.a.2.0, where the 8th LINCOLNSHIRE REGT. were in touch with 112th Infantry Brigade. New Zealanders were reported to be in touch on the Right and were also advancing through the wood with only slight resistance.

At 3.25 pm the New Zealanders were reported to have reached S.E. corner of wood and to hold edge of same to where touch was maintained with 8th SOMERSET L.I.

8th LINCOLNSHIRE REGT. were reported at 4.25 pm to have reached SHROPSHIRE RESERVE, 2 platoons in HUBERT AVENUE and remainder of that company in QUADRANGLE RESERVE. The 8th SOMERSET L.I. were believed to be in SHROPSHIRE RESERVE and QUADRANGLE TRENCH but not in touch with 8th LINCOLNSHIRE REGT. O.C. 8th SOMERSET L.I. reported having ordered forward company of 4th MIDDLESEX REGT. placed at his disposal.

112th Infantry Brigade when asked what battalion was to be put at the disposal of 63rd Infantry Brigade replied 1/1st HERTS REGT. Arrangements were therefore made over the 'phone for two companies to move forthwith to P.2.b.& d. and two companies into road through P.2.b. & d. (2 Machine Guns of 'B' M.G.Coy to stay attached) to replace companies of 4th MIDDLESEX REGT. which had moved forward in support of the leading battalions.

At 7.15 pm 8th SOMERSET L.I. reported they were held up as Q.3. strongly held by the enemy and O.C. 8th SOMERSET L.I. had decided to draw in his posts from Q.3. and E. of BANBURY HILL ROAD.

At 7.15 pm 1/1st HERTS REGT. reported their move completed and that they were located as ordered (see above).

One Company of Pioneers and a detachment of 153rd Field Co. R.E. were arranged for to dig a strong point about P.12.b. (SOMERSET SPUR) in case of an enemy counter attack through the wood.

At......

At 7.30 pm arrangements were made with 92 Brigade Heavy Artillery to shell Q.3. Col.CROFTON also arranged to barrage this square for 10 minutes and to keep it under fire during the night.

At 8.15 pm one our line ran QUADRANGLE TRENCH to Q.2.d.9.1. - due W. to Q.2.c.8.2. - Q.2.c.8.5. - Q.2.a.5.1. - Q.2.b.5.5. - up SHROPSHIRE RESERVE to junction with HUBERT AVENUE - CHEETHAM SWITCH - HENLEY LANE. S.O.S. lines were arranged with the Group Commander to be 300 - 400 yards in front of this line.

At 10.45 pm 63rd Infantry Brigade Order No.A.B.9 was issued. To-morrow (3th) would be spent in reorganising the front line and certain withdrawals would be made to enable a systematic bombardment of Q.3, Q.2.b. & d. and K.32.d. Nothing of interest occurred during the remainder of the night.

8th Septr.

At 11 a.m. Brigade Headquarters moved to P.11.b.0.3.

Energetic patrolling was carried out and patrols of 8th SOMERSET L.I. worked up OXFORD ALLEY and TUPNELL AVENUE. No enemy were met and post was to be established at Q.3.d.1.5.

The position of our patrols at this time was rather obscure and accordingly the action of our Artillery had to be very carefully controlled.

8th LINCOLNSHIRE REGT. were told to push posts to SHROPSHIRE SUPPORT and in SHROPSHIRE RESERVE, and after dark to relieve 8th SOMERSET L.I. in the latter trench as far South as the junction in LEAD STREET.

9th Septr.

Situation was reported quiet during the night except for considerable gas shelling - Blue and Yellow Cross in Q.2, Q.7, Q.8 - throughout the night till 7 am. In a telephone conversation on the evening of the 8th with G.S.O. , the Brigade was told to definitely establish the line QUADRANGLE TRENCH - TUPNELL AVENUE - to Q.3.b.7.7 - QUEER STREET - KNIFE TRENCH - KITTEN TRENCH - K.32.b.65.00 - Cross Roads K.32.b.75.85 - K.26.c.9.2. - advanced posts at Q.3.b.6.0 - Q.4.a.2.1 - Q.4.a.35.80 - Q.3.b.7.7 by the afternoon of the 10th inst. The G.O.C. called a Commanding Officers Conference at 9.30 am at H.Q. of 8th SOMERSET L.I. Whilst this Conference was in progress 37th Division Warning Order No.G.533 and letter No.G.532 were received. The Brigade would probably take over the Divisional Front on the right 9,10th instant. All Commanding officers were warned and ordered to be ready to push forward strong patrols. 4th MIDDLESEX REGT. would relieve troops of 8th SOMERSET L.I. South of E. and W. grid line through Q.1. and Q.2. central. 63rd Infantry Brigade Order No.254 was issued at 3.15 approx.

At 12.55 pm our line was reported to run K.32.b.2.0 - HUBERT AVENUE - along SHROPSHIRE TRENCH - BUTLER TRENCH - to Q.3.c.80.95 - then BUTLER SUPPORT to TUPNELL AVENUE at Q.3.d.10.65 - then South along TUPNELL AVENUE to boundary. Strong patrols were pushing out to KITTEN and KNIFE TRENCH and along TUPNELL and QUEER STREET.

At 5.50 pm the 8th SOMERSET L.I. reported having killed 1 enemy in a patrol encounter at Q.3.a.70.90 - identification 240 I.R.

At 6.15 pm 8th SOMERSET L.I., continuing their very energetic patrolling, forced their way to BUTLER CROSS and captured 2 O.Rs of the 239th I.R. and one machine gun - Patrols working down TRESCAULT TRENCH.

Heavy hostile shelling of OXFORD ALLEY, YORKSHIRE BANK, KITTEN TRENCH.

At 7.30 pm O.C. 8th SOMERSET L.I., who was up forward, reported very heavy enemy shell fire on the whole of his sector and a Machine Gun barrage being put down on his forward trenches. He suspected enemy might be massing for an attack in the wood South of HAVRINCOURT. O.C. 8th LINCOLNSHIRE REGT. reported heavy hostile shelling shortly after, and also estimated that the enemy might be going to attack. Accordingly Col.CROFTON, commanding the Group, who was at this time at Brigade H.Q., was asked to arrange for as many guns as possible to fire on suspected areas.

All was reported to be quiet at 10.45 pm.

10th...

10th Septr.

At 1.10 am O.C. 8th SOMERSET L.I., who had just returned from the front line, reported that his Battalion was very nearly on the objective given in Brigade Order 254. 4th MIDDLESEX REGT. had taken over Southern Sector and relief was complete. 4th MIDDLESEX REGT. had to pass through some heavy shelling on their way to the line, luckily suffering no casualties.

At 5.50 am O.C. 8th LINCOLNSHIRE REGT. reported he had taken over the line from the 112th Infantry Brigade to the Northern Divisional boundary - his new line reported to run K.32.b.6.0 - K.32.b.75.80 - along N. edge of SLAG HEAP, thence along W. bank of Canal.

Dispositions at this time were -

4th MIDDLESEX REGT. - Two Companies in line (Q.9.a. & 3.c.)
　　　　　　　　　　　One Company in Support in vicinity of CLAYTON CROSS.
　　　　　　　　　　　One Company in Reserve in P.3.b.& d.
　　　　　　　　　　　Battalion H.Q. P.6.d.4.8.
8th LINCOLNSHIRE REGT. Three Companies in Line (One Coy. N. of Canal in K.25.d. - One Company SLAG HEAP and vicinity, and One Company K.32.d.)
　　　　　　　　　　　One Company in Reserve, BANBURY HILL Q.2.a.
　　　　　　　　　　　Battalion H.Q. J.3.b.9.6.
1/1st HERTS REGT. - Battalion disposed One Company North of Canal in J.3.b. and J.30.c. Three Companies in Line P.12. central - J.36.central.
　　　　　　　　　　　Battalion H.Q. J.36.c.1.4.

63rd T.M.BATTERY at this time working under O.C. 8th SOMERSET L.I. with 2 mortars - each with 60 rounds of ammunition. Battery H.Q. Q.8.a.4.6. 'C' COMPANY, 37th M.G.Btn. had all guns well forward owing to the nature of the ground and the thickness of the wood.

During the night the enemy made several strong bombing attacks against the positions of the 8th LINCOLNSHIRE REGT. on the SLAG HEAP. When these attacks were repulsed he contented himself by very heavy shelling of our trenches on the Heap.

At 10 am two strong fighting patrols were sent out by 4th MIDDLESEX REGT., the Southerly patrol starting from N.Z. area and working up SHERWOOD TRENCH met strong resistance and was fired on and forced to withdraw, suffering casualties of 1 Officer and 2 O.Rs wounded, 3 O.Rs missing. The Northerly patrol reached a point Q.4.d.5.7. without opposition, no enemy having been seen. Three enemy posts were located at this time by Green Very Lights being fired from them owing to enemy short shelling at Q.10.a.60.45 - Q.10.b.4.2. - Q.10.b.4.3. 8th SOMERSET L.I. had pushed out patrols to K.33.c.8.8. and had met no opposition except slight sniping from West of HAVRINCOURT.

At 4 p.m. 8th LINCOLNSHIRE REGT. reported their line K.33.c.5.5. - K.32.d.60.95 - K.32.b.5.5. - K.32.b.75.80 - K.32.b.00.95 - K.26.c.70.10 - K.26.c.75.70. A very successful encounter took place in the fighting on the SLAG HEAP at this time, a post of 11 enemy being accounted for by 8 killed and 3 prisoners. 8th SOMERSET L.I. were in touch on their left and line ran KNIFE TRENCH - QUEER STREET - TUFNELL AVENUE - TUFNELL TRENCH - with posts established in Q.4.a. at North and South ends of BURNLEY AVENUE. 4th MIDDLESEX REGT. line unchanged down TUFNELL TRENCH to South boundary.

At 7.15 pm considerable enemy movement was observed on road running E. and W. in K.26.d. and 27.c., estimated about 150 of the enemy moving towards WIGAN COPSE. These parties were engaged by Artillery, Lewis Gun and Rifle Fire and commenced dribbling back towards HAVRINCOURT. It is considered without doubt that the enemy had intended to attack the SPOIL BANK but that the attack was prevented from materialising owing to the fire brought to bear and the heavy casualties inflicted on them.

At 7.18 pm 8th SOMERSET L.I. reported very heavy Trench Mortar fire and shelling of the whole of Q.3. Group were asked to retaliate. Enemy barrage was reported on front of Left two battalions. All was reported quiet by 8.30 pm except for desultory shelling of HAVRINCOURT WOOD.

11th Septr.

At 2 am 'Q' Special Co. R.E. successfully projected 300 drums of gas on the S.W. edge of HAVRINCOURT and at 3.30 am another 170 drums on the same target.

At......

- 7 -

At about 10 am Division Order No.241 was received ordering the relief of the Brigade by 62nd Division on the Left and by the 111th Infantry Brigade on the Right. 63rd Infantry Brigade Order No.256 was issued at 1.30 pm.

The relief of the 4th MIDDLESEX REGT. on the Right Sector of the Brigade Front was carried out during the afternoon by the 13th K.R.R.V., 111th Infantry Brigade, who unfortunately suffered some casualties owing to heavy enemy shelling. 63rd Infantry Brigade was to be accommodated on relief in the VELU - LEBUCQUIERE area.

The day passed quietly and reliefs were successfully carried out of all troops in rear of the outpost line. The latter were ordered to withdraw at ZERO - 1 hour except the post of the 8th LINCOLNSHIRE REGT. on YORKSHIRE BANK who were to remain in position until ZERO - ½ hour. ZERO was notified later to be 5.25 am on the 12th September.

12th Septr.

All Brigade Group was reported complete in the VELU - LEBUCQUIERE area at 8.10 am on the 12th inst. Units were located as follows:-

Brigade Headquarters	-	I.30.a.9.8.
8th Somerset L.I.	-	LEBUCQUIERE, I.30.a.8.8.
8th Lincolnshire Regt.	-	I.29.b.0.0.
4th Middlesex Regt.	-	VELU CHATEAU.
153rd Field Co. R.E.	-	I.23.a.
'C' Co. 37th M.G.Bn.	-	LEBUCQUIERE.
63rd T.M.Battery	-	I.29.b.

---oOo---

Casualties suffered by the Brigade throughout the whole period from 3rd September to morning of the 12th September were very slight, details of which are subscribed:-

	Killed.	Wounded.	Missing.	Gassed.	S.I.W.	NYDN.	TOTAL.
8th Lincolns...	9	31	-	16	2	-	58
8th Somersets..	7	58	2	36	1	1	105
4th Middlesex..	6	24	3	4	-	-	37
					TOTAL FOR BRIGADE..		200.

Officers.

KILLED - 2/Lieut. G.JONES.   8th Lincolns.
            Lieut.   B.W.GAUNT.   63rd T.M.Battery.

WOUNDED - Lieut.   L.T.MARSHALL.   4th Middlesex.
             Lieut.   E.S.DASHFIELD.   4th Middlesex.
             Captain W.J.BENNETT.   8th Somerset L.I.
             Lieut.   K.G.WOODMANSEY.   8th Somerset L.I.
             2/Lieut. G.MATTHEWS.   8th Somerset L.I.

---oOo---

Owing to the nature of the fighting and the type of country to be traversed during the whole of the operations, the Machine Guns were kept well forward in the front line in order to avail themselves of fleeting targets and to cover the advancing Infantry.

Major BEECHMAN carried out all the tasks allotted to him with the greatest alacrity and showed a good grasp of the situation in the siting of his guns.

This type of fighting was not particularly suited to Trench Mortars, but the 63rd Trench Mortar Battery did some excellent work in conjunction with the 8th SOMERSET L.I. in Q.3., silencing a machine gun nest. It is much regretted that Lieut.B.W.GAUNT, York & Lanc. Regt. attd. 63rd T.M.Battery, whilst advancing with one of the guns was killed by a M.G. bullet. This officer had done extremely good work with the battery previous to and during this action.

I again wish to thank all ranks of the Artillery Group commanded by Lt.Col.CROFTON, DSO, for their willing assistance and the good results obtained from their fire.

                                                   Challenor.
                                                   Brigadier General.
24th September, 1918.   Commdg. 63rd Inf. Brigade.

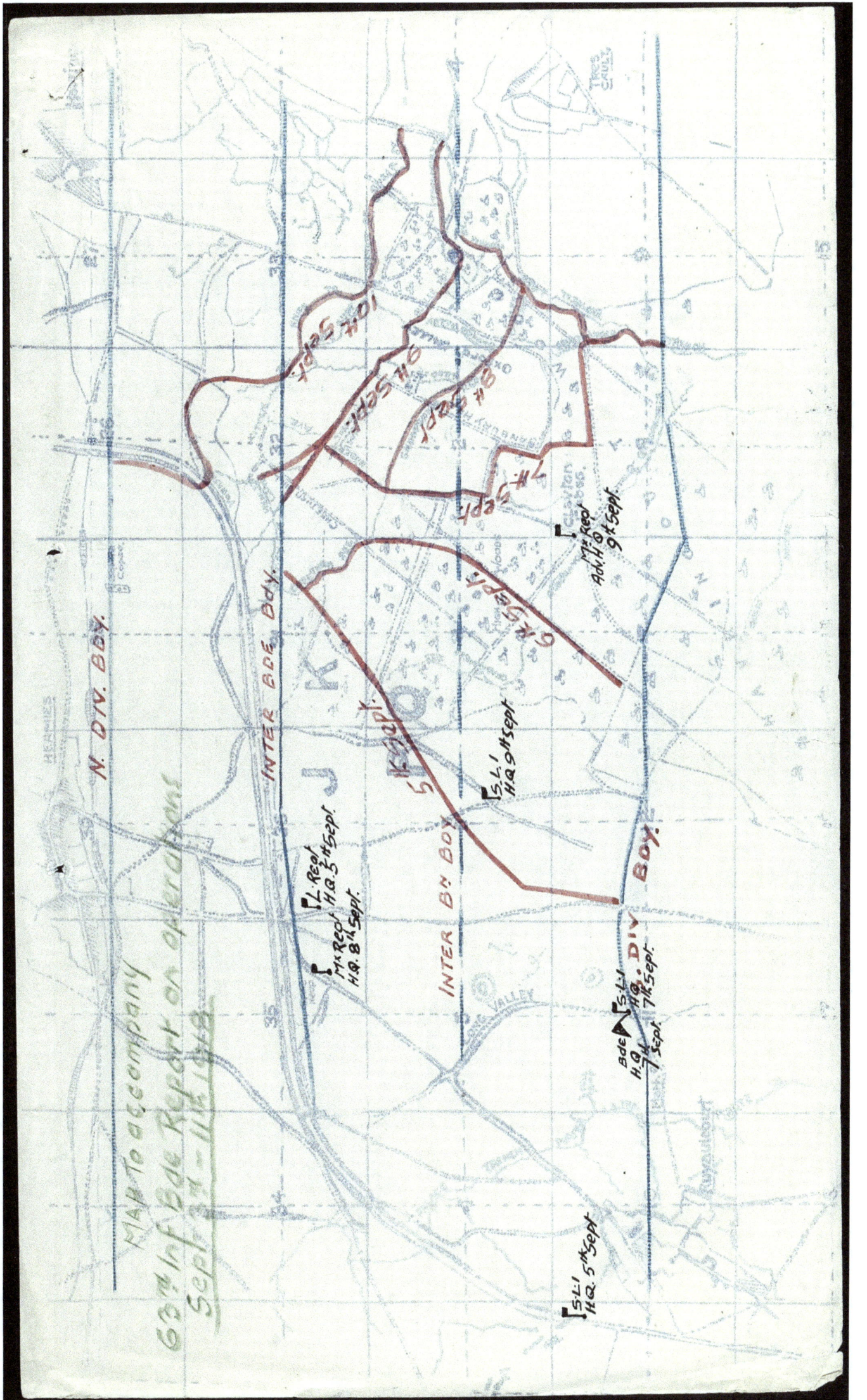

O.C. 8th Somersets
8th Lincolns
4th Middlesex

W.D.

I wish to thank you, your Officers, N.C.Os and Men, and to place on record, my appreciation of the exceptionally good work, great endurance and determination displayed by all ranks in the operations around HAVRINCOURT WOOD from 3rd September to 11th September, 1918.

The duties of clearing up the wood and establishing a line East and North of it, presented many difficulties owing to the nature of the ground and heavy enemy shelling. That this was done so successfully, and with such light casualties, reflects the greatest credit on all ranks.

Your Battalion has again, therefore, added to its already long list of honours, and I feel sure will continue to do so with the same gallantry and devotion to the end, which is now in sight.

13th September, 1918.

Brigadier General.
Commdg. 63rd Inf. Brigade.

Copy.

REPORT ON OPERATIONS CARRIED OUT ON 21st SEPTEMBER, 1918

by

63rd INFANTRY BRIGADE.

At 9 pm on 19th September 37th Division letter No.G.780 of 19th instant was received.

20th Septr.
G.O.C. went round Battalions and saw Commanding Officers, telling them of the proposed operation. In the G.O.C's absence the Divisional Commander visited Brigade Headquarters and pointed out the urgency of the operation.

The following objectives were ordered to be taken:- Posts at junction BURTON LANE - DERBY TRENCH, and one in BILHEM-CHAPEL WOOD SWITCH, North of TRESCAULT-RIBECOURT Road.

At 4.30 pm a Conference of Group Commanders was held at Brigade Headquarters, and various targets were worked out, ZERO hour to be 3 am 21st September.

At 6.30 pm G.S.O.2, 37th Division, arrived at Brigade H.Q. and the scheme was told him. G.S.O.1 was told roughly on the 'phone what was proposed, and then the G.O.C. spoke to G.O.C. 37th Division on the 'phone. The operation as proposed was cancelled, and the new scheme was to be more in the nature of a heavy artillery bombardment to destroy all wire and obstacles in the area, Infantry being withdrawn and a four hours bombardment being arranged.

Details of above were worked out in conjunction with G.S.O.2 of the Division. The C.R.A. was to coordinate the action of the R.F.A. and Heavy Artillery (63rd Infantry Brigade Order No.260).

ZERO HOUR (hour at which Artillery were to open) was decided on as 12 noon 21st September.

21st Septr.
The withdrawal of the Infantry was successfully carried out by 12 noon, and the bombardment commenced at that hour.

On again advancing at 3.45 pm the 8th SOMERSET L.I. (on the right) regained original line without difficulty, being in a position to push forward down BASS LANE at 4 pm, and BURTON LANE at 4.3 pm.

A. The platoon working down BASS LANE found this trench to be blocked at intervals - necessitating clearing and surmounting these obstacles. Two blocks were successfully surmounted but at the third further movement forward was delayed for a matter of 10 minutes whilst the block, which was extremely elaborate, was cleared. In the meantime the entire first section became casualties from stick bombs and rifle grenades, which were fired with great accuracy on our party. At this time the enemy's Field Artillery fired salvoes on BASS LANE and DERBY SUPPORT, impeding the bringing up of supports. The second section on being brought up also became casualties, so the Officer ordered patrol to fall back to DERBY TRENCH, where he reported to his Company Officer. Owing to the fact that our Artillery bombardment had made no impression on the wire it was found impossible to leave the trench and work forward on the flanks. Three enemy Machine Guns were very active, firing trained on top of the blocks, and our men crossing them came under heavy fire.

B. BURTON LANE. Patrol started at 4.3 pm. This party found on reaching our original block that it had been worked on by the enemy and strongly reinforced during our bombardment. The moment they attempted to cross this block heavy Machine Gun and Rifle Grenade fire was opened on them and further advance was impracticable.

A platoon from the right Company got into STAFFORD SUPPORT (after crossing the open for 40 yards - the trench being filled in) and moved on down to a point within about 30 yards of QUEENS LANE. On attempting

to.....

to cross a similar block to other parties at this point they came under heavy Machine Gun fire. This party, having been ordered to exploit and not advance against opposition, returned to our lines. This trench had always been reported clear, and as it is very shallow and in view from BEAUCAMP it was decided not to leave a post at this point.

In the course of the bombardment one of the enemy from an advanced post crawled forward at Q.11.a.7.1. to avoid our bombardment, got lost and found himself a prisoner.

8th LINCOLNSHIRE REGT. had great difficulty in advancing to even their original line owing to being under observation from the FLESQUIERES Ridge. The trenches up which they had to advance were blocked in several places as the result of our shell fire, especially TRESCAULT TRENCH towards its junction with DERBY SUPPORT. Parties came under considerable Machine Gun fire going up this trench and also in re-occupying 'A' Sap.

In attempting to cross TRESCAULT-RIBECOURT ROAD by DERBY TRENCH and DERBY SUPPORT patrol came under very heavy Machine Gun fire from direction of K.36.c.0.0.

Touch was gained with 8th SOMERSET L.I. in DERBY SUPPORT at about 4.30 pm, and it was learnt that they had been unable to advance.

Enemy Machine Guns were noticed to be firing from their usual positions.

Before withdrawing, dumps of Bombs and S.A.A. had been left on either side of the TRESCAULT-RIBECOURT ROAD; unfortunately the one on the South side was destroyed by a shell.

A party proceeded along DERBY TRENCH (which was very much damaged) and reached a point between the two branches of AEROPLANE TRENCH (Q.5.c.6.9.) and were suddenly subjected to a hail of stick bombs, the enemy evidently being in wait in their old position in BILHEM-CHAPEL WOOD SWITCH. Party fell back, having suffered casualties, and after a pause a second attempt was made with the same results, but a block was established at Q.5.c.6.9. between the two branches of AEROPLANE TRENCH. This block was handed over to 42nd Division on relief.

Bombardment seems to have been very short. When bombardment increased at last moment enemy retaliated very heavily and caught our party moving up, and it is thought same rate of fire should have been maintained the whole time. It was quite impossible to have gone over the top as it is all on forward slope.

The fact that posts were not established as ordered is attributed to :-

1. The Artillery bombardment which was to have obliterated the enemy's wire and trenches did not succeed in its object, wire and trenches remaining practically intact.

2. The only part of the bombardment which was really heavy was during the last quarter of an hour, and it is thought this increase in fire merely served to put the enemy on his guard. During the last quarter of an hour the enemy's Artillery opened heavy fire on TRESCAULT TRENCH and 'A' SAP, making reoccupation very difficult. ~~Owing to lack of time in the preparation of the scheme this fact was omitted. It had been intended that the Artillery fire should grow intense at intervals during the bombardment.~~

3. The bombardment did not dislodge the enemy from his positions, the enemy being found in all his original posts and reported by the attacking parties to be in considerable strength.

4. The fact that the wire had not been cut patrols were unable to leave the trenches, the enemy evidently expecting our men to move by these trenches had them very carefully registered, and on the slightest sign of movement opened a very heavy fire.

5. On the left of the front our Artillery seems to have been very short, much damage being done to West end of TRESCAULT TRENCH and DERBY SUPPORT.

------------oOOo------------

Original Copy.

WAR DIARY

63rd Infantry Brigade

OCTOBER, 1918

Army Form C. 2118.

WAR DIARY
or
INTELLIGENCE SUMMARY
(Erase heading not required.)

Instructions regarding War Diaries and Intelligence Summaries are contained in F. S. Regs., Part II. and the Staff Manual respectively. Title pages will be prepared in manuscript.

Place	Date October	Hour	Summary of Events and Information	Remarks and references to Appendices
E. of METZ-en-COUTURE	1st		Brigade moved to area GOUZEAUCOURT WOOD - HX S.E. of HAVRINCOURT WOOD. Brigade H.Q. ½ mile east of METZ-en-COUTURE.	
,,	2nd			
,,	3rd		Specialist training, musketry and working parties on roads.	
,,	4th			
GOUZEAUCOURT	5th		At 1800 hrs Brigade moved to LA VACQUERIE - GOUZEAUCOURT Area.	
,,	6th		Resting.	
,,	7th		Resting. 4th Middlesex Regt. moved at 2200 hrs to cross SCHELDT CANAL at FACTORY BRIDGE N. of BANTEUX and came under command of G.O.C. 112th Inf. Bde. Bde. H.Q. moved at 1800 hrs to dugout 1000 yds N.W. of BANTEUX.	
BANTEUX	8th		8th Lincolnshire Regt. crossed SCHELDT CANAL by trestle bridge S.W. of VAUCELLES and 8th Somerset L.I. by FACTORY BRIDGE near BANTEUX at 0630 hrs and proceeded to vicinity of SLATE COPSE. At 1208 hrs Bde. H.Q. moved across canal to dugout 800 yds from RED FARM.	
BELLEAISE FARM			At 1410 hrs Bde. H.Q. moved to BELLEAISE FARM. 8th Somerset L.I. and 8th Lincolnshire Regt. moved to S.W. PELU WOOD.	
			At 1800 hrs 8th Somerset L.I. on left and 8th Lincolnshire Regt. on right attacked high ground S.E. of ESNES under an artillery barrage, 4th Middlesex Regt. in support. Attack lost direction in dark and did not attain crest; right ran back to N.E. corner BRISIEUX WOOD.	
BRISIEUX WOOD	9th		At 0400 hrs Bde. H.Q. moved to N.W. corner of BRISIEUX WOOD.	
			At 0520 advance continued. 63rd Bde. attained objective - ridge S.E. of HAUCOURT and 112 Bde. passed through them to second objective west of LIGNY-en-CAMBRESIS. S.E.	
HAUCOURT			At 1030 hrs Bde. HQ moved to BRISIEUX Chateau; battalions in position xxxx of HAUCOURT.	
			At 1400 hrs Bde. HQ moved to HAUCOURT. Brigade in billets and bivouacs in and S. of HAUCOURT.	
,,	10th		At 0115 hrs 4th Middlesex Regt. moved to LIGNY and came under command of G.O.C. 112th Inf. Bde.	
LIGNY-en-CAMBRESIS CAUDRY			At 0630 hrs Brigade HQ moved to LIGNY and Brigade Group (less 4th Middlesex) to South of CAUDRY.	
			At 1940 hrs Brigade HQ moved to CAUDRY, 8th Somerset L.I. to N.W. and 8th Lincolnshire Regt. to S.W. of AUDENCOURT. Report centre in village.	
			At 1200 hrs 8th Somerset L.I. moved to PONT CAUDRY and 8th Lincolns to N. of AUDENCOURT.	
AUDENCOURT			1245 hrs Bde. HQ at AUDENCOURT; 4th Middlesex Regt. at CLERMONT Chateau reverted to command of G.O.C. 63rd Inf. Bde. Advance continued by 8th Somerset L.I. and 8th Lincolnshire Regt. who	

Army Form C. 2118.

WAR DIARY
or
~~INTELLIGENCE SUMMARY~~
(Erase heading not required.)

Instructions regarding War Diaries and Intelligence Summaries are contained in F. S. Regs., Part II. and the Staff Manual respectively. Title pages will be prepared in manuscript.

Place	Date	Hour	Summary of Events and Information	Remarks and references to Appendices
	11th		passed through 112th Inf. Bde. and reached ridge west of R. SELLE by 1800 hrs in touch left and right. Heavy barrage and M.G. fire on slope overlooking river and men very tired. Patrols worked down to bank of River SELLE during night. 8th Somerset L.I. threw two platoons across river near BRIASTRE and 8th Lincolnshire Rgt. one platoon across near NEUVILLY. In touch on left but right uncertain.	
	12th	At 1030 hrs	4th Middlesex Regt. moved to valley S.E. of VIESLY. 2 companies 8th Somerset L.I. and one company 8th Lincolnshire Regt. across river.	
		1000	patrol of 8th Lincolnshire Regt. North of NEUVILLY unable to proceed. Considerable shelling and M.G. fire all day in SELLE valley and slope W. of river. 3 bridges made.	
		0430 hrs,	4th Middlesex Regt. formed up E. of River SELLE for attack on high ground.	
		0445 hrs,	8th Somerset L.I. and 8th Lincolnshire Regt. withdrawn W. of River SELLE.	
		0600 hrs	3 leading companies 4th Middlesex Regt. reached high ground E. of River SELLE; not in touch with 50th Bde. N. of NEUVILLY but left refused to keep in touch with N.Z. who had not attained N. end of ridge owing to M.G. fire from BELLE VUE.	
		0730 hrs	4th Middlesex support Company unable to cross railway owing to M.G. in culverts which had not been mopped up. In touch on right.	
		1200 hrs	1 coy. 1/1 Herts ordered to mopup railway but did not arrive there owing to M.G. in embankment. 2 coys 8th Somerset L.I. and 1 coy. 1/1 Herts ordered to relieve left coy. 4th Middlesex who were required to strengthen remainder of 4th Middlesex line.	
		1515 hrs	enemy ~~KRKENE~~ counter attack on our right and wheel right behind 4th Middlesex. Heavy barrage. 4th Middlesex Regt. retire from crest on to railway and mop up most of it. Very heavy shelling. Our guns and M.Gs punish the enemy. All bridges now broken. Possible to cross river on trees fallen across it.	
		1800 hrs	N.Z. attack BELLE VUE with barrage. 8th Somerset L.I. (2 companies) cooperate on their right and link up with 4th Middlesex near practice trenches. Brigade relieved by 13th Inf. Bde., 5th Div. and billeted in CAUDRY.	
			For all orders for and report on operations Sept. 30th – Oct. 12th, 1918, see Appendix 1.	1.
CAUDRY	13th) 14th) 15th) 16th (17th) 18th)		-----Resting and Cleaning up. -----Training.	

Army Form C. 2118.

WAR DIARY
or
INTELLIGENCE SUMMARY.
(Erase heading not required.)

Instructions regarding War Diaries and Intelligence Summaries are contained in F. S. Regs., Part II. and the Staff Manual respectively. Title pages will be prepared in manuscript.

Place	Date	Hour	Summary of Events and Information	Remarks and references to Appendices
CAUDRY	19th 20th 21st		Inspection by Divisional Commander Church parade. Command of 63rd Inf. Bde. taken over from Brigadier General OAKLEY, D.S.O. by Brigadier-General A.B. HUBBACK, C.M.G. Training.	
	22nd		Training. Warning order received for Brigade to move to BRIASTRE Area. Billeting parties sent forward by units.	
BRIASTRE	23rd	0900 hrs.	63rd Inf. Bde. moved by march route to BRIASTRE - VIESLY Area. 8th Somerset L.I. and 8th Lincolnshire Regt. in BRIASTRE, 4th Middlesex Regt. in VIESLY, in billets. 63rd Inf. Bde. Order No. 266	2
BEAURAIN	24th	0700 hrs.	Advance continued. 63rd Inf. Bde. moved to BEAURAIN in the morning. O. No. 267 ...... In the afternoon 63rd Inf. Bde. relieved 111th Inf. Bde. in support, 8th Somerset L.I. forming defensive flank along railway N.E. of SALESCHES, 4th Middlesex Regt. in NEUVILLE and 8th Lincolnshire Regt. IN SALESCHES. 63rd Inf. Bde. Order No. 268	3 4
SALESCHES MILL	25th		2 companies 8th Lincolnshire Regt. relieve 2 companies 8th Somerset L.I. in area along railway N.E. of SALESCHES. Slight shelling of support area. Area N. of GHISSIGNIES reconnoitred by officers.	
	26th		Some shelling of support area in vicinity of SALESCHES Station. Reconnoitring continued. Battalions carried out Lewis Gun training and musketry.	
	27th		On night 27/28th 63rd Inf. Bde. relieved 112th Inf. Bde. in the line, 8th Somerset L.I. on left and 8th Lincolnshire Regt. on the right with 4th Middlesex Regt. in support in the SALESCHES Area. 63rd Inf. Bde. Order No. 269	5
	28th		Counter preparation shelling by enemy on GHISSIGNIES in early morning. Quiet until after-noon when considerable shelling of GHISSIGNIES Area.	
	29th		Enemy artillery quieter. Intermittent shelling of forward area. Harassing fire on SALESCHES at night. 63rd Inf. Bde. Defence Instructions issued, No. 3026 G	6
	30th 31st		Occasional bursts by enemy field guns on forward area. At 0330 hrs a raid was carried out by 8th Somerset L.I. in conjunction with a battalion of 3rd N.Z. (Rifle) Bde. under an artillery barrage on trenches in R.35.a. and c. 1 prisoner 83rd I.R., 22nd Div. captured and 30 - 40 enemy killed. Our casualties, 2 slightly wounded. Little retaliation. Our T.Ms cooperated and M.Gs fired on S.O.S. lines. 63rd Bde. O. 270 ...... On night Oct. 31/1 Nov. 4th Middlesex Regt. relieved 8th Somerset L.I. on the left subsector of 63rd Bde. front. 8th Somerset L.I. withdrew to SALESCHES Area. Relief complete 2130 hrs ...... Order No. 271	7 8

Army Form C. 2118.

WAR DIARY
or
INTELLIGENCE SUMMARY.

(*Erase heading not required.*)

Place	Date	Hour	Summary of Events and Information	Remarks and references to Appendices
	November 2nd 1918		Owing to the general tactical situation, warfare had become more or less stationary during this tour in the line, but the enemy was constantly harassed by all arms.	

[signature] Capt.
for BM
Brigadier General,
Comdg. 63rd Infantry Brigade.

REPORT ON OPERATIONS SEPT. 30TH, 1918 - OCT. 12TH, 1918.

30th Sept.

63rd Inf. Bde. moved from the LE BARQUE - THILLOY Area to BERTINCOURT, RUYAULCOURT and NEUVILLE in accordance with 37th Divn. Order No. 249 and 63rd Inf. Bde. Order No. 262. All units were in new area by 1300 hrs, Brigade H.Q. being in ruined huts and Battalions in ruined huts, shelters and trenches.

1st Oct.

63rd Inf. Bde. moved in accordance with 37th Div. Instruction No. G 1010/1, H.Q. to dugout on road 1000 yards east of METZ-EN-COUTURE. The Brigade group was accommodated as follows :-
153rd Field Coy. R.E. in Q.22.
8th Somerset L.I. in Q.15.
8th Lincolnshire Rgt. in Q.28.
4th Middlesex Regt. and T.M.Battery in Q.16.
Units found a certain amount of cover in ruined shelters but were without blankets.

2nd, 3rd and 4th Oct.

Resting, specialist training and working on roads. Blankets arrived on 2nd Oct. for all units except 8th Lincolnshire Regt. who received theirs on the 3rd.

4th Oct.

A phone message was received from Division giving warning of move of Brigade via CREVECOEUR for attack thence S.E. Commanding Officers' Conference ordered by G.O.C for 0900 hrs on 5th Oct.

5th Oct.

Commanding Officers' Conference at Brigade H.Q. at 0900 hrs. G.O.C., Brigade Major and Commanding Officers left to reconnoitre at 10.55 hrs but were recalled by phone and cyclist orderlies and information given that attack via CREVECOEUR would be made by 112th Inf. Bde.
At 11.30 hrs the Brigade received orders to occupy H.Q. and locations being vacated by 112th Inf. Bde. in Q.17 and Q.19. This was cancelled by phone and the Brigade put on half an hour's notice to move.
A phone message was received at 1630 hrs from G.S.O.1. ordering Brigade to move HQ troops to 112th Inf. Bde. H.Q. and area R.19, 20, 21 and 27. Units sent advanced parties at once and followed immediately. They arrived in new area after dark and spent a very bad night owing to there being no blankets or shelters, and the rain.
One platoon of 4th Middlesex Regt. was ordered by Divn. to proceed by lorry to GATEAU WOOD to clean up Div. H.Q. This platoon did not rejoin until after the first phase of the operations.

6th Oct.

The day was spent in reconnoitring by Brigade and Regimental Staffs and in making shelters by the men. The Brigade Commander was informed that G.O.C. 37th Division would probably confer with Brigadiers at R.24.a.3.0 at 1200 hrs. At 1230 hrs the Brigadier was informed by G.S.O.3. that the conference would not take place but would be held at 1500 hrs. At the conference G.O.C. 37th Division outlined scheme of attack on the MASNIERES - BEAUREVOIR Line and the operations to follow
Trench shelters were issued.

7th Oct.

At 10.15 hrs 37th Divn. Order No. 256 for attack on the MASNIERES - BEAUREVOIR Line was received, and a warning order, 63rd Inf. Bde. No. 2086 G, was issued.
At 15.30 hrs the Brigade Major was told on the phone that 4th Middlesex Regt. would be at the tactical disposal of G.O.C. 112th Inf. Bde. O.C. 4th Middlesex Regt. was informed by phone and told to report himself at once for instructions to 112th Inf. Bde. H.Q.
At 16.00 hrs 37th Divn. No. G.1102/1 - 2 - 3 and 4 were

received, giving Zero hour for 8th Oct. and details of forward moves Units were informed of Zero hour (B.M.238); the move forward was ordered in 63rd Inf. Bde. Order No. 263 issued at 19.15 hrs.

At 19.47 Brigade H.Q. opened at R.24.a.3.0, N.W. of BANTEUX

At 22.00 4th Middlesex Regt. moved from their bivouacs, crossed canal by Factory Bridge at EM.01.45 hrs and came under command of G.O.C. 112th Inf. Bde.

8th Oct.

8th Somerset L.I. crossed canal at 06.30 hrs by Factory Bridge and moved to west of VAUCELLES WOOD (M.27.b, c, d).

8th Lincolnshire Regt. crossed by pontoon bridge at 06.40 hrs. and moved to vicinity of SLATE COPSE.

At 11.00 hrs G.S.O.I. informed Brigade Major that the Brigade might move forward at any time after 12.00 hrs, and gave, generally, boundaries and successive bounds. Units were informed in B.M.244 issued at 11.15 hrs and Brigade H.Q. moved to M.27.b.2.8 forthwith. 37th Divn. G 829 confirmed.

At 14.00 hrs a phone message was received saying Battalions were to rendezvous near PELU WOOD ready to attack the BLUE DOTTED LINE N.11.b. - N.5.central at 16.00 hrs. Battn. Commanders were at Brigade H.Q. and were told the scheme which was confirmed in B.M.246. Both battalions had 7 miles to go to reach the rendezvous in PELU WOOD. There, Lewis Guns were removed from limbers and Battalions moved on at 17.10 hrs.

The time of attack was changed to 18.00 hrs by 37th Divn. G 836 which was received at 15.56 hours and transmitted to Battns. forthwith by runner, being received by Battns. in time.

The time of attack was changed at 16.18 hrs to 18.30 hrs by 37th Div. G.8.61. Battalion Commanders were informed and arranged in conjunction with the Brigade Major the Battalion Boundaries, forming up places, etc. This was very difficult as the attack had to be arranged for and carried out in the dark over ground which had not been previously reconnoitred and which was deficient in prominent landmarks. It was found that the valley N.10.b and d was impassable from west to east in many places owing to steep banks.

8th Somerset L.I. attacked on the left and 8th Lincolnshire Regt. on the right, bearing in a S.E. direction. Battalions got to within 400 yards of their objective on the left and centre but were held up on the right as GUILLEMIN had not been taken by 21st Divn. and the right ultimately ran back to the S.E. corner of BRISIEUX WOOD.

A forward report centre was formed at the N.W. corner of BRISIEUX WOOD. Only the cramped accommodation near BELLE AISE FARM could be found for Brigade H.Q. and this had to be shared with 112th Infantry Brigade.

On completion of the above operation 63rd Inf. Bde. took over the front line, with 112th Inf. Bde. in support (37th Divn. G.A. 38 dated 8th Oct.).

At 19.07 hrs a warning order (G.840) for the continuation of the advance the next day was received. First objective O.7.d. - HAUCOURT (inclusive) was allotted to 63rd Inf. Bde. and second objective, LIGNY - L.27.a.0.0 to 112th Inf. Bde. Battalions were informed with details in B.M.247, sent out at 20.15 by runners in duplicate and received by battalions about midnight.

Owing to the barrage arrangements the forward troops had to be withdrawn. This was difficult in the unknown country and in the dark, and also because orders had previously been issued for the left Battalion to push down N.11.a. and c. and clear enemy from house at N.11.a.2.0.

9th Oct.

At 05.20 hrs 8th Lincolnshire Regt. on right and 8th Somerset L.I. on left advanced according to orders and secured their objectives without any opposition. 112th Inf. Bde. passed through on this line to the second objective.

Brigade H.Q. moved to the N.W. corner of BRISIEUX WOOD at 04.00 hrs and to BRISIEUX CHATEAU at 10.30 hrs, thence to HAUCOURT at 14.00 hrs. On receipt of G.849 at 09.30 hrs the Brigade was disposed for the night on its objective, each of the leading Battns. on a 2 company front with 4th Middlesex Regt. in support in HAUCOURT all Battalion H.Q. being located in HAUCOURT.

At 20.00 hrs G 857, warning order of continuation of advance, was received.

10th Oct.

At 00.01 hrs G.S.O.1 phoned that 4th Middlesex Regt. were to rendezvous West of LIGNY-en-CAMBRESIS (0.33.c.) at 03.00 hrs and would be at disposal of G.O.C. 112th Inf. Bde. The remainder of 63rd Inf. Bde. Group were to be at the same place by 02.00 hrs, ready to pass through 112th Inf. Bde. when the latter had cleared up CAUDRY, and to exploit towards the River SELLE. Battalions were told at once over the phone and in B.M.261 issued at 00.50 hrs. In each case Battalions were in position punctually. Brigade H.Q. joined 112th Inf. Bde. H.Q. in LIGNY at 07.30 hrs after seeing G.S.O.1 at Divnl. H.Q.

The 112th Inf. Bde. had no news of the situation at 07.30 hrs. The Brigade Major, 112th Inf. Bde. was out reconnoitring and cyclist and cavalry patrols had not yet sent any information. A phone message was received from Division saying that 63rd Inf. Bde. was not to pass through 112th Inf. Bde. until the latter met with resistance. At 09.30 hrs the situation was still obscure. 63rd Inf. Bde. was concentrated S.E. of CAUDRY (I.30.b and d) pending a situation report from 112th Inf. Bde..

At 10.00 hrs Brigade H.Q. moved to L.29.d.central. S. of CAUDRY. Battalions were told (B.M.267) to gain touch with leading Battalions of 112th Inf. Bde. by means of officer patrols and were informed that they would go through 112th Inf. Bde. as soon as the situation was cleared up. At this time the situation had become complicated for the following reasons :-
The 50th Inf. Bde. had advanced more rapidly than 112th Inf. Bde. and had been enfiladed by artillery and machine gun fire from near CLERMONT CHATEAU. In an untimed message from 50th Inf. Bde. information of this arrived at Brigade H.Q. too late for action. 2 companies of 50th Inf. Bde. had been sent across the 112th Inf. Bde. front to mop up and the leading troops of 37th Division did not know whether they were expected to half left wheel or to carry on in their original direction.

At 12.00 hrs the G.O.C. considered it advisable for 63rd Inf. Bde. to pass through 112th Inf. Bde. (B.M.271), the situation however still being obscure. 112th Inf. Bde. were roughly on a line CLERMONT CHATEAU - BETHY. 4th Middlesex Regt. reverted to command of G.O.C. 63rd Inf. Bde.. This Battalion was very tired as it had been in close support on two successive days and it was considered it should have as much rest as possible before moving forward in support of the leading Battalions. Battalions were ordered to move straight to the River SELLE, to cross the stream and gain the high ground in E.25.a., 8th Somerset L.I. on the left and 8th Lincolnshire Regt. on the right. 63rd Inf. Bde. H.Q. now moved to AUDENCOURT.

A phone message was received from 17th Divn. saying they were preparing to attack NEUVILLY and asking 63rd Inf. Bde. to cooperate. It was too late to issue fresh orders but Battalions were told to be as quick as possible and to cooperate as far as possible.

Touch was immediately gained on both flanks and the advance proceeded rapidly up to the line VIESLY - J.12.central. Here there was a heavy barrage and machine gun fire from high ground J.6.c. - D.30.c. This ridge was gained after having sustained many casualties, Captain MADDEN, M.C., 8th Somerset L.I.,

-4-

being severely wounded, and further advance was prevented by casualties from heavy shellfire and it was decided to wait for dusk before pushing down to the river.

Early in this advance a forward report centre was established at the house J.10.b.4.1. Situation reports of great value were received from here and also from Cavalry and Cyclist patrols.

At 13.00 hrs it was ascertained that 17th Divn. were to attack at 17.00 hrs to gain the railway East of NEUVILLY. 8th Lincolnshire Regt. and 8th Somerset L.I.were told (B.M.274) to protect the flanks of 50th Inf. Bde. and to cooperate according as the situation developed, maintaining touch with both flanks. This attack was unsuccessful but during the night 1 platoon of 8th Lincolnshire Regt. crossed the river in the direction of NEUVILLY CEMETERY and 2 platoons of 8th Somerset L.I. crossed south of BRIASTRE by a footbridge erected by 153rd Field Coy., R.E. at about E.25.c.2.6.

B.M.278 issued at 21.00 hrs ordered 4th Middlesex Regt. to concentrate in the valley J.5.central by 05.00 hrs 11th inst.. This was cancelled after attack on 12th had been countermanded.

37th Divn. G.981 received at 20.18 hrs ordered a bridgehead to be formed east of the River SELLE. The artillery arrangements were phoned by G.S.O.1 at 20.45 hrs and confirmed by G.986 received at 00.35 hrs. Orders for this attack were issued to the Brigade Group in O.264.

11th Oct.

At 01.55 hrs the attack for 05.00 hrs was cancelled (B.M. 279) after a phone conversation between the Brigadier and the Divnl. Commander. This was confirmed in G.995 at 02.45 which also ordered strong patrol action and exploitation (B.M.280).

During the morning patrols across the river were unable to proceed owing to M.G.fire. Touch was maintained with left on E. side of river but not with right. 4th Middlesex Regt. were moved forward to J.5. by 10.05 hrs and got in touch close touch with forward battalions (B.M.281 and phone message from 4th Middlesex).

About 15.00 hrs a conference was held at Brigade H.Q. at which G.O.C. Division., G.S.O.1 and Artillery Brigade Commanders were present. Details of the attack and artillery action for the 12th were arranged. 37th Divn. Order No. 251 for the attack was issued at 19.00 hrs but was not received until after the issue of 63rd Inf. Bde. B.M.365 at 18.15 hrs which had been hastened in order to give Battalions time to make the necessary arrangements.

The attack was to be carried out by 4th Middlesex Regt. at 05.00 hrs in cooperation with troops of flank Divisions under an artillery barrage. They were to be formed up east of the River SELLE by 04.30 hrs and such troops of 8th Lincolnshire Regt. and 8th Somerset L.I. who were east of the river were to be withdrawn west of the river by 04.45 hrs. The 1/1st Herts. Regt. were put at the tactical disposal of G.O.C. 63rd Inf. Bde.

During this day and the following night two additional footbridges and one artillery bridge were constructed by 153rd Field Coy., R.E. Fairly heavy shelling hampered both the work and also the getting up of material.

12th Oct.

At 05.00 hrs 4th Middlesex Regt. advanced from their forming up position with three companies in front line. They were heavily fired on by machine guns from along the railway from BELLE VUE and from NEUVILLY. The machine guns along the railway were silenced by the artillery and by 10 rounds rapid from the centre company who then at once moved forward. At BELLE VUE the artillery effect was poor. The left flank suffered heavily from this and from the inability of the New Zealanders to reach their objectives.

Little opposition was met after crossing the railway but the left flank had to be refused to link up with the N.Z. Divn., the enemy retiring to the immediate front in disorder. By 07.30 hrs the battalion was digging in on the high ground and were in touch on the right with 17th Divn. The support company had advanced across the river and were echeloned to the left, except for one platoon on the right who moved up with the leading wave. They were not able to cross the railway owing to enfilade machine gun fire from machine guns which had not been sufficiently mopped up. These machine guns in BELLE VUE, and others in NEUVILLY which had not been cleared prevented reinforcements and messages from reaching the front line, making the situation extremely difficult.

In B.M.296 issued at 10.00 hrs one company 1/1st Herts Regt. and one company 8th Somerset L.I. were ordered to cross the river on the south and attempt to mop up the railway northwards. These companies were prevented from crossing however owing to machine gun fire from NEUVILLY.

An attack had been arranged with one company 1/1st Herts and 2 companies 8th Somerset L.I. against BELLE VUE on the left. As this attack was developing the enemy counterattacked at 15.05 hours on the right. The enemy attacked in strength with a very heavy barrage on the front line and the line of the river, driving in the Division on the right and exposing both flanks of 4th Middlesex Regt. who were forced to withdraw to the line of the river. Before retiring 4th Middlesex Regt. inflicted casualties on the enemy with machine gun, Lewis gun and rifle fire. He also suffered from our artillery and from machine guns west of the river.

A fresh attack was ordered by N.Z.Division against BELLE VUE at 18.00 hrs. 2 companies 8th Somerset L.I. and one company 1/1st Herts. Regt. then in BRIASTRE were ordered to cooperate and gain the line of the railway. 63rd Trench Mortar Battery did very good work against BELLEVUE and greatly helped in making the attack a success firing over 30 rounds. This attack was entirely successful, the line of the railway being gained and patrols being pushed south along railway. Opposition was met however at the Signal Box at E.25.central The line swung back from this point towards E.25.c.central to where touch was gained with 4th Middlesex Regt. who had also pushed forward patrols and gained the line of the railway in K.1.b.70.90 and E.25.d.60.50.

The relief by 13th Inf. Bde., 5th Division was ordered to be carried out in 37th Divn. O 252 and the line was handed over as above. Owing to the small number of troops pushed east of the river by 13th Inf. Bde. positions gained by patrols of 4th Middlesex Regt. on the railway were not taken over. Battalions were successfully withdrawn and the Brigade was complete in CAUDRY by 07.00 hrs on the 13th, all battalions being close to Brigade H.Q. in the centre of the town in good billets.

I wish to place on record my appreciation of the work done by 'A' Squadron, 3rd Hussars, and the Company of IV Corps Cyclists who were attached to the Brigade during the latter phase of the operations. Their duties were extremely arduous but all orders were carried out with intelligence and rapidity to my entire satisfaction.

I also wish to thank the officers and men of 37th Divisional Artillery for the excellent support they afforded the Brigade - in particular, Major THORNE, M.C., who commanded the mobile battery which did excellent shooting in the vicinity of BELLE VUE.

Bunkell
Brigadier General,
Comdg. 63rd Infantry Brigade.

October 19th 1918.

The following casualties were incurred during the operations of Oct. 1st - Oct. 12th :-

	KILLED		WOUNDED		MISSING	
	Offs.	O.Ranks	Offs.	O.Ranks	Offs.	O.Ranks
8th Lincolnshire Regt.	-	11	6	77	-	1
8th Somerset L.I.	-	4	3	56	-	1
4th Middlesex Regt.	2	30	5	132ˣ	1	18@
TOTAL	2	45	14	265	1	20

ˣ Includes 1 gassed (shell)

@ Includes 1 wounded and missing
and 2 wounded, believed prisoners.

Oct. 19th 1918

Rockley
Brigadier General,
Comdg. 63rd Infantry Brigade.

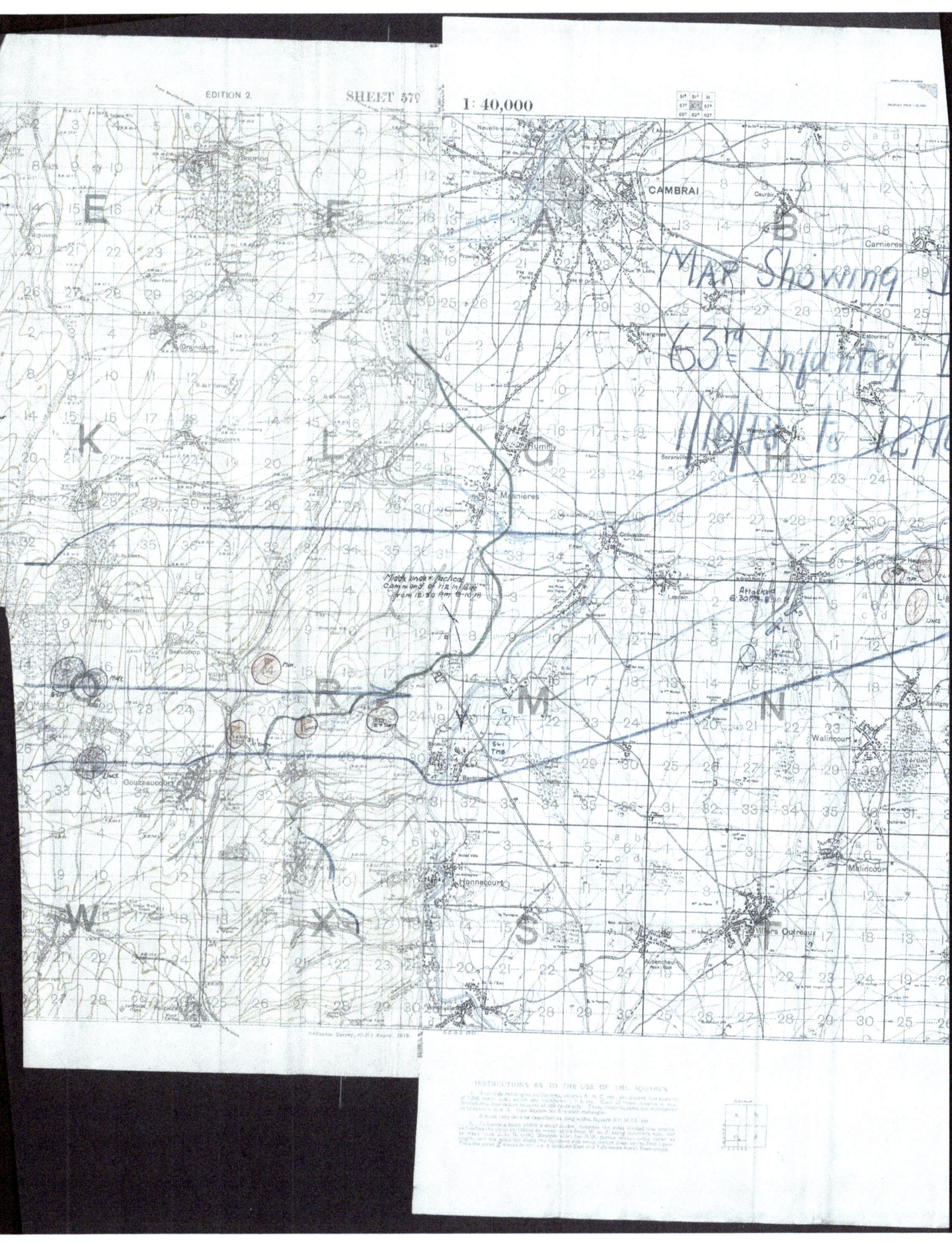

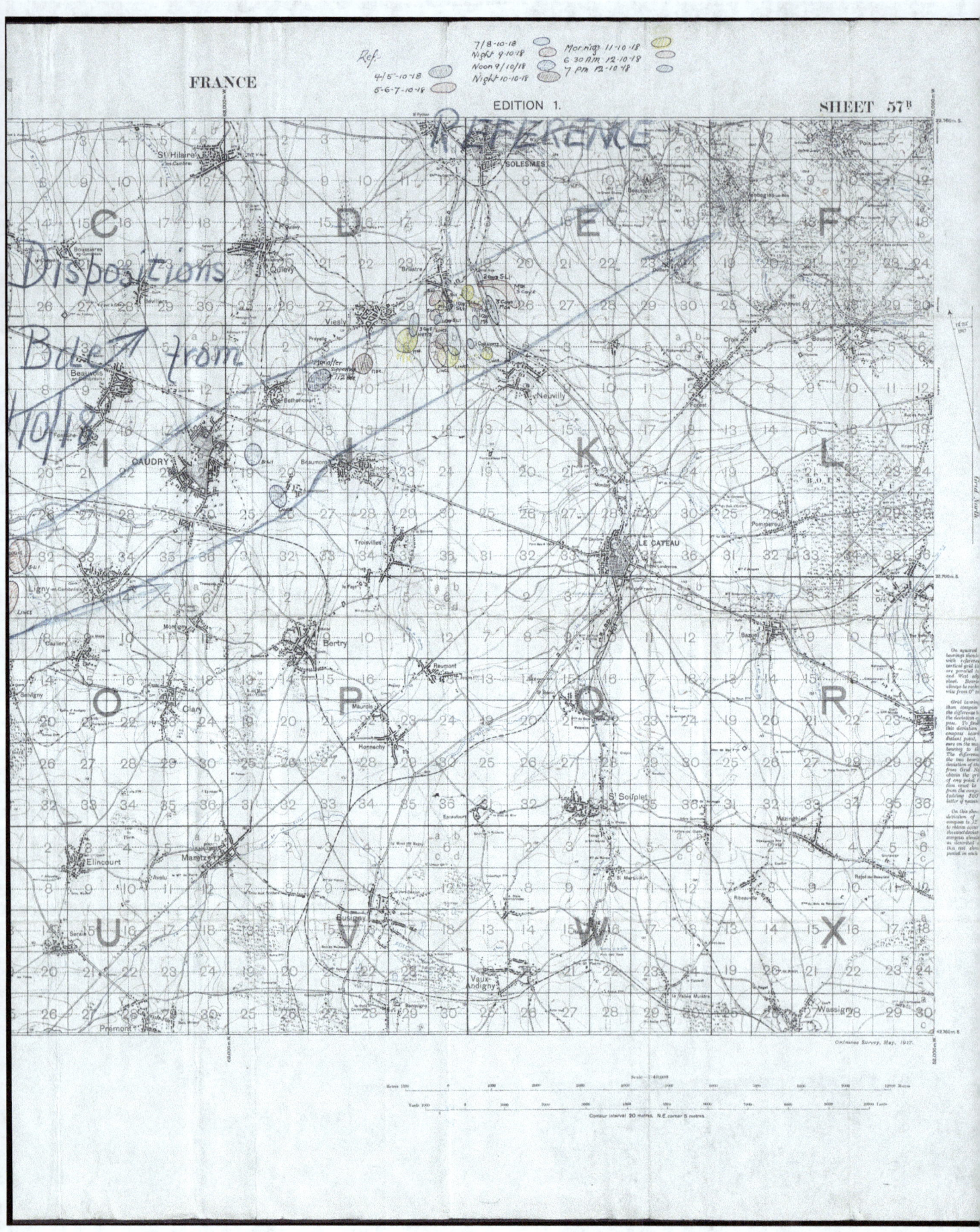

GLOSSARY

	Abbey.
	Watering-place.
	Custom-shelter.
	Steel works.
	Posts (Ry.)
Abbᵉ, Barrow	
	Old.
	Aqueduct.
Tree	
	fan-shaped
	bare
	forked
	isolated
	leaning
	Small tree.
	Arch.
	Slate quarry.
	Halt.
	Asylum.
Asiles	Lunatic asylum
	Inn.
	Alder-tree.
	Ferry.
	Baths.
	Bathing place.
	Boom, Beacon.
	Sand-bank.
	Mud-bank.
	Hut.
	Dam.
	Gate, Stile.
	Weigh-bridge.
	Dock, Pond.
	Tidal dock.

Bassin de radoub	Dry dock.
Bateau phare	Light-ship.
Blanchisserie	Laundry.
B.M. (borne militaire)	Mile stone.
Bᵗ (borne kilométrique)	
Boulangerie	
Fabᵗ de boutons	Bolt Factory.
Bouée	Buoy.
Brasserie, Brass	Armoury.
Briqueterie, Brique	Brickfield.
Brise-lames	Breakwater.
Bureau de poste	Post office.
„ de douane	Custom house.
Butte	Butt, Mound.
Cabane	Hut.
Câbleᵗ, Cableᵗ	Inn.
Câble sous-marin	Submarine cable.
Calvaire, Calᵉ	Calvary.
Canal de	
„ dessèchement	Drainage canal.
Canal d'irrigation	Irrigation canal.
Fabᵗ de caoutchouc	Rubber factory.
Carrière, Carʳᵉ	Quarry.
„ de gravier	Gravel-pit.
Caserne	Barracks.
Champ de courses	Race-course.
„ „ manœuvres	Drill-ground.
„ „ tir	Rifle range.
Chantier	Ship yard.
	Dock yard.
Chantier de construction	Slip-way.
Chapelle, Chᵉˡˡᵉ	Chapel.
Charbonnages	Colliery.
Château d'eau	Water tower.
Chaussée	Causeway.
Chemin de fer	Railway.
Cheminée, Chᵉᵉ	Chimney.
Chêne	Oak tree.
Cimetière, Cimᵉ	Cemetery.
Clocher	Belfry.
Clouterie	Nail factory.
Colombier	Dove-cot.

Coron	Workmen's dwellings.
Cour des marchandises	Goods yard.
Couvent	Convent.
Crassier	Slag heap.
Croix	Cross.
Darse	Inner dock.
Démolie	Destroyed.
Détruit - e, Détᵗ	
Déversoir	Weir.
Digue	Dyke, causeway.
Distillerie, Distᵉ	Distillery.
Douane	Custom-house.
Bureau de douane	
Entrepôt de douane	Custom warehouses.
Dynamitière, Dynamⁿ	Dynamite magazine.
Dynamiterie	Dynamite factory.
Écluse	Sluice, Lock.
Échassette, Eclᵗᵉ	Sluice.
École	School.
Écurie	Stable.
Église	Church.
Émaillerie	Enamel works.
Embarcadère, Embᵉ	Landing place.
Établisst, Etabᵗ	Inn.
Étang	Pond.
Fabrique, Fabᵗ	Factory.
Fabᵗ de produits chimiques	Chemical works.
Fabᵗ de faïence	Pottery.
Faïencerie	
Ferme, Fᵐᵉ	Farm.
Filature, Filᵗᵉ	Spinning mill.
Fonderie, Fondᵗ	Foundry.
Fontaine, Fontᵉ	Spring, fountain.
Forêt	Forest.
Forme de radoub	Dry dock.
Forge	Smithy.
Fosse	Mine, Pit.
Fossé	Moat, Ditch.
Four	Kiln.
„ à chaux	Lime-kiln.

Four à coke	Coke oven.
Ganterie	Glove Factory.
Gare	Station.
Garenne	Warren.
Garnison	Garrison.
Gazomètre	Gasometer.
Glacerie	Mirror Factory.
Fabᵗ de glaces	
Glacière	Ice factory.
Grue	Crane.
Gué	Ford.
Guérite	Sentry-box, Turret.
„ à signaux	Signal-box (Ry.)
Halte	Halt.
Hangar	Shed, Hangar.
Hôpital	Hospital.
Hôtel-de-Ville	Town hall.
Houillère	Colliery.
Huilerie	Oil factory.
Imprimerie, Imprᵉ	Printing works.
Jetée	Pier.
Laminerie	Rolling mills.
Ligne de hante	
Laisse	marée
„ de basse marée	Low
Maison Forestière Mon ᶠᵉ	Forester's house.
Malterie	Malt-house.
Marbrerie	Marble works.
Marais	Marsh.
Marais salant	Salt marsh
Marché	Market.
Mare	Pool.
Meule	Rick.
Minière	Mine.
Monastère	Monastery.
Moulin, Mⁿ	Mill.
„ à vapeur	Steam mill.
Mur	Wall.
„ crénelé	Loop-holed wall.

Nacelle	Ferry.
Orme	Elm.
Orphelinat	Orphanage.
Oseraie	Osier-bed.
Ouvrage	Fort.
Ouvrages hydrauliques	Water works.
Papeterie	Paper-mill.
Parc	Park, yard.
„ d'aérostation	Aviation ground.
„ à charbon	Coal yard.
„ à pétrole	Petrol store.
Passage à niveau P.N.	Level-crossing.
Passerelle, Psᵉˡˡᵉ	Foot-bridge.
Pépinière	Nursery-garden.
Peuplier	Poplar tree.
Phare	Light-house.
Pilier, Pilᵉ	Post.
Plaine d'exercice	Drill ground.
Pompe	Pump.
Ponceau	Culvert.
Pont	Bridge.
„ levis	Drawbridge.
Poste de garde	Coast-guard
Station côte	station.
Poteau Pᵗ	Post.
Poterie	Pottery.
Poudrière, Poudʳᵉ	Powder magazine.
Magasin à poudre	
Prise d'eau	Water supply.
Puits	Pit-head, Shaft, Well.
„ artésien	Artesian well
„ d'aérage	Ventilating shaft.
„ ventilateur	
„ de sondage	Boring.
Quai	Quay, Platform.
„ aux bestiaux	Cattle platform.
„ aux marchandises	Goods platform.
Raccordement	Junction.
Raffinerie	Refinery.
„ de sucre	Sugar refinery.
Râpier	Beet root factory.

ORIGINAL COPY.

WAR DIARY

63rd Infantry Brigade

NOVEMBER, 1918

Army Form C. 2118.

WAR DIARY
or
INTELLIGENCE SUMMARY

(Erase heading not required.)

Instructions regarding War Diaries and Intelligence Summaries are contained in F. S. Regs., Part II. and the Staff Manual respectively. Title Pages will be prepared in manuscript.

Place	Date	Hour	Summary of Events and Information	Remarks and references to Appendices
SALESCHES MILL	Nov. 1		Enemy artillery quiet during the day. Harassing fire on roads and approaches in early morning.	
	2		On the night of 1/2nd Nov. 4th Middlesex Regt. took over part of the front held by the left platoon of 8th Lincolnshire Regt. 8th Lincolnshire Regt. took over the left company front of the battalion on its right. This adjustment was made in readiness for a general advance due E. Considerable shelling, green and yellow cross gas, on area S.W. of GHISSIGNIES. A battalion of 3rd N.Z. Bde. took over the front held by two platoons on the left of 4th Middlesex Front.	
	3		At 2345 hrs 8th Lincolnshire Regt. carried out a raid with artillery barrage on the enemy positions on railway in A.5.a. They evidently antidipated the raid and very heavy machine gun fire was encountered throughout. The raiders penetrated to the railway and 30 - 40 casualties are reported to have been inflicted on the enemy. Our casualties were 3 killed, 16 wounded and 10 missing believed killed. Enemy artillery retaliation very slight. O. No. 272. From 0345 to 0500 hrs the enemy put down a very heavy C.P. barrage on the support area south of GHISSIGNIES with calibres up to 15 cm. GHISSIGNIES Road also shelled.	1
Chateau, GHISSIGNIES, A.5.c.2.2	4		On the night 3/4th, 63rd Inf. Bde. were relieved by 111th Inf. Bde. Outposts were kept out by 63rd Inf. Bde. until zero at 0530 hrs, 4th. 63rd Inf. Bde. withdrew to cellars in GHISSIGNIES and shelters on E. edge of SALESCHES. Constant touch was kept with the enemy until 0400 hrs. 8th Somerset L.I. were attached to 112th Inf. Bde. for the attack. The advance was continued due E. 2 platoons 8th Lincolnshire Regt. assisted 112th Inf. Bde. in mopping up enemy position in vicinity of the Chapel, X.5.a., taking prisoners. At 10.00 hrs 63rd Inf. Bde. (less 8th Somerset L.I.) assembled in the area S.E. of GHISSIGNIES. At midday orders were received for 63rd Inf. Bde. to consolidate the area between the blue and the blue dotted lines in reserve and battalions proceeded by march route to LOUVIGNIES. Orders were received during the afternoon that the division would be withdrawn to the BEAURAIN Area. 63rd Inf. Bde. then marched back and billeted for the night in GHISSIGNIES. In the evening the Brigade was notified to withdraw to NEUVILLE Area.	
NEUVILLE X.25.b.3.4.	5		63rd Inf. Bde. proceeded by march route to NEUVILLE where battalions were billeted. 8th Somerset L.I. rejoined the Brigade during the afternoon. Very wet day. For report on and all orders for operations from Oct. 23rd - 5th Nov. see appendix. 1	1
	6		Bathing and cleaning. Very wet day.	
	7.		Staff ride in area round BELLE VUE (Battle of River SELLE).	
	8		Training and bathing. Inspection of 4th Middlesex Regt. by Brigade Commander.	

2449 Wt. W14957/M90 750,000 1/16 J.B.C. & A. Forms/C.2118/112.

Army Form C. 2118.

WAR DIARY
or
INTELLIGENCE SUMMARY
(Erase heading not required.)

Instructions regarding War Diaries and Intelligence Summaries are contained in F. S. Regs., Part II. and the Staff Manual respectively. Title Pages will be prepared in manuscript.

Place	Date	Hour	Summary of Events and Information	Remarks and references to Appendices
CAUDRY	9.		Warning order received for 63rd Inf. Bde. to move to CAUDRY on the 11th inst.	
	10.		Church parades. Billeting parties sent forward to CAUDRY.	
	11.		63rd Inf. Bde. proceeded by march route to CAUDRY, being accommodated in billets. O. 274	2
	12.		Hostilities ceased at 1100 hours.	
	13.		Training. Presentation of medal ribands by Corps Commander in the afternoon in the Square, CAUDRY. 63rd Inf. Bde. No. 3169 G.	3
	14.		Training. Inspection of 63rd T.M.Battery by Brigade Commander in the morning and of 8th Somerset L.I. in the afternoon. G.O.C. very pleased with the turnout of each.	
	15.		Inspection of 8th Lincolnshire Regt. in the afternoon by the Brigade Commander.	
	16.		Training.	
	17.		Church parades. Special Divisional thanksgiving service and church parade in CAUDRY Theatre. Warning order received that G.O.C. 37th Division would inspect 63rd Bde. on the 19th. Conference of Commanding Officers at Brigade Headquarters.	
	18.		Preliminary Brigade parade.	
	19.		Inspection of 63rd Inf. Bde. by G.O.C. 37th Division. 63rd Inf. Bde. No. 3204 G	4
	20.		Training and Recreation.	
	21.		Training and Recreation.	
	22.		Training and Recreation. Divnl. Commander reviewed the Division. 63rd Bde. O. 275	5
	23.		Training and Recreation.	
	24.		Church Parades.	
	25.		Training and Recreation.	
	26.		Training and Recreation.	
	27.		Brigade Route March (CAUDRY - BEAUVOIS - BOIS TRANCOURT - CATTENIERES - FONTAINE-AU-PIRE - CAUDRY). 63rd Inf. Bde. Order No. 276	6
	28.		Training and Recreation.	
	29.		Warning order received of the move of 63rd Inf. Bde. to the VILLERS-POL Area, 63rd Bde. to stage for the first night in the HAUSSY Area. Billeting parties sent forward to each of the above areas.	
	30.		During the period at CAUDRY, the education scheme was started and battalion arrangements made accordingly. The afternoons were chiefly devoted to recreation.	

3.11.18

A. Hubback
Brigadier General,
Comdg. 63rd Infantry Brigade.

WAR DIARY

63rd Infantry Brigade.

NOVEMBER, 1918

List Of Appendices.	No. of Appendix.
Report on operations, Oct. 23rd – Nov. 5th, (including 63rd Inf. Bde. Orders Nos. 272 and 273)	1
63rd Infantry Brigade Order No. 274	2
63rd Infantry Brigade Order No. 3169 G	3
63rd Infantry Brigade Order No. 3204 G	4
63rd Infantry Brigade Order No. 275	5
63rd Infantry Brigade Order No. 276	7
Casualties during November, 1918	8
Reinforcements during November, 1918	9
Strength of units, Nov. 30th, 1918	10

63rd Infantry Brigade
========================

REPORT ON OPERATIONS, OCT. 23RD TO NOV. 4TH, 1918.

Oct. 23rd   In accordance with Divnl. Order No. 253 of 22nd Oct., 63rd Inf. Bde. Group moved from CAUDRY to VIESLY - BRIASTRE Area during the morning; owing to very dense traffic the march was considerably delayed, a Brigade of N.Z. Division moving at the same time along the road from PONT CAUDRY to VIESLY.

Dispositions on arrival were - 8th Somerset L.I. and 4th Middlesex Regt. in VIESLY, and Brigade H.Q., 63rd T.M.Battery and 8th Lincolnshire Regt. in BRIASTRE. During the afternoon 8th Somerset L.I. were moved to BRIASTRE in accordance with telephone instructions received from 37th Division, 63rd Inf. Bde. being in Divisional Reserve. Warning was received that the Brigade would probably not be required to move that night and the men spent a good night in billets, the Brigade remaining in Divnl. Reserve.

Oct. 24th.   In accordance with Divnl. Order G.58 received at 2000 hours, on 23rd inst., the Brigade moved forward to the BEAURAIN Area. This move was completed by 0930 hours, Brigade H.Q. at E.11.b.3.0.

At 1000 hours a telephone message was received from G.S.O.1. that one battalion would move forthwith to area just west of NEUVILLE (X.25.a.). 8th Lincolnshire Regt. moved off at once accompanied by one section of machine guns. 4th Middlesex Regt. and 8th Somerset L.I. had dinners and were to be prepared to move at any time after 1200 hrs.

37th Div. G.80 was received at 1339 hrs ordering the Brigade to relieve 111th Inf. Bde. in support and form a defensive flank facing S.E. along the railway.

On completion of this relief the dispositions of the Brigade were as follows :-

<u>8th Lincolnshire Regt.</u>   One Company along railway X.16. ; 2 companies in SALESCHES ; 1 company X.15.c. ; H.Q., SALESCHES.

<u>8th Somerset L.I.</u>   One company X.15.d - X.21.b. ; one company VITERLAN; one company on railway X.27.a. - X.21.d. ; one company round CHAPEL, X.27.a.; H.Q., VITERLAN.

<u>4th Middlesex Regt.</u>   In Brigade Reserve with 2 companies F.1.a.; 2 companies X.26.a., b. and d. ; H.Q. NEUVILLE.

The question of accommodation was somewhat difficult owing to the fact that 111th Inf. Bde. retained the accommodation then occupied by them in NEUVILLE and SALESCHES.

Brigade H.Q. remained the night 24/25th Oct. in BEAURAIN.

Oct. 25th.   Brigade H.Q. opened at the MILL, X.20.c.central, at 0900 hrs. It was decided to relieve the one company of 8th Somerset L.I. in X.15.d and X.21.b. and one company on railway X.27.a. and X.21.d. by 2 companies 8th Lincolnshire Regt. from SALESCHES. The two companies 8th Somerset L.I. so relieved were accommodated in cellars in SALESCHES. This relief was carried out in daylight without incident and was completed by 1630 hours.

On the 24th and 25th Oct., patrols from Battalions forming the right defensive flank had been keeping in close touch with the situation of 21st Division on the right and much information as to their line and dispositions was obtained and sent on to Division.

Oct. 26th.   Advantage was taken of the various banks in the vicinity and Battalions carried out training in musketry and Lewis Gun, and all ranks were instructed how to fire the German machine gun.

Oct. 27th.   Warning was received on the telephone that the Brigade would be required to relieve 112th Inf. Bde. in the front line on night 27/28 Oct. This was confirmed by G.151 rec[eived at ?]302 hours. The afternoon was spent by Commanding Officers [in reconnaissance ?] and making arrangements for the relief. The rel[ief was comple]ted by 2240 hours on the 27th inst. Dispositions on c[ompletion of reli]ef were :-

<u>Brigade H.Q.</u>   Remained at MILL, X.20[...]

(2)

2 battalions in line each on a 2 company front disposed in depth, and one battalion in reserve Brigade reserve in SALESCHES with one company in practice trenches in X.9.a.

The following were the detailed dispositions :-
8th Somerset L.I. on left holding line of road R.34.c. to cross roads R.34.d.8.2, with 2 companies in depth; support company in X.4.a.8.8; reserve company in cellars, X.4.c. Battalion H.Q. GHISSIGNIES.
8th Lincolnshire Regt. on right, line through orchards X.4.b.8.6 - X.5.a.5.2 to halt on Railway X.11.a.5.8, with 2 companies in depth; one company in support along railway X.10.c - X.11.a; one company in reserve in cellars X.4.d.6.2. Battalion H.Q., GHISSIGNIES.
4th Middlesex Regt. 3 companies in cellars, SALESCHES, and one company X.9.a.9.1. Battalion H.Q., SALESCHES.

Inter-battalion boundary was line X.10.a.5.2 - X.4.d.40.35 - R.35.c.0.0.

Oct. 28th. The night was passed without incident except for heavy enemy shelling of GHISSIGNIES during early morning.

As N.Z. Div. had been holding posts to R.34.central, it was arranged that 8th Somerset L.I. would extend to the left, taking over posts from N.Z. Div. to R.34.b.5.6. This relief was carried out on night 28/29th, being complete about 0345 hours 29th Oct.

Enemy shelling of GHISSIGNIES continued throughout the day, otherwise the situation was quiet.

Active patrolling had been carried out during the night and much useful information was gained regarding the enemy's method of holding the railway line along the Brigade front.

Oct. 29th. The day passed quietly with no change in the situation. The enemy's activity consisted mainly of artillery harassing fire on the approaches to GHISSIGNIES.

Oct. 30th. Situation remained unchanged. Enemy artillery somewhat less active except in the vicinity of SALESCHES Station and CHAPEL X.15.b. In the evening a practice manning of Battle Positions was carried out by 4th Middlesex Regt., 3 companies moving from SALESCHES to line of old German rifle pits X.14.c. and X.21.a. This practice was carried out in good time in the dark.

Oct. 31st. At 0330 hours, in accordance with 63rd Inf. Bde. Order No. 270, 8th Somerset L.I. carried out a successful raid on the enemy's positions on the railway about R.35.a.40.15. Two platoons were employed, the leading platoon working North and South along the railway whilst the support platoon mopped up and reconnoitred the ground just east of the railway. This raid was carried out in conjunction with 2 platoons of 1st Bn. N.Z.R.B. on the left. One prisoner was taken, identification 83rd I.R., 30 to 40 enemy were estimated to have been killed and several machine guns destroyed. Our casualties were very slight, consisting of one officer and one other rank slightly wounded. The artillery barrage was very regular and the troops were able to approach within 12 yards of the railway before the barrage lifted clear. 3" Stokes Mortars and 6" Medium T.Ms cooperated, forming a block to the south and engaging suspected enemy M.G. emplacements.

Two fighting patrols from 8th Lincolnshire Regt. attempted silently to mop up enemy posts on railway X.5.c. just before the above raid, but were unable to do so owing to the alertness of the enemy and concentrated machine gun fire.

During the morning of Oct. 31st N.Z. Div. were reported to have pushed forward posts to the railway. 8th Somerset L.I. were ordered to cooperate but N.Z. Div. posts were afterwards withdrawn and the situation remained unchanged.

The day passed quietly except for occasional shelling of GHISSIGNIES and front line in R.34.d.

In accordance with 63rd Inf. Bde. Order No. 271, 4th Middlesex Regt. relieved 8th Somerset L.I. in the left sector of the Brigade front during night Oct. 31st/1st Nov. This relief was carried out without incident and was completed by 2030 hours. 8th Somerset L.I. were withdrawn complete to SALESCHES, with Battalion H.Q. at FME. BERNIER. 4th Middlesex Regt. held the line on a two-company front with support company in area X.4.a.8.0, their reserve company being in practice trenches X.9.a. Battalion H.Q. GHISSIGNIES

Owing to ....

(2)

Owing to the relief, patrolling had been somewhat interrupted on the left of the Brigade front but patrols of 8th Lincolnshire Regt. were again very active pushing forward and occupying night posts of the enemy, but were unable to secure any prisoners owing to his alertness.

Nov. 1st. Situation remained unchanged. During the night, in accordance with Divisional Orders, the Brigade boundaries had been slightly re-adjusted, 8th Lincolnshire Regt. relieving troops of 21st Division as far south as X.11.d.0.0. In order to allow this to be carried out 4th Middlesex Regt. were ordered to relieve troops of 8th Lincolnshire Regt. as far south as X.5.a.3.8, inter-battalion boundary becoming the GHISSIGNIES - CHAPEL (X.5.a) road, inclusive to 4th Middlesex Regt. This adjustment was completed by 2055 hours.

Nov. 2nd. Situation quiet except for some T.M. fire on the front posts of the right company of the right Battalion during the night. At 1830 hours a message was received from Division to the effect that troops of 4th Middlesex Regt. North of an East and West line through R.34.d.7.6. were to be relieved by troops of N.Z.Division. Owing to the lateness in receiving these orders, the relief was not complete until 0345 hrs 3rd inst.

At 2345 hours 8th Lincolnshire Regt. raided the enemy's positions on the railway about the Chapel, X.5.a., under an artillery and trench mortar bombardment. This raid was carried out on a one platoon front with one platoon in close support. The railway was entered by the leading platoon and several casualties were inflicted on the enemy. 3 prisoners were taken but subsequently escaped. The supporting platoon was unable to reach the railway owing to heavy hostile machine gun fire from the railway cutting. Our casualties were somewhat heavy, including 12 other ranks reported missing. In the subsequent advance on the 4th inst., the bodies of 11 were found buried by the enemy in the railway cutting. On being examined the bodies were found to have been terribly disfigured. One, the body of No. 241136 Corpl. G.A.DICKENSON, had six bayonet wounds, and one hand cut off. In addition both eyes were missing and had apparently been gouged out. It is not thought possible that these wounds could have been inflicted in the course of actual fighting.

Enemy artillery retaliation to our barrage was very slight.

The maps of this area had been found to be very misleading; what was taken to be a level crossing at X.5.a.5.5 was proved to be a very steep railway cutting fully 12 feet deep with a destroyed road bridge over the railway.

Nov. 3rd. During the morning, commencing at 0345 hrs and lasting until 0500 hrs, the enemy fired a heavy counter-preparation on the area X.9, X.10, X.15 and X.16, and practice trenches, especially along crest X.9.b, Green, Yellow and Blue Cross gas shell being much in evidence.

In accordance with 37th Div. Order 255 received at 1345 hrs 2nd Nov., 111th Inf. Bde. were to pass through 63rd Inf. Bde. in the front line on the early morning of the 4th Nov. and continue the advance in a due E. direction. All information possible found out by reconnaissance was given to the assaulting battalions by 8th Lincolnshire Regt. and 4th Middlesex Regt. Information was received from Division during the day that touch had been lost with the enemy on the front of the First Army and it was of the utmost importance that during the night 3/4th Nov. constant touch be maintained with the enemy along the whole Brigade front. Both Battalions in the line were ordered to send out patrols, keeping in very close touch with either flank, every patrol being ordered to gain definite information regarding disposition and line of enemy posts. Reports were received hourly from both battalions that the enemy was holding the line of the railway strongly along the whole Brigade front. These reports were sent direct to 111th Inf. Bde.

During the evening parties from both battalions were employed taping out forming up places for the assaulting battalions of 111th Inf. Bde. Each Battalion also supplied officer guides to assist 'C' Company, 14th Bn., Tank Corps, in taping out tracks. As 111th Inf. Bde. took up their positions, 8th Lincolnshire Regt. and 4th Middlesex Regt. were withdrawn to cellars in GHISSIGNIES and shelters in SALESCHE area.

It had.............

(4)

It had been arranged that 2 platoons of 8th Lincolnshire Regt would form up in rear of 13th Rifle Brigade and help mop up the railway and neighbourhood of CHAPEL, (X.5.a) after 13th Rifle Brigade had passed through on morning of 4th Nov.

Nov. 4th.   63rd L.T.M.Battery cooperated at Zero (0530 hrs) to Zero plus 4 minutes in a hurricane bombardment with 6 mortars on the Chapel,X.5.a

The two platoons 8th Lincolnshire Regt. met considerable opposition in mopping up the railway cutting and Chapel area and it was not until the cooperation of a tank was secured that the cutting was finally cleared, 21 prisoners and several machine guns having previously been taken by 8th Lincolnshire Regt.

8th Somerset L.I. were attached to 112th Infantry Brigade who were to follow 111th Infantry Brigade. 8th Somerset L.I. were not actually employed until late in the afternoon when they had to push through difficult country and the FORET DE MORMAL which they successfully cleared, managing to push through to the Eastern edge of the wood by early morning of 5th Nov.

At 1000 hours troops of 4th Middlesex Regt. and 8th Lincolnshire Regt. which had been withdrawn to SALESCHES were moved up to the GHISSIGNIES Area, being at half an hour's notice. Brigade H.Q. opened at the Chateau, GHISSIGNIES, at 1200 hours.

A Commanding Officers' Conference was held at 1430 hours at Brigade H.Q., during which a message was received from Division that the Brigade would move forthwith to LOUVIGNIES. Whilst the troops were on the move to LOUVIGNIES, a message was received that the Division would be relieved that night by 5th Division and permission was received from Division for the Brigade to return to GHISSIGNIES where the night was spent, the men being accommodated in billets in the village.

Nov. 5th.   63rd Inf. Bde. (less 8th Somerset L.I.) was withdrawn to the NEUVILLE Area, the move being completed by 1200 hrs. 8th Somerset L.I rejoined the Brigade at 1630 hours, Brigade H.Q., the three battalions and 63rd T.M.Battery being billeted in NEUVILLE.

Nov. 9th 1918

Brigadier General,
Comdg. 63rd Infantry Brigade.

ORIGINAL COPY.

WAR DIARY

63rd Infantry Brigade

DECEMBER, 1918.

Army Form C. 2118.

WAR DIARY
or
INTELLIGENCE SUMMARY.
(Erase heading not required.)

Instructions regarding War Diaries and Intelligence Summaries are contained in F. S. Regs., Part II. and the Staff Manual respectively. Title pages will be prepared in manuscript.

Place	Date	Hour	Summary of Events and Information	Remarks and references to Appendices
HAUSSY	Dec.1		63rd Inf. Bde. moved by march route to the HAUSSY Area, 8th Lincolns being in billets in Montrecourt; 4th Middlesex Regt. and 8th Somerset L.I. at HAUSSY. 63 d Inf. Bde. Order No. 277	1.
VILLERS-POL	2		63rd Inf. Bde. moved by march route to VILLERS POL Area; 8th Lincolns and 4th Middlesex in billets at VILLERS POL - 8th Somerset L.I. at ORSINVAL. 63rd Infantry Brigade Order No. 277.	
	3		Resting.	
	4.		Visit of His Majesty. Troops of the Brigade lined the road through ORSINVAL.	
	5		Recreation and Education.	
	6		Recreation and Education.	
	7		Parades; recreation and education.	
	8.		Church parades.	
	9		Education and recreation.	
	10.		Education and Recreation. G.O.C. 37th Division visited billets of 4th Middlesex Regt. and spoke to the men.	
	11.		G.O.C., Staff Captain and Lieut. MATTHEWS proceeded to the new area by car, Lieut. MATTHEWS remaining.	
	12.		Education.	
BAVAI	13.		63rd Inf. Bde. Group, consisting of 37th M.G.Bn., 49th Field Ambulance, No. 2 Coy. Train and 63rd Inf. Bde. moved by march route to the BAVAI Area.	
SOUS-LE-BOIS	14		63rd Inf. Bde. moved by march route to SOUS-LE-BOIS (near MAUBEUGE) area.	
	15.		Day spent in billets at SOUS LE BOIS.	
GRAND RENG	16		Brigade Group moved by march route to GRAND RENG Area. Marched past the Corps Commander at GRANDXXXNX VIEUX RENG. Corps Commander remarked that the brigade had marched past him better than any other brigade he had seen so far during the advance.	
	17		37th M.G. Battalion moved to BOUSSOIS independently.	
BINCHE	18		Brigade Group moved by march route to the BINCHE Area; 4th Middlesex Regt. to RESSAIX.	
COURCELLES	19		Brigade Group moved by march route to COURCELLES (near CHARLEROI).	
	20		The Brigade Group less 4th Middlesex Regt. and 63rd Inf. Bde. HQ and 63rd T.M.Bty. moved to the final area as under :-	
			8th Lincolnshire Regt.) FRASNES-lez-GOSSELIES.	
			8th Somerset L.I.)	
			49th Field Ambulance. LIBERCHIES.	
HOUTAIN-LE-VAL	21		37th Division reverted to Divisional Troops. 63rd Inf. Bde. HQ and 4th Middlesex Regt. moved to final area and were located as under :- 63rd Inf. Bde. H.Q. KM ... Chateau, HOUTAIN-LE-VAL 63rd T.M.Battery, HOUTAIN LE VAL. 4th Middlesex Regt. - REVES.	

Army Form C. 2118.

WAR DIARY
or
INTELLIGENCE SUMMARY.
(Erase heading not required.)

Instructions regarding War Diaries and Intelligence Summaries are contained in F. S. Regs., Part II. and the Staff Manual respectively. Title pages will be prepared in manuscript.

Place	Date	Hour	Summary of Events and Information	Remarks and references to Appendices
HOUTAIN-LE-VAL	22		Nothing to report. All units settling down and rearranging very scattered billets. For all orders for the march from VILLERS POL Area to HOUTAIN-LE-VAL Area see 63rd Infantry Brigade Order No. 278, and Amendments Nos. 1 &b2 and Addenda Nos. 1, 2, 3 and 4.	2
	23		Nothing to report. (and 3229 G - details of men falling out etc.,	2a
	24		do.	
	25		Christmas dinners, etc.	
	26		Nothing to report.	
	27		Captain H.A.MAYNARD, M.C., Staff Captain 63rd Infantry Brigade proceeded to 5th Division as Acting D.A.Q.M.G. Lieut. A.H.MATTHEWS assumed the duties of Staff Captain.	
	28		Nothing to report.	
	29		do.	
	30		do.	
	31		do.	
			Education classes were continued during the month and a number of lectures of general interest were given. Recreation was somewhat interfered with owing to the wet weather. By the end of the month a considerable number of men (chiefly pivotal) had been demobilised.	3

January 3rd 1919

N.W.Bally Capt B/4.
for Lieutenant Colonel,
Comdg. 63rd Infantry Brigade.

ORIGINAL COPY

W A R   D I A R Y

63rd Infantry Brigade

January, 1919

Army Form C. 2118.

WAR DIARY
or
INTELLIGENCE SUMMARY
(Erase heading not required.)

Instructions regarding War Diaries and Intelligence Summaries are contained in F. S. Regs, Part II. and the Staff Manual respectively. Title Pages will be prepared in manuscript.

Place	Date	Hour	Summary of Events and Information	Remarks and references to Appendices
HOUTAIN LE VAL	Jan. 2nd		Brigadier General A.B.HUBBACK, C.M.G., D.S.O., proceeded to England on leave. Command of the Brigade was taken over by Lieut.-Col. R.A.SMITH, D.S.O., M.C., Royal Fusiliers.	
	3rd to 8th		Nothing to report.	
	9th		Conference of Commanding Officers at Divisional Headquarters.	
	10th to 19th		Brigadier General A.B.HUBBACK, C.M.G., D.S.O., returned from leave and took over command of the Brigade.	
	20th to 31st		Nothing to report.	
			During the period under review, a small amount of training was carried out; most of the time was devoted to Educational and Recreational training.	
			During the month 31 officers and 698 other ranks were demobilized from the Brigade, making a total of 31 officers and 850 other ranks demobilized since the armistice.	1

A.Hubback Brigadier General,
Comdg. 63rd Infantry Brigade.

2449 Wt. W14957/M90 750,000 1/16 J.B.C. & A. Forms/C.2118/12.

63rd Infantry Brigade

WAR DIARY

January, 1919.

List of Appendices	No. of Appendix
Numbers demobilized	1
Reinforcements received	2
Strength of Units, January 31st, 1919	3

63rd Infantry Brigade

DEMOBILIZATION.

Unit	Numbers demobilized during January, 1919		Numbers demobilized up to Jan. 31st 1919	
	Offs.	O.R.	Offs.	O.R.
8th Lincolnshire Regt.	11	234	11	277
8th Somerset L.I.	8	238	8	329
4th Middlesex Regt.	10	213	10	227
63rd T.M. Battery	1	10	1	14
Headquarters, 63rd Infantry Brigade.	1	3	1	3
T O T A L	31	698	31	850

63rd Infantry Brigade

REINFORCEMENTS RECEIVED DURING JAN, 1919.

	Officers	Other Ranks	Date
8th Lincolnshire Regt.	1		5.1.19
		3	6.1.19
	1	11	7.1.19
			9.1.19
		8	10.1.19
		2	13.1.19
		4	16.1.19
		1	25.1.19
	2	29	
8th Somerset L.I.	1		1.1.19
	1	16	3.1.19
		18	10.1.19
		6	14.1.19
		2	25.1.19
	2	42	
4th Middlesex Regt.		1	31.12.18
		12	7.1.19
		9	11.1.19
		3	25.1.19
		25	

Total Reinforcements received during January 1919 :-

<u>4 officers, 96 other ranks.</u>

63rd Infantry Brigade

STRENGTH OF UNITS, JAN. 31st 1919.

Unit	Strength		Details included	
	Offs.	O.R.	Offs.	O.R.
8th Lincolnshire Regt.	33	672	11	214
8th Somerset L.I.	35	613	17	195
4th Middlesex Regt.	29	666	9	188
63rd T.M. Battery	3	31		12
63rd Inf. Bde. H.Q.	5	41	1	12
	105	2023	38	621

ORIGINAL

63rd Infantry Brigade.

W A R   D I A R Y

February, 1919.

Army Form C. 2118.

WAR DIARY
or
INTELLIGENCE SUMMARY
(Erase heading not required.)

Instructions regarding War Diaries and Intelligence Summaries are contained in F. S. Regs., Part II. and the Staff Manual respectively. Title Pages will be prepared in manuscript.

Place	Date	Hour	Summary of Events and Information	Remarks and references to Appendices
HOUTAIN-LE-VAL.	February.		On February 3rd, 1919, the Corps Commander, Lieut.-General Sir G.M.HARPER, K.C.B., D.S.O., Commanding IV Corps, presented Union Colours on parade to 8th Battalion Lincolnshire Regiment and 8th Battalion Somerset Light Infantry. After the presentation, all three battalions of 63rd Infantry Brigade marched past the Corps Commander.	
			During the month Educational and recreational training were carried on, but owing to demobilization became somewhat restricted. (See Education Report for February..............	1
			From February 7th to February 14th a guard consisting of four officers and 250 other ranks was provided by 8th Battalion Lincolnshire Regt. for duty on Supply Trains.	
			During the month 7 officers and 614 other ranks of the Brigade were demobilized, making a total of 37 officers and 1450 other ranks since the commencement of demobilization..........	2
			[signature]	
			Brigadier General, Comdg. 63rd Infantry Brigade.	
	March 4th 1919			

63rd Infantry Brigade

STRENGTH OF UNITS, February 28th 1919.

Unit	Strength Offrs.	Strength O.R.	Details Included Offrs.	Details Included O.R.
8th Lincolnshire Rgt.	27	473	11	135
8th Somerset L.I.	34	473	19	193
4th Middlesex Regt.	25	424	9	119
TOTAL	86	1370	39	447

63rd Infantry Brigade

REINFORCEMENTS RECEIVED DURING FEBRUARY, 1919

	Offrs.	O.R.	Date
8th Lincolnshire Regt.		1	5.2.1919
		2	13.2.1919
		6	15.2.1919
		9	
8th Somerset Light Infantry	1		15.2.1919
		1	2.2.1919
		1	6.2.1919
		1	11.2.1919
		1	26.2.1919
	1	4	
4th Middlesex Regt.		2	11.2.1919
		1	14.2.1919
		5	18.2.1919
		2	19.2.1919
	1	1	22.2.1919
		2	26.2.1919
	1	13	

Total Reinforcements received during February 1919:-

2 officers, 26 other ranks.

63rd Infantry Brigade No. E 234

Education Officer,
37th Division

Ref. G.E.82 dated 27th Feb., 1919

     Owing to rapid demobilization during this month, the attendance at the educational classes has been greatly reduced. In the early part of January, the average number of students on the roll in each unit, for general subjects, was 500. Now the average number is 150.

     The education scheme suffered greatly owing to the general demobilization in January of Teachers and students. Under their guidance the classes were well organised and well attended. Good work was done both in general and special subjects, and lectures on various subjects were given two or three times a week.

     After their release, the work of instruction devolved mainly on the Platoon Commanders. These officers carried on as well as they could, but the majority, though possessed of sound general knowledge, had little idea of teaching, and consequently were unable to impart their information to the students with confidence.

     As demobilization continued, many of the students lost interest in the work and discontinued their attendance at the special classes. During this month owing to the large number of men released platoons have been amalgamated for instruction in general subjects - e.g., English, Arithmetic, History and Citizenship. Very few general lectures have been given as most of officer lecturers or no longer available.

     Special subjects - e.g., Shorthand, French and Book-keeping are being taught in all battalions, but the classes are very small.

(sd) C.J.MANSELL, Lieut.,
for Brigade Major,
63rd Infantry Brigade.

28th February 1919

ORIGINAL

WAR DIARY

63rd Infantry Brigade

MARCH, 1919

Army Form C. 2118.

WAR DIARY
or
INTELLIGENCE SUMMARY.
(Erase heading not required.)

Instructions regarding War Diaries and Intelligence Summaries are contained in F.S. Regs., Part II. and the Staff Manual respectively. Title pages will be prepared in manuscript.

Place	Date	Hour	Summary of Events and Information	Remarks and references to Appendices
JUMET-Heigne			During the month, demobilization was carried on, a total of 10 officers and 75 other ranks being demobilized during March, making a total of 48 officers and 1525 other ranks since demobilization began.	
			On March 10th, 11th, 12th and 13th, the Brigade moved from the FRASNES-lez-GOSSELIES, REVES and HOUTAIN-LE-VAL Area to JUMET, where the Cadres of the Division were to be concentrated. (See 63rd Infantry Brigade No. 3277	1
			During the month two drafts of 80 O.R. each from 8th Lincolnshire Regt. were sent to No. 28 and No. 39 P.O.W.Companies respectively, and 108 other ranks 4th Middlesex Regt., were transferred to 18th Bn. Middlesex Regt. on the 26th March and 5 officers and 130 other ranks 4th Middlesex Regt. were transferred to 18th Bn. Middlesex Regt. on 10th March	
			Large guards on supply trains and equipment stores were provided by 8th Lincolnshire Regt. and 8th Somerset L.I. during the month.	
	April 2nd 1919		A.W.Kitch. Lieutenant Colonel, Comdg. 63rd Infantry Brigade.	

WAR DIARY

63rd Infantry Brigade.

MARCH 31st, 1919

List of Appendices	No. of Appendix
63rd Infantry Brigade No. 3277 ... (Move to JUMET Area)	1
Reinforcements during March, 1919 ...	2
Numbers demobilized during March, 1919	3
Strength of Units, March 31st, 1919	4

<u>S E C R E T.</u>

63rd Infantry Brigade No. 3277

37th Division
8th Lincolnshire Regt. }
8th Somerset L.I.   } for information
4th Middlesex Regt.   }
99999----------------

Ref. Administrative Instructions No. 93
Concentration of Division in 111th Inf. Bde. Area.
----

1. I propose to move one Battalion a day commencing Monday 10th inst. This is necessitated by the sale and demobilization of animals. All the animals of the Brigade will be pooled and will be used to move each Battalion in turn.

2. O.C. No.2 Coy. Train reports that he is unable to supply baggage wagons for the move; therefore one lorry will be required instead.

3. Two lorries will be required to move the blankets of each Battalion, and two lorries to move the S.A.A. - approximately 5½ tons per Battalion, making a total of 5 lorries required each day on the 11th, 12th and 13th inst.

4. The S.A.A. limbers will be used for the conveyance of the harness and saddlery of animals disposed of and other equipment that had already been oiled for handing into Ordnance.

5. Can arrangements be made for lorries to report as under :-

    8th Lincolnshire Regt,   10th inst.   1000 to 1100 hours
    8th Somerset L.I.   11th inst.   do.
    4th Middlesex Regt.   12th inst.   do.

and 3 lorries to 63rd Infantry Brigade Headquarters 1000 to 1100 hours on 13th inst. to move stores and personnel.

March 7th 1919
(sd) A.B.HUBBACK, Brigadier General,
Comdg. 63rd Infantry Brigade.

-2-

8th Lincolnshire Regt.
8th Somerset L.I.
4th Middlesex Regt.
Brigade Transport Officer

Forwarded. Units of the Brigade will move independently in accordance with para. 5 above unless lorries are not available in which case notification will be sent as soon as received.
Ref. para. 1 the Brigade Transport Officer will arrange for the pooling of animals for the move of each unit.

March 8th 1919
(sd) A.H.MATTHEWS, Lieut.,
A/Staff Captain,
63rd Infantry Brigade.

63rd Infantry Brigade

REINFORCEMENTS RECEIVED DURING

MARCH, 1919

	Offs.	O.R.	Date
8th Lincolnshire Regt.		1	24.3.19
		1	27.3.19
		2	
8th Somerset Light Infantry	1		14.3.19
4th Middlesex Regt.		3	2.3.19
	1		5.3.19
		3	12.3.19
		2	15.3.19
		1	25.3.19
		1	28.3.19
		10	

Total Reinforcements received during March 1919 :-

2 officers. 12 other ranks

63rd Infantry Brigade

STRENGTH OF UNITS, MARCH 31st 1919

UNIT	Strength		Details Included	
	Offrs.	O.R.	Offrs.	O.R.
8th Lincolns	19	226	6	105
8th Somerset L.I.	23	400	7	88
4th Middlesex Regt.	17	54	5	8
TOTAL	59	680	18	201

63rd Infantry Brigade

DEMOBILIZATION.

Unit	Numbers demobilized During March		Total to date	
	Offrs.	O.R.	Offrs.	O.R.
8th Lincolnshire Regt.	3	6	19	443
8th Somerset L.I.	7	55	17	520
4th Middlesex Regt.	-	10	11	548
H.Q. 63rd Inf. Bde.		4	1	14
Total	10	75	48	1525

www.ingramcontent.com/pod-product-compliance
Lightning Source LLC
Chambersburg PA
CBHW080814010526
44111CB00015B/2558